The French and British in the Old Northwest

The French & British

In the Old Northwest

A Bibliographical Guide

to Archive and Manuscript Sources

by Henry Putney Beers

National Archives and Records Service

Wayne State University Press
Detroit, 1964

Second Printing, 1965
Library of Congress Catalog Card Number 64-13305

Grateful acknowledgement is made to the
DETROIT HISTORICAL SOCIETY
and the SOCIAL SCIENCE RESEARCH COUNCIL
for financial assistance in publishing this book

To Alice Tharpe Beers

Contents

Preface

THIS VOLUME presents an historical account of the acquisition, preservation, and publication by American and Canadian institutions of the original records created by French and British officials in the Old Northwest (the region south of the Great Lakes) chiefly during the eighteenth century, and of officials and governing bodies of Canada relating to that region.

The records include administrative papers of commandants, judicial records, notarial records, and land records. To facilitate a proper understanding of the records, the government of the region and the land grant system have been defined and described, as well as the ecclesiastical organization of Catholic missions, churches and some Protestant denominations in the old Northwest region. The papers of officials, trading and land companies, and traders, containing communications from governmental sources and copies of official documents, are also included. Since most of the region was connected for governmental purposes with New France, the Province of Quebec, and Upper Canada (Ontario), successively, a description of pertinent records of those jurisdictions has been presented. The area covered by this study includes Michigan, Ohio, Indiana, Illinois, Wisconsin, Minnesota, and the Dakotas, with some reference to the western portions of Pennsylvania and New York. The principal settlements, however, were those in southern Illinois, Vincennes, Mackinac, and Detroit. The Illinois settlements were connected for a time with French Louisiana. The records of that province are not described, since I have a separate work under way on the records of Louisiana during the French and Spanish regimes and of the Floridas during the Spanish and British regimes.

The preparation of this work would not have been possible without the data afforded by the publications of the archival and manuscript depositories in the Midwest and Canada. Many of these institutions have also provided additional information by letter on specific points; acknowledgments for such assistance appear in the footnotes. Research has been carried on primarily in the Library of Congress and in the National Archives; to their staffs I extend my thanks. I am indebted to William G. Orsmby, head of the Manuscript Division of the Canadian Public Archives and to Barbara Wilson of that division for making available in 1962 unpublished finding aids, inventories, and catalogs, permitting a perusal of the shelves of records, and supplying others for examination. A visit to the Burton Historical Collection of the Detroit Public Library in 1958 was rendered more profitable by the assistance given by its director, James M. Babcock. A careful reading of the manuscript by Handy Bruce Fant of the National Archives has enabled me to make various improvements and corrections. For the faults that remain I alone am responsible.

H.P.B.

Arlington, Va.
November 1963

I   The Records

of the French Regime

History

The colony of New France, as Canada was known during the French period, included the country along the St. Lawrence River on which the early settlements were made in what is now the province of Quebec. As a result of the activities recounted in the following pages, the Great Lakes region became a dependency of New France, and Canada, a word of Indian origin, became the popular name for New France, as distinct from Acadia, the region encompassing present-day Nova Scotia and eastern New Brunswick. This designation did not come into official use until 1791, when it was adopted for Lower Canada and Upper Canada; those provinces formed a single government in 1840 (United Canada), and in 1867 they joined with New Brunswick and Nova Scotia to form the nucleus of a federation known as the Dominion of Canada, to which other provinces were later added.

Expeditions sent out from the St. Lawrence River in Canada (where Samuel de Champlain had established a French colony at Quebec in 1608) gradually explored the country of the Great Lakes as well as the Mississippi River and its tributaries. In 1615, Champlain traveled with a small party up the Ottawa River, a northern branch of the St. Lawrence, through Lake Nipissing and Georgian Bay to Lake Huron. Jean Nicolet, Champlain's agent, made the first passage of the straits of Mackinac from the northern end of Lake Huron, and of Lake Michigan to the head of Green Bay and the Fox River in 1634, thus becoming the discoverer of Wisconsin.[1]

[1] Milo M. Quaife, *Wisconsin; Its History and Its People, 1634-1924* (Chicago, 1924. 4 vols.), I, 93; John B. Brebner, *The Explorers of North America, 1492-1806* (New York, 1933), 188-89.

1

The discoverers of Lake Superior were two Jesuit missionaries, Isaac Jogues and Charles Raymbault, who went to Sault Ste. Marie in 1641 to work among the Indians.[2] In 1659, the Indian traders Radisson and Groséilliers passed over the Ottawa River and Lake Nipissing route and visited Chequamegon Bay on Lake Superior and the region southwest of that lake.[3] Returning from Sault Ste. Marie in 1669 with an Iroquois guide, Andrien Jolliet made the first voyage through Lake Huron, the St. Clair River, Lake St. Clair, and the Detroit River to Lake Erie and followed a trail along the northern shore of Lake Erie to Lake Ontario. Jolliet's journey showed it was possible to travel by water all the way from the upper St. Lawrence River to Lake Michigan, except for a portage around the Niagara River.[4] In 1670, two Sulpician missionaries, François Dollier de Casson and René de Bréhant de Galinée traveled west from Lake Erie over Jolliet's route to Sault Ste. Marie. Robert René Cavelier, Sieur de la Salle, who had journeyed with Dollier and Galinée to Lake Ontario in 1669, probably reached the Allegheny and Ohio rivers in the winter of 1669-70.[5] In 1673, Louis Jolliet, Father Jacques Marquette and a few voyageurs traversed the Fox-Wisconsin route to the Mississippi River, which they followed as far as the Arkansas River, demonstrating that the Mississippi flowed into the Gulf of Mexico rather than the Pacific Ocean.[6] La Salle and a canoe party of Frenchmen and Indians traveled from the Chicago portage down the Illinois River and the Mississippi River to its mouth in 1682, completing the first journey by Frenchmen from the Great Lakes to the Gulf of Mexico.

The French declared sovereignty over the regions they explored

[2] Quaife, *Wisconsin*, I, 76.

[3] *Ibid.*, 63-69. The principal work on these men is Grace L. Nute, *Caesars of the Wilderness: Médard Chouart, Sieur des Groséilliers, and Pierre Esprit Radisson, 1618-1710* (New York, London, 1943).

[4] Jean Delanglez, *Life and Voyages of Louis Jolliet (1645-1700)* (Chicago, 1948), 7-10.

[5] Beverley W. Bond, Jr., *The Foundations of Ohio* (*The History of the State of Ohio,* ed. by Carl Wittke, vol. I, Columbus, 1941), 65; Carl Wittke, *A History of Canada* (New York, 1933), 10. See however, Frances Krauskopf, "The Documentary Basis for La Salle's Supposed Discovery of the Ohio River," *Indiana History,* XLVII (June 1951), 143-53.

[6] Brebner, *Explorers of North America*, p. 254-55; Quaife, Wisconsin, I, 97.

and discovered through acts of possession. In June 1671, in the presence of a number of Indian tribes, Simon François Daumont, Sieur de Saint-Lusson, planted a wooden cross at Sault Ste. Marie, raised the arms of Louis XIV, and proclaimed French sovereignty over the region. In July 1679, a similar ceremony was performed at a Sioux village on Mille Lacs, west of Lake Superior, by Daniel Greysolon, Sieur Duluth, probably the first white man on Minnesota soil. On reaching the mouth of the Mississippi in 1682, La Salle took possession in the name of the French king. Other explorers such as La Vérendrye and Céloron de Blainville (whose explorations will be mentioned later), kept journals of their expeditions and buried lead plates with inscriptions asserting possession of the areas traversed in the name of the French king.[7]

The French attempted to solidify their claim to the Great Lakes region and the Mississippi Valley by establishing forts and promoting settlement and trade.[8] La Salle secured approval from France to erect forts at strategic places in order to connect the settlements on the St. Lawrence with the new areas in the West. In 1679, he embarked from a base at Niagara for the Illinois country, where he built Fort Miami (Mich.) at the mouth of the St. Joseph River,[9] and in the next year established Fort Crevecoeur on the south side of the Illinois River a mile below Lake Peoria.[10] But the powerful Iroquois of New York, who attempted to keep the tribes south of the Great Lakes in subjection in order to control the Indian trade, destroyed the Indian village, forcing the commandant, Henri de Tonty to retire from Fort Crevecoeur with the Recollect missionaries who had been stationed there to Green Bay, on Lake Michigan. Fort St. Louis, established by La Salle in 1682 at Starved Rock

[7] A photograph of a lead plate found at the mouth of the Kanawha River, now in the Virginia Historical Society, is in Bond, *Foundations of Ohio*, p. 116. The article by DeLand, cited below, contains a photograph of the La Vérendrye plate found in Fort Pierre, S. Dak. in 1913.

[8] Percy J. Robinson, *Toronto during the French Régime: A History of the Toronto Region from Brûlé to Simcoe, 1615-1793* (Toronto, Chicago, 1933), 43 *et. seq.*

[9] Bessie L. Pierce, *A History of Chicago* (New York, 1937-57. 3 vols.), I, 8.

[10] Clarence W. Alvord, *The Illinois Country, 1673-1818* (Springfield, 1920), 81-82.

on the Illinois River near present-day Utica, was moved to Peoria ten years later by his successors, Tonty and François Dauphin de la Forest. With the seating of French settlers around this fort, it became the first permanent village in the Illinois country.[11]

Other forts were constructed by the French during this period. About 1680 a military detachment arrived at St. Ignace on the strait of Mackinac.[12] The post here was known at first as Fort de Buade, but was soon called Fort Michilimackinac. In 1680 the French built Fort Miami at the foot of the rapids of the Maumee River (present-day Maumee, Ohio), rebuilt it in 1693, and later deserted it. The Sieur Duluth was dispatched from Canada in 1686 to erect a post at the Strait of Lake Erie, but instead of that location he chose one at present-day Port Huron and built Fort St. Joseph, which was abandoned two years later.[13] Another temporary site, Fort St. Joseph, was founded somewhat later on the St. Joseph River (present-day Niles, Mich.) to prevent Iroquois incursions, and soon abandoned.[14] For a time in 1685 and again in 1691-92 small French forces were garrisoned at Chicago, but despite its advantageous location this point did not become a permanent fortification.[15]

In the latter part of the seventeenth century the leading trader on the Upper Mississippi was Nicolas Perrot, who had traded earlier at Green Bay and on the Fox River. After being appointed commandant at La Baye (Green Bay) in 1684, he expanded trading operations to the Upper Mississippi River. Passing over the Fox-Wisconsin waterway and turning north on the Mississippi, he spent the winter of 1685-86 at Trempealeau Bluffs, where he built a trading post. He erected Fort Antoine on the east shore of Lake Pepin in 1686, and conducted a profitable trade there with the Sioux Indians. In the same year he established Fort St. Nicolas at the mouth

---

[11] Alvord, *Illinois Country*, p. 100.

[12] Roger Andrews, *Old Fort Mackinac on the Hill of History* (Menominee, Mich., 1938), 14.

[13] Clarence M. Burton, and others, eds., *The City of Detroit, Michigan, 1701-1922* (Detroit, Chicago, 1922. 5 vols.), I, 83, II, 857.

[14] George Paré, "The St. Joseph Mission," *Mississippi Valley Historical Review*, XVII (June 1930), 33-37.

[15] Pierce, *History of Chicago*, I, 9-11.

of the Wisconsin River, at or near Prairie du Chien,[16] and in 1689 took formal possession of the region for the French king at Fort St. Antoine. Trade prospered for a time, but after the outbreak of war with the Iroquois in 1689, the forts on the Upper Mississippi were abandoned, and Perrot withdrew to the Fox River until 1698, when on orders from the government, he and other traders were recalled to Montreal.

Pierre Charles le Sueur, who had previously spent some time on the Upper Mississippi River, was designated in 1693 as commander of Fort La Pointe on Chequamegon Bay.[17] Besides keeping peace between the Sioux and the Chippewa, he was to protect the Bois Brulé-St. Croix waterway, which afforded passage from the western end of Lake Superior to the Mississippi River. In 1695 he established Fort Le Sueur on Prairie Island opposite the present town of Red Wing, on the west side of the Mississippi River between Lake Pepin and the St. Croix River. In 1699, after an absence of several years, during which he visited France in an unsuccessful effort to obtain permanent command over Lake Superior and the Upper Mississippi, he returned to North America with the Sieur d'Iberville. He left Louisiana in 1700 and ascended the Mississippi and Minnesota rivers, and built Fort L'Huillier on the Blue Earth River near present-day Mankato. When he departed in 1701, he left behind a detachment which followed him to the Gulf of Mexico in the next year.

The military arrangements of the French in the Upper Country were disastrously affected by a war with the Iroquois that began in 1689.[18] At first, reinforcements were sent to the western forts to save them from Indian attack. An evacuation of the posts in the West was decided upon in 1696 and executed two years later.[19]

---

[16] Kellogg, *French Régime in Wisconsin*, p. 232.

[17] William W. Folwell, *A History of Minnesota* (St. Paul, 1921. 4 vols.), I, 38.

[18] In the seventeenth century the region of the upper Great Lakes and the northeastern part of the Mississippi Valley was referred to as the Northwest and the Upper Country (*pays en haut*). Today this area is known as the Midwest.

[19] Kellogg, *French Régime in Wis.*, p. 257-67.

Missionaries and *coureurs de bois,* or bushrangers, thereafter represented the French in the West.

After the conclusion of peace with the Iroquois in 1700, the French determined to regarrison the West. Instead of re-establishing the old posts, they occupied three strategic places with large garrisons and concentrated French settlers and Indian allies there. The points selected were the straits between Lake Huron and Lake Erie, the Illinois country, and the mouth of the Mississippi.[20] While commandant at Fort Michilimackinac from 1694 to 1698, Antoine Laumet de la Mothe Cadillac learned about the country along the Detroit River and, with royal permission, established Fort Pontchartrain at Detroit in July 1701.[21] Because of its strategic position on the best route to the West, Detroit became the most important French post. French activities in the West were blocked for a time by the outbreak of The Queen's War in 1701, the earliest of a series of struggles that embroiled France and England in Europe and in North America during the eighteenth century.

The establishment of peace by the Treaty of Utrecht of 1713 permitted the restoration of the western posts, and by 1715 the Sieur de Lignery had rebuilt Fort Michilimackinac on the south side of the straits (present-day Mackinaw City). In the same year, Fort St. Joseph was rebuilt among the Miami Indians on the St. Joseph River. In 1717, after a punitive expedition led by the Sieur de Louvigny against the Fox Indians who had closed the Fox-Wisconsin waterway to French traders, Fort La Baye was erected near the mouth of the Fox River. Fort La Pointe was rebuilt in 1718 on the southwestern tip of Madeline Island in Chequamegon Bay, where the main villages of the Chippewa Indians were located.[22] Fort de Chartres was completed on the bank of the Mississippi sixteen miles above Kaskaskia in 1720 by a detachment sent to Illinois from Louisiana.[23] These garrisons were soon supplemented by a chain of forts along the Maumee and Wabash rivers, which afforded a channel of transportation from Lake Erie to the

[20] *Ibid.,* p. 269.
[21] Burton, ed., *City of Detroit,* I, 84-86.
[22] Kellogg, *French Régime in Wis.,* p. 291-300; Alvord, *Illinois Country,* p. 149.
[23] Alvord, *Illinois Country,* p. 153.

Mississippi. Fort Miami (present-day Fort Wayne, Ind.), established in 1715 at the head of the Maumee, was the first link in the chain of forts.[24] Fort Ouiatenon was founded in 1720 a short portage away on the headwaters of the Wabash.[25] Farther down the Wabash, François Marie Bissot, Sieur de Vincennes, erected Fort Vincennes in 1732 or 1733.[26] These military posts, particularly Fort Ouiatenon, became important in furthering trade with the Miami and in combatting the aggression of the Iroquois and the English, who were struggling for control of the area.

Later, the network of forts was further strengthened. In 1738, some of the Huron who had been living near Detroit migrated to Sandusky Bay on the southwestern shore of Lake Erie and established a village which became the scene of both French and English trading activity.[27] Fort Sandusky was built there in 1751 and replaced by Fort Junundat in 1754.[28] As an additional means of checking trade between the Indians and the English, the French fortified Sault Ste. Marie in 1751.[29] In 1757 they constructed Fort Massac on the north bank of the Ohio a few miles below the mouth of the Tennessee to prevent raids by the English.

An expedition led by René Boucher de la Perrière effected a resumption of French activities on the Upper Mississippi River by founding Fort Beauharnios in 1727 on the western shore of Lake Pepin, near present-day Frontenac, Minn.[30] The post was occupied intermittently thereafter and was reconstructed in 1736 on the east side of the lake by Jacques le Gardeur de St. Pierre. Another fort built at Trempealeau Bluffs on the Mississippi River by René

24 Kellogg, *French Régime in Wis.*, p. 291.

25 *Ibid.*, p. 82; Logan Esarey, *History of Indiana from Its Exploration to 1922* (Dayton, Ohio, 1922-23, 3 vols.), I, 19-20. Fort Ouiatenon was near present-day Lafayette, Ind.

26 Paul C. Philips, "Vincennes in Its Relation to French Colonial Policy," *Indiana Magazine of History*, XVII (Dec. 1921), 322.

27 W. E. Shiels, "The Jesuits in Ohio in the Eighteenth Century," *Mid-America*, XVIII (Jan. 1936), 36-39.

28 Lucy E. Keeler, "Old Fort Sandoski of 1745 and the 'Sandusky Country,' " *Ohio Archaeological and Historical Society Publications*, XVII (1908), 365.

29 Otto Fowle, *Sault Ste. Marie, and Its Great Waterways* (New York, 1925), 194-96.

30 Kellogg, *French Régime in Wis.*, p. 308-311.

Godefroy de Linctot in 1731 was occupied until approximately 1736.

Paul de la Marque, Sieur Marin, came to the region in 1729 to complete the conquest of the western Indians.[31] He continued in command for over twenty years, expanding French influence and trade in the Minnesota region and building Fort Marin opposite the mouth of the Wisconsin River in 1739, and Fort La Jonquière on the Upper Mississippi in 1750. Later, he built Fort Duquesne on the west bank of the Mississippi at the mouth of the Crow Wing River, and Fort Vaudreuil on the west bank of the river below the mouth of the Wisconsin River. On his death in 1752, he was succeeded by his son, Joseph de la Marque.[32] Another father-son combination, Louis Denis and Philippe Denis, the Sieurs de la Ronde, commanded at La Pointe from 1727 onward and besides trading for furs initiated copper mining in the Northwest.[33] The fur-trading centers at Green Bay, the headquarters of the Sieurs Marin, Prairie du Chien, and La Pointe developed into permanent settlements, but the more remote and less strategically located posts in Minnesota did not survive the fur-trading era.

While the Marins operated on the Upper Mississippi, Pierre Gaultier de Varennes, Sieur de la Vérendrye and his sons extended French trade north and west of Lake Superior and searched for a route to the western sea. La Vérendrye reached Grand Portage on the Pigeon River in Minnesota in 1731, and in the next year established his headquarters at Fort St. Charles at what is now the northernmost point in Minnesota.[34] A party sent out by La Vérendrye in 1732 built Fort St. Pierre at the outlet of Rainy Lake, and Fort Maurepas, constructed in the same year near the mouth of the Red River, was soon moved to the mouth of the Winnipeg River. La Vérendrye led an expedition overland in 1738 to the village of and Mandan Indians in what is now North Dakota, and sent his son,

[31] *Ibid.*, p. 324.

[32] A diary by the Sieur de Marin for the trading year 1753-54 is in Grace L. Nute, ed., "Marin versus La Verendrye," *Minnesota History*, XXXII (Winter 1951), 226-38. See also her "Posts in the Minnesota Fur-Trading Area, 1660-1855," *Minn. Hist.*, XI (Dec. 1930), 353-85.

[33] Kellogg, *French Régime in Wis.*, 351.

[34] Arthur S. Morton, "La Vérendrye; Commandant, Fur-Trader and Explorer," *Canadian Historical Review*, IX (Dec. 1928), 292.

the Chevalier, to the Missouri River.[35] The Chevalier and another son journeyed south again in 1742 to the Black Hills of South Dakota, but though they found the Missouri River, the La Vérendryes failed to discover a route to the western sea.

The French were long prevented from developing the Allegheny-Ohio route because of the domination of the area by the powerful and hostile Iroquois. This route was finally traversed from Lake Erie to the mouth of the Ohio in 1739 by a military detachment led by Maj. Charles Le Moyne, Baron de Longueuil.[36] In 1749 Governor La Galissonière of Canada sent out a reconnoitering expedition to the upper Ohio under Capt. Pierre Joseph Céloron de Blainville as an initial step in the campaign to win back the allegiance of the Indians south of Lake Erie and to oppose the English.[37] In 1753 a military force commanded by Capt. Pierre Paul Marin and Capt. Michel Pean built Fort Presque Isle (now Erie, Pa.), Fort Le Boeuf (now Waterford, Pa.) on the upper waters of French Creek, and Fort Machault, or as it was sometimes called, Venango (now Franklin, Pa.), at the junction of French Creek and the Allegheny River.[38] Still another expedition under Capt. Claude-Pierre de Contrecoeur founded Fort Duquesne at the forks of the Ohio in 1754. The area was an appendage to New France, the home base of the occupying forces.

By the mid-eighteenth century, the French had established permanent settlements on the Great Lakes and on the Mississippi River and its tributaries, and had gained title to the region by right of occupation as well as discovery. The English by this time were carrying on an extensive trade from their Atlantic seaboard colonies with the Indians on the Ohio River and its northern affluents, but had established no settlements beyond the Allegheny Mountains. The English colonies, however, claimed title to the region

[35] *Ibid.,* p. 296; John B. Brebner, *Explorers of North America, 1492-1806,* p. 359.

[36] George A. Wood, "Céloron de Blainville and French Expansion in the Ohio Valley," *Miss. Valley Hist. Rev.,* IX (Mar. 1923), 303.

[37] Bond, *Foundations of Ohio,* p. 115-20; Wood, "Céloron de Blainville," p. 311-12.

[38] Donald H. Kent, *The French Invasion of Western Pennsylvania, 1753* (Harrisburg, 1954); Solon J. and Elizabeth H. Buck, *The Planting of Civilization in Western Pennsylvania* (Pittsburgh, 1939), 69-70.

south of the Great Lakes by virtue of their charters from the English crown.

The century-old rivalry between the French and the English in North America was part of a larger struggle that had resulted in a series of European and North American wars, and had been brought to a head by the determination of the English to oust the French from the Ohio Valley. In 1753, the colony of Virginia sent George Washington to warn off the French and demand their withdrawal from the Ohio Valley, but when he returned in 1754 to occupy the forks of the Ohio, he was obliged to surrender at Fort Necessity to a larger French force commanded by Coulon de Villiers.

English preparations for military campaigns in North America included an expedition against Fort Duquesne.[39] Gen. Edward Braddock invaded the Ohio Valley in 1755 with a force of British soldiers and colonial troops, but was defeated on the Monongahela River. In November 1758, threatened by a superior force led by Brig. Gen. John Forbes, the French evacuated and burned Fort Duquesne, and after the English capture of Fort Niagara in 1759, they withdrew from forts Presque Isle, Le Boeuf, and Machault. The English victory over the French at Quebec in September 1759 was followed by the French capitulation at Montreal on September 8, 1760, by which Canada and its dependencies were surrendered to the English.

Government

Authority at the posts in the interior was chiefly in the hands of the commandants.[40] They were appointed by the King upon the recommendation of the governor-general at Quebec and exercised a combination of administrative, judicial, and legislative powers. The posts were so distant from Quebec that the commandants' sway over the military and civil population was autocratic, although ap-

---

[39] The background of the ensuing conflict, known in American annals as the French and Indian War, and in European history as the Seven Years' War, can be traced in Bond, *Foundations of Ohio*, and in general histories of the United States.

[40] Caldwell, *French in the Miss. Valley*, p. 12; Burton, ed., *City of Detroit*, I, 163, II, 1123.

peal could be made to Quebec. The commandants handled Indian relations, managed the King's domain and his storehouse, regulated justice in posts without a deputy of the intendant of New France, and performed marriages. Besides their official duties, they had certain social obligations, such as participating in festivities and acting as godfathers. Subordinate officials included the chaplain, surgeon, interpreter, missionary, the storekeeper, and sometimes, a smith. The administrative expenses at the post were paid by the proceeds from the sale of licenses to traders.[41]

The royal notaries who functioned in the settlements of the Upper Country were responsible for the preservation of documents recording legal agreements between individuals. Primarily official recorders of legal acts in France, where the functionary had come into widespread employment since the twelfth century,[42] the notaries broadened out their duties in the posts to include some other activities. Notaries served at Kaskaskia, Fort de Chartres, Detroit, Vincennes, and Michilimackinac. They drew up and authenticated documents according to the form and regulations prescribed by the *coutume de Paris* (custom of Paris). The acts were copied into registers so there would be a public record for the use of notaries, judges, intendants, and others.[43] The documents that they preserved include acts of supervision of minors, agreements of all kinds, apprenticeship papers, arbitration decisions, auctions, bonds, business contracts, certificates, chancery acts, contracts of hire, conveyances of land, debts, deeds, donations, emancipations, exchanges, gifts, inventories of property, lawsuit papers, leases, loans of money, marriage contracts, mortgages, partnerships, powers of attorney, renunciations, receipts, sales of property, settlements of estates, testaments, transfers of real estate, and wills. Further occupation was provided for the notaries as common magistrates and justices of the peace.[44] In Illinois, the notary functioned generally as royal solicitor (*procureur*) and clerk of the court.[45]

[41] Caldwell, *French in the Miss. Valley*, p. 31-32.
[42] Jacques Monicat, "Les archives notariales," *Revue historique*, CCXIV (juillet-sept. 1955), 1-2.
[43] Caldwell, *French in the Miss. Valley*, p. 17-18.
[44] *Ibid.*, p. 18.
[45] Alvord, *Illinois Country*, p. 196.

The Sieur d'Iberville, who founded the new French colony of
Louisiana at Biloxi Bay on the Gulf Coast in 1699, claimed jurisdiction over the Illinois country after its abandonment by the forces
of New France. He and his brother, the Sieur de Bienville, who
later became governor of Louisiana, sent expeditions to the Illinois
country but were unable for many years to effect a permanent settlement there. In August 1717, control over Louisiana passed to
the Company of the West (or Mississippi Company), and an
amendment to the charter of the company incorporated the Illinois
country into Louisiana and bestowed upon the company the right
to exploit its resources.[46] Set up in September 1721 as one of nine
military districts in the province of Louisiana, the Illinois district
constituted a narrow strip from the Alleghenies to the Rockies, that
embraced the country between the Ohio and the Illinois River.[47]
Though separated from Quebec rule, the Illinois commandant
would on occasion receive instructions from Canada.[48] The northern boundary was never definitely established, but New France
was regarded as lying beyond the Chicago portage and Fort
Ouiatenon on the Wabash River, thus placing Fort Vincennes and
later Fort Massac within the Illinois district. The districts were
grouped into four commandaries; the Arkansas and Illinois districts
were united into a commandery whose headquarters was in Illinois. Through its headship of the commandery, the jurisdiction of
the Illinois government extended to Arkansas Post and Natchi-
toches on the Red River.[49] In later years when the occupation of the
upper Ohio was undertaken by the forces of Canada, the portion of
the upper Ohio Valley east of the Wabash was transferred from the
Illinois district to Canada.[50]

The new status imposed upon the Illinois country through its
association with Louisiana and the distance of that district from

[46] *Ibid.*, p. 151, 169, 191.

[47] Alvord, *Illinois Country*, p. 152, 190-91.

[48] Lawrence H. Gipson, *Zones of International Friction; North America,
South of the Great Lakes Region 1748-1754* (*The British Empire before the
American Revolution*, vol. IV, New York, 1942), 137.

[49] Caldwell, *French in the Miss. Valley*, p. 12.

[50] Gipson, *Zones of International Friction, South of the Great Lakes*, p. 135.

New Orleans necessitated the formation of a more elaborate governmental organization. The new commandant, Pierre Duqué, Sieur de Boisbriant, arrived at Kaskaskia in December 1718, accompanied by an entourage of military and other officials, a hundred troops, employees of the Company of the West, mining engineers, and workingmen.[51] The erection of Fort de Chartres as the seat of government was quickly undertaken. The government organized by the charter company consisted of the commandant, chief clerk, keeper of the storehouse, under-clerk, engineer, captain of the troops, a lieutenant, two second lieutenants, and a council.[52] At the head was the major commandant who was both the principal military and administrative officer of the district and the commandery. In addition to his military functions the major commandant supervised agriculture, the fur trade and Indian relations, the building of churches, census taking; issued permits for the use of land; and adjudicated disputes. The positions already named were usually combined with others, since the duties for most offices were not burdensome and the individual positions did not provide adequate financial support. The keeper of the storehouse (the commissary) also functioned as the notary for a time, thus continuing a task that had been performed by the Jesuit missionaries.[53] Employment as chaplains was given to the missionaries upon the completion of Fort de Chartres in 1720. Second in importance to the major commandant was Marc Antoine de la Loëre des Ursins, the principal clerk and director of the company.

The provincial council instituted in 1722 acted in a dual capacity. It assisted in administrative affairs by providing advice, officiated as a court of first instance in both civil and criminal cases, and in rendering justice was subordinate to the higher court of the colony at New Orleans. Its membership included the major commandant as president, the principal clerk, the keeper of the storehouse, and the secretary. The council also executed land grants,

---

[51] Alvord, *Illinois Country*, p. 152-53; Sister Mary B. Palm, *The Jesuit Missions of the Illinois Country, 1673-1763* (St. Louis, 1931), 49-50.

[52] Belting, *Kaskaskia*, p. 16-20.

[53] Palm, *Jesuit Missions*, p. 51.

regulated titles, and administered estates.[54] The royal notary also came to function as the clerk of the council, thus combining the two chief record-keeping positions.

Although control of the Louisiana colony was returned to the crown in 1731, the government of the Illinois commandery underwent little alteration in its general composition, with one important exception: the judicial duties of the provincial council were transferred to Louis Auguste de la Loëre Flancour, who arrived in 1734 as the local representatives of the French government's Department of the Marine, and as the *commissaire ordonnateur* of Louisiana.[55] In effect he was subdelegate or deputy intendant, and had charge of justice, police, and finances.. As the judge he decided cases without a jury according to the custom of Paris. After Flancour's death in 1746, Joseph Buchet, who had been the royal storekeeper, served as subdelegate of the intendant until 1757. He had two successors, Jean Arnold Valentine Bobé Descloseaux and Joseph Lefebvre.

The civil communities that developed around the forts and missions in Illinois exercised a degree at self-government. The habitants of the village of Kaskaskia elected a syndic, and as parishioners of the church of the Immaculate Conception they elected *marguilliers* or church wardens.[56] The assemblies that occurred after the mass were presided over by the syndic when matters of a civic character were considered and by the curé when religious questions were involved. The syndic represented the village in lawsuits and attended to certain local matters such as the repair of the fences about the commons. The church wardens supervised burials and controlled the administration of church property. Such officials were also elected at the mission village of Cahokia, and probably at New Chartres, the village that developed about the new Fort de Chartres. The new fort was completed in stone in 1755, at a greater distance from the Mississippi than the two previous forts of the same name. The captain of militia who represented the comman-

---

[54] Edward G. Mason, "Old Fort Chartres," in *Illinois in the Eighteenth Century* (*Fergus Historical Series*, No. 12, Chicago, 1881), 27.

[55] Alvord, *Illinois Country*, p. 194.

[56] *Ibid.*, p. 221; Belting, *Kaskaskia*, p. 21. For further data on the mission in Illinois, see the last section of the chapter.

dant in the villages supervised road work by the citizens and executed the decisions of the judge.

The early settlements in Illinois were located on the low land along the Mississippi River that became known as the American Bottom. Always subject to flooding by the river, Kaskaskia was permanently inundated near the end of the nineteenth century when the Mississippi River cut through the peninsula separating it from the Kaskaskia River and changed its course. Cahokia still exists as a small hamlet a short distance south of East St. Louis, which because of its proximity to St. Louis, Missouri, prospered and outstripped the older settlements in the area after its founding early in the nineteenth century.

Detroit was governed by a succession of commandants under the jurisdiction of the government of New France.[57] Less important in its governmental aspect than Fort de Chartres, this post never had a comparable array of officials. Robert Navarre, a recent arrival in the community, was appointed notary in 1734 and developed into something of a factotum, becoming judge, general scrivener, surveyor, school teacher, tax collector, collector of tithes and church dues, and village and church treasurer.[58] He remained in office until the surrender of Detroit to the British in 1760 and continued for a time under them.

In 1742, Céloron de Blainville went to Detroit as the permanent resident commandant. The French Government believed that a permanent commandant would be more interested in increasing agricultural output, and thereby reducing administrative expenses as well as strengthening control over the Indians. Other officials appointed to serve under Céloron de Blainville included a deputy of the intendant who was to be concerned with legal and financial matters, an almoner, a chaplain, an interpreter, and a surgeon. The

---

[57] The most detailed treatment of the French period at Detroit is to be found in Burton's *City of Detroit,* I. For biographical sketches of the commandants there, see his "Detroit Rulers, French Commandants in this Region from 1701 to 1760," Michigan Pioneer and Historical Society, *Historical Collections,* XXXIV (1905), 303-40. This publication was variously titled; hereafter it will be cited as *Mich. Hist. Colls.* The Society became in 1929 the Michigan State Historical Society.

[58] Burton, ed., *City of Detroit,* I, 106, 165-66.

governor-general of Canada abolished the new system on the grounds that the post should be continued as a reward for distinguished officers and Céloron de Blainville was consequently transferred from Detroit in 1744.[59] By order of the home government, however, he was returned to Detroit in 1749 in the same capacity, and a renewed effort was made to build up the settlement there as an Indian trade center and a bulwark against English aggression.[60] Detroit was given a larger stockade, a bigger garrison, and jurisdiction over forts Miami and Ouiatenon.

Though exploration and evangelization were strong incentives, the chief motive of the French in the Northwest was the development of the fur trade, since together with the allied water transportation industry it provided the bulk of the income of New France. In the early days of the colony, Indian tribes (especially Huron and Ottawa) came down from their villages on the Great Lakes to the French settlements on the St. Lawrence to barter furs for the firearms and hardware on which they had become dependent. These tribes served as middlemen between Indians from regions further west and the French traders, bringing down furs and taking back merchandise. The Iroquois Indians inhabiting the region south of Lake Ontario also served as middlemen between the western Indians and the Dutch, and later with the English at Albany (N.Y.). To preserve their stake in the Northwest, the Iroquois attacked the Huron and then the Ottawa during the mid-seventeenth century, forcing those tribes to flee to more remote areas of the West, and reducing their role as middlemen in the fur trade. Because of this, individual traders were allowed to go to the rich fur country of the Great Lakes, and in the last quarter of the seventeenth century these independent traders or *coureurs de bois* (bushrangers) included such significant figures in western history as Radisson, Groséilliers, Duluth, Perrot, Tonty, La Forest, and Le Sueur. Traders such as these eventually displaced the Indian tribes as middlemen in the fur trade. They established themselves at the trading posts mentioned earlier, and formed a link between the western Indians who trapped beaver and other fur-bearing animals and the commercial companies in Quebec and Montreal,

59 Caldwell, *French in the Miss. Valley*, p. 43.
60 *Ibid.*, p. 44; Wood, "*Céloron de Blainville*," p. 313-14.

whose warehouses contained the manufactured goods imported from France.[61] The beaver pelts were used in France and in other parts of Europe to make felt hats, a very popular headgear at that time.

After the crown took over the control of New France in 1663, it attempted to promote and regulate the fur trade. To prevent un-licensed *coureurs de bois* from encroaching on the trade, a regula-tion of 1673 kept men from the woods, and in 1676 the governor was prohibited from issuing licenses.[62] A limited return to the license system was adopted in 1681, when twenty-five permits were issued to favored persons, and the number of licenses was grad-ually increased until four hundred men were in the Indian coun-try with legal sanction. In 1698, in another effort to suppress the *coureurs de bois* and to force the Indians to bring their furs to the villages on the St. Lawrence, the issuance of licenses was discon-tinued by the crown. Some *coureurs de bois* returned from the woods, but other remained there and received goods with which to continue trade with the Indians. The discontinuance of the In-dian trade was an important factor in the abandonment of the west-ern posts in 1698; when these posts were reestablished early in the eighteenth century their commandants (who received trade mo-nopolies) became the chief figures in the fur trade. Cadillac re-ceived such a privilege at Detroit and had to pay for the mainte-nance of the garrison and the mission out of his profits. He obtained his greatest income from the sale of licenses to *voyageurs* and to resident traders.[63] Although the crown obtained funds for main-taining other posts by leasing trading privileges at the posts to the highest bidders, the commandant at Fort Ouiatenon was allowed only a simple license to trade. Special arrangements were made at other places such as La Pointe, where the right to trade was extended with the understanding that copper would be mined. With the reinstitution of the license system in 1715, the trade was

---

[61] William B. Munro, "The Coureurs de Bois," Massachusetts Historical Society, *Proceedings*, LVII (Oct. 1923-June 1924), 193-95.

[62] Harold A. Innis, *The Fur Trade in Canada; an Introduction to Economic History* (Toronto, 1956), 85; Alvord, *Illinois Country*, p. 72.

[63] Lawrence H. Gipson, *Zones of International Friction; the Great Lakes Frontier, Canada, the West Indies, India, 1748-1754* (*The British Empire before the American Revolution*, Vol. V, New York, 1942), 45.

carried on only at specific posts and the holders could sell licenses to *voyageurs*.[64] During the ensuing years when both the leasing and licensing systems were in effect, the region south of the Great Lakes extending from Ohio to Iowa and Minnesota became the great source of beaver pelts in North America.

The French developed a trade system in the Great Lakes area that was continued by the British: the licenses (*congés*) permitted trade at certain posts, designated the number of canoes to be taken, and the kinds of goods to be carried. Birch bark canoes originally devised by the Indians were enlarged to carry bigger crews and more cargo. The owner of the goods and of the license was the *bourgeois* (employer); the hired men were the *engagés*, and some who paddled the canoes were called *voyageurs* (canoemen); others were blacksmiths, canoe builders, and warehousemen. The *engagés* signed contracts or *engagements* that were filed by the notaries. Fleets of canoes departed from Montreal in the spring or in the middle of September, following the Ottawa River-Lake Nipissing route or the St. Lawrence River and Great Lakes route to Michilimackinac.[65] There the canoes separated into smaller parties and followed the various river routes to the Indians' hunting grounds, where the experienced *voyageurs* traded with the Indians. In the late eighteenth century there were possibly as many as 5,000 *engagés* in the Northwest in any one season. In the spring, the *engagés* met at Michilimackinac, sorted out their furs, and started on the long journey to Montreal.

Unlicensed *coureurs de bois* who obtained their goods clandestinely from merchants in Montreal or in the English colonies also traded among the Indians in the Northwest. Retired *voyageurs* and *coureurs de bois* were the earliest French settlers in the West.[66]

---

[64] *Ibid.*, p. 45; Innis, *Fur Trade in Canada*, p. 106.

[65] Caldwell, *French in Miss. Valley*, p. 51; Alvord, *Illinois Country*, p. 72; Kellogg, *French Régime in Wis.*, p. 268.

[66] On the fur trade see also Arthur S. Morton, *A History of the Canadian West to 1870-71* (London, [1939]); Bernard DeVoto, *The Course of Empire* (Boston, 1952); Grace L. Nute, *The Voyageur's Highway; Minnesota's Border Lake Land* (St. Paul, 1941); Paul C. Phillips and J. W. Smurr, *The Fur Trade* (Norman, Okla., 1961. 2 vols.). A monograph could still be devoted, however, to the French fur trade in the Old Northwest.

Land Grants

Early in the French regime in Canada the seigniorial system of land tenure of Old France was introduced into the colony. The crown made grants of land (seigniories) varying in size with river frontage to seigniors who were obligated to defend their domains.[67] The settlers paid rent and performed certain feudal duties, such as military service and labor, for the seigniors. Such seigniorial grants were made by the French in the West.

Land grants were made in the West to encourage settlement and cultivation, because of the necessity of maintaining the garrisons and the traders as far as possible from local production. The earliest entrepreneurs in Illinois, La Salle and his successors, Tonty and La Forest, were given grants by the crown to assist them in getting established.[68] In 1719 the Sieur de Boisbriant, first commandant of Illinois under the authority of Louisiana, began making grants of land.[69] He laid out a common and confirmed the titles of the villagers of Kaskaskia to land they had appropriated. Ownership of the common, which was used for pasturage and woodlands, was in the parish; the common fields were narrow strips of individually-owned farming land fronting on the rivers adjacent to the villages.[70] A number of large concessions were granted by the commandant and the company director, La Loëre des Ursins. In 1722, the Seminary of Foreign Missions at Cahokia received a grant of four square leagues to be divided into common field concessions among the

[67] The principal work on this system is William B. Munro, *The Seigniorial System in Canada; A Study in French Colonial Policy* (New York, 1907).

[68] In 1683 La Salle made several seigniorial grants at Fort St. Louis to his lieutenants, and in 1690 his grant at that place was transferred to Tonty and La Forest; the texts of these grants are printed in Theodore C. Pease and Raymond C. Werner, eds., *The French Foundations, 1680-1693* (*Collections* of the Illinois State Historical Library, Vol. XXIII, *French Series*, Vol. I, Springfield, Ill., 1934), 19-44, 228-34.

[69] Alvord, *Illinois Country*, p. 207; Palm, *Jesuit Missions*, p. 50.

[70] Plats of the common fields and of the commons of the villages of Illinois, prepared by American surveyors, are in Walter Lowrie and Matthew St. Clair Clarke, eds., *American State Papers, Documents, Legislative and Executive, of the United States* (Washington, Gales and Seaton, 1832-61. 38 vols.), *Public Lands*, II, 182 *et seq.* Hereinafter cited as *A.S.P., Pub. Lands.*

villagers.[71] The mining engineer, François Renault, was given in 1723 a concession north of Fort de Chartres where the village of St. Philippe was founded. De Boisbriant himself became seignior of a concession that became the village of Prairie du Rocher. A common was provided for each of these new villages.[72] The habitants occupying the common fields around the villages were required to pay a tithe to the church amounting to 1/26 of their produce. They did not live in the fields, but rather in dwellings erected on lots within the villages granted to them by the proprietors or by the commandant. During the period of the company government, the council, and later the commandant, made grants at Fort de Chartres.[73] From 1732 onward, after the dissolution of the Company of the Indies, which had succeeded the Mississippi Company in 1719, all concessions of land emanated from the royal officers.[74] The practice of issuing papers with inexact descriptions of the bounds of grants and of making transfers of land by delivery of possession or informal paper grants which were not recorded subsequently caused trouble for the American authorities.[75] Land grants in Illinois were confirmed by the Superior Council of Louisiana in whose registers they were recorded.[76]

[71] John F. McDermott, *et al*, eds., *Old Cahokia; A Narrative and Documents Illustrating the First Century of Its History* (St. Louis, 1949), 15, 95. An English translation of the text of the grant appears on p. 63.

[72] Frederick Beuckman, "The Commons of Kaskaskia, Cahokia, and Prairie du Rocher," *Illinois Catholic Historical Review*, I (Apr. 1919), 407-08.

[73] Edward G. Mason, "Old Fort Chartres," p. 27-32.

[74] *A.S.P., Pub. Lands,* II, 189.

[75] Francis S. Philbrick, ed., *The Laws of Indiana Territory, 1801-1809* (*Colls*. Ill. State Hist. Lib. Vol. XXI, *Law Series*, Vol. II, Springfield, Ill., 1930), lxv-lxvi, lxix-lxx; "Journal of Executive Proceedings . . . ," July 18, 1790, in Clarence E. Carter, ed., *The Territorial Papers of the United States, Volume III, The Territory Northwest of the River Ohio, 1787-1803* (Washington, 1934), 322.

[76] Thompson, "The Cahokia Mission Property," *Ill. Cath. Hist. Rev.,* V (Jan.-Apr. 1923), p. 99; An English text of the confirmation, Aug. 14, 1743, of the grant of the common to Kaskaskia is in Sidney Breese, *The Early History of Illinois from Its Discovery by the French in 1673, until Its Cession to Great Britain in 1763* (Chicago, 1884), 294-96. The text of a petition by inhabitants of Kaskaskia, Feb. 9, 1727, for the confirmation of the grants made by Boisbriant eight years before can be found in the Breese book mentioned above, p. 286-92.

The granting of land at Fort Vincennes is said to have been initiated by its founder, the Sieur de Vincennes.[77] Most of the grants at the fort were made by Capt. Louis St. Ange de Bellerive, who commanded the post from 1736 to 1764. He gave concessions in writing for house lots in the village, farm lands in the form of narrow strips running back from the Wabash River, and gave oral permission to others to occupy land.[78] The concessions were written on small pieces of paper which were filed with the notary or given to the individual. No register of either the written or the verbal grants was kept. A verification of titles, prepared at Vincennes in 1774 at the request of General Haldimand from such documents as could then be found, shows the names of the grantees, the condition of their titles, the dates of the grants, the names of the commandants, and the names of the governors general of Louisiana by whom the concessions were confirmed.[79] Such concessions as were put into writing gave only the meagerest information.[80]

On his seigniory on the Detroit River, Cadillac, under authority given him by the King in 1704, granted lots in the village and for farms on neighboring lands.[81] Grants were made only to those who would occupy or cultivate the lots in person or by tenant, and an annual payment had to be made to the seignior. Later comman-

[77] F. Bosseron and others to Winthrop Sargent, July 3, 1790, Carter, ed., *Terr. Papers, N.W. Terr.,* II, 283.

[78] Certificate of Louis St. Ange, in Jacob P. Dunn, ed., "Documents Relating to the French Settlements on the Wabash," Indiana Historical Society *Publications,* Vol. II, No. 11 (1894), 430; Leonard Lux, *The Vincennes Donation Lands* (reprinted from the Indiana Historcial Society *Publications,* Vol. 15, No. 4, Indianapolis, 1949), 430-31.

[79] Dunn, ed., "Documents French Settlements," p. 425-27.

[80] Examples are printed in Lux, *Vincennes Donation Lands,* p. 434-35; John Law, *The Colonial History of Vincennes under the French, British and American Governments* (Vincennes, 1858), 136-37.

[81] Burton, ed., *City of Detroit,* I, 94-95; 274; Clarence M. Burton, "Cadillac's Village," or "Detroit under Cadillac" with List of Property Owners, and a History of the Settlement from 1701-1710 (Detroit, 1896), 6 *et seq.* Besides the list of the names of property owners, this publication contains a map showing the lots conveyed by Cadillac in Detroit. A list of the sites of land granted by Cadillac can be found in the "Cadillac Papers," *Mich. Hist. Colls.,* XXXIII (1904), 373-82.

dants at Detroit conceded land on the Detroit River and its tributaries, but confirmations were usually not obtained from the
Crown.[82] Some of the grants made by the governor of Canada were
confirmed by the King, and others were not.[83] Few settlers who obtained land under the French regime on the Detroit River and its
branches had documentary titles to that land.[84] Detroit also had a
common used as a pasture from the beginning of the settlement.

Sometime after the reestablishment of Fort Michilimackinac on
the south side of the strait, the fort was considerably enlarged and
plots of land were granted within the enclosure for private use.[85]
Under the terms of the capitulation of Montreal of 1760, these
grants remained in French hands and the British were obliged to
pay rent for the use of some of them.

A seigniory was granted at Sault Ste. Marie in 1750 as a military
and agricultural establishment. With the requirement that a post
be constructed, a grant on the south bank of the St. Mary's River
was made to two officers, the Chevalier de Repentigny and Captain
de Bonne. The former reached the site during the summer of 1751
and before winter completed a stockade, remaining until 1755.
The two officers served with the French forces during the French
and Indian War; De Bonne was killed, and De Repentigny remained loyal thereafter to France. Heirs to the claim brought suit
over a hundred years later in the United States District Court
at Detroit, Mich., which decided they were entitled to 214,000
acres. On appeal to the United States Supreme Court, however, an
adverse decision was rendered in December 1866.[86]

[82] Silas Farmer, *The History of Detroit and Michigan* (Detroit, 1884), 19-
20. In this publication (p. 977-82) appears "A descriptive list of French farms
or private claims in Wayne County"; Ernest J. Lajeunesse, ed., *The Windsor
Border Region, Canada's Southernmost Frontier; a Collection of Documents*
(Toronto, 1960), xlii-xliii, lxx.

[83] Augustus Woodward to Albert Gallatin, Jan. 4, 1806, *A.S.P., Pub. Lands*,
I, 264-65.

[84] Burton, ed., *City of Detroit*, I, 274.

[85] Moreau S. Maxwell and Lewis H. Binford, *Excavation of Fort Michilimackinac, Mackinac City, Michigan, 1959 Season* (East Lansing, Mich.,
1961), 12-13.

[86] Fowle, *Sault Ste. Marie*, p. 193-95; Daniel L. Crossman, "How the Last
French Claim to a Michigan Farm Was Extinguished," (*Mich. Hist. Colls.*,
XIV, Lansing, 1890), p. 644-50.

Illinois Country

Upon the departure of the French from Illinois after its cession to the British at the close of the French and Indian War most of the records of a purely local character were left behind in the places where they had been accumulated. In 1772, the British moved the garrison and the records of Fort de Chartres to Kaskaskia. The abandonment of Fort de Chartres at this time was the result of encroachment by the Mississippi River. What was left of the fort was destroyed by the British upon their departure. In 1915 the State of Illinois acquired the site for a park; the foundations of the fort have been uncovered and some of the original buildings have been reconstructed. The two principal collections of French records were thus brought together in one depository, and since Kaskaskia also served as the county seat of the county of Illinois under Virginia, the French and British records remained there.

Custody of the records was transferred in June 1790 to William St. Clair, recorder of the newly created St. Clair County of the American Northwest Territory by François Carbonneaux.[87] When a segment of St. Clair County became Randolph County in 1795, Kaskaskia became the county seat of the latter county, and the colonial records remained there. Some of the Kaskaskia records were copied at this time by the officials of Cahokia and can be found in "Record A" of the recorder's office at Belleville. To save the county records from the Mississippi River floods which frequently inundated Kaskaskia, the seat of Randolph County was moved to Chester in 1847. The removal of the records took place in March 1848, and as the office of the circuit clerk and recorder was too small to contain all of the documents, the colonial records and other old papers were left in the boxes in which they had been moved and placed in the hall of the county building.[88] Here they remained for years exposed to manuscript hunters. Sometime before 1878 the old records were sacked or packaged and set on top of the book case in the office of the deputy circuit clerk.

In the summer of 1905 Clarence W. Alvord, a young instructor

---

[87] Clarence W. Alvord, "The Old Kaskaskia Records," *Chicago Historical Society Proceedings,* III (1906), 37, 44.

[88] *Ibid.,* p. 38.

at the University of Illinois, was sent by the Illinois State Historical Library to the southern part of the state to search for the old French records. On top of some book shelves in the office of the circuit clerk at Chester, he located three large sacks and four packages of papers.[89] These proved to be the records that had accumulated during the French and British periods at Kaskaskia. Arrangements were made with the county commissioners for the University of Illinois to borrow the French records and part of the British ones in order that they could be arranged and studied. They were deposited in the university library, where Alvord was able to use them for a period of over ten years in his research on early Illinois history.

During the period of 115 years from 1790 to 1905, when steps were at last taken for the proper preservation of the French records of Illinois, the collection was seriously depleted. The receipt given by St. Clair in 1790 refers to three bundles of land papers, six record books in mutilated condition, and 1308 bills of sale dated from 1722 to 1790.[90] Of three registers found by Alvord at Chester he could identify only one of them with those described by St. Clair— a register of the Kaskaskia collection dating from the British period. He also reported the sales papers as about one-third missing. From lists which were found with the records, it is evident that only part of the French records of Illinois survived into the twentieth century. Alvord estimated that there should have been over 7,000 of the types of papers found and that in addition there should have been 2,000 others of an administrative character embracing instructions to the commandant and military and judicial papers. Allowing a total of 9,000, less than a third of the records which probably existed were preserved.[91] There were 2,950 papers dated from 1720 to 1790, and of these, 2,180 related to the French period.

---

[89] *Ibid.*, p. 41; Clarence W. Alvord, "The Finding of the Kaskaskia Records," *Transactions* of the Illinois State Historical Society, 1906, *Publication* No. 11 of the Illinois State Historical Library (Springfield, 1906), 27; Clarence W. Alvord, "Eighteenth Century French Records in the Archives of Illinois," American Historical Association, *Annual Report*, 1906, I, 353.

[90] The text of the receipt is in Alvord, "18th Century French Records," p. 356-57.

[91] *Ibid.*, p. 357-58.

The bulk of the Kaskaskia records are the notarial instruments drawn up at Fort de Chartres and at Kaskaskia. These records are valuable for family, economic, social, and administrative history of the Illinois country.[92] The notorial and judicial records reveal the mode of life which developed in that region during the French regime. An incomplete register kept by the various notaries accompanies the records. There are also two volumes of translations for the years 1723-1802.

Records also exist for the court which operated from 1722 onward. The judicial papers include reports of civil and criminal trials, declarations before the notaries, depositions, reports of the execution of decisions, and petitions for justice.[93] Documents relating to the settlement of estates include authentications with seals, inventories, appointments of guardians, specifications of property and renunciations of community goods by wives or widows.

Such administrative records as had been accumulated by the commandant and the council and which remained on hand at the time of the transfer of sovereignty in 1765, were largely carried off by the French. The papers left behind consist of edicts of the officials, correspondence, and community acts.[94]

Another record that had been kept at Kaskaskia and Fort de Chartres during the French period was found at Belleville. The seat of St. Clair County had been moved there from Cahokia in 1814 and with it the records that had been preserved in the latter village. The record book was bound in hog hide and contained registrations of donations made at Kaskaskia from 1737 to 1754 and and at Fort de Chartres from 1754 to 1764.[95] The last keeper of this book, Joseph Labuxière, took it with him to St. Louis in 1767, and made five entries in it at that place between Sept. 1, 1768 and June 6, 1769. He brought it back with him on his return to Illinois in 1782 or 1783, hoping to be paid by interested parties for copies from the

[92] Alvord, "Kaskaskia Records," p. 29; Alvord, "18th Century French Records," p. 359.

[93] Alvord, "18th Century French Records," p. 359.

[94] *Ibid.*

[95] Clarence W. Alvord, "Illinois in the Eighteenth Century; A Report on the Documents in Belleville, Illinois," Illinois State Historical Library *Bulletin*, I, no. 1 (1905), 12-16; Alvord, "18th Century French Records," p. 363-64.

French register. The volume was preserved in the court records at Cahokia and was finally carried to Belleville. John Nicholas ("Nick") Perrin, lawyer and historian of that place, found this record in 1890 and described it years later.[96] Entitled "Registre des Insinuations des Donations aux Siege des Illinois," it is a record of civil contracts, mostly marriage contracts and donations of property in payment of old age care.[97] It also contains some partnership contracts, provisions for dowries, and the 1768 settlement of property by Pierre Laclede upon Madame Chouteau. The original register was transferred from Belleville, St. Clair County to the Illinois State Archives in 1940. Found in legible condition, it has been calendared, indexed, and translated. Microfilm and typewritten copies of the register are in the custody of the Illinois Historical Survey at Urbana.

Not all of the papers that disappeared from the Kaskaskia records were lost. The collection had not been completely unknown and unused. In 1884 Sidney Breese reported that he had found the records of the court of the royal jurisdiction of Illinois among the lumber in the county recorder's office.[98] Another Illinois historian, Edward G. Mason, visited Chester about 1879, and apparently as a result, part of the Kaskaskia records found their way to the Chicago Historical Society.[99] These records, 135 in number, covered the years 1737-84 and included deeds, partnerships, transfers, engagements, sales, and concessions of land at Kaskaskia, Fort de Chartres, and other places.[1] The custodians of the records at Chester were

[96] John Nicholas Perrin, "The Oldest Civil Record in the West," *Trans.* Ill. State Hist. Soc., 1901, *Pub.* No. 6, Ill. State Hist. Lib. (Springfield, 1901), 63-65; J. N. Perrin, *Perrin's History of Illinois* (Springfield, Ill., 1906), 69. Another description was published by a member of the faculty of the University of Chicago; see Edwin E. Sparks, "Record of a Lost Empire in America," *Chautauquan,* XXXIII (Aug. 1901), 478-86.

[97] Margaret C. Norton "The Oldest Extant Civil Record West of the Alleghanies," *Illinois Libraries,* XXXI (Apr. 1949), 187. Some facsimile pages from the register consisting of marriage contracts for 1737 are on p. 188-89 of this article.

[98] Sidney Breese, *The Early History of Illinois* (Chicago, 1884), 217.

[99] Alvord, "Old Kaskaskia Records," p. 40.

[1] Canada, Public Archives, *Report on Canadian Archives,* 1905 (Ottawa, 1905), I, xliii. Rev. P. M. O'Leary transcribed these records for the Public Archives of Canada in 1906.

apparently not adverse to using the old records for lighting fires[2] or to allowing visitors to carry away documents that interested them.[3]

After the transfer of the Kaskaskia records to the University of Illinois Library, steps were taken for their repair and preservation. Alvord remedied the state of disorder and disrepair to which the records had been reduced by neglect and mishandling by arranging them in chronological order under subject headings and placing them in large envelopes. Work on the collection was facilitated by the creation in the graduate school in 1910 of the Illinois Historical Survey, whose task under the direction of Alvord was the collection of source materials on the history of Illinois. Documents in need of repair were reinforced with silk, mounted on sheets of paper, and placed in covers before being boxed. The collection was classified into three groups: commercial papers, 1718-97 (12 boxes); private papers, 1739-96 (7 boxes); and public papers, 1720-1816 (5 boxes).[4] Other work performed upon the manuscripts included the preparation of a calendar, an incomplete biographical index, and transcripts, abstracts, and translations.[5] The collection was returned to Randolph County in two installments, the second one being made in 1935. The Survey subsequently acquired a microfilm of part of the records for the French period made by Natalia B. Belting in 1939 for use in her book on *Kaskaskia under the French Regime*.[6]

The most important measure for the preservation of the Kaskaskia records was taken in 1952 when the Illinois State Archives

[2] Mason, "Old Fort Chartres," p. 42.

[3] Alvord, "Old Kaskaskia Records," p. 44.

[4] Ernest E. East and Margaret C. Norton, "Randolph County Records; an Inventory of Microfilm Copies in the Illinois State Library," *Illinois Libraries,* XXXV (June 1953), 256-58. See also the inventory by M. J. Pease cited below.

[5] "Report of the Editor," in Illinois State Historical Library, *Report,* 1914, 20; Ernest E. East, "Historical Treasures of Randolph County," *Illinois Libraries,* XXXV (Apr. 1953), 162.

[6] The Canadian Archivist, Arthur G. Doughty, inspected the Kaskaskia records while they were at Urbana and arranged for copies to be made (Doughty to J. F. Jameson, Feb. 6, 1906, Carnegie Institution of Washington, Department of Historical Research, Correspondence Files).

microfilmed selected documents on 47 reels.[7] Copies of this microfilm have since become available at the Illinois Historical Survey of the University of Illinois and at Southern Illinois University at Carbondale, and persons interested in doing research on the French period of Illinois are encouraged to use these photographic reproductions instead of the fragile originals at Chester. Selections from the Kaskaskia records have been microfilmed by the National Park Service for use in its studies of historic sites.

John Allen, the curator of history of the Southern Illinois University Museum, found some additional Kaskaskia records at Chester in 1950 and removed them to that institution for examination and microfilming.[8] These records included a few miscellaneous documents for 1737-44, and others of later dates. When the microfilming was completed by the university, the original records were returned to the circuit court at Chester.

In 1959 an important group of Kaskaskia manuscripts was found among the personal papers left by Alvord at the University of Illinois when he departed for the University of Minnesota in 1920.[9] He was probably preparing these together with documents from other sources for publication. A record book for 1736-82 contains deeds and other legal documents, and among some 270 loose documents, 1718-1834, are other notarial papers on the French regime. The documents were calendared and microfilmed and a revised inventory of the Randolph county records was published. The officials of that county accepted an offer of the Illinois State Archives to laminate and bind the documents, and they were later returned to the circuit court clerk.

John Nicholas Perrin spent so much time working with the old records in the courthouse at Belleville that they became known as the "Perrin collection." He used the records for historical research,

[7] Illinois University, Illinois Historical Survey, *Guide to Manuscript Materials of American Origin in the Illinois Historical Survey,* comp. by Marguerite J. Pease (Urbana, June 1956), 85-86.

[8] Norman W. Caldwell, "Additional Kaskaskia Manuscripts," *Illinois Libraries,* XXXIV (May 1952), 194-202. For further treatment of this collection, see Chapter III.

[9] Marguerite Jenison Pease, "Archives in Randolph County; a Revised Inventory," *Illinois Libraries,* XLIII (June 1961), 437, 446.

arranged them, and prepared an index which is still in use. He was in charge of the records as county archivist of St. Clair County during the 1930's. After his death they were cared for by the local historical society until their transfer on a permanent loan in 1940 to the Illinois State Archives.[10] That institution has repaired the records, arranged them in chronological order in legal size folders, translated, calendared, and indexed them.[11] A microfilm of the collection is in the Illinois Historical Survey at Urbana.[12] The years covered are 1722 to 1809, but most of the records for the French period have disappeared.[13] The accumulation of records at Cahokia would not have been great, however, since it was not the seat of government.

In Illinois, through the efforts of the Illinois Historical Survey and the Illinois State Archives, most of the essential steps for the proper preservation of the valuable records on the colonial history of the state have been taken. But there is still need for detailed inventories of the French and British records and of the archival reproductions arranged according to provenance and covering all depositories.

Alvord initiated a program for the procurement of reproductions from the French archives for the University of Illinois in 1906 in order to recover the missing administrative papers and to complete the documentation for the French period.[14] Little was accomplished, however, before the creation of the Illinois Historical Survey in 1910, when an arrangement was made with Waldo G. Leland, the agent of the Carnegie Institution of Washington in France, for the selection and copying of documents relating to Illinois. After an interruption caused by the European War, work

[10] Margaret C. Norton, "The J. Nick Perrin Collection," *Illinois Libraries,* XXII (Oct. 1940), 22-24.

[11] Icko Iben, "Notes from the Work Shop, Marriage in Old Cahokia," *Illinois Libraries,* XXVI (Nov. 1944), 473.

[12] Illinois University, Ill. Hist. Survey, *Guide to MS, Materials of Amer. Origin,* p. 90.

[13] McDermott, *Old Cahokia,* p. 93-94.

[14] Henry P. Beers, *The French in North America; A Bibliographical Guide to French Archives, Reproductions, and Research Missions* (Baton Rogue, 1957), 161-65.

was resumed in March 1916 and carried on for a year and a half in the Archives des Colonies. Transcripts from the same source in the Library of Congress were photographed. The addition of these numerous reproductions to the Kaskaskia records formed a broad documentary basis and enabled Alvord to present in his *Illinois Country* the first consecutive account of the French occupation of the upper Mississippi Valley. He planned to do a more complete study of the French regime in Illinois but was unable to accomplish it.

Publication of the documents had to await the completion of volumes on the British regime and the procurement of additional reproductions. Theodore C. Pease, Alvord's successor, and Raymond C. Werner edited some of these reproductions together with others from the notarial archives of Montreal, the Otto L. Schmidt collection of the Chicago Historical Society, and from the Newberry Library and published them in 1934 as *The French Foundations, 1680-1693*. This compilation dealt with the financial and commercial aspects of the colonization of Illinois. To select additional documents for the continuation of the French series, Pease visited Paris in 1933 and again in 1937. Photostats obtained during 1934-40 through Abel Doysié became the basis of two additional volumes.[15] The collection of transcripts, photostats, and microfilm, derived from the Archives des Colonies, the archives of the Ministries of Marine, War, and Foreign Affairs, the Hydrographic Service, and the Bibliothèque Nationale to which further additions were made in 1946-1948, covers the years 1669 to 1796.[16] There is a gap in the published series from 1694 to 1746, but so far as they go, the documents which appear in both French and English are an excellent contribution to the history of the state. The reproductions from the

[15] Theodore C. Pease, ed., *Anglo-French Boundary Disputes in the West, 1749-1763* (*Colls.* Ill. State Hist. Lib. vol. XXVII, *French Series*, vol. II, Springfield, 1936); and Pease and Ernestine Jenison, eds., *Illinois on the Eve of the Seven Years' War, 1747-1755* (*Colls.* Ill. State Hist. Lib., vol. XXIX, French Series, vol, III, Springfield, 1940). The Illinois Historical Survey plans to publish additional documents.

[16] For complete information, see Illinois University, Illinois Historical Survey, *Guide to Manuscript Materials Relating to Western History in Foreign Depositories Reproduced for the Illinois Historical Survey*, comp. by Marguerite J. Pease, (Urbana, Ill., 1956), 53-98.

Archives des Colonies, series C11A, relate to the whole of the Northwest with some material on Louisiana and include many letters and other documents by officers and Jesuit priests who served at Fort de Chartres, and Fort Ouiatenon, as well as communications from the officials of New France relating to that area. The copies from the Archives des Colonies, series B (outgoing letters) contain instructions about the western posts which would have been forwarded by the governors of Canada and Louisiana.

Censuses were taken in the Illinois country during the eighteenth century, but some of them were merely statistical in content.[17] A transcript of the census of Jan. 1, 1732 from the French Archives des Colonies, series G1, vol. 464 in the Manuscript Division of the Library of Congress contains the names of heads of families, and the numbers of children, Negro and Indian slaves, farm animals, mills, houses, and barns in the different settlements. A copy of this census is also in the Canadian Public Archives.

Though an earlier start had been made in Indiana in procuring reproductions from French archives, only a small quantity was ever obtained.[18] The first acquisition was from the Canadian Public Archives,[19] and others were later obtained from Paris.[20] A fuller documentation relative to Indiana will be found in the reproductions at Urbana, in the Library of Congress, and in the Canadian Public Archives.

The University of Chicago has a large collection of manuscript reproductions in depositories in the United States, Canada, and

[17] Statistical data from the censuses of 1723, 1724, 1732, and 1752 relating to Illinois are in Margaret C. Norton, ed., *Illinois Census Returns, 1810, 1818* (*Colls*. Ill. State Hist. Lib., Vol. XXIV, *Statistical Series*, Vol. II, Springfield, 1935), xxi-xxv. See also Evarts B. Greene and Virginia D. Harrington, *American Population Before the Federal Census of 1790* (New York, 1932), 186-92. Concerning the 1752 census see the description of the Vaudreuil papers in this chapter. A publication containing all of the censuses relating to the Old Northwest would be a valuable source of genealogical and economic data.

[18] Beers, *French in North America*, p. 169.

[19] Jacob P. Dunn, ed., "Documents Relating to the French Settlements on the Wabash," Ind. Hist. Soc., *Pubs.*, II, No. 11 (1894), 403-42.

[20] Jacob P. Dunn, ed., "The Mission to the Ouabache," Ind. Hist. Soc., *Pubs.*, VIII, No. 2 (1924), 253-330; Caroline Dunn and Eleanor Dunn, trans., "Indiana's First War," Ind. Hist. Soc., *Pubs.*, VIII, No. 2 (1924), 71-143.

Europe relating to early white men and Indians in the Mississippi Valley.

Detroit

No original records of the French period remained in official custody at Detroit at the time of the transfer to the United States. The notarial records had been sent to Quebec in 1784 by order of Governor Haldimand, and remained there until 1790 when William D. Powell, the first judge of the court of common pleas for the District of Hesse, brought them back to Detroit.[21] They came into the custody of William Monforton in his capacity as notary public. Instead of surrendering these records to the American authorities at the time of the transfer of sovereignty in 1796, he took them across the Detroit River to Sandwich. Pursuant to an Ontario statute of 1871, volumes A, B, and C of the notarial registers were returned to Detroit where they were placed in the registrar's office of Wayne County. Volume A of these registers covers the French period, but it contains only 10 pages for 1737 to 1767.[22] Copies of the notarial acts are in the Burton Historical Collection of the Detroit Public Library, which has made an index, and in the Canadian Public Archives at Ottawa.[23] Other copies of notarial documents retained by the individuals concerned will be found in collections of personal papers described elsewhere.

A record of notarial transactions at Detroit for 1707-10 with some

[21] Burton, ed., *City of Detroit*, I, 206; Milo M. Quaife, ed., *The John Askin Papers* (Detroit, 1928, 1931. 2 vols.), I, 107; Lajeunesse, ed., *Windsor Border Region*, p. lxiv, 74; Quebec (Province) Council Committee, "Report of the Committee of Quebec on the Ancient Archives [March 1790]," in Canada, Public Archives, *Report Concerning the Public Archives*, 1904 (Ottawa, 1905), Appendix D, 127 (hereafter cited as "Report of the Committee of Quebec").

[22] Letter from James M. Babcock, Chief, Burton Historical Collection, July 9, 1958, with report by Dorothy V. Martin. The texts of two land grants of 1751 in the notarial records are in Lajeunesse, ed., *Windsor Border Region*, p. 58-59.

[23] Floyd B. Streeter, "The Burton Historical Collection of the Detroit Public Library," *Americana Collector*, I (Jan. 1926), 129; Canada, Public Archives, *Report*, 1904, 53; David W. Parker, *Guide to the Materials for United States History in Canadian Archives* (Washington, 1913), 105.

earlier documents relating to Cadillac executed at Quebec was found in the archives at Quebec and published in English by Clarence M. Burton.[24] It consist largely of sales of houses in Fort Pontchartrain, but it contains also some marriage contracts, a contract between Cadillac and the Ursulines for the care of his daughter, and an inventory of Cadillac's property.[25]

One original record of the French regime is in the Burton Historical Collection of the Detroit Public Library. Long in the possession of the Cicotte family, it is known as the "Cicotte ledger." It is a register of families that settled in Detroit and in Windsor, Ont. during 1749-51 under a special government program and gives information relating to the families, the extent and location of the land grants, and the assistance afforded by the government in rations, farming equipment, animals, and loans.[26]

Other materials relating to Detroit and Michigan were also collected by Clarence M. Burton, the owner of a title and abstract company in Detroit, whose investigations in land titles developed an interest in historical manuscripts. From Quebec he obtained copies of judicial papers and of documents in the registers of the Superior Council concerning the settlement of Detroit. During 1895 to 1898 he employed a copyist in the notarial archives in the courthouse at Montreal to copy all documents relating to the Old Northwest and to extract all other documents.[27] The result was

[24] Clarence M. Burton, "Cadillac's Records," *Mich. Hist. Colls.*, XXXIV (1905), 215-77.

[25] Data from these records are incorporated into an alphabetical list entitled "Citizens and Families of Early Detroit—Directory of Cadillac's Village, 1701-1710," in Burton, ed., *City of Detroit*, II, 1314-37. Another list of the inhabitants of Detroit in 1710 is in *Mich. Hist. Colls.*, XXXIII (1903), 492-95. A list of the men who were with Cadillac in 1701 is in Jean Delanglez, "The Genesis and Building of Detroit," *Mid-America*, XXX (Apr. 1948), 99-104.

[26] L. O. [Woltz], "Source Material of the Detroit Public Library as Supplied by the Acquisition of the Burton Historical Collection," *Michigan History Magazine*, VI (1922), 389. The Burton Historical Collection has clippings from the Detroit *Evening News*, Aug. 15, 22, 29, 1903, containing a list of the names of the colonists who settled in Detroit under this program. An extract from the record containing entries relating to a few settlers is in Lajeunesse, ed., *Windsor Border Region*, p. 49-53.

[27] C. M. Burton to Waldo G. Leland, Dec. 27, 1904, Carnegie Instit. Wash., Dept. Hist. Research, Corresp. Files.

twenty-two volumes of transcripts consisting of seven thousand pages for the years 1678-1819.[28] These voluminous copies consist of contracts or agreements between Montreal merchants and *voyageurs*, soldiers, and interpreters, to whom they had committed their goods, for the conduct of trade with the Indians in the Upper Country.[29] The collection also comprises bills of lading, invoices, deeds of sale, partnerships, official appointments, marriage contracts, powers of attorney, and occasional personal correspondence. An index to the collection was prepared by the Work Projects Administration in 1939-40. These thousands of documents form one of the best sources for the life of the early white men in the West. Information may be derived from them regarding the names of the *voyageurs*, their posts, dates of visits, the conduct of the trade, and the Indians. At Ottawa, Mr. Burton secured copies of documents collected by the first Dominion Archivist, Douglas Brymner.

Burton's collecting activities also extended to the archives of France. Between 1893 and 1897 he obtained twelve volumes of transcripts through Benjamin F. Stevens from the Archives des Colonies (series C11).[30] From translations of these prepared by Stevens, Burton edited and published an important collection of documents for 1686 to 1741 relating to the founding of Detroit and the early years of Michigan.[31] The documents concern administration, military affairs, Indian trade and relations, Jesuit missions, and land grants. The volumes embody in many instances information regarding Mackinac and Illinois as well as Detroit. On a personal visit to France in 1907, Burton procured additional copies of Cadillac papers, and in subsequent years he arranged for transcribing others. A translation of the extensive compilation by Pierre

[28] Canada, Public Archives, *Report*, 1905, I, xxiv, xxvii; Letter from James M. Babcock, Chief, Burton Historical Collection, July 9, 1958, with report by Dorothy V. Martin.

[29] A *voyageur's* contract of July 1749 is in Lajeunesse, ed. *Windsor Border Region*, p. 48-49. See the discussion of the notarial records of Quebec in Chapter II.

[30] Beers, *French in North America*, p. 113-16.

[31] "Cadillac Papers," *Mich. Hist. Colls.*, XXXIII-XXXIV (Lansing, 1904-05), 36-715, 11-214.

Margry,[32] containing much relating to Detroit and the Northwest, was also made by B. F. Stevens and Brown, Ltd., of London, at the instance of Burton. A microfilm of the translation is in the University of Chicago Library. Burton's acquisitions were presented in 1914 to the Detroit Public Library, and in 1921 the collection was established as The Burton Historical Collection. Its staff is presently assembling data for a guide to its materials.

A neighboring institution, the William L. Clements Library at Ann Arbor, contains a collection of transcripts from the Archives des Colonies, series C11A. Obtained by Clements in 1921 through Abel Doysié, this collection of 2,720 pages concerns affairs in Canada, the Great Lakes region, and the Illinois country. It duplicates to a considerable extent the collections of Burton and of the Illinois Historical Survey.[33]

The Burton Historical Collection later acquired photostats from the Archives des Colonies concerning the Sieur de Cadillac, Indians, military posts (particularly Detroit and Mackinac), Jesuits, fur trade, and campaigns against the Foxes and Chickasaw, 1686-1752. Reproductions of documents relating to the Sieur de Cadillac have also been obtained from the Institut Généalogique Drouin at Montreal and the McCord Museum of McGill University. The Burton Historical Collection has obtained a few original Cadillac documents from different sources, and a census of the inhabitants of Detroit of Sept. 1, 1750. In 1958 it bought a collection of 66 *arrêts*, edicts, *déclarations*, ordinances, and memoirs issued by the French Government during 1671-1769, most of which have probably been printed in the compilation published by the province of Quebec.[34] The collection also has rare French publications many of which are documentary in character.

---

[32] *Mémoires et documents pour servir à l'histoire des origines françaises des pays d'outre-mer; découvertes et établissements des français dans l'ouest et dans le sud le l'Amérique septentrionale (1614-1754)* (Paris, 1879-88. 6 vols.). Concerning the preparation of this work, see Beers, *French in North America*, p. 102-10.

[33] Beers, *French in North America*, p. 181-82.

[34] New France, Laws, Statutes, etc., *Édits, ordonnances royaux, déclarations et arrêts du Conseil d'État du roi concernant le Canada* (Québec, 1854-56. 3 vols.).

The Michigan Pioneer and Historical Society obtained copies of French documents from the Canadian Public Archives during the 1890's, including transcripts from the French archives in Paris.[35] A few of these were apparently published in various volumes of the Society's *Historical Collections*, but the bulk of the documents remained unpublished and were destroyed in the burning of the State Office Building at Lansing in 1951.

Censuses giving the names of inhabitants were taken infrequently at Detroit during the French regime. A census believed to be of 1706 and to have been acquired from the library of Peter Force is in the Manuscript Division, Library of Congress. Besides the names of heads of families, it gives ages, birthplaces, numbers of boys, girls, *engagés*, slaves, quantity of land, and property owned. A copy of a census of Sept. 1, 1750, obtained from the Archives des Colonies, series G1, v. 461, is in the Canadian Public Archives, from which the Burton Historical Collection apparently acquired a photostat. It shows the names of heads of families, the number of women, boys and girls under and over 15, and slaves in each household, and statistics as to agricultural production and farm animals. This census has been published,[36] and statistical data on the population of Detroit is available for other years.[37] A Detroit census for 1760, giving information similar to that of the 1750 census, is in the Burton Historical Collection.

The State Historical Society of Wisconsin also has reproductions from French and Canadian archives. The secretary of the Society, Lyman C. Draper, obtained a small quantity of transcripts consisting chiefly of journals of military expeditions against the Indians during 1690 to 1730 from the Library of Parliament of Canada and published them.[38] His successor, Reuben G. Thwaites, published a larger collection of French documents consisting of

---

[35] "Report of the Committee of Historians," *Mich. Hist. Colls.*, XXI (1892), 30.

[36] Lajeunesse, ed., *Windsor Border Region*, p. 54-56.

[37] Greene and Harrington, *American Population before 1790*, p. 190-91.

[38] Lyman C. Draper, ed., "Canadian Documents," (*Collections* of the State Historical Society of Wisconsin, V, Madison, 1907), 64-108. Originally published in 1868.

acts of possession filed by French explorers.[39] Thwaites employed a copyist in the French Archives des Colonies during 1896-99 and in later years obtained additional transcripts.[40] He edited selections from these, from copies of French transcripts and original records in Canada, and from a number of printed sources and published an extensive compilation.[41] Though composed more largely of communications which passed between the officials of Canada and those of the French government in Paris, this compilation, from 1684 to 1760, contains numerous documents originating with commandants and missionaries in the West. The documents concern discoveries, Indian trade and relations, missions, military affairs, posts, and geography—not only of Wisconsin but of all the Old Northwest. Louise P. Kellogg, a research associate of the State Historical Society of Wisconsin, utilized these documents in preparing a scholarly work on the *French Régime in Wisconsin and the Northwest*. The study, published in 1925, was written from a new angle—that of the western posts.

Although the State of Pennsylvania has not considered it necessary to procure reproductions directly from the French archives, the Pennsylvania Historical and Museum Commission has an extensive collection of copies consisting of reproductions borrowed from the Canadian Public Archives as well as copies of documents in other Canadian depositories and in the Library of Congress.[42] The Frontier Forts and Trails Survey, a Works Projects Administration program sponsored by the State published translations of some documents.[43] Dr. Alfred P. James prepared for the Western Pennsylvania Historical Survey in Paris in 1932 a calendar of docu-

[39] Reuben G. Thwaites, ed., "Important Western State Papers," (*Colls.* State Hist. Soc. Wis., XI, Madison, 1888), 26-63.

[40] Beers, *French in North America*, p. 158.

[41] Reuben G. Thwaites, ed., *The French Régime in Wisconsin, 1634-1760,* (*Colls.* State Hist. Soc. Wis., XVI-XVIII, Madison, 1902, 1906, 1908. 3 vols.).

[42] Donald H. Kent, "Preserving Pennsylvania's Historical Heritage Photographically," *Pennsylvania History,* XVII (Oct. 1950), 305-06.

[43] *Journal of Chaussegros de Léry,* edited by Sylvester K. Stevens and Donald H. Kent (Harrisburg, 1940); *Wilderness Chronicles of Northwestern Pennsylvania,* edited by Sylvester K. Stevens and Donald H. Kent (Harrisburg, 1941). See also Beers, *French in North America*, p. 170-72.

ments which is deposited in the Darlington Memorial Library of the University of Pittsburgh.[44]

The collections of reproductions from French archives in Midwest depositories provide valuable sources for data concerning the French era. But since they were acquired on a selective basis and consist of transcripts, they are incomplete and sometimes inaccurate. Investigators should supplement them by using the photographic reproductions which can be borrowed from the Library of Congress and from the Canadian Public Archives. The documentary compilations published in Michigan, Wisconsin, Illinois, and Indiana are selective and incomplete even for the years they cover, but they provide a beginning for many areas of investigation.

Land Records

Records relating to land grants in the Old Northwest suddenly became of interest to the United States when it undertook the settlement of the land claims derived from the former governments. The problem of the lands in the territory northwest of the Ohio River came up in the Congress of the Confederation even before the Treaty of Paris of 1783 acknowledged that region to be a part of the United States. Upon the urgings of the Congress, the states having claims to the region under the terms of their colonial charters from the British Government executed deeds of cession during 1781-86 surrendering those claims.[45] Congressional resolves for June 20 and Aug. 29, 1788 required that measures be taken to confirm in their titles and possessions the French and Canadian inhabitants of the settlements on the Mississippi River and at Vincennes.[46]

[44] Franklin J. Holbrook, "The Survey in Retrospect," *Western Pennsylvania Historical Magazine*, XIX (Dec. 1936), 297.

[45] Frederic L. Paxson, *History of the American Frontier, 1763-1893* (Boston, 1924), 49-55. The acts of cession are printed in Carter, ed., *Terr. Papers, N.W. Terr.*, II, 3-12, 22-24. The Virginia document stipulated that the possessions and titles of the French and Canadian inhabitants and other settlers of Kaskaskia, Vincennes, and neighboring villages were to be confirmed to them (*ibid.*, II, 8).

[46] Carter, ed., *Terr. Papers, N.W. Terr.*, II, 112-15, 145. See also Payson J. Treat, *The National Land System, 1785-1820* (New York, 1910), 203.

Pursuant to instructions of Aug. 29, 1788,[47] Governor St. Clair undertook early in 1790 the examination of claims to land at those places. Besides requiring the settlers to exhibit documentary proof of their claims, he apparently utilized the "Papiers Terriers" in the custody of the notary, François Carbonneaux. Three bundles of these land papers were receipted on June 12, 1790 by William St. Clair, who had been appointed recorder of deeds for St. Clair County in the preceding month.[48] The report by the governor was accompanied by a list of land claims at Kaskaskia and a list of the inhabitants there, at Cahokia, and at Prairie du Pont.[49]

When Randolph County was formed from the southern portion of St. Clair County in October 1795, the French land records remained at Kaskaskia, which became the seat of the new county. In 1848 the records were taken to Chester, the new county seat.

The state legislature took a well-conceived measure for the preservation of the old French records when, on Feb. 14, 1855, it designated William Henry, of Prairie du Rocher, to translate them into English and to record them in well-bound books.[50] Translations so recorded were to be entered into the index and entry books kept by the county recorder. The translation thus authorized makes up two volumes of documents for the years 1723-1802.[51] It was fortunate that the translations were recorded, since during the next fifty years the original land records disappeared, and Alvord's search in 1905 brought to light only four badly torn leaves of the three bundles of papers taken over by William St. Clair in 1790.[52]

[47] Carter, ed., *Terr. Papers, N.W. Terr.,* II, 146.

[48] Alvord, "Old Kaskaskia Records," p. 44.

[49] The report made to the Secretary of State, Feb. 10, 1791, is printed in Carter, ed., *Terr. Papers, N.W. Terr.,* II, 323-37 (the lists on p. 253-61). Extracts from the report are in *A.S.P., Pub. Lands,* I, 18-19. The act of Congress of Mar. 3, 1791 confirmed 400 acres of land to each head of a family resident in the Illinois country or at Vincennes in 1783 (1 Stat. 221-22).

[50] Illinois, Laws, *Private Laws,* 1855, p. 677-78.

[51] Theodore C. Pease, comp., *The County Archives of the State of Illinois* (*Colls.* Ill. State Hist. Lib., Vol. XII, *Bibliog. Ser.,* Vol. III, Springfield, 1915), 556.

[52] Alvord, "18th Century French Records," p. 357; Alvord, "Old Kaskaskia Records," p. 45.

Investigations in the archives in Paris have failed to uncover concessions or petitions relating to land grants in Illinois.[53] The examination of the land claims at Vincennes was undertaken in 1790 by Winthrop Sargent, secretary of the Northwest Territory. He found an incomplete collection of land records, owing to the careless record-keeping methods that had been followed by the French and the British.[54] The practice of filing concessions written on small pieces of paper in the notary's office without taking the trouble to record them in bound volumes had resulted in the loss of many of the papers. Sargent learned that at the end of the French regime one notary, indifferent to the interests of the settlers, had carried off all papers in his possession.[55] Such French papers as survived were probably taken over from Jean M. P. LeGras, the commandant of the village, who had shown them to Col. Josiah Harmar, the commander of the United States Army, upon his appearance there in August 1787.[56] John Mills, appointed the recorder of deeds of Knox County on July 3, 1790,[57] soon after the formation of the county, became the new custodian of the records. Sargent's examination was based also on documents presented by claimants, which were returned to them. For inclusion in his report and for the guidance of the surveyor he had appointed to lay out the claims, Sargent drew up a list of claims which he recommended for confirmation.[58]

The activities of the board of land commissioners at Kaskaskia

[53] Alvord, *Illinois Country*, p. 207 n. 48.

[54] Winthrop Sargent to the President, July 31, 1790, *A.S.P., Pub. Lands*, I, 9-11.

[55] *Ibid.*, 10. J. E. Phillibert, one-time notary at Vincennes, certified on Aug. 12, 1773, that in 1761 the flight of Baumer, his successor as notary, and the removal of the record office of the post in the same year to an Illinois post had caused the loss of a number of concessions and contracts of sale (Dunn, ed., "French Settlements," p. 428).

[56] Josiah Harmar to Henry Knox, Aug. 7, 1787, Smith, ed., *St. Clair Papers*, II, 27.

[57] Carter, ed., *Terr. Papers, N.W. Terr.*, III, 316.

[58] Sargent to Samuel Baird, July 31, 1790, *A.S.P., Pub. Lands*, I, 12-15. Baird was also supplied on July 13, 1790 with a list of the heads of families resident at Vincennes in 1783 and entitled to donations of land authorized by Congress (*ibid.*, p. 11; Carter, ed., *Terr. Papers, N.W. Terr.*, II, 285-87).

resulted in the accumulation of records relating to the French and British land grants in the Illinois settlements. During the course of their investigations, the commissioners ascertained that most of the records relating to the private land claims had disappeared.[59] They utilized the records in the custody of the recorder of Randolph County, including a record of grants made between 1722 and 1740,[60] recorded documents presented by claimants and oral testimony from knowledgeable settlers regarding other claims. Robert Robinson, who was engaged as clerk, interpreter and translator for the board on Jan. 1, 1805, remained in its employ for five years.[61] In 1810, on the basis of these records, the commissioners prepared and forwarded to the Treasury Department reports on all claims to town lots, farms, and the village commons in the Illinois country.[62] Numerous lists of claimants and plans of the villages are included in the reports.

More important than the published source mentioned above for the history of the settlement of Illinois during the eighteenth century are the records collected in the land office at Kaskaskia. They remained there until the office was abolished in 1855, when they were transferred to the Springfield land office.[63] An act of Congress of July 31, 1876, abolished the Springfield office and provided for the transfer of the records to the state of Illinois.[64] A custodian provided by the state in 1879[65] remained in charge of the records until June 1882, when they passed into the custody of the Auditor of

[59] See statements by the commissioners, Elijah Backus and Michael Jones, published in their reports in *A.S.P., Pub. Lands*, II, 124, 182, 183, 189.

[60] *Ibid.*, p. 189.

[61] Robinson to Return J. Meigs, Apr. 20, 1810, Carter, ed., *Terr. Papers, Ill. Terr.*, XVI, 90-93; Petition to Congress by Robert Robinson, no date, 1810, *ibid.*, p. 93-94. Robinson was allowed $500 compensation for his extra services, including the conveyance of the reports of the commissioners to Washington (Act of May 1, 1810, 6 Stat. 94).

[62] *A.S.P., Pub. Lands*, II, 123-209. A subsequent report dated Jan. 4, 1813, appears *ibid.*, p. 210-41.

[63] Thomas A. Hendricks to Register and Receiver, Kaskaskia, Nov. 16, 1855, Records of the Department of the Interior, General Land Office, Register and Receiver, Letter Record, v. 48. National Archives.

[64] 19 Stat. 121.

[65] Act of May 21, 1879, Illinois, *Statutes,* 1879, 238.

Public Accounts.[66] Besides many volumes of field survey notes,
township plats, tract books, and records of the sale of lands from
the various Federal land offices in the state, the collection includes
a register of documents relating to the French and British land
claims. The register contains four volumes of grants, deeds, affidavits, etc., entered in French and English during the years 1804-
14.[67] A fifth volume contains English translations of the French
documents recorded in the other volumes. One bundle contains
papers which are mostly recorded in registers one and two. The
land records are now housed in the Illinois State Archives, but
they remain under the control of the Auditor. The registers are
valuable for the local history and genealogy of the colonial period.

When Detroit and Mackinac were taken over by the United
States from the British in 1796, they were placed under the jurisdiction of the Northwest Territory. The treaty with Great Britain of
Nov. 19, 1794 provided for the transfer of the frontier posts, and
stipulated that the land holdings of the citizens of either of the two
countries within the territories of the other country were to be respected.[68] In Michigan, the recorder of newly created Wayne
County was directed in August 1796 to take over the land records
from a Mr. Rowe at Detroit.[69] This effort was apparently unsuccessful, since it was later stated that the records had been carried
off by the British and that much of the original evidence had been
lost.[70]

The land offices opened at Detroit, Vincennes, and Kaskaskia
pursuant to a Congressional act of Mar. 26, 1804, were charged with

[66] Illinois, State, Auditor of Public Accounts, Biennial Report, 1882
(Springfield, 1882), xi. This report contains a brief inventory of the records.

[67] Clarence W. Alvord and Theodore C. Pease, "Archives of the State of
Illinois," Amer. Hist. Asso. Ann. Rep., 1909, 430-33; Survey of Federal Archives, Illinois, Inventory of Federal Archives in the States, Series VIII, The
Department of the Interior, No. 12, Illinois (Chicago, 1941), 30. Both inventories describe the entire collection of land records.

[68] Hunter Miller, ed., Treaties and Other International Acts of the United
States of America (Washington, 1931-48. 8 vols.) II, 246, 253-54.

[69] Winthrop Sargent to Peter Audrain, Aug. 17, 1796, Carter, ed., Terr.
Papers, N.W. Terr., III, 448.

[70] Petition to Congress by Inhabitants of Wayne County, Sept. 2, 1800,
ibid., p. 104-05.

the task of settling the private land claims within those districts.[71] French and British claimants were required to file notices of their claims and to present documentary evidence for recording by the register of the land office. The registers and receivers of the respective districts were to constitute boards of land commissioners for the examination and settlement of the land claims. Subsequently the registers of the three offices were allowed five hundred dollars additional compensation for translating and recording grants, deeds, or other land documents in the French language.[72]

In the Detroit district the Board of Land Commissioners employed Peter Audrain in 1805 as clerk, interpreter, and translator.[73] He recorded documents submitted as evidence of claims and translated deeds and other instruments. All of the French documents relating to claims which were pretended to be based upon legal grants were translated, but for claims based upon purchases or conveyances only summaries were abstracted in English.[74] Audrain continued to serve in the foregoing positions until July 1, 1811.[75] Since he had been appointed register of the land office in April 1806, he continued to have custody of the records until his death in 1820. An inventory of the records listing an item for eleven packages of deeds alphabetically arranged[76] was prepared in the following year when they were delivered by Francis Audrain, who had temporarily succeeded his father, to the new register.

Other records of land ownership in the Detroit area based upon French grants exist in a variety of forms. Transcripts of conveyances which were forwarded by Cadillac to the French Ministry of the

[71] Carter, ed., *Terr. Papers, Ind. Terr.,* VII, 173-75; 2 Stat. 277-78.

[72] Act approved Mar. 3, 1805, *ibid.,* p. 265; 2 Stat. 345.

[73] George Hoffman to Albert Gallatin, Dec. 1, 1805, *A.S.P., Pub. Lands,* I, 267.

[74] Hoffman to Gallatin, Apr. 3, 1806, Carter, ed., *Terr. Papers, Mich. Terr.,* X, 51.

[75] Audrain to Gallatin, July 6, 1808, *ibid.,* p. 229-30; see also p. 239, 308-09. Special acts of Congress approved Feb. 26, 1811 and Apr. 30, 1816 appropriated $1,700 to compensate him for the balance due for his services as clerk and interpreter from July 1, 1807 to July 1, 1811 (6 Stat. 98, 180).

[76] Enclosure in Henry B. Brevoort to Josiah Meigs, Aug. 16, 1822, Carter, ed., *Terr. Papers, Mich. Terr,* XI, 261.

Marine are in the Burton Historical Collection.[77] In the same collection are copies from the registers of the intendant and of the
Superior Council of Quebec pertaining to land grants at Detroit.[78]
The notarial registers of Detroit, already described, contain records
of land conveyances. The names of persons to whom concessions
were made between 1734 and 1750 appear in one of the parish registers of Fort Pontchartrain in the records of the church of Ste.
Anne at Detroit.[79] The previously described "Cicotte ledger" gives
information relative to the extent and location of the land grants
made during 1749-50. Besides the notarial registers, the registrar of
Wayne County, at Detroit, has a series of huge folios in which are
recorded deeds and other documents on land transfers in Detroit
and Wayne County, 1703-1869. A typewritten digest of the series,
prepared by the Michigan Works Progress Administration Vital
Records Project, is available in the Burton Historical Collection,
and contains one volume for the period 1703-96.

An agent was sent to Green Bay and Prairie du Chien in 1820 to
investigate titles and claims to land. He was instructed to receive
and record deeds and other documentary evidence of grants made
before the treaty of Paris of 1763 by the French government or between that time and the treaty of peace of 1783 between Great
Britain and the United States.[80] Isaac Lee, a resident of Michigan
Territory familiar with the French language, was selected for this
task. Finding no documentary evidence of either French or British
grants in the hands of the inhabitants, he took testimony of claimants at Prairie du Chien in October 1820 and during the following
winter at Green Bay.[81] The testimony of claimants and witnesses
as to occupancy and possession at those places was presented by

[77] Burton, *Cadillac's Village*, p. 7.

[78] Streeter, "Burton Historical Collection," p. 129.

[79] A list derived from this source of grants at Detroit from 1734 to 1753 is
in Ontario, Department of Public Records and Archives, *Third Report*, 1905
(Toronto, 1906), 85-88; see also *ibid.*, xlvii, 120-21, 129.

[80] William Woodbridge, Peter Audrain, and J. Kearsley to I. Lee, Aug. 8,
1821 [1820], *A.S.P., Pub. Lands*, V, 306-07; Frederick N. Trowbridge, "Confirming Land Titles in Early Wisconsin," *Wis. Mag. Hist.*, XXVI (Mar. 1943),
316.

[81] Lee to the Land Commissioners [extract], no date, *A.S.P. Pub. Lands*, V,
307.

Lee to the land commissioners at Detroit and has been published together with plans by Lee of the settlements at Prairie du Chien and Green Bay showing the individual land claims.[82]

For the locations of the French and British land grants in the Old Northwest, investigators are obliged to use the survey records prepared by the United States surveyors-general who functioned in that region. The remaining original documents did not usually provide exact descriptions of the boundaries of the tracts.[83] The execution of surveys was rendered difficult by the lack of documents.[84] To make up for these deficiencies, the registers of the land offices were required to furnish the surveyor-general with transcripts of the decisions of the land commissioners boards.[85] The commissioners did not always supply adequate information, and it had to be supplemented through inquiries by deputy surveyors who were engaged on the actual surveys.

The accumulation of survey materials was begun by the Surveyor-General Northwest of the Ohio, a position originally created in 1796, but with the appointment of other surveyors-general and the completion of surveys in the various states the records were transferred to other custodies. Upon the appointment of William Rector as Surveyor-General of Illinois and Missouri Territories in 1816, instructions were sent out for the transfer of pertinent records to his custody.[86] Other records were transferred to the newly appointed Surveyor-General of Wisconsin and Iowa Territories in

[82] *Ibid.*, p. 283-328. The documents are also published in the Duff Green (1834) edition of *A.S.P., Pub. Lands*, IV. The manuscript from which the printing was done is in the records of the General Land Office in the National Archives. Papers of Lee as land commissioner are in the William Woodbridge papers in the Burton Historical Collection.

[83] Jared Mansfield to Albert Gallatin, Oct. 12, 1804, Carter, ed., *Terr. Papers, Ind. Terr.*, VII, 221; George Hoffman to Gallatin, Dec. 6, 1806, Carter, ed., *Terr. Papers, Mich. Terr.*, X, 76. Mansfield served as Surveyor-General from 1803 to 1812.

[84] Mansfield to Gallatin, June 21, 1806, Carter, ed., *Terr. Papers, Ind. Terr.*, VII, 361; Mansfield to Aaron Greeley, Jan. 30, 1808, Carter, ed., *Terr. Papers, Mich. Terr.*, X, 195.

[85] Act of Mar. 26, 1804, 2 Stat. 279, Sec. 4.

[86] Act of Apr. 29, 1816, 3 Stat. 325-326; Josiah Meigs to Edward Tiffin, May 11, 1816, Carter, ed., *Terr. Papers, Ill. Terr.*, XVII, 335-36.

November 1838.[87] When the office of the Surveyor-General Northwest of the Ohio moved from Cincinnati to Detroit in 1845, the
records pertaining to the state of Ohio were left behind for delivery
to its custodian.[88] The collection at Detroit was further reduced in
December 1849 by the shipment of other records to state authorities
at Indianapolis.[89] A further division of the records at Detroit occurred in May 1857 when those relating to Michigan were sent to
Lansing,[90] and those relating to Minnesota were sent to St. Paul.[91]
The Surveyor-General also removed to St. Paul, and concerned himself thereafter only with surveys within the state of Minnesota.[92]
When the office of the Surveyor-General of Wisconsin and Iowa at
Dubuque was closed in 1866, the records concerning Wisconsin

[87] Act of June 12, 1838, 5 Stat. 243; E. S. Haines to James Whitcomb, Nov.
27, 1838, Records of the Department of the Interior, General Land Office,
Letters Received from the Surveyor General Northwest, National Archives.
(Hereinafter cited as DI, GLO, Lets. Recd. SG, NW.) An inventory of the
records is present.

[88] Act of Mar. 3, 1845, 5 Stat. 758; Lucius Lyon to John Wilson, July 15,
1845, Feb. 21, Aug. 3, 1846, DI, GLO, Lets. Recd., SG, NW, 522, 6159,
10586; Lyon to James H. Piper, Nov. 7, 1846, printed in "Report of the Commissioner of the General Land Office," Nov. 30, 1846 *House Doc.* 9, 29 Cong.,
2 sess., p. 39. This transfer was made on July 29, 1846, pursuant to an act of
June 12, 1840 (5 Stat. 384-185), which provided that whenever the surveys
and records of any state were completed the surveyor-general was required to
deliver over to the state all of the field notes, maps, records and other papers
pertaining to land titles. The foregoing act was amended by one of Jan. 22,
1853 (10 Stat. 152), which vested in the Commissioner of the General Land
Office the authority to make the transfer of the records, permitted free access
to the records after their delivery to the states by deputy surveyors or other
agents of the United States, and required the states to make proper provision
by law for the reception and safe keeping of the records and for free access
to them. These acts were the legal basis for numerous transfers of records to
states.

[89] Lucius Lyon to James Butterfield, Dec. 20, 1849, DI, GLO, Lets. Recd.,
SG, NW, 11977.

[90] Charles L. Emerson to Thomas A. Hendricks May 11, May 26, 1857, DI,
GLO, Lets. Recd., SG, Minn., D85566, D88576. An inventory accompanies
the second letter.

[91] Thomas A. Hendricks to Charles L. Emerson, Apr. 1, 1857, Records of
the Department of the Interior, General Land Office, Letters Sent to Surveyors-
General, v. 17.

[92] Emerson to Hendricks, Apr. 13, May 23, 1857, DI, GLO, Lets. Recd.,
SG, Minn., D82100, D88308; act of Mar. 3, 1857, 11 Stat. 212.

were delivered on August 1 to an agent of that state.[93] These collections now in state custody contain field notes of surveys, plats, maps, contracts, records of private surveys, and correspondence relating to the private land claims derived from the French and British governments.[94]

The adjudication, survey, and patenting of private land claims resulted in the accumulation in the General Land Office[95] of consolidated files relating to those claims in the various territories and states. The pertinent records include the reports, lists of claims, abstracts of patent certificates, registers, journals of proceedings, etc. sent in by the boards of land commissioners.[96] Much of these materials have been printed in the several editions of the *American State Papers, Public Lands.* The surveyors' field notes and the survey plats (maps or graphic representations) prepared from them identify the private land grants as well as the areas sold at public sale.[97] Transcripts of these plats were furnished by the surveyors-

[93] William Johnson to Joseph S. Wilson, Aug. 2, Aug. 9, 1866, DI, GLO, Lets. Recd., SG, Ia., G84633; "Special Report by Joseph S. Wilson in Regard to Surveying Archives of Missouri, Iowa, and Wisconsin," May 26, 1866, in *Report of the Secretary of the Interior*, Nov. 19, 1866, *House Exec. Doc. 1*, 39 Cong., 2 sess., p. 404-06.

[94] Inventories or descriptions of these records can be found in the following places: Alvord and Pease, "Archives of Illinois," p. 424-26; Survey of Federal Archives, Illinois, *Inventory of Federal Archives in the States, Series VIII, The Department of the Interior, No. 12, Illinois* (Chicago, 1941), 57-60; John L. Conger, "Report on the Public Archives of Michigan," Amer. Hist. Assoc., *Ann. Rep.*, 1905, I, 373; Survey of Federal Archives, Minnesota, *Inventory of Federal Archives in the States, Series VIII, The Department of the Interior, No. 22, Minnesota* (St. Paul, 1941), 6-9; Survey of Federal Archives, Wisconsin, *Inventory of Federal Archives in the States, Series VIII, The Department of the Interior, No. 48, Wisconsin* (Madison, 1939), 6.

[95] Originally established in the Treasury Department in 1812, transferred to the Interior Department in 1849, this office was consolidated in 1946 with the Grazing Service to form the Bureau of Land Management.

[96] A list of the records relating to Illinois Territory appears in Carter, ed., *Terr. Papers, Ill. Terr.*, XVII, 19-20n.

[97] Clark L. Gumm, "The Foundation of Land Records," *Our Public Lands*, VII (Oct. 1957), 4-5; William D. Pattison, "Use of the U.S. Public Land Survey Plats and Notes as Descriptive Sources," *Professional Geographer*, n.s., VIII (Jan. 1956), 10-11. The field notes and survey plats have been retained by the Bureau of Land Management, except those for Ohio, Indiana, and Illinois, which are in the National Archives.

general. Both kinds of lands were also shown upon the township plats covering the six-mile square areas which were surveyed according to the rectangular system of land surveys. Tract books containing a record of the manner of disposal of the lands were maintained in the local land offices and in the General Land Office.[98] Record copies of the patents to lands issued by the Federal Government are maintained in a huge series of volumes, to which there is an index available for the patents for private land claims. Among the case files or land entry papers in the National Archives which document separate actions relating to the lands is a file of Private Land Claim Papers, or Dockets.[99] Filed alphabetically by state in heavy jackets bearing identification data, these case files include notices and evidences of claims, patent certificates, survey plats, affidavits, deeds, abstracts of title, testimony, copies of federal court decisions, appeals, correspondence, and related papers. This is the most important file relating to individual claims, containing not only the histories of the claims listed above, but also much local history of a more general nature.

These federal land records constitute important sources for various fields of research. To make the most of them their interrelationships must be studied; the tract books can be used as an index to the case files, and the latter as an index to the patents.[1] The federal surveys of the foreign land grants reveal the pattern of settlement in areas peopled by the French, Spanish, British, and Mexicans. They disclose the condition of the land at the time of the transfer to the United States and even of previous times, since they show not only the farm lands, towns, commons, but also water courses, Indian and pioneer trails, traces of prior settlements by the Indians (archaeological sites), and vegetation.[2]

[98] Robert W. Harrison, "Public Land Records of the Federal Government," *Miss. Valley Hist. Rev.,* XLI (Sept. 1954), 280-81.

[99] U.S. National Archives, *Preliminary Inventory of the Land-Entry Papers of the General Land Office,* comp. by Harry P. Yoshpe and Philip P. Brower (*Preliminary Inventory* No. 22, Washington, 1949), 12. For Illinois there are 600 cases in 4 boxes; for Indiana 542 cases in 4 boxes; and for Michigan and Wisconsin 960 cases in 9 boxes.

[1] Harrison, "Public Land Records," p. 285.

[2] Pattison, "Public Land Survey Plats and Notes," p. 12-13.

Manuscript Collections

The public archives can be supplemented by manuscript collections containing documents of an official character in depositories in the United States and Canada. In the Chicago Historical Society are three groups of papers that were brought together by collectors among its members. The collection of Edward G. Mason, a president of the Society and author of works on the history of Illinois, includes letters, 1742-1800, signed by explorers of Illinois, governors of New France, and Louis XIII.[3] In 1905, Otto L. Schmidt, a physician with broad civic and cultural interests, presented a collection of manuscripts to the Society, chiefly on the conduct of the fur trade from the 1750's to the early nineteenth century.[4] Transcripts from this collection are in the State Historical Society of Wisconsin and the Illinois Historical Survey,[5] and some of the documents have been published.[6] The Indian trade and land transfers in early Illinois are illuminated by materials in the large Charles F. Gunther collection, which also includes correspondence about New France.[7] Gunther was a candy manufacturer and public official of Chicago, and after his death in 1920 funds were raised for the purchase of his manuscripts and other materials for the Chicago Historical Society. Some papers of Charles de Langlade,

---

[3] George B. Utley, "Source Material for the Study of American History in the Libraries of Chicago," Bibliographical Society of America, *Papers*, XVI, pt. I (1922), 34.

[4] Theodore C. Pease, "Otto Leopold Schmidt: 1863-1935," Illinois State Historical Society, *Journal*, XXVIII (Jan. 1936), 225-36.

[5] Illinois, University, Illinois Historical Survey, *Guide to Manuscript Materials of American Origin in the Illinois Historical Survey*, comp. by Marguerite J. Pease (Urbana, 1956), 92.

[6] Pease and Werner, eds., *French Foundations, passim;* Pease and Jenison, eds., *Illinois on the Eve of the Seven Years' War, passim.*

[7] Utley, "Source Material in the Libraries of Chicago," p. 36-37; Honorius Provost, "Inventaire des documents concernant l'histoire du Canada conservés aux archives de Chicago," *Revue d'histoire de l'Amérique française*, IV déc. 1950, mars 1951), 453-58, 591-600; "Charles F. Gunther Collection," Ill. State Hist. Soc., *Jour.*, XIII (Oct. 1920), 401-03.

a trader and militia officer at Michilimackinac and Green Bay, are in the State Historical Society of Wisconsin.[8]
Depositories outside of the Old Northwest also have pertinent documents. The papers of the Marquis de Vaudreuil, governor of Louisiana from 1743 to 1753 and of New France from 1755 to 1760, are in the Henry E. Huntington Library, San Marino, Calif.[9] These papers include letters, 1752-53, from Major de Makarty-Mactique, commandant of Illinois, and from François Saucier, the engineer charged with rebuilding Fort de Chartres, orders, lists of troops, and census lists.[10] Photostats of the items in the Vaudreuil papers concerning Illinois are in the Illinois Historical Survey,[11] and some of them have been published.[12] The papers of Michel Chartier, Marquis de Lotbinière, a French engineer officer, in the New York Public Library (photostats in the Canadian Public Archives) include a journal of a trip to Michilimackinac in 1749 and a memoir on the country between that place and the Mississippi River.[13] The same period is covered by a collection of his letters in the New York Historical Society.[14] In 1937, the New York Public Library purchased over 15,000 French ordinances, edicts, and decrees concerning North America.[15] Documents relating to Fort de

[8] Wisconsin, State Historical Society, *Guide to Manuscripts of the Wisconsin Historical Society*, comp. by Alice E. Smith (Madison, 1944), 123; "Langlade Papers—1737-1800," (*Colls*. State Hist. Soc. Wis., VIII, 1877-79, Madison, 1879), 209-23.

[9] Stanley M. Pargellis and Norma B. Cuthbert, "Loudoun Papers, (a) Colonial, 1756-58, (b) French Colonial, 1742-53," *Huntington Library Bulletin*, No. 3, (Feb. 1933), 104-05.

[10] Notes based upon a 1752 census of Illinois in the Vaudreuil papers are published in Belting, *Kaskaskia*, p. 86-120. According to this author not all of the residents of the Illinois settlements were listed in this census.

[11] Illinois Historical Survey, *Guide to MS. Material of American Origin*, p. 112.

[12] Pease and Jenison, eds., *Illinois on the Eve of the Seven Years' War* contains 34 documents.

[13] Canada, Public Archives, Manuscript Division, *Preliminary Inventory, Manuscript Group 18, Pre-Conquest Papers* (Ottawa, 1954), 21.

[14] New York Historical Society, *Survey of the Manuscript Collections in the New York Historical Society* (New York, 1941), 12.

[15] Lawrence C. Wroth and Gertrude L. Annan, *Acts of French Royal Administration Concerning Canada, Guiana, the West Indies, and Louisiana, prior to 1791* (New York, 1930).

Chartres and Kaskaskia are in the Missouri Historical Society at St. Louis, Mo. Documents on Canada from 1642 and others on Indians east of the Mississippi River are in the Henry E. Huntington Library. Narratives of travel, including journals, diaries, reports, accounts, and autobiographies of explorers, soldiers, officials, missionaries, and traders are important primary sources.[16] Such documents contain much descriptive and narrative information. These documents have long been of interest to investigators and consequently have been much sought after in archival and manuscript depositories. The journals and accounts that have appeared in print are too numerous to be described individually; they can be found listed in various bibliographies.[17] They constitute an important supplement to other types of documents; without them there would be

[16] On the subject of exploration see Winsor, ed., *Narrative and Critical History of America*, IV; Lawrence J. Burpee, *The Search for the Western Sea; the Story of the Exploration of North-western America* (Toronto, 1935. 2 vols.); Lawrence J. Burpee, *The Discovery of Canada* (Toronto, 1924); Nellie M. Crouse, *In Quest of the Western Ocean* (New York, 1928); Jean Delanglez, "A Mirage: the Sea of the West," *Revue d'histoire de l'Amérique française*, I (déc. 1947, mars 1948), 346-81, 541-68; Bernard De Voto, *The Course of Empire* (Boston, 1952); Brebner, *Explorers of North America*.

[17] The chief bibliographies are as follows: Appleton P. C. Griffin, "Discovery of the Mississippi; Bibliographical Account of the Travels of Nicolet, Alloüez, Marquette, Hennepin, and La Salle in the Mississippi Valley," *Magazine of American History*, IX (Mar., Apr., 1883), 190-99, 273-80; Winsor, ed., *Narrative and Critical History of America*, IV; Appleton P. C. Griffin, "Bibliography of the Discovery and Exploration of the Mississippi Valley," in Knox College, Library, *An Annotated Catalogue of Books Belonging to the Finley Collection on the History and Romance of the Northwest* (Galesburg, Ill., 1924), 47-67; Frances M. Staton and Marie Tremaine, eds., *A Bibliography of Canadiana; Being Items in the Public Library of Toronto, Canada, Relating to the Early History and Development of Canada* (Toronto, 1934), 1-64; Jean Delanglez, "The Discovery of the Mississippi; Primary Sources," *Mid-America*, XXVII (Oct. 1945), 219-31; William Matthews, *American Diaries, an Annotated Bibliography of American Diaries Written Prior to the Year 1761* (Berkeley, Los Angeles, 1945); William Matthews, *Canadian Diaries and Autobiographies* (Berkeley, Los Angeles, 1950); Robert R. Hubach, *Early Midwestern Travel Narratives: an Annotated Bibliography, 1634-1850* (Detroit, 1961); Beers, *French in North America*, p. 121-22, 134, 244-46; Henry P. Beers, *Bibliographies in American History; Guide to Materials for Research* (New York, 1942), 38-44; Leland, *Guide to Materials for Amer. History*, I, *passim*.

many lacunae in the history of the Old Northwest.[18] The activities
of explorers and engineer officers accompanying expeditions have
produced maps and charts which are a further source of basic information.[19]

[18] Compilations not cited elsewhere include Louise P. Kellogg, ed., *Early
Narratives of the Northwest, 1634-1699* (New York, 1917); Milo M. Quaife,
ed., *The Development of Chicago, 1647-1914, Shown in a Series of Contem-
porary Original Narratives* (Chicago, 1916); Milo M. Quaife, ed., *The Western
Country in the 17th Century; Memoirs of Lamothe Cadillac and Pierre Liette*
(Chicago, 1947).

[19] Henry Harrisse, *Notes pour servir à l'histoire à la bibliographie et à la
cartographie de la Nouvelle-France et des pays adjacents, 1545-1700* (Paris,
1872); Francis Parkman, "Early Unpublished Maps of the Mississippi and the
Great Lakes," in *La Salle and the Discovery of the Great West* (Boston, 1879),
449-58; Edward D. Neill, *The History of Minnesota: from the Earliest French
Explorations to the Present Time* (Minneapolis, 1882), 799-802; Justin Winsor, "The Maps of the Seventeenth Century Showing Canada," in *Narrative
and Critical History*, IV, 377-94; Gabriel A. Marcel, *Cartographie de la Nou-
velle-France; supplément à l'ouvrage de M. Harrisse* (Paris, 1885); Narcisse
E. Dionne, *Inventaire chronologique des cartes, plans, atlas relatifs à la Nou-
velle-France et à la province de Québec, 1508-1908* (Québec, 1909); Canada,
Public Archives, *Catalogue of Maps, Plans and Charts in the Map Room of the
Dominion Archives*, classified and indexed by H. R. Holmden (Ottawa, 1912);
Louis C. Karpinski, "Manuscript Maps Relating to American History in
French, Spanish, and Portuguese Archives," *Amer. Hist. Rev.*, XXXIII (Jan.
1928), 328-30; Jean Delanglez, "Franquelin Mapmaker," *Mid-America*, XXV
(Jan. 1943), 29-74; Louis C. Karpinski, "Michigan and the Great Lakes upon
the Map, 1636-1802," *Mich. Hist. Mag.*, XXIX (July, Sept. 1945), 291-312;
Richard R. Rogers, "Historical Cartography of the Great Lakes (1569-1746),"
Michigan Academy of Sciences, *Papers*, XXXIV (1948), 175-84; Jean De-
langlez, "The Sources of the Delisle Map of America, 1703," *Mid-America*,
XXV (Oct. 1943), 275-98; Raphael N. Hamilton "The Early Cartography
of the Missouri Valley," *Amer. Hist. Rev.*, XXXIX (July 1934), 645-62; Aubrey
Diller, "Maps of the Missouri River before Lewis and Clark," in M. F. Ashley
Montagu, ed., *Studies and Essays in the History of Science and Learning
Offered in Homage to George Sarton* (New York, 1946), 503-19; Carl I.
Wheat, *Mapping the Trans-Mississippi West, Volume One, The Spanish En-
trada to the Louisiana Purchase, 1540-1804* (San Francisco, 1957); Emerson
D. Fite and Archibald Freeman, *A Book of Old Maps, Delineating American
History from the Earliest Days Down to the Close of the Revolutionary War*
(Cambridge, 1926); Louis C. Karpinski, *Historical Atlas of the Great Lakes
and Michigan, to Accompany the Bibliography of the Printed Maps of Michi-
gan* (Lansing, 1931). Maps from depositories in both Canada and the United
States appear in Sara Jones Tucker, *Indian Villages of the Illinois Country*
(*Scientific Papers*, Illinois, State Museum, vol. II, pt. I, *Atlas*, Springfield,
1942). See also the titles on cartography in the chapter on the British regime
in the present work.

Ecclesiastical Records

The Catholic Church was active in New France from its earliest years. In return for a considerable measure of financial support from the French Government, the Church was expected to inculcate a spirit of obedience among the populace. Some Recollects of the Franciscan order arrived in the colony under Champlain's sponsorship in 1615.[20] At their invitation, Jesuits began appearing in 1625 to assist in evangelizing the Indians. When the Recollects were recalled in 1632, the Jesuits remained and became a prominent force in the affairs of the colony. No Indians were too remote for the missionary efforts of the Jesuits, and they were among the earliest Frenchmen to enter the Upper Country. Missionaries of the Sulpician order arrived to join in the missionary work in 1657. The head of the mission became one of the first seigniors of Montreal when a seminary was established there. Returning to the colony in 1670, the Recollects founded a college at Three Rivers.

Jurisdiction over the religious affairs of the colony was claimed by the Bishops of St. Malo and Rouen in France during its early years.[21] The arrival of the Sulpicians in 1657 with a superior who was also a vicar general of Rouen resulted in a conflict with the superior of the Jesuits. In the next year the Jesuits secured the appointment of one of their own members, François de Montmorency-Laval de Montigny, as vicar apostolic of New France with the title of Bishop of Petraea. Armed with a papal consecration and instructions from the King of France, Laval established himself in 1659 as the principal church dignitary in New France.[22] He became a member of the Sovereign Council, but after the establishment of royal government in the colony his influence in the political sphere soon declined. His authority over the religious orders and clergy

[20] A. Leblond De Brumath, *Bishop Laval* (Toronto, 1926), 1-5; Canon Scott, "The Catholic Church in the Province of Quebec, from Its Beginning to Our Time," in William C. H. Wood, ed., *The Storied Province of Quebec, Past and Present* (Toronto, 1931-32. 5 vols.), I, 477; McInnis, *Canada*, p. 71.

[21] Scott, "The Catholic Church in the Province of Quebec," p. 482; McInnis, *Canada*, p. 72.

[22] De Brumath, *Bishop Laval*, p. 26; McInnis, *Canada*, p. 72.

of New France was enhanced in 1674 upon his appointment by the Pope as Bishop of Quebec, with a diocese extending over the entire French domain in North America.[23] Control over the parochial clergy as well as the religious orders was in Laval's hands. He founded the Seminary of Quebec in 1663 to train Canadians for the priesthood and to create a disciplined community from which parish priests could be dispatched on orders of the bishop.[24] The seminary became associated with the Seminary of Foreign Missions of Paris, which had been formed about 1650 to promote foreign missions.

The Jesuits entered the field of the upper lakes in the 1660's by establishing a mission at Sault Ste. Marie and another at La Pointe, on Chequamegon Bay.[25] The mission was moved to St. Ignace on Mackinac strait in 1671, and then withdrawn in 1706 because of the further removal of the Hurons to Detroit. A mission located among the Potawatomi at Green Bay in 1669[26] sent out word of the Illinois Indians, and in 1674 Father Marquette established a mission among the Kaskaskia, the first in the Illinois country.[27] Irregularly occupied, the mission to the Kaskaskia was at first located near present-day Utica, Illinois, and was later moved to Peoria when Tonty built Fort St. Louis there. In 1700 this mission accompanied the Kaskaskia to the Des Pères River opposite Cahokia and in the spring of 1703 again moved with the Indians to a permanent site on the Kaskaskia River.[28] A Jesuit mission established at Chicago in 1696 was abandoned in 1702, apparently because the Indians moved to the east away from the Sioux. Priests of the Seminary of Foreign Missions of Quebec founded a mission among the

---

[23] De Brumath, *Bishop Laval*, p. 129, 136; Gilbert J. Garraghan, "The Ecclesiastical Rule of Old Quebec in Mid-America," *Catholic Historical Review*, XIX (Apr. 1933), 17; Ivanhoë Caron, "Le Diocèse de Québec; divisions et subdivisions de 1674 à 1844," Société canadienne d'histoire de l'église catholique, *Rapport*, 1937-38, 11.

[24] Mason Wade, *The French Canadians, 1760-1945* (London, 1955), 38-39.

[25] Fowle, *Saulte Ste. Marie*, p. 96-98.

[26] *Ibid.*, p. 98; Quaife, *Wisconsin*, I, 86.

[27] Palm, *Jesuit Mission*, 13-14; Alvord, *Illinois Country*, p. 67, 132.

[28] Palm, *Jesuit Missions*, p. 36-37; Belting, *Kaskaskia*, p. 10-12.

Cahokia Indians in 1699, and later served also the parish church of St. Anne at Fort de Chartres.[29] This church maintained the chapel of St. Joseph at Prairie du Rocher and probably another at St. Philippe.

The earliest religious official to function in Detroit was the Recollect chaplain who arrived in 1701 with Cadillac.[30] The church of St. Anne was erected and a regular parish inaugurated. Until the end of the French regime St. Anne's served as the parish church for the French on both sides of the Detroit River.

Registers of baptisms, marriages, and burials were kept by the Roman Catholic Church long before governmental edicts made them official records. In the fifteenth century certain bishops of France required the registering of baptisms and burials by the clergy.[31] In 1548 the Council of Trent imposed the function of registering baptisms and marriages on the entire Catholic Church, and in 1614 the priests were further required to register burials.[32] The information recorded was needed for the execution of canonical laws in the administration of sacraments.

Incomplete church registers for the Illinois settlements are extant. The records of the Church of Our Lady of the Immaculate Conception at Kaskaskia have been deposited by the Diocese of Belleville in St. Louis University Archives, and include a baptismal register, 1695-1719, 1732, 1733, 1735, 1758-1834, a marriage register, 1741-1835, and a burial register, 1721-27.[33] Extracts from the

[29] Alvord, *Illinois Country*, p. 200-01.

[30] Richard R. Elliott, "The Recollect Priests Who Officiated at the Church of Saint Anne, Detroit, from 1701-1782, and as Chaplains at Fort Pontchartrain, during the French Regime," (*Mich. Hist. Colls.*, Vol. XXXV, Lansing, 1907), 267.

[31] Jacques Levron, "Les registres paroissiaux et d'état civil en France, *Archivum*, IV (1959), 55.

[32] Léon Roy, "The Keeping of Church Registers of Juridical Status in the Province of Quebec," in Quebec (Province) Archives, *Rapport de l'archiviste de la province de Québec*, 1959-1960 (Québec, 1961), 169.

[33] Historical Records Survey, Missouri, *Guide to Depositories of Manuscript Collections in the United States: Missouri* (St. Louis, 1940), 11; Palm, *Jesuit Missions*, p. 80, 82, 120, 121, 125; Edward G. Mason, "The Kaskaskia Parish Records," *Mich. Hist. Colls.*, Vol. 5 (Lansing, 1884), 94-109.

baptismal register of Kaskaskia, 1692-1735, have been published,[34] as have extracts from the marriage register, 1723-63.[35] The original register of baptisms, marriages, and burials of Ste. Anne of Fort de Chartres, including entries for the dependent chapels of St. Joseph of Prairie du Rocher and Notre Dame of the Visitation of St. Philippe, 1721-65, are in the St. Joseph Church at Prairie du Rocher.[36] Extracts of the registers of Kaskaskia, 1695-1834, and copies of the register of Ste. Anne of Fort de Chartres, prepared by Oscar W. Collet, are in the Chicago Historical Society.[37] Copies of the registers of those churches are also in the Missouri Historical Society, Jefferson Memorial Building, St. Louis, Mo.,[38] and the Society has prepared a name index to the Kaskaskia registers. Abstracts of the registers of Kaskaskia and Fort de Chartres prepared by Rev. P. M. O'Leary are in the Canadian Public Archives and copies are in the Provincial Archives of Quebec. Register entries for St. Philippe, 1761-65, have been published.[39] The register of the church at Cahokia was destroyed by fire in 1783.

The registers for other missions in Indiana and Michigan have also been preserved. Those for Vincennes, 1749-86, are in the old cathedral library of the Church of St. Francis Xavier.[40] Copies are in the Missouri Historical Society, the Burton Historical Collection of the Detroit Public Library, the Canadian Public Archives (indexed), the Shea Collection in the Georgetown University Archives, and the Indiana State Library. A translation has been pub-

[34] C. J. Eschmann, "Kaskaskia Church Records," Ill. State Hist. Soc., *Trans.,* 1904, Ill. State Hist. Lib., *Pub.* No. 9, 394-413; Belting, *Kaskaskia,* p. 79.

[35] Belting, *Kaskaskia,* p. 80-85.

[36] C. J. Eschmann, "Prairie du Rocher Church Records," Ill. State Hist. Soc., *Trans.,* 1903, Ill. State Hist. Lib., *Pub.,* No. 8, 128-49.

[37] George B. Utley, "Source Material for the Study of American History in the Libraries of Chicago," Bibliographical Society of America, *Papers,* XVI, pt. I (1922), 34.

[38] Historical Records Survey, Missouri, *Guide to Depositories,* 11.

[39] Wilfred Bovey, "Some Notes on Arkansas Post and St. Philippe in the Mississippi Valley," Royal Soc. Canada, *Procs. and Trans.,* 3d ser., XXXIII, sect. II (May 1939), 41-47.

[40] Cora C. Curry, *Records of the Roman Catholic Church in the United States as a Source for Authentic Genealogical and Historical Material* (Washington, 1935), 10.

lished of some of the registers of baptisms, marriages, and burials, 1749-73.[41] The baptismal register of St. Joseph mission passed into private hands after the burning of the fort and was presented eventually in 1857 to Jacques Viger, in whose collection of manuscripts it can now be found in the Seminary of Quebec of Laval University. A translation of this register, 1720-73, has been published.[42] Photostats of the St. Joseph registers are in the Burton Historical Collection and the Canadian Public Archives. The entries in the register of the Church of St. Anne on Mackinac Island are chiefly for marriages and baptisms, 1741-1821, but there are also abstracts of earlier entries beginning in 1695, copied from an older register which is now lost, and some entries for burials, 1743-1806.[43] Copies are in the State Historical Society of Wisconsin and in the Canadian Public Archives. The registers of St. Anne's Church of Detroit, containing entries for baptisms, marriages, and deaths, begin in 1704 and are still in its possession.[44] Transcripts and translations, 1704-1848, are in the Burton Historical Collection, which has indexed registers, and transcripts, 1703-1800, are also in the Canadian Public Archives. A "Genealogy of French Families of Detroit" (twenty-five volumes) prepared from these registers and other records of Detroit by Christian Denissen is in the Burton Historical Collection, and a copy is in the Canadian Public Archives.

Registers kept by chaplains who served at French military posts in western Pennsylvania have also come to light. John D. G. Shea

[41] Edmond J. P. Schmitt, trans., "The Records of the Parish of St. Francis Xavier at Post Vincennes, Ind.," American Catholic Historical Society, *Records,* XII (Mar., June, Sept. 1901), 41-60, 193-211, 322-36.

[42] George Paré and Milo M. Quaife, trans. and ed., "The St. Joseph Baptismal Register," *Miss. Valley Hist. Rev.,* XIII (Sept. 1926), 205-39.

[43] Reuben G. Thwaites, ed., "The Mackinac Register," (*Colls.,* State Hist. Soc. Wis., Vol. XVIII-XIX, Madison, 1908, 1910), 469-513, 1-162. Abstracts of earlier entries back to 1695, which were prepared from an old register now lost, are included in the publication. See also Reuben G. Thwaites, "At the Meeting of the Trails: the Romance of a Parish Register," Mississippi Valley Historical Association, *Proceedings,* VI (1912-13), 198-217.

[44] Historical Records Survey, Michigan, *Inventory of the Church Archives of Michigan, The Roman Catholic Church: Archdiocese of Detroit* (Detroit, July 1941), 45; Elliott, "Recollect Priests," p. 267.

obtained a copy of the register of Fort Duquesne and published it.[45] It was later republished in French and English by Andrew A. Lambing, a Catholic priest who wrote a history of the church in western Pennsylvania.[46] A copy of the register of Fort Duquesne is in the Canadian Public Archives. A list of names derived from the burial register of Fort Presque Isle, which was found among the registers of the parish of Notre Dame of Montreal, has been published,[47] and upon the rediscovery of the register years later it was republished.[48]

Church registers are valuable sources of information. They antedate the public vital statistics records and provide a continuous record about individuals and families. They are useful for population growth, local history, infant mortality, slavery, religious, cultural, and social history. Baptismal registers contain the names and sex of infants, the date of birth or the approximate date, names of parents and godparents, and sometimes information as to where the parents were from and their occupations. The nicknames of fathers are occasionally recorded. Entries are included for illegitimate children and the offspring of slaves and Indian women. The names of the missionary, priest, or chaplain, and the date of recording are given. Marriage registers contain the names of parties, parents, witnesses, and officiating priests. Burial registers give the names of the deceased and of the parents, time of death, age, place of burial, and the names of attendants. Entries for slaves include

[45] John D. G. Shea, *Registres des baptesmes et sepultures qui se sont faits au Fort Duquesne pendant les années 1753, 1754, 1755 & 1756* (Nouvelle York, 1859). The register had been published in English in the Pittsburgh *Daily Gazette* for July 1858. For his historical work Shea also procured copies of some of the registers of Detroit, Vincennes, Ouiatenon, and Kaskaskia.

[46] Andrew A. Lambing, trans. and ed., "Register of the Baptisms and Interments Which Took Place at Fort Duquesne During the Years 1753-1756," *The American Catholic Historical Researches,* I (1884), 60-73, 109-18, 138-54; II (1885), 18-25, and separately as *The Baptismal Register of Fort Duquesne (from June, 1754, to Dec., 1756),* (Pittsburgh, 1885). Lambing obtained a copy of the register from the original in the archives of the Supreme Court of Montreal.

[47] Ovide-M.-H. Lapalice, "Registre du Fort de la Presque Isle," *Canad. Antiq. and Numismat. Jour.,* XI, 3d ser. (Oct. 1914), 168-70.

[48] Père Hugolin Lemay, éd., "Le registre du fort de la Presqu'île pour 1753," *Bull. recherches hist.,* XLIV (juillet 1938), 204-11.

the names of owners. The former place of residence and the marital status of the deceased are usually indicated. The specific causes of death are usually not stated though vague references are sometimes made to sickness or wounds. The signatures of attendants sometimes follow that of the priest.

II The Records

of Quebec on the French Regime

Government

The government of New France was an absolute paternalism characterized by central control and close royal supervision.[1] During more than the first half century of the colony an attempt was made to exploit it through the grant of charters to private individuals and companies. After several earlier grants, control of the colony was bestowed in 1627 upon the Company of New France, which was given monopoly of trade and governmental rights.[2] The trading monopoly was transferred in 1645 to the Company of the Inhabitants, an association of traders at Quebec. The companies proved to be poor instruments of colonization, however, for they neglected the promotion of settlement for the exploitation of the fur trade.

New France became a royal colony in 1663 when the crown cancelled the charter of the Company of New France. It was given the customary government of a French province, consisting of a governor, an intendant, a bishop, and a sovereign council. But in the following year when Jean Baptiste Colbert, the controller-general, divided French colonial activities between the Company of the East Indies and the Company of the West Indies, governmental rights, ownership of the land, and a monopoly of trade were vested in the Company of the West Indies. But because of its greater interest in the French colonies in the West Indies, the crown retained

[1] Carl Wittke, *A History of Canada*, p. 13; William P. M. Kennedy, *The Constitution of Canada 1534-1937; an Introduction to Its Development, Law and Custom* (London, 1938), 1.

[2] Wittke, *History of Canada*, p. 13; Kennedy, *Constitution of Canada*, p. 7-9; Herbert L. Priestley, *France Overseas through the Old Regime; a Study of European Expansion* (New York, 1939), 71.

61

political control over New France and to a considerable extent supervised commercial affairs.[3] This company likewise proved unsuccessful as a colonizing agent, and direct royal government was formally instituted in New France in 1674.

By governing New France the crown sought to exercise close supervision over its affairs, since in France as well as in the French colonies, authority was being centralized in the crown.[4] Direction over the colonies involved not only matters of general policy but also the regulation of the life of the colonists. This was accomplished by the issuance of instructions to the royal officials and the promulgation of decrees which constituted legislation for the colony. At the time of the institution of royal government in the colony the body of laws prescribed was the Custom of Paris.

The head of the colony was the governor, who was commissioned to maintain the royal authority as the representative of the king. He commanded the military forces, conducted relations with the Indians and foreign colonies, and ordered extraordinary expenditures arising from emergencies.[5] In theory he was governor-general of all the French provinces in Canada and of Louisiana, but the officials in those places received their orders directly from the king.[6]

The position of intendant became a regular part of the government of New France after the colony was taken over by the crown.[7] Expanding upon his original function as a check or spy upon the activities of the governor and the bishop, the intendant

[3] Priestley, *France Overseas*, p. 130-33; George M. Wrong, *The Rise and Fall of New France* (New York, 1928. 2 vols.), I, 365-68; Edgar McInnis, *Canada, A Political and Social History* (New York, Toronto, 1959), 43.

[4] McInnis, *Canada*, p. 47.

[5] Kennedy, *Constitution of Canada*, p. 14; Caldwell, *French in the Miss. Valley*, p. 23, 33, 64; Francis H. Hammang, *The Marquis de Vaudreuil; New France at the Beginning of the Eighteenth Century* (Bruges, 1938), 29-35; Raphael Bellemare, "Vice-rois et lieutenants généraux des rois de France en Amérique," Société historique de Montréal, *Mémoires et documents relatifs à l'histoire du Canada* (Montréal, 1859), III, 97-122; Pierre-Georges Roy, "Les secretaires de gouverneurs et intendants de la Nouvelle-France," *Bull. recherches hist.*, XLI (fév. 1935), 74-107.

[6] Hammang, *Marquis de Vaudreuil*, p. 30.

[7] Regis Roy, "Les intendants de la Nouvelle-France," *Proceedings and Transactions of the Royal Society of Canada*, 2d ser., IX (1903), 65-107 contains biographical sketches of the intendants.

assumed a wide variety of powers over finance, justice, and police affairs. He supervised the colony's finances, including both expenditures and taxation. He attended to matters of supply, the issuance of munitions and other materials in the king's stores for use as presents for the Indians and equipment for military expeditions. As a judge the intendant decided seigniorial disputes and commercial and criminal cases. Appeals from his decisions were made to the king in council. The ordinances and regulations issued by the intendant constituted the legislation governing the everyday life of the people in their relations with each other. He also enforced royal decrees and orders of the Superior Council. The intendant replaced the governor as presiding officer of the Superior Council in 1674; he also attended councils of war and was a member of courts-martial. The governor and the intendant worked together in the preparation of the budget, the promotion of religion and its extension to the Indians, and the granting of seigniories.[8] The governor could intervene in the administration of justice in the case of decrees which he considered contrary to royal orders. He was obliged to furnish assistance in the execution of the intendant's judgments.

Other government agencies established at Quebec late in the seventeenth century had little or no connection with the administration of the western posts. The Prévôté of Quebec was a court of justice which judged civil and criminal cases in the first instances and appeals from private jurisdictions (seigniories), both of which could be carried to the Superior Council.[9] The Department of the Marine maintained a deputy at Quebec to perform the routine work connected with the administration of the colonial finances. Attended to at first by the intendant, admiralty matters were soon entrusted by that busy official to the Prévôté of Quebec which handled them until an admiralty court began functioning at Quebec in 1719.[10]

[8] Hammang, *Marquis de Vaudreuil*, p. 33-35.

[9] Pierre-George Roy, "La maréchaussée de Québec sous le régime français," *Procs. and Trans.*, Royal Soc. Canada, 3d ser., XII, sect. I (May 1918 and Mar. 1919), 189-92.

[10] Louis-Guillaume Verrier, "Les registres de l'amirauté de Québec," Quebec (Province) Archives, *Rapport de l'archiviste de la province de Québec*, 1920-1921 (Québec, 1921), 108-09.

The Sovereign Council was composed initially of the governor, the bishop, and five councilors chosen by those officials. Attached to the council were the attorney-general who brought complaints before the tribunal, the secretary or registrar who kept the records, and bailiffs. A notary registered wills, contracts, and other legal documents. Upon his arrival in 1665 the intendant was added to the council. A change in name from Sovereign Council to Superior Council occurred in 1674, when Louis XIV took over complete authority from the Company of the West Indies. The Superior Council performed legislative, administrative, and judicial functions. It issued local regulations relating to finance, trade, and police. In registering the king's decrees it placed them in operation; it also registered the governor's orders, and the intendant's ordinances. The council acted in an advisory capacity to the administrative officers. Judicially the council was the highest court of appeal in the colony, hearing both civil and criminal cases. Appeal from its decisions could be made to the royal council in Paris. The powers of the council connected with the finances and legislation were largely taken over by the intendant, who also encroached upon its judicial powers. Attendance upon the council by the bishop became irregular, and after 1703 he was represented by a deputy.[11]

After the establishment of settlements farther up the St. Lawrence River at Three Rivers in 1634 and at Montreal in 1642, administrative districts were set up at those places and at Quebec. Montreal became of special importance for the Upper Country, for it developed into a base for military operations against the Iroquois, a depot for the outlying posts, and a center for the fur trade whence *coureurs de bois* departed for the Indian country.[12] The district had as governor an officer who was charged particularly with the conduct of military affairs and who was assisted by

[11] Pierre-Georges Roy, "Les conseillers au conseil souverain de la Nouvelle-France," *Procs. and Trans.* Royal Soc. Canada, 3d ser., IX, sect. I (Sept. 1915), 173-87, gives the names of the councilors, the attorneys general, and the registrars.

[12] Stephen B. Leacock, *Montreal, Seaport and City* (New York, 1942), 58; Caldwell, *French in the Miss. Valley*, p. 11; E. R. Adair, "The Evolution of Montreal under the French Regime," Canadian Historical Association, *Report*, 1942, 29.

several subordinate officers.[13] Civil affairs were attended to by a judge, a crown attorney (*procureur fiscal*), a recorder (*greffier*), a sheriff (*huissier*), a syndic or mayor, an interpreter, storehouse guards, and a road supervisor.[14] The Sulpician priest in charge of the mission at Montreal as seignior had the right of appointing the judge between 1648 and 1693 when the appointment became a royal prerogative.[15] A *mauréchaussée* or police force with executive and judicial authority over criminal offenses and responsibility for the public safety was established in 1677.[16] A commissary of the marine, who was concerned with navigation matters, also attended the council of war and served as subdelegate of the intendant and keeper of the king's storehouse.[17]

Provincial Records

Among the most important sources for the history of the region south of the Great Lakes during the French regime are the records of New France. The close connections between that colony and the West during the seventeenth and eighteenth centuries and the part played by its officials in governing that region have been indicated in the preceding pages. Those years in the history of the West can still be illuminated by the records of New France.

The capitulation of Montreal of Sept. 8, 1760, at which time Canada was surrendered to the British, made provision in regard to the French records. The pertinent articles read as follows:

[13] Leacock, *Montreal*, p. 63; Edouard-Zotique Massicotte, "Mémento historique de Montréal, 1636-1760," *Procs. and Trans.* Royal Soc. Canada, 3d ser., XXVII, sect. I (May 1933), 111-14. This publication also lists the names of civil and religious officials at Montreal.

[14] Leacock, *Montreal*, p. 63-64. Edouard-Zotique Massicotte, who was archivist of the judicial archives at Montreal for many years, has published lists of the judges, attorneys, coroners, notaries, recorders, sheriffs, and syndics, of which the titles are in the bibliography.

[15] Edouard-Zotique Massicotte, "Les tribunaux et les officiers de justice à Montréal, sous le régime français, 1648-1760," *Procs. and Trans.* Royal Soc. Canada, 3d ser., X, sect. I (Dec. 1916), 273.

[16] Edouard-Zotique Massicotte, "La maréchaussee à Montréal," *Bull. recherches hist.* XXII (jan. 1916), 16.

[17] Pierre-Georges Roy, "Les commissaires ordinaires de la marine en la Nouvelle-France," *Bull, recherches hist.*, XXIV (fév. 1918), 51; Caldwell, *French in the Miss. Valley*, p. 11.

Article XLIII. The Papers of the Government shall remain without exception, in the power of the Marquis de Vaudreuil and shall go to France with him. These papers shall not be examined on any pretence whatsoever.—"Granted, "with the reserve already made."
Article XLIV. The papers of the Intendancy, of the offices of Comptroller of the Marine, of the ancient and new treasurers, of the Kings magazines, of the offices of the Revenues and forges of St. Maurice, shall remain in the power of M. Bigot, the Intendant; and they shall be embarked for France in the same vessel with him; these papers shall not be examined.— "The same as "in this article."
Article XLV. The Registers, and other papers of the Supreme Council of Quebec, of the Prévoté, and Admiralty of the said city; those of the Royal Jurisdictions of Trois Rivieres and of Montreal; those of the Seignorial Jurisdictions of the colony; the minutes of the Acts of the Notaries of the towns and of the countries; and in general, the acts, and other papers, that may serve to prove the estates and fortune of the Citizens, shall remain in the colony in the rolls of the jurisdictions on which these paper depend. "Granted."[18]

The commissary for the King's provisions or his deputy was to be allowed to remain in the colony for a year to settle his business and at the end of that period he was to leave, and to carry off his papers with him.

The principal officials of Canada, including the Marquis de Vaudreuil-Cavagnal, the governor, François Bigot, the intendant, the Chevalier de Lévis and other military officers departed before the end of 1760 with their papers.[19] The intendant deposited his records at La Rochelle. Part of these records and the papers of the governor were subsequently transferred to Versailles and are today in the Archives des Colonies.[20] Many of the refugees from

[18] Adam Shortt and Arthur G. Doughty, eds., *Documents Relating to the Constitutional History of Canada, 1759-1791* (Ottawa, 1918. 2 vols.), I, 34.

[19] Joseph-Edmond Roy, *Rapport sur les archives de France relatives à l'histoire du Canada* (Ottawa, 1911), 433, 518.

[20] Paul Roussier, "Les origines du dépôt des papiers publics des colonies: le dépôt de Rochefort (1763-1790)," *Revue de l'histoire des colonies françaises*, XVIII (1st trimestre 1925), 22; Carlo Laroche, "Les archives d'outre mer et l'histoire coloniale française," *Revue historique*, CCVI (oct.-déc., 1951), 218-19.

Canada who settled in the neighborhood of La Rochelle and Rochefort between 1758 and 1763 brought with them family papers, curés and notaries their registers, and clerks of courts their dossiers.[21] Records also came into this area from Louisiana and other French colonies in America. The requirement by the government of documentary evidence with applications for relief led to the establishment in 1765 of a Dépôt des Archives des Colonies at Rochefort where all of these records could be deposited for safekeeping.[22] Gui-Louis Haran, an old employee of the Marine Department, was appointed keeper, and he transported from La Rochelle the records of the intendancy. A fire at Rochefort in 1786 is believed to have destroyed some of the colonial records deposited there. In 1790, after the death of Haran, the depot at Rochefort was abolished, and the records were transferred to Versailles where a Dépôt des Papiers Publics des Colonies had been established in 1776.[23] A part of the Archives de la Marine et des Colonies, this depot was moved in 1837 to Paris and placed in the building occupied by the Ministry of the Marine and the Colonies on Rue Royale. When the Ministry of the Colonies was created in 1894, the Archives des Colonies, including the Dépôt des Papiers Publics des Colonies, moved to the Pavillon de Flore in the Louvre.

In carrying off the papers of their offices, the last governor and intendant of New France were following the custom that had always been practiced in that colony. The administrative papers including the letters and instructions received, and the copies of dispatches sent to France were regarded as the property of the officials themselves and were taken away by them.[24] Consequently such records are not to be found in the archives preserved at Quebec and, since in most cases the private collections have dis-

---

[21] Paul Roussier, "Le dépôt des papiers publics des colonies," *Revue d'histoire moderne*, IV (juillet-août, 1929), 243.

[22] *Ibid.*

[23] Roussier, "Origines du dépôt des papiers publics des colonies," p. 47-48. It became principally a depository for duplicate copies of records of French colonies and is still in existence in the Ministère de la France d'Outre-Mer.

[24] Arthur G. Doughty, *The Canadian Archives and Its Activities* (Ottawa, 1924), 14.

appeared,[25] the searcher must turn to the archives of France for these important sources of information. A few letters of the Marquis de La Jonquière and of Pierre de Rigaud, Marquis de Vaudreuil-Cavagnol are in the Canadian Public Archives.[26] That institution reported in 1949 the purchase of 600 letters, reports, etc., relating to François de Beauharnois, intendant of New France from 1702 to 1705.[27]

According to the capitulation of Montreal in 1760, records relating to the property and legal rights of individuals, including registers and papers of the Superior Council, the Prévôté, the Admiralty of Quebec, the royal jurisdictions of Three Rivers and Montreal, seignorial jurisdictions, and the minutes and acts of notaries, were to remain in Canada.[28] Part of these records passed into the custody of the provincial secretary of the Province of Quebec and others into the hands of the clerk of the court of common pleas. A report of March 1790 submitted by a committee which had been appointed by Lord Dorchester in December 1787 to investigate the ancient records of the province, contains data as to the custody and condition of the records of New France and valuable inventories.[29] Consideration of the facts revealed in the report of the committee resulted in the concentration of all of the records in the vaults of the provincial secretary.[30]

During the nineteenth century the records of New France were seriously despoiled while in the custody of the provincial secretary by persons who were allowed too free an access to them, so

[25] Roy, *Rapport sur les archives de France*, p. 448, 1029.

[26] Canada, Public Archives, Manuscript Division, *Preliminary Inventory, Manuscript Group 18, Pre-conquest Papers* (Ottawa, 1954), 15-16. Some letters and extracts of others of De La Jonquière are published in Camille La Jonquière, *Marquis de La Jonquière, Le chef d'escadre Mis de la Jonquière, gouverneur general de la Nouvelle-France, et le Canada de 1749 à 1752* (Paris, 1896).

[27] Canada, Public Archives, *Report*, 1949, x.

[28] Shortt and Doughty, eds., *Docs. Const. Hist. Canada*, I, 34.

[29] Quebec (Province), Legislative Council. "Report of the Committee of Quebec on the Ancient Archives [Mar. 1790]," in Canada, Public Archives, *Report Concerning the Public Archives*, 1904 (Ottawa, 1905), Appendix D, 82-189. The report was originally published at Quebec in 1791.

[30] Fernand Ouellet, *L'Histoire des archives du gouvernement en Nouvelle-France* (Extrait de *La revue de l'Université Laval*, XII, no. 5, jan. 1958, Québec), 15.

that extensive gaps developed in many of the files.[31] The loss might have been even greater had not transcribing of records, as a preservative measure, been undertaken in 1845 and carried on thereafter for many years. A number of lists and inventories published in the reports of the provincial secretary are useful for the history of the records and could be useful in rebuilding the incomplete files.[32] Some judicial and intendancy records and transcripts were transferred from the Literary and Historical Society of Quebec to the custody of the provincial secretary in 1888.[33] An Archives Branch was created in the government of the province in 1920, and the records passed into the care of a professional archivist.[34] The Canadian Public Archives has transcribed many of the French records at Quebec, so that copies are now at Ottawa.[35]

The records of New France now preserved in the Provincial Archives at Quebec contain material relating to many places in the United States. Certain records of the Superior Council and of the intendant are primarily of value for the administration of the colony and its constitutional, legal, social, political and economic history. The record of proceedings (*Jugements et Délibérations*) of the Superior Council do not contain much relating to the United States, but its registers of the official texts of royal and

---

[31] Quellet, *L'Histoire des archives,* p. 17-19. Some of these missing archives are known to be in depositories in Montreal, Ottawa, Toronto, Boston, New York, Chicago, and New Orleans, (Pierre-Georges Roy, "Les archives de la Province de la Québec," *Bull. recherches hist.,* XXXII (avril 1926), 204.

[32] Quebec (Province), Secretary, *Report of the Secretary and Registrar,* 1886-87 (Québec, 1888), 61-66; *ibid.,* 1887-88 (Québec, 1889) 9-13; *ibid.,* 1888-89 (Québec, 1890), 128-29; "Chronological List or Index of Grants en Fief and Royal Ratifications of Grants en Fief made in New France to the Time of Its Cession to the British Crown in 1760," *ibid.,* 1892 (Québec, 1893), 120-66; "List of the Historical Volumes and Registers in the Vault of the Department of the Registrar of the Province of Quebec," *ibid.,* 1904 (Sessional Papers, XXXVIII, pt. 2, Québec, 1905), 6-18.

[33] *Ibid.,* 1887-88 (Québec, 1889), 7-8; Literary and Historical Society of Quebec, *The Centenary Volume of the Literary and Historical Society of Quebec, 1824-1924,* (Québec, 1924), 43-44.

[34] William Wood, "The New Provincial Archives of Quebec," *Can. Hist. Rev.* II (June 1921), 126.

[35] Numerous references to these transcripts can be found in the *Reports of the Public Archives* as early as 1884 and as late as 1946. See also Biggar, "Public Archives at Ottawa," II, 70-71.

other decrees, edicts, orders, etc. (*Registres des Insinuations*) contain documents bearing on the history of the United States.[36] Calendars of both series are available,[37] and many of the documents in the proceedings have been published.[38] Naturalization papers were also registered by the council.[39] Permits to trade given at Quebec by the governor and intendant in 1736 and 1737, including many for places in the United States, are registered in a volume with other documents.[40] Among the orders of the intendant for 1705-59 are some concerning administrative matters, the fur trade, and fisheries in American territory.[41] An inventory of the ordinances for 1705-60 has been published.[42] Those for earlier years have disappeared, but the texts have been recovered insofar as possible from other collections in France and in Canada and have been published.[43]

[36] Parker, *Guide to the Materials for U.S. History*, p. 206-07. A list of the more important documents concerning the United States (1663-1755) among those registered appears *ibid.*, p. 207-10.

[37] New France, Conseil supérieur de Québec, *Inventaire des jugements et délibérations du Conseil supérieur de la Nouvelle-France de 1717 à 1760*, par Pierre-Georges Roy (Beauceville, 1932-35. 7 vols.); New France, Conseil supérieur de Québec, *Inventaire des insinuations du Conseil souverain de la Nouvelle-France*, par Pierre-Georges Roy (Beauceville, 1921).

[38] New France, Laws, Statutes, etc., *Édits, ordonnances royaux, déclarations et arrêts du Conseil d'état du roi, concernant le Canada* (Québec, 1803-06, 2 vols.). A revised and enlarged edition of this publication, embracing documents omitted from the earlier edition, appeared in 1854-56. The proceedings of the council are in New France, Conseil supérieur de Québec, *Jugements et délibérations du Conseil souverain de la Nouvelle-France, 1663-1710* (Québec, 1885-91. 6 vols.). Publication of the texts was suspended because of the considerable expense involved.

[39] Pierre-Georges Roy, "Les lettres de naturalité sous le régime française," *Bull. recherches hist.*, XXX (août 1924), 225-32, giving a list of the names of natives of Ireland, England, New England, Germany, and others who were naturalized.

[40] Parker, *Guide to Materials for U.S. History*, p. 210. An inventory of *congés* issued during 1739-52 is in Quebec (Province) Archives, "Les congés de traite sous le régime français au Canada," *Rapport de l'archiviste de la province de Québec*, 1922-23 (Québec, 1923), 191-265.

[41] Parker, *Guide to Materials for U.S. History*, p. 211-14.

[42] New France, Intendant, *Inventaire des ordonnances des intendants de la Nouvelle-France, conservées aux Archives provinciales de Québec*, par Pierre-Georges Roy (Beauceville, 1919. 4 vols.).

[43] New France, *Ordonnances, commissions, etc.; etc., des gouverneurs et intendants de la Nouvelle-France, 1639-1706*, par Pierre-Georges Roy (Beauceville, 1924. 2 vols.).

Judicial Records

The records of the Prévôté of Quebec, 1666-1759, consisting principally of minutes of the court sessions, are valuable for legal history, social life, and economic matters.[44] Registers of the Prévôté of Quebec also contain commissions issued to the judicial officers, marriage contracts, wills, deeds, issuances of the King and the council, and ordinances and regulations of the Prévôté.[45] An inventory of the registers opens the way into these sources for the genealogist and the student. Material of American interest is scattered and relates chiefly to individuals and to cases connected with the Indian trade.[46]

The judicial archives in the courthouse at Quebec contain several groups of papers. These include notarial acts from 1635, consisting in general of documents relating to property and personal and business relationships, such as agreements, concessions, deeds, leases, marriage contracts, receipts, sales, wills, etc.[47] These records are arranged by notaries (*études*) for each of which there is an inventory.[48] Some of the notarial records of Quebec have

[44] J.-B. Gareau, "La Prévôté de Québec; ses officers—ses registres," Quebec (Province) Archives, *Rapport de l'archiviste de la province de Québec,* 1943-44 (Québec, 1944), 60.

[45] New France, Cour de la prévôté de Québec, *Inventaire des insinuations de la prévôté de Québec,* par Pierre-Georges Roy (Beauceville, 1936. 3 vols.).

[46] Parker, *Guide to Materials for U.S. History,* p. 217.

[47] A list of the notaries appears in Joseph Edmond Roy, *Histoire du notariat au Canada* (Lévis, 1899-1902. 4 vols.), and in Pierre-Georges Roy, "Les notaires au Canada sous le régime français," Quebec (Province) Archives, *Rapport de l'archiviste de la province de Québec,* 1921-22 [Québec, 1922] 1-58, and in André Vachon, "Inventaire critique des notaires royaux des gouvernements de Québec, Montréal et Trois-Rivierès (1663-1764)," *Revue d'histoire de l'Amérique française,* IX-XI (1955-57). See also the following inventories: Quebec (province) Judicial Archives, *Inventaire des contrats de mariage du régime français conservés aux archives judiciaires de Québec,* par Pierre-Georges Roy (Québec, 1937-38. 6 vols.); Quebec (Province) Archives, *Inventaire des geffes des notaires du régime français,* par Pierre-Georges et Antoine Roy (Québec, 1942-53. 17 vols.) Quebec (Province) Judicial Archives, *Inventaire des testaments, donations et inventaires du régime français conservés aux archives judiciaires de Québec,* par Pierre-Georges Roy (Québec, 1941. 3 vols.).

[48] Quebec (Province) Judicial archives, *Inventaire des registres de l'état civil conservés aux archives judiciaires de Québec,* par Pierre-Georges Roy (Beauceville, 1921).

found their way to the Chicago Historical Society.[49] A file of papers relating to the appointment of guardians and family councils dates from 1639.

Other records that came to be deposited in the judicial archives were the registers of civil status. An ordinance adopted by the Sovereign Council of New France in November 1678 required the priests in charge of parishes throughout the province to prepare duplicates of the registers of baptisms, marriages, and burials.[50] These were to be collated with the original registers at the end of each year, authenticated, and deposited in the archives of each judicial district. Thus the government became possessed of registers of civil status that supplied it with means of ascertaining information about individuals whenever it was required for legal purposes.[51]

The Institut Généalogique Drouin in Montreal (4184, rue St.-Denis) where genealogical compilations are prepared, has micro-reproductions of the birth, marriage, and death records of French Canada from 1621 totaling sixty-one million documents.

Land Records

Several series of records concern land grants. The registers of the intendant contain the concessions and ratifications of the intendants.[52] Registrations of the titles of concessions, ratifications and other acts under orders issued by the intendant, Michel Bégon, during 1722-25 are also available. Titles from these sources, but mostly from the registers of the intendants, were published in

---

[49] "Calendar of Manuscripts in the Archives of the Chicago Historical Society," *Report on Canadian Archives*, 1905, I, xxxii-xlvii.

[50] A. S. Archambault, "Les registres de l'état civil de la province de Québec," *Revue trimestrielle canadienne*, IV (mai 1918), 56.

[51] The priests of the Roman Catholic Church, other local religious institutions, and city clerks are still required to maintain registers of civil status. Detailed and explicit regulations for keeping registers are in the Civil Code of the Province of Quebec (Léon Roy, "The Keeping of Church Registers of Juridical Status in the Province of Quebec," in Quebec (Province) Archives, *Rapport de l'archiviste de la province de Québec*, 1959-60, Québec, 1961, 187-221). The registers are more valuable for establishing identity than in proving the exact dates of birth, marriage, and death.

[52] Parker, *Guide to Materials for U.S. History*, p. 214.

1854.[53] Another file is the *"aveux et dénombrements,"* (acknowledgments of vassalage and enumerations), which are descriptions of the grants deposited by the seigniors. Containing lists of the habitants in addition to the physical details of the grants, these records are valuable for local history.[54] A compilation of documents derived from these records contains topographic and geographic data relative to Quebec, Montreal and Three Rivers.[55] The seigniors were also required to make declarations of fealty and homage (*"actes de foi et hommage"*) to the governors. An inventory of these records constitutes a valuable tool for local history and genealogy.[56] It gives not only exact archival references but also indicates where printed copies of the deeds may be found. A selection of documents relating to the seigniorial system has been published.[57] The first register became so damaged and fragile from use that it was put into print to save the original.[58] A sample in print of an *aveu et dénombrement* shows it to have value not only for genealogy but also for social and economic history.[59] Transcriptions of the land records of Quebec are in the

53 Quebec, (Province), Parliament, *Pieces et documents relatifs à la tenure seigneuriale, demandés par une adresse de l'assemblée législative* (Québec, 1852-54. 2 vols.).

54 Pierre-Georges Roy, "Les archives de la Province de Québec," *Bull. recherches hist.*, XXXII (avril 1926), 200.

55 Quebec, (Province), *Cadastres abrégés des seigneuries* (Québec, 1863. 6 vols.).

56 Quebec, (Province) Archives. *Inventaires des concessions en fief et seigneurie, fois et hommages et aveux et dénombrements conservés aux archives de la province de Québec*, par Pierre-Georges Roy (Québec, 1927-29. 6 vols.); Canada, Public Archives, "Abstracts of the actes de foy et hommage (Fealty Rolls)," *Report on Canadian Archives*, 1884-85 (Ottawa, 1885, 1886), 1-29, 31-76. A partial list of land grants lying within or adjacent to the United States is in Parker, *Guide to Materials for U.S. History*, p. 216-17.

57 William B. Munro, ed., *Documents Relating to the Seigniorial Tenure in Canada, 1598-1854* (Toronto, 1908).

58 Quebec (Province) Archives, *Papier terrier de la Compagnie des Indes Occidentales, 1667-1668* (Beauceville, 1931).

59 Quebec (Province) Archives, "Aveu et dénombrement de messire Louis Normand, prêtre du séminaire de Saint-Sulpice de Montréal, au nom et comme fondé de procuration de messire Charles-Maurice le Pelletier, supérieur du séminaire de Saint-Sulpice, de Paris pour la seigneurie de l'île de Montréal (1731)," *Rapport de l'archiviste de la province de Québec*, 1941-42 (Québec, 1942), 1-176.

Canadian Public Archives. Personal information about inhabitants of Quebec can be found in the land records.[60]

Montreal District

There are a number of records in Montreal containing documents relating to the region south of the Great Lakes that became part of the United States.[61] The records at Montreal are concentrated in the courthouse, which by regulation became the depository for notarial acts and registers of civil status as well as for the strictly judicial records.[62] The collection of edicts, ordinances, and regulations which emanated from the governments of France, New France, and the district of Montreal are of interest primarily for the development of the town and district of Montreal and for the social life of the area.[63] The civil and criminal court proceedings

---

[60] A list of copyholders in one section of Quebec is in Ivanhoë Caron, "Les censitaires du côteau Sainte-Geneviève (banlieue de Québec) de 1636 à 1800," *Bull. recherches hist.*, XXVII (avril, mai, juin 1921), 97-108, 129-46, 161-76.

[61] See the "Statement of Documents, Registers, Court Records (procedures) &c. in the Archives of Montreal from the establishment of the Judicial District down to the Conquest of 1760," in "Report of the Committee of Quebec," Canada, Public Archives, *Report*, 1904, 149-56. This list was prepared in 1790 by the committee appointed by the governor-general in 1787. Eudore Evanturel, an archival clerk in the office of the secretary of the Province of Quebec, was sent to Montreal and Three Rivers in 1889 to investigate the records at those places. As a result of this visit, he prepared a catalog of the judicial archives preserved in the courthouse at Montreal, which is published in Quebec (Province), Secretary, *Report . . .*, 1888-89 (Québec, 1890). 131-35 and an incomplete index for 1651-95, *ibid.*, 1889-90, 1890-91 (Québec, 1890-91), p. 73-91, 79-298.

[62] Edouard-Zotique Massicotte, "Les archives judiciaires de Montréal." *Bull. recherches hist.*, XXXII (avril 1926), 226-28.

[63] Edouard-Zotique Massicotte, *Montréal sous le régime française; répertoire des arrêts, édits, mandements, ordonnances et règlements, conservés dans les archives au Palais de justice de Montréal, 1640-1760* (Montréal, 1919). Published also in *Procs.* and *Trans.* Royal Soc. Canada, 3d ser. XI, sect. I (Dec. 1917 and Mar. 1918), 147-74, XII (Dec. 1918 and Mar. 1919), 209-23. A subsequent inventory lists additional documents: E.-Z. Massicotte, "Les arrêts, édits, ordonnances, mandements et règlements, conservés à Montréal, *Bull recherches hist.*, XXXIV (sept. 1928), 520-27.

contain little on American history.[64] The registers of civil status, which are valuable for genealogical data, begin in 1642.[65] The notarial records document personal and family relationships and business transactions.[66] Acts of faith and homage were also filed by the notaries.[67] Transcripts from the notarial records are in the Burton Historical Collection of the Detroit Public Library and in the Canadian Public Archives.[68] In addition to administration, biography,[69] and genealogy, these records are the primary source of information for commerce and industry and for the manners and customs of the time.[70]

Two types of documents among the notarial records at Montreal are of especial interest for American history. These are the *congés*, or permits to trade issued to traders and the *engagements*, or contracts between traders and *voyageurs*. They are valuable for information on the fur trade carried on in American territory,

[64] Parker, *Guide to Materials for U.S. History*, p. 271.

[65] Ovide-M.-H. Lapalice, "Le premier registre d'état civil de Montréal," *Canadian Antiquarian and Numismatic Journal*, 3d ser., VIII (Oct. 1911), 171-98.

[66] "Statement of Documents, Registers, . . . ," in Canada, Public Archives, *Report*, 1904, 124, 150-156. The Montreal notarial records are inventoried in P.-G. Roy and Antoine Roy, *Inventaire des greffes des notaires du régime français* (Québec, 1942-53. 17 vols.) See the table at the front of vol. 17. E.-Z. Massicotte, "Les actes des trois premiers tabellions de Montréal, 1648-1657," *Procs. and Trans.* Royal Soc. Canada, 3d ser., IX sect. I, (Sept. 1915), 189-204. The texts of a few notarial documents will be found in Pease and Werner, eds., *French Foundations, passim.* An inventory of property, Feb. 8, 1662, is printed in E.-Z. Massicotte, "L'Inventaire des biens de Lambert Closse," *Bull. recherches hist.*, XXV (jan. 1919), 16-31. An index to marriage contracts in the Montreal notarial records is in the Canadian Public Archives.

[67] E.-Z. Massicotte, "Inventaire des actes de foi et hommage conservés aux Archives judiciaires de Montréal," in Quebec, (Province), Archives, *Rapport*, 1921-22 (Québec, 1922), 102-08.

[68] Henry P. Biggar, "The Public Archives at Ottawa," *Bulletin* of the Institute of Historical Research, II (Feb. 1925), 71.

[69] Documents concerning Duluth, his brother, and his uncle in the archives at Montreal are listed in E.-Z. Massicotte, "Daniel de Greysolon, sieur de Lhut, Claude de Greysolon, sieur de la Tourette et Jean-Jacques Patron," *Bul. recherches hist.*, XXXIII (mars 1927), 139-47.

[70] A sample of another type of record in the archives is a "rôle de cotisation" or list of habitants, the oldest one for 1673 is printed in E.-Z. Massicotte, "La population de Montréal en 1673," *Canad. Antiq. Numis. Jour.*, 3d ser., XI (oct. 1914), 141-67.

and they afford genealogical data not to be found in the registers of civil status. Both series cover the British as well as the French period. A chronological inventory in print of the *congés* issued during 1681-1737 gives the name of the official issuing the permit, the name of the person to whom issued, the number of men in the canoe, its destination, and cargo.[71] Inventories of the *engagements* list over thirteen thousand of these documents for the years from 1670 to 1760 and a total of nearly twenty thousand up to 1821.[72] These inventories provide merely the date of execution, the names of the parties to the contract, and the notarial file. The documents themselves also state places of residence, occupations, dates of voyages to the west, times and terms of employment, and sometimes data as to the value of services and commodities and the volume of trade, and the names of witnesses. Numerous *engagements* from the Montreal files made by La Forest and Tonty with various *voyageurs* and others for voyages to Illinois are in print.[73] Transcripts of thousands of the agreements are among the copies of the notarial records of Montreal in the Burton Historical Collection. Other copies for the years 1727-35 are in the Minnesota Historical Society.

Three Rivers District

Material relating to explorers and *coureurs des bois* who were active in American territory can also be found in the archives in

[71] E.-Z. Massicotte, "Congés et permis déposés ou enregistrés à Montréal sous le régime français," en Quebec (Province) Archives, *Rapport,* 1921-22 (Québec, 1922), 189-225.

[72] E.-Z. Massicotte, "Répertoire des engagements pour l'ouest conservés dans les Archives judiciaires de Montréal," en Quebec, (Province) Archives, *Rapport,* 1929-30, 1930-31, 1931-32, 1932-33 (Québec, 1930-33), 191-466, 353-453, 243-365, 245-304, 260-397.

[73] Pease and Werner, eds., *The French Foundations, passim.* A permit to trade at Vincennes, May 1754, is printed in Pease and Jenison, eds., *Illinois on the Eve of the Seven Years' War,* 853-57. A lease of Apr. 10, 1747 for the post at Green Bay is in Thwaites, ed., *French Regime in Wis.,* XVII, 451-55. The value of the trading licenses for local history is demonstrated in Peter L. Scanlan, *Prairie du Chien: French, British, American* (Menasha, Wis., 1937). He gives (p. 237-45) a list of licenses issued from 1716 to 1779 for Mackinac, Green Bay, Mississippi River, and the Sioux country.

the courthouse at Three Rivers. The registers of civil status date from 1634, but are incomplete for the years before 1654.[74] The notarization of acts for Three Rivers was performed at Quebec before 1650, but there are some originals and copies of notarial records at Three Rivers going back to 1636.[75] The notarial acts have been calendared.[76] The judicial proceedings of civil and criminal cases date from 1653; many are so faded that they are difficult to read and should be transcribed. Other records of Three Rivers are in Quebec in the museum of the Province of Quebec. Transcripts from the archives at Three Rivers are in the Public Archives of Canada at Ottawa.

Documentary Publications

The Provincial Archives of Quebec has rightly concentrated upon the publication of calendars of its extensive and valuable archives. Such a program has been successfully and competently executed and has produced the largest body of calendars of any archival institution in North America. Toward the end of the nineteenth century when the provincial government first became energetically interested in its archives, it published a four-volume collection of documents in 1883-85 from the provincial archives and copies of transcripts from French archives, and in 1893 issued the first volume of a projected series of historical documents, which

[74] Raymond Douville, "Short Sketch of the Archives of Three Rivers," *American Archivist*, X (July 1947), 263.

[75] *Ibid.*, p. 266; J.-B. Meilleur-Barthe, "Inventaire sommaire des archives conservées au Palais de Justice des Trois-Rivières," in Quebec (Province) Archives, *Rapport de l'archiviste de la province de Québec*, 1920-21 (Québec, 1921), 340. Other descriptions of the archives at Three Rivers can be found in Quebec (Province), Legislative Council, "Report of the Committee of Quebec on the Ancient Archives [Mar. 1790]," in Canada, Public Archives, *Report Concerning the Public Archives*, 1904 (Ottawa, 1905), Appendix D, p. 110, 135, 138, 140-41, 156, 159, 162, 164, 173, 177, and in Quebec (Province), Secretary, *Report of the Secretary and Registrar . . .* 1904 (Quebec, 1904), 15-18.

[76] Quebec (Province) Archives, *Inventaire des greffes des notaires du régime français*, par P.-G. Roy et Antoine Roy, (Québec, 1942-53. 17 vols.). See the table at the front of vol. 17.

was not continued.[77] Numerous documents which are hard to locate even with the index volumes, can be found scattered in the many-volumed *Bulletin des Recherches Historiques,* and in the *Rapport de l'Archivist de la Province de Québec,* for which there is no index at all. It is unfortunate that the Provincial Archives did not persevere in the publication of a separate documentary series, which by this time might have amounted to several volumes.

Reproductions from French Archives

For papers of an administrative character, including those of governors, intendants, commandants, and other officials, investigators have had to have recourse to the archives of France and family papers. Such papers are largely missing in Canada and in the collections of the American states, for it was the custom of the officials, including the commandants of the posts in the Upper Country, to carry off their papers at the conclusion of their terms of service. Through the vicissitudes of time these papers have largely disappeared, although some important ones have been brought to light.[78]

The Ministry of the Marine accumulated correspondence and other documents relating to the administration of New France and Louisiana. Now preserved in the Archives Nationales in Paris and known as the Archives des Colonies, these records contain letters received from officials in Canada (series C11A) among which are many communications originating at the western posts.[79] In this

[77] Quebec (Province) Archives, *Collection de manuscrits contenant lettres, mémoires, et autres documents historiques relatifs à la Nouvelle-France, recueillis aux archives de la province de Québec, ou copiés à l'étranger; mis en ordre et édités sous les auspices de la législature de Québec, avec table etc.* (Québec, 1883-85. 4 vols.); Quebec (Province) Parliament, Nouvelle-France, *Documents historiques; correspondance echangée entre les autorités françaises et les gouverneurs et intendants, Volume I* (Québec, 1893).

[78] Roy, *Rapport sur les archives de France,* p. 445, 448, 1029 *et seq.*

[79] *Ibid.,* p. 470-71. Further description of the pertinent records with bibliography can be found in Beers, *French in North America,* 12 *et seq.* A calendar of series C11A by Joseph Marmette is in *Report on Canadian Archives, 1885-87.* Documents from both that series and series C13A are calendared in Nancy M. Surrey, *Calendar of Manuscripts in Paris Archives and Libraries Relating to the History of the Mississippi Valley to 1803* (Washington, 1926, 1928. 2 vols.).

file are many bills and vouchers authorized by the commandants for services and supplies furnished at the western posts. These are valuable for information relative to the activities of the French and the Indians, and for trade and business.[80] A similar file of letters received (series C13A) concerns Louisiana. Dispatches and orders sent to these colonies constitute series B, Archives des Colonies.[81] Pertinent documents are in the archives of other French ministries, including those of War, Foreign Affairs, and various departments, cities, ports, and naval districts.[82] The manuscript collections of the Bibliothèque Nationale and other libraries, and family papers contain correspondence and other documents. Replacements for the lost administrative papers can be made to a large degree from the foregoing sources, but such a file if it were reconstructed would not be entirely complete, for the local files contained documents of local origin for which there would have been no reason to send on copies to France and which would therefore be unique.

For over a hundred years American and Canadian archival insti-

[80] Caldwell, *French in the Miss. Valley,* p. 25, 30-31, 34, 89 n. 9, 103. Expense accounts are published in Pease and Werner, eds., *French Foundations,* p. 60-67 and in Burton, ed., *Cadillac Papers,* XXXIII, 568, 593-94.

[81] A calendar of series B prepared by Édouard Richard is in *Report on Canadian Archives, 1899, Supplement, 1904, 1905.* See also France, Ministère de la France d'Outre-Mer, Service des Archives, *Inventaire analytique de la correspondance générale avec les colonies, départ, série B (déposée aux Archives nationales), I-, registres 1 à 37 (1654-1715),* par Étienne Taillemite (Paris, 1959) [to be continued].

[82] Further description of these records can be found in Beers, *French in North America, passim.* See also M. Baudot, "Les archives départementales, centres de la documentation historique régionale," *La gazette des archives,* n.s., num. 9 (jan. 1951), 46-55; René Baudry, "Les archives de France et l'histoire du Canada," en *Mélanges offerts par ses confrères étrangers, à Charles Braibant* (Bruxelles, 1959), p. 31-42; Étienne Taillemite, "Les archives de la France d'Outre-Mer," *La gazette des archives,* n.s., num. 22 (juillet 1957), 6-22; France, Direction des Archives de France, *État des inventaires de archives nationales, départementales, communales et hospitalières; supplement (1937-1954)* (Paris, 1955); France, Archives Nationales, *Registres de Trésor des chartes* (Paris, 1958-); France, Direction des archives de France, *Guide des recherches dans les fonds judiciaires de l'ancien régime,* par Michel Antoine, et al. (Paris, 1958); France, Archives nationales, *Le fonds du Conseil d'état du roi aux Archives nationales; guide des recherches,* Michel Antoine (Paris, 1955). Current bibliography regarding the French archives is in *La gazette des archives; organe de l'Association amicale professionnelle des archivistes français,* n.s., num. 1, jan. 1947- (Paris, 1947-).

tutions, historical societies, libraries, historians, collectors, and others have drawn on the archives of France for materials relating to the history of the United States and Canada.[83] The Canadian Public Archives at Ottawa has the largest and most varied collection of transcripts and microfilm from French archives.[84] In the United States the largest assemblage of reproductions in the form of transcripts, photostats, and microfilm is in the Division of Manuscripts of the Library of Congress.[85] Reproductions obtained by the Archives of the Quebec Province from both Paris and Ottawa have been the basis of published collections of the correspondence of the Count de Frontenac,[86] the Marquis de Vaudreuil,[87] Jean Talon,[88] the journals, memoirs, and papers of the Chevalier de la

[83] My purpose here is merely to call attention to the principal collections and documentary publications. A history of these various reproduction activities is in Beers, *French in North America, passim.*

[84] *Ibid.,* p. 230 *et seq.* Descriptions of the numerous archival reproductions obtained by the Canadian Public Archives are in Canada, Public Archives, Division des Manuscrits, *Inventaire provisoire, fonds des manuscrits no 1, Archives nationales, Paris Archives des colonies* (Ottawa, 1952): Canada, Public Archives, Division des manuscrits, *Inventaire provisoire, fonds des manuscrits, no. 2, Archives de la marine, no. 3, Archives nationales, no. 4, Archives de la guerre, Paris* (Ottawa, 1953); Canada, Public Archives, Division des manuscrits, *Inventaire provisoire, fonds des manuscrits no. 6, Archives departmentales, municipales, maritimes* (to be published).

[85] Beers, *French in North America,* p. 198 *et seq.* The Library of Congress has published no inventory of its reproductions from French archives, but see Surrey's *Calendar of MSS. in Paris Archives;* Waldo G. Leland, *Guide to Materials for American History in the Libraries and Archives of Paris, Volume I, Libraries* (Washington, 1932); Waldo G. Leland and John J. Meng, and Abel Doysié, *Guide to Materials for American History in the Libraries and Archives of Paris, Volume II, Archives of the Ministry of Foreign Affairs* (Washington, 1943).

[86] Quebec (Province) Archives, "Correspondance échangée entre la Cour de France et le gouverneur de Frontenac, pendant sa première administration (1672-1682)," in *Rapport de l'archiviste de la province de Quebec,* 1926-27 (Québec, 1927), 3-144; Quebec (Province) Archives, "Correspondance échangée entre la Cour de France et le gouverneur de Frontenac, pendant sa seconde administration (1689-1699)," *ibid.,* 1927-28, 1928-29, 3-211, 247-384.

[87] Quebec (Province) Archives, "Correspondance entre M. de Vaudreuil et la Cour," *ibid.,* 1938-39, 1939-40, 1942-43, 1946-47, 10-179, 355-463, 399-443, 371-460.

[88] Quebec (Province) Archives, "Correspondance échangée entre la Cour de France et l'intendant Talon pendant ses deux administrations dans la Nouvelle-France," *ibid.,* 1930-31, 1-182.

Pause, whose duties and observations as a military officer during 1755-60 extended to New York, Pennsylvania, the Great Lakes, and the Illinois country.[89]

The collections of transcripts in the depositories mentioned above include materials on exploration and cartography.[90]

Both the Canadian Public Archives and the Library of Congress are continuing their reproduction activities in French archives. The activities of the former institution include the photographing of manuscript maps to replace earlier hand drawn copies. Neither institution has sponsored extensive documentary publications based upon its holdings, though both have afforded aid to other compilers.

The Province of Ontario, originally a part of Quebec, has recently undertaken the sponsorship of a documentary series based on transcripts and microreproductions in the Canadian Public Archives and other sources. One volume on the French period consists of nearly 200 pages of documents (with English translations) by explorers, missionaries, intendants, governors, officers, engineers, and visitors relating to Fort Frontenac during 1668-1759.[91] These documents supply data about persons who served in the Old Northwest and information regarding various places in that area. There is still need for similar collections for posts such as Michilimackinac and Vincennes.

Censuses derived from the French archives are a valuable source of information not only for genealogy but also for economic and social history. Data can be obtained from them regarding the men who went to the Upper Country, names of their household members, servants employed, and farm animals owned. Numerous censuses were taken in New France between 1666 and 1760, but not all of them contain the names of heads of families; many were

[89] La Pause, Jean-Guillaume-Charles de Plantavit de Margon, Chevalier de, "Mémoire et observations sur mon voyage au Canada," *ibid.*, 1931-32, 3-46; "Les mémoires du Chevalier de la Pause," *ibid.*, 1932-33, 305-91; "Les papiers La Pause," *ibid.*, 1933-34, 65-231.

[90] Beers, *French in North America*, p. 121-24, 127-29.

[91] Richard A. Preston and Leopold Lamontagne, ed. and trans., *Royal Fort Frontenac* (*Publications* of the Champlain Society, Ontario Series, No. 2, Toronto, 1958).

merely statistical in character.[92] Copies of the censuses were filed in the archives in Paris, and the Canadian Public Archives has obtained reproductions from the Archives des Colonies, series G1 and series B.[93] Censuses of Quebec for 1666, 1667, 1681,[94] 1716,[95] and one of the Three Rivers for September 1760 have been published.[96] The Bureau of Statistics of the Dominion of Canada planned some years ago to bring out a volume containing all of these early censuses. The idea is still a good one; it would make a valuable addition to the source material on New France.[97]

[92] Lists of the censuses prepared from manuscript and printed sources are available in Canada, Department of Agriculture, "Censuses of Canada, 1665 to 1871," in *Census of Canada, 1870-71* vol. IV (Ottawa, 1876); Canada, Bureau of Statistics, "Chronological Summary of Population Growth in Canada, with Sources of Information, 1605-1931," *Seventh Census of Canada, 1931*, vol. I (Ottawa, 1933), 133-53; and a revised list in processed form: Canada, Bureau of Statistics, Demography Branch, *Chronological List of Canadian Censuses* (Ottawa, [1942]).

[93] Canada, Public Archives, Division des manuscrits, *Inventaire provisoire, fonds des manuscrits, no. 1*, p. 17.

[94] The censuses of 1666, 1667, and 1681 are in Benjamin Sulte, *Histoire des canadiens-français, 1608-1880* (Montréal, 1882-84. 8 vols.), IV, 52-78; V, 53-88. A more exact text of the 1666 census is in Quebec (Province), "Le premier recensement de la Nouvelle-France [1666]," *Rapport de l'archiviste de la province de Québec, 1935-1936* (Québec, 1936), 1-154. The 1666 census with notes regarding the individuals mentioned also appears in Pierre-Georges Roy, ed., "Le premier recensement nominal de Québec," *Bulletin des recherches historiques*, XXXVII (juin, juillet 1931), 321-31, 385-404.

[95] Abbé Louis Beaudet, ed., *Recensement de la ville de Québec pour 1716* (Québec, 1887).

[96] Canada, Public Archives, "Recensement des habitans de la ville & gouvernement des Trois Rivières, tel qu'il a ete pris au mois de septembre mil sept cent soixante," *Report of the Public Archives, 1918* (Ottawa, 1920), 158-89; Quebec (Province) Archives, "Recensement des habitants de la ville et gouvernement des Trois-Rivières," *Rapport de l'archiviste de la province de Québec, 1946-47* (Québec, 1947), 3-53.

[97] A worth-while project for the archival and manuscript depositories of the Midwest to undertake on a cooperative basis would be the procurement on microfilm of all of the records at Quebec, Montreal, and Three Rivers bearing on the history of that region. Such reproductions as are now available in Midwest depositories are not complete. The Public Archives of Canada has transcripts from the records of New France, but it might be possible to interest it in participating in a program for microfilming those records. Some collections of original records are already on hand in depositories of the Midwest. Reproductions from the French archives can be borrowed from the Library of Congress for scholarly use. If some of the institutions of the Midwest also had on

Manuscript Collections

Manuscript collections in Canadian depositories contain documents relating to the region south of the Great Lakes. Jacques Viger, a public official and antiquary of Montreal,[98] assembled a valuable collection of manuscripts which passed into the hands of Abbé Hospice A. Verreau, another collector who presented the Viger-Verreau collection to the archives of the Seminary of Quebec at Laval University. Among the manuscripts are the papers of several military officers, including Claude-Pierre Pécaudy, Sieur de Contrecoeur; Pierre-Paul de la Malgue, Sieur de Marin; Daniel-Hyacinthe-Marie de Beaujeu; and Jacques Le Gardeur, Sieur de Saint-Pierre, who participated in the occupation of the Ohio Valley and the defense of Fort Duquesne, 1753-55. Selections from the papers have been published,[99] and microreproductions of the entire collection are in the custody of the Pennsylvania Historical and

---

hand microfilm of the records of New France, all of the most important records for the history of the French regime in that region would be available for the use of interested scholars. It would be to the interest of depositories at Quebec, Montreal, and Three Rivers to cooperate, since they could then require searchers to use the microfilm or enlargements made from it and thereby lessen wear and tear on the original records. Such a program should also cover the records of the British regime in the Old Northwest. Once accomplished, the microreproductions assembled by this program would enable Midwestern historians to work with greater ease and efficiency on the history of the French and British regimes. It would also be possible to produce documentary compilations such as have been and are still being published by states on the Atlantic seaboard (See Jack P. Greene, "The Publication of the Official Records of the Southern Colonies," *The William and Mary Quarterly*, 3d ser., XIV [Apr. 1957], 268-80. Other records which are not in print will be found on microfilm, see William S. Jenkins, comp. and Lillian A. Hamrick, ed., *A Guide to the Microfilm Collection of Early State Records*. Prepared by the Library of Congress in Association with the University of North Carolina [Washington, 1950], and a *Supplement,* 1951. There are many subjects connected with the history of the French period on which monographs need to be written, e.g., the fur trade, Indian relations and wars, private land grants, missions and churches, military affairs, governmental administration, and social, cultural, and economic life.

[98] Victor Morin, "Esquisse biographique de Jacques Viger," *Mémoires Société Royale du Canada*, sér. 3, XXXII, sect. 1 (mai 1938), 183-90.

[99] Fernand Grenier, ed., *Papiers Contrecoeur et autres documents concernant le conflit anglo-français sur l'Ohio de 1745 à 1756* (Québec, 1952).

Museum Commission, and the Canadian Public Archives.[1] Besides first hand accounts by the officers of their activities, the papers contain instructions and orders from Governor Duquesne and the intendant Bigot. In the Viger-Verreau collection are journals of tours by Joseph-Gaspard Chaussegros de Léry, an engineer officer, to Detroit in 1749, and to Fort Niagara, Fort Duquesne, and Detroit in 1754-55.[2] Part of his journal of a voyage down the Ohio River with the De Longueil expedition in 1739 is in print.[3] He made the first compass survey of that river, and a reproduction of his map in the French Hydrographic Survey is in the Library of Congress.[4] The papers of several other officers in the Viger-Verreau collection also contain letters relating to operations in western Pennsylvania during the 1750's, and among the letters are many from Governor Duquesne and other officials of Canada. One of these officers was Jacques Daneau Demuy who was appointed commandant of Detroit in 1754 and served in that post until his death in 1758. Another was Jacques Le Gardeur, Sieur de Saint-Pierre, whose papers for 1731-55 also cover his services as commandant of Fort Beauharnois (1735-37), of Fort Michilimackinac (1747), and explorations in the West after 1749.

[1] Pennsylvania Historical and Museum Commission, *Preliminary Guide to the Research Materials of the Pennsylvania Historical and Museum Commission* (Harrisburg, 1959), 22. A microfilm is also in the General Library of Laval University. The two institutions cooperated on both the microfilm and the publication projects.

[2] "Les Journaux de campagne de Joseph-Gaspard Chaussegros de Léry [1749]," Quebec (Province) Archives, *Rapport de l'archiviste de la Province de Québec*, 1926-1927 (Québec, 1927), 331-405; "Journal de Joseph-Gaspard Chaussegros de Léry, lieutenant des troupes, 1754-1755," *ibid.*, 1927-1928, p. 355-429. An English rendering of the journal for 1754-55 by S. K. Stevens and Donald H. Kent appeared in 1940.

[3] "Journal de la campagne faite par le détachment du Canada sur les Chicachas en février 1740 au nombre de 201 français, et 337 sauvages de Canada, Illinois, Missouris et 58 Chactas faisant en tout 596 hommes," *ibid.*, 1922-1923, p. 157-65. Other documents and a map by Chaussegros de Léry are in Frontier Forts and Trails Survey, *The Expedition of Baron de Longueuil; a Preliminary Report Commemorating the 200th Anniversary* (*Northwestern Pennsylvania Historical Series*, ed. by Sylvester K. Stevens and Donald H. Kent) (Harrisburg, 1940).

[4] U.S. Library of Congress, *Report of the Librarian of Congress*, 1937, p. 132-37.

There is a published inventory of a part of the Viger collection called the "saberdache," a miscellany in forty-three volumes containing some material relating to the United States.[5]

Scattered manuscripts exist in other depositories such as the Canadian Public Archives, the Provincial Archives of Quebec, the Historical Society of Montreal, the Seminary of St. Sulpice at Montreal, and no doubt at other places. But until more guides and inventories are published, or the national union catalog of manuscripts is compiled, these manuscripts will continue to be difficult to locate. The names and addresses of depositories that might have materials are in directories.[6]

Ecclesiastical Records

The church registers of the Quebec Province which supply data like that in the registers described in the preceding chapter are valuable for the information they offer about the Frenchmen who journeyed to the Upper Country. Registers begun in Quebec in 1621 were burned in 1640, but were reconstructed by one of the Jesuit priests on the basis of data supplied by the persons concerned. The registers of chief interest are those of Quebec and Montreal, 1642-date, in the churches (both named Notre Dame) at those places,[7] and those of Three Rivers, 1634-date, in the custody of the Bishop of Three Rivers.[8] Copies of the registers of Quebec, 1621-1816, Montreal, 1642-1778, and Three Rivers, 1634-1763, are in the Cana-

[5] Fernand Ouellet, "Inventaire de la saberdache de Jacques Viger," en Quebec, Province Archives, *Rapport de l'archiviste de la province de Québec*, 1955-1956 et 1956-1957 (Québec, [1958]). p. 31-176.

[6] American Association for State and Local History, *Directory of Historical Societies and Agencies in the United States and Canada, 1961* (Madison, Wis., 1961), and the latest edition of the *American Library Directory*, which includes Canadian libraries.

[7] Montreal, Notre-Dame Church, *Premier registre de l'église Notre-Dame de Montréal*," *Canadian Antiq. and Numis. Jour.*, 3d ser., X (Oct. 1913), 214- p. xxii; Ovide-M.-H. Lapalice, "Les premières pages du régistre de la paroissee de Montréal," *Canadian Antiq. and Numis, Jour.*, 3d ser., X (Oct. 1913), 214- 37.

[8] J.-B. Meilleur Barthe, "Inventaire sommaire des archives conservées au palais de justice des Trois- Rivières," en Quebec (Province) Archives, *Rapport de l'archiviste de la province de Québec*, 1920-1921 (Québec, 1920), 338.

dian Public Archives.[9] Index cards to the registers of the church of Notre Dame of Montreal are in that church, and a microfilm is in the Canadian Public Archives.

Other records relating to the missions and churches of the Old Northwest are in the archives of the religious orders in Canada. The extant archives of the Society of Jesus in Canada are in the Archives of St. Mary's College in Montreal.[10] Numerous relations, reports, letters, and journals from these archives and other depositories concerning Jesuit missions in the Old Northwest, Louisiana, New York, and New England have been published under the edi-

---

[9] Arthur G. Doughty, "Sources for the History of the Catholic Church in the Public Archives of Canada," *Cath. Hist. Rev.*, XIX (July 1933), 166; Canada, Public Archives, *Report of the Public Archives*, 1909, 103; 1910, 105; 1929, 12. A table of parishes in the Province of Quebec in 1764 is in Ivanhoë Caron, *La colonisation de la province de Québec; débuts du régime anglais, 1760-1791* (Québec, 1923), 242-50, 288-301. Ovide-M.-H. Lapalice, "Le premier régistre d'état civil de Montréal," *Canad. Antiq. and Numis. Jour.*, 3d ser., VIII (Oct. 1911), 171-98; Barthe, "Inventaire sommaire," p. 328-49; Quebec (Province), Judicial archives, *Inventaire des registres de l'état civil conservés aux Archives judiciaires de Québec*, par Pierre-Georges Roy (Beauceville, Québec, 1921). Much data derived from the registers of Quebec parishes is contained in Cyprien Tanguay, *Dictionnaire généalogique des familles canadiennes depuis la fondation de la colonie jusqu'à nos jours* (Montréal, 1871-90. 7 vols.). This compilation is not without errors and gaps, and the compiler failed to use the registers of several parishes in the Montreal region. Citations to public and ecclesiastical archives are to be found in Père Archange Godbout, "Nos Ancêtres au XVIIe siècle, dictionnaire généalogique et bibliographique des familles canadiennes," Quebec (Province) Archives, *Rapport de l'archiviste de la Province de Québec*, 1951-1952 et 1952-1953 [Québec, 1954], 447-544. *ibid.*, 1953-1954 et 1954-1955 [Québec, 1956], 443-536; *ibid.*, 1955-1956 et 1956-1957 [Québec, 1958], 377-489. See also Quebec (Province) Archives, "Bibliographie de généalogies et histoires de familles," *Rapport de l'archiviste de la province de Québec*, 1940-1941 (Québec, 1941), 95-332. References to archival sources relating to individuals who served in the militia are in Claude de Bonnault, ed., "Le Canada militaire; état provisoire des officers de milice de 1641 à 1760," Quebec (Province) Archives, *Rapport de l'archiviste de la province de Québec*, 1949-1950 et 1950-1951 (Québec, 1951), p. 261-527.

[10] Beers, *French in North America*, p. 28; Rev. P. M. O'Leary, Report on the Archives of the Society of Jesus, St. Mary's College, Montreal, Revd. Father Jones, S.J., Archivist (Montreal, Oct. 1911). This manuscript report in the Canadian Public Archives lists considerable material on the activities of Jesuits in the Old Northwest.

torship of Reuben G. Thwaites.[11] The transcripts obtained by Thwaites for his publication are in the State Historical Society of Wisconsin. Thwaites was the secretary of this society.[12] An extensive collection of records relating to the Sulpicians is preserved in the Seminary of St. Sulpice at Montreal,[13] and copies of them have been obtained by the Canadian Public Archives.[14] The Archives of the Quebec Seminary at Laval University contain records of the seminary itself, some records of the Archbishopric of Quebec, and collections of manuscripts presented by persons who had been interested in the history of the Catholic Church.[15] Transcripts of letters and other documents in these archives regarding the mission of Tamaroa at Cahokia, 1680-1735, have been procured by the Illinois Historical Survey, Urbana, Ill.[16] English translations of documents from those archives on that mission, 1698-1763, have been printed from photostats in the possession of the National Park Service and transcripts in the archives of the Bishop of Belleville.[17]

In the Archives of the Archbishopric of Quebec can be found other letters which originated in the missions and churches of the Upper Country and Louisiana as well as correspondence with

[11] Reuben G. Thwaites, ed., *The Jesuit Relations, and Allied Documents: Travels and Explorations of the Jesuit Missionaries in New France, 1610-1791* . . . (Cleveland, 1896-1901. 73 vols.). For an account of the preparation of this work with additional bibliography, see Beers, *French in North America,* p. 29-30, 117-19. A reprint of Thwaites' compilation was issued by The Arthur H. Clark Company, Glendale, Calif., in 1959.

[12] Thwaites, ed., *Jesuit Relations,* LXXI, 225-33.

[13] M. R. Bonin, "Les archives sulpiciennes, source d'histoire ecclésiastique," Société canadienne d'histoire de léglise catholique, *Rapport* (1934-35), 39-50.

[14] Canada, Public Archives, *Report of the Public Archives,* 1912 (Ottawa, 1913), 3, 15-17.

[15] Arthur Maheux, "Les archives du séminaire de Québec," *Le Canada français,* XXVII (fev. 1940), 503-08. A manuscript inventory in two volumes is available at the seminary, and a copy is in the Canadian Public Archives at Ottawa.

[16] Illinois Historical Survey, University of Illinois, *Guide to MS. Materials in Foreign Depositories,* p. 108.

[17] McDermott, *Old Cahokia,* p. 57-83.

church and public officials of Canada, France, and Rome.[18] Since the curés in the West did not usually preserve their files, the only copies available are those in Quebec, which are contained in eight boxes—a treasure of data on religious history.[19] Secretaries kept these records in orderly condition and facilitated their use by arranging extensive inventories.[20] In addition to the correspondence there are other documents relating to the church administration throughout the diocese entered in registers from which a selection of the most important register entries has been published.[21]

Another church official whose correspondence is of value for the Great Lakes and the Mississippi Valley was the grand vicar of the Bishop of Quebec at Paris. Pierre de la Rue, the Abbé de l'Isle Dieu, occupied this post from 1734 to 1777 and conducted a correspondence with the Ministry of the Marine concerning the religious affairs of New France and Louisiana.[22] A collection of these docu-

[18] Lionel St. G. Lindsay, "The Archives of the Archbishopric of Quebec," *Records* of the American Catholic Historical Society, XVIII (1907), 10-11; Ivanhoë Caron, "Les archives de l'archevêché de Québec," Société canadienne d'histoire de l'église catholique, *Rapport*, (1934-35), 69; Parker, *Guide to Materials for U.S. History*, p. 224-70.

[19] Caron, "Archives de l'archevêché de Québec," p. 71.

[20] Ivanhoë Caron, "Inventaire de la correspondance de Mgr. Jean-Olivier Briand, évêque de Québec (Province), Archives, *Rapport de l'archiviste de la province de Québec*, 1929-30 (Québec, 1930), p. 47-136; Ivanhoë Caron, "Inventaire de la correspondance de Mgr. Louis-Philippe Mariaucheau d'Esgly, évêque de Québec, 1740 à 1791, *ibid.*, 1930-31, 185-98; Ivanhoë Caron, "Inventaire des documents concernant l'église du Canada sous le régime français," *ibid.*, 1939-40, 1940-41, 1941-42 (Québec, 1940-42), 155-353, 333-473, 178-298. The last inventory covers not only the episcopal archives but also the provincial archives of Quebec, the Canadian Public Archives, the Bibliothèque Nationale in Paris, Vatican archives, and in the Archives Nationales of France the series Moreau de Saint-Méry, Archives des Colonies, series B and Cll. A list of the names of colonists who were converted to Catholicism and whose acts of adjuration are to be found in a register in the archiepiscopal archives of Quebec, is in Roland-J. Auger, "Registre des abjurations (1662-1757)," *Mémoires de la société généalogique canadienne-française*, V (juin 1953), 243-46.

[21] Caron, "Archives de l'archevêché de Québec," p. 66-67; Henry Tetu et Charles O. Gagnon, eds., *Mandements, lettres pastorales et circulaires des évêques de Québec* (Québec, 1887-88. 4 vols.).

[22] Ivanhoë Caron, "Les Évêques de Québec, leurs procureurs et leurs vicaires généraux à Rome, à Paris, et à Londres, (1734-1834)," Royal Soc. Can., *Procs. and Trans.*, 3d ser., XXIX, Sect. I (May 1935), 153.

ments derived from the archives of the Archbishop of Quebec has been published.[23]

The religious orders that served in Canada, the Northwest, and Louisiana came under the jurisdiction of provincials of those orders in France and of their generals in Rome, the seat of authority of the Catholic Church throughout the world. The archives of the Jesuit Province of France were largely destroyed following the expulsion of the society from that country in 1764, but a remnant which was saved by Father Gabriel Brotier is now housed in the Séminaire Missionaire, "Les Fontaines" at Chantilly (Oise) near Paris.[24] Of this collection of 199 volumes, 26 relate to the missions in North America. Transcripts of other reproductions from the collection are in the St. Mary's College Archives, Montreal; the State Historical Society of Wisconsin, Madison, Wis. (Thwaites transcripts); the Canadian Public Archives and the Institute of Jesuit History of Loyola University, Chicago.[25] St. Louis University plans to obtain a complete reproduction on microfilm of these Jesuit archives.[26] The university also has microfilmed materials relating to Jesuit activities in the French colonies on North America from the Archivum Romanum Societatis Iesu (Archivum Generale), the general archive of the Jesuits in Rome. Other documents on that area are in the Fondo Gesuitico al Gesù, the archive of the Procurator-General, who was the treasurer of the order and its liaison officer with the papal congregations. Microfilms from this archive are in the St. Louis University Archives. Another organization of the Jesuit Generalate is the Institutum Historicum Societatis Iesu, whose function is the publication of documents from the archive, which is building up its resources by collecting reproductions from other Jesuit archives. An American Division of the Institutum, estab-

---

[23] Quebec (Province), Archives, "Lettres et mémoires de l'Abbé de l'Isle-Dieu," *Rapport de l'archiviste de province de Québec,* 1935-36, 1936-37, 1937-38 (Québec, 1936, 1937, 1938), 275-410, 331-459, 147-253.

[24] A brief history of these records is given in Beers, *French in North America,* p. 32-33.

[25] *Ibid.,* p. 117-19, 133-34, 242-43.

[26] John F. Bannon, "The Saint Louis University Collection of Jesuitica Americana," *Hispanic American Historical Review,* XXXVII (Feb. 1957), 85-86.

lished at St. Louis University in 1957, will undertake the editing of documentary publications bearing on the Jesuits in North America. Of far less importance because of lesser involvement in French North American affairs are the records in Paris of the Séminaire de Saint-Sulpice which controlled the seminary at Montreal, the Séminaire des Missions Etrangères, which was connected with the Seminary of Quebec, and the Séminaire du Saint-Esprit which provided personnel for the missions in Canada.[27] Transcripts and microfilms from the collections in these institutions, from the records of the Archbishop of Paris and from the Generalate of the Society of Jesus in Rome are in the Canadian Public Archives.[28] In the Archives Nationales are some records relating to the Recollects,[29] but the Roman archives of the Friars Minor, of which the Recollects were a branch, were largely destroyed during an invasion by the French army in 1798.[30]

Other sources relating to the religious history of New France and Louisiana are in the Archives Nationales in Paris. Some of these records are in the files accumulated by the ministries of the French government, and others are in the files of archbishops, bishops, colleges, religious orders, and seminaries which under laws of the French Republic were deposited in the public archives. Various series of the Archives des Colonies and the Archives de la Marine contain relevant documents; others are in the records of the archbishops of Paris and Rouen and in the records of the seminaries of Paris which had connections with Canada.[31] Still other records are in the possession of the archbishops, seminaries, the

---

[27] Doughty, "Sources for the History of the Catholic Church," p. 152-55; Bernard Mahieu, "Les archives de l'église catholique en France," *Archivum,* IV (1954), 102.

[28] Doughty, "Sources Catholic Church," p. 152-55; Biggar, "Public Archives at Ottawa," III, 44; Canada, Public Archives, *Report,* 1913, 9; 1929, 9; 1949, 458; 1953-54, 25. Descriptions of these sources will be in the preliminary inventory of manuscript group 17.

[29] Marie Hugolin Lemay, *Le Père Joseph Denis, premier récollet canadien (1657-1736)* (Québec, 1926, 2 vols.), I, 24-25.

[30] Basile Pandzic, "Les archives générales de l'ordre des frères-minuers," *Archivum,* IV (1954), 154.

[31] Beers, *French in North America,* p. 31. Individual documents relating to the Northwest and Louisiana are listed in Surrey, *Calendar of Manuscripts in Paris Archives,* and in Caron, "Inventaire de documents concernant l'église du Canada." Frère Achille Gingras (Les Frères de l'Instruction Chrétienne, Mai-

Bibliothèque Nationale, and other libraries, and in departmental archives.[32] Reproductions from many of these sources are in the Canadian Public Archives as well as in other institutions.[33]

During 1960-61, Thomas T. McAvoy obtained microfilm copies of documents relating to American Catholic history from the archives of the Sacred Congregation of the Propaganda and other collections in Rome. These copies are now in the University of Notre Dame Archives.

The first Catholic church in the Province of Ontario was originally founded by Father Armand de La Richardie in 1728 as a Jesuit mission among the Huron Indians encamped across the Detroit River from Fort Pontchartrain.[34] It became known as the Mission of the Assumption, was moved in 1742 to Bois Blanc Island, and in 1749 was rebuilt at La Pointe de Montréal in present Sandwich. Some sixty French families that had settled on the east side of the Detroit River were given permission in 1765 to build a new church, and in 1767 Father Pierre Potier who had come to the Huron mission in 1744 as an assistant to Father de La Richardie was designated as pastor of the Church of the Assumption. By the time another church was built in 1787 most of the Huron Indians had removed from the area. For their benefit the mission had maintained in its earlier days a farm, a store, and a blacksmith's forge.

The archives of the Church of the Assumption, Windsor, Ontario, contain the original registers of baptisms, burials, and marriages. The baptismal register begins in 1728 and in the early years the entries pertain to infants of Huron parentage. The children of French parents were ordinarily baptized in the church of St. Anne's at Detroit, but for convenience baptisms were sometimes per-

son Notre-Dame de Saint-Laurent, Saint-Romuald, Lévis,, Province de Quebec) has recently concluded a two-year investigation of the manuscript sources in Europe for the religious history of Canada from 1608 to 1860. A summary of his findings has been issued in mimeographed form with the title *Répertoire des sources manuscrites de l'histoire religieuse canadienne en Europe, surtout à Paris, à Rome et à Londres, de 1608 à 1860.*

[32] Guy Duboscq, "Inventaire des archives departementales communales et hospitaliéres se rapportant à l'histoire ecclésiastique," *Revue d'histoire de l'église de France*, XXXVI (1950), 70-75; XXXVIII (1952), 90-91.

[33] Doughty, "Sources for the History of the Catholic Church," p. 149-52.

[34] E. C. LeBel, "History of Assumption, the First Parish in Upper Canada," Canadian Catholic Historical Association, *Report* 1954.

formed at the Mission of the Assumption, and seventeen entries for white children appear in the account book of the mission during 1751-56.[35] The entries for the years 1756 to 1761 have been lost, but from 1761 a continuous record was kept of baptisms, marriages and burials. Copies of the registers in the Burton Historical Collection have been indexed; other copies are in the Essex Historical Society, Windsor, Ontario, and copies for 1761-67, 1781-99 are in the Canadian Public Archives, which has alphabetical name indexes. Part of the registers for the eighteenth century have been published.[36] Since many of the early settlers on the east bank of the Detroit River had moved over from Detroit, the registers of Assumption Church are useful for personal data concerning those persons (including some who had been officials) as well as for pioneer settlers in southwestern Ontario, whose descendants are numbered among the inhabitants of that province today.

Other records produced at the mission are also of value for the history of both sides of the Detroit River. An account book of 1733-51, 1775-1859, the original of which is in the Burton Historical Collection, relates to the operations of the farm, the store, and the forge and is of interest for the economic history of the area, including trade carried on with the people of Detroit.[37] Other manuscripts

[35] Lajeunesse, *Windsor Border Region,* p. lxvi.

[36] Reuben G. Thwaites, ed., "Mission des Hurons du Detroit, 1733-56," in *The Jesuit Relations,* (Cleveland, 1900), LXX, 70-77. A list of the baptisms 1751-56 appears in Lajeunesse, ed., *Windsor Border Region,* p. 78-79. In Francis Cleary, ed., "Baptisms (1761-86), Recorded in the Parish Registers of Assumption, Sandwich," Ontario Hist. Soc. *Papers and Records,* VII (1906), 31-97 are a list of baptisms, 1761-86 giving the date, name of child, names of parents, names of sponsors, and officiating priest; list of marriages, 1782-86, giving date, names of contracting parties, names of parents, residence, names of witnesses, and officiating priest; list of deaths, 1768-86, giving date, name of deceased, age, witnesses, officiating priest. Summaries of marriages recorded during 1760-81 are in Lajeunesse, ed., *Windsor Border Region,* p. 343-55. A briefer list for those years is in Margaret C. Kilroy, "In the Footsteps of the Habitant on the South Shore of the Detroit River," Ontario Hist. Soc., *Papers and Records,* VII (1906), 26-29.

[37] Published in Reuben G. Thwaites, ed., "Mission des Hurons du Detroit, 1733-56," in *The Jesuit Relations* (Cleveland, 1900), LXIX, 245-77, LXX, 19-70; and in Richard R. Elliott, ed., "Account Book of the Huron Mission at Detroit and Sandwich (1740-51)," in Ontario, Dept. of Public Records and Archives, *Fifteenth Report* 1918-19 (Toronto, 1920), 689-715.

of Father Potier were carried away and deposited in the Archives of St. Mary's College, Montreal, by Father Félix Martin. The collection includes a diary for 1743-81, correspondence, and a Huron grammar.[38] The Loyola University Library of Chicago, Ill., has obtained photostats of these manuscripts from the Archivum Generale of the Society of Jesus in Rome.[39] A typewritten copy of the part of his diary covering 1743-44, recording journeys from Quebec to Detroit, Detroit to St. Joseph, Mich., and St. Joseph to Illinois, is in the Burton Historical Collection and photostats are in the custody of the Pennsylvania Historical and Museum Commission, Harrisburg, Pa. The Gagnon Collection in the Montreal Municipal Library includes other Potier papers consisting of a census of 1747 of the Huron village on Bois Blanc Island and Huron-French vocabularies.

[38] Ontario Dept. of Public Records and Archives, *Fifteenth Report*, p. xiii, xix.

[39] E. R. Ott, trans. and ed., "Selections from the Diary and Gazette of Father Pierre Potier, S.J. (1708-1781)," *Mid-America*, n.s., VII (July, Oct. 1936), 199-207, 260-65. Extracts appear in Lajeunesse, ed., *Windsor Border Region*, p. 37-41.

III   The Records

of the British Regime

History

The French posts on the upper lakes, already partially isolated by the British capture of Forts Niagara and Frontenac, were surrendered by the French capitulation at Montreal on Sept. 8, 1760. Maj. Robert Rogers received Detroit from the French commandant, Capt. Marie François Picote de Bellestre, on Nov. 29, 1760;[1] and during the following winter British troops occupied Forts Sandusky, Miami, Ouiatenon, and St. Joseph. Fort Massac was not ocupied by the British. British forces occupied Forts Michilimackinac and La Baye in September and October 1761, respectively.[2] A detachment at Sault Ste. Marie was obliged to seek refuge at Michilimackinac following the destruction of the old French stockade by fire in 1762.[3] La Pointe on Chequamegon Bay had been abandoned by the French in 1759 and was not regarrisoned by the British.

The British occupation of the lake posts was abruptly terminated in the spring of 1763 at the opening of Pontiac's War. All of the western posts were lost to the Indians in May and June 1763, with the exceptions of Niagara, Detroit, and Fort Pitt (Pittsburgh). British control of the West was recovered through campaigns waged during 1763-64 by Col. Henry Bouquet and Col. John Brad-

[1] Louise P. Kellogg, *The British Régime in Wisconsin and the Northwest* (Madison, 1935), 6; Nelson V. Russell, *The British Régime in Michigan and the Old Northwest, 1760-1796* (Northfield, Minn., 1939), 10-11.

[2] Kellogg, *British Régime*, p. 12.

[3] Alexander Henry, *Alexander Henry's Travels and Adventures in the Years 1760-1776*, ed. by Milo M. Quaife (Chicago, 1921), 64.

street. Michilimackinac was reoccupied in September 1764 by Capt. William Howard's detachment from Detroit. This was the only point northwest of Detroit held by British military forces in the years that followed; it served, as it had under the French, as a fur trading center for the whole area.[4]

The Illinois country was not occupied by the British until after the suppression of Pontiac's conspiracy. Since that district appertained to the province of Louisiana, it was not surrendered to the British by the capitulation of Montreal in 1760. The treaty of Paris of Feb. 10, 1763, however, transferred the sovereignty over New France and the Louisiana territory east of the Mississippi to the British. Repeated attempts by the British during 1763-65 to reach the Illinois country failed because of Indian hostility. Capt. Thomas Sterling and a detachment of troops from Fort Pitt finally took possession of Fort de Chartres on October 10, 1765.[5] Capt. Louis St. Ange (who had been called from Fort Vincennes to succeed Pierre Joseph Neyon de Villiers in command of Fort de Chartres in 1764) withdrew after Sterling's arrival with his small detachment of troops to the newly established village of St. Louis, on the opposite side of the Mississippi River.

The British effected a number of changes in military arrangements throughout the Northwest during the 1770's. Since Fort de Chartres had been flooded by the Mississippi and abandoned in 1772, a detachment of troops was left at Kaskaskia under Capt. Hugh Lord until arrangements could be made for civil government.[6] The building which had been occupied by the Jesuits was fortified by Captain Lord and named Fort Gage. The fort at Detroit was replaced by a new one in 1778 at another location and named Fort Lernoult after Capt. Richard B. Lernoult, the officer

[4] Kellogg, *British Régime*, p. 36-37.

[5] Alvord, *Illinois Country*, p. 264.

[6] Alvord, *Illinois Country*, p. 297-98; Kellogg, *British Régime*, p. 124, 132. Regarding the military problem in the West at this time, see Paul O. Carr, "*The Defense of the Frontier, 1760-1775*" (University of Iowa, *Studies in the Social Sciences*, X, no. 3, Nov. 1, 1934, Iowa City, 1935?), 46-59; Clarence E. Carter, ed., *The Correspondence of General Thomas Gage with the Secretaries of State, and with the War Office and the Treasury 1763-1775* (New Haven, London, 1933. 2 vols.), *passim*.

then commanding the station. During 1780-81 the dilapidated fort on the mainland at Michilimackinac was replaced by a new military work on Mackinac Island, which afforded greater security.

Government

The Great Lakes region was governed during the early years of the British occupation by the military commandants of the forts. These army officers were subordinate to the British commander in chief at New York.[7] Like their French predecessors, the commandants concerned themselves with civil affairs as well as military matters. Their orders were supreme in both spheres, and their authority unlimited. By British custom and in tacit conformity with the terms of the capitulation of Montreal, the custom of Paris and the laws and usages followed during the French regime were continued in force.[8] The commandants controlled Indian trade and managed Indian affairs.[9] In their civil capacity they adjudicated disputes and performed marriages.

After the formal transfer of sovereignty over New France and Eastern Louisiana to Great Britain and the transfer of the Floridas by Spain by the treaty of Paris in 1763, a new arrangement was made for the government of this vast territory. Most of this region had been in dispute not only with France and Spain but also among the British colonies of the Atlantic seaboard possessing conflicting claims based upon their colonial charters. Besides settling the boundary disputes, it was also desirable to pacify the Indians, to regulate settlement by whites, and to gain time in which to decide upon an Indian trade policy.[10] The proclamation of Oct. 7, 1763

[7] Alvord, *Illinois Country,* p. 264; Burton, ed., *City of Detroit,* I, 181, II, 1124; Kellogg, *British Régime,* p. 41.

[8] William R. Riddell, *Michigan under British Rule; Law and Law Courts, 1760-1796* (Lansing, 1926), 27-28.

[9] Instructions on the latter subject were issued by Sir William Johnson on Sept. 8, 1761 (*The Papers of Sir William Johnson,* ed. by James Sullivan, Alexander C. Flick, Almon W. Lauber, and Milton W. Hamilton, Albany, 1921-62. 13 vols., III, 473-74.)

[10] Kellogg, *British Régime,* 28-30; Paxson, *History of the American Frontier,* p. 8-10.

created three new provinces and an Indian preserve, all under royal control.[11]

The province of Quebec embraced the drainage basin of the St. Lawrence River to Lake Nipissing and the region to the north. South of this province and west of a line drawn through the heads of the rivers flowing into the Atlantic was the Indian Country extending to the northern boundary of the Floridas, which were constituted as separate provinces of East Florida and West Florida. The seaboard colonies were not to make grants of land in the Indian Country, and persons illegally settled there were to be removed. The Northwest was thus included in the Indian Country, and no provision was made by the proclamation for the government of the scattered settlements in the region. In effect the authority that had been established by the British Army upon its original occupation of the western country was continued.

The civil communities about the western posts and other settlements were governed by the British much as they had been by the French. At the military posts a succession of army officers held sway. Though the personnel was generally changed, some of the same positions were continued. Robert Navarre was retained as notary at Detroit, and functioned as an intermediary between the new regime and the French population. In 1767, however, the commandant appointed Philip Dejean to the position of judge and notary.[12] When Dejean went with Hamilton to Vincennes in 1778, he was succeeded by Thomas Williams. William Montforton was appointed upon Williams' resignation in 1784. Not long after the British assumed jurisdiction in Illinois in 1765, the two remaining civil officials, Joseph Lefebre, the judge, attorney-general, and keeper of the royal warehouse, and Joseph Labuxière, the clerk and notary, left for St. Louis with Captain St. Ange.[13] The position

[11] The text is in Clarence W. Alvord and Clarence E. Carter, eds., *The Critical Period, 1763-1765* (*Collections* of the Illinois State Historical Library, Vol. X, *British Series*, Vol. I, Springfield, Ill., 1915), 39-45, and in Shortt and Doughty, eds., *Docs. Const. Hist. Canada*, I, 163-68.

[12] Burton, ed., *City of Detroit*, I, 123, 167, 170, 173, II, 913, 1124.

[13] Clarence C. Carter, *Great Britain and the Illinois Country, 1763-1774* (Washington, 1910), 49.

of notary was continued at Kaskaskia and at Vincennes. The captains of militia were retained to try petty cases, to enforce decrees, and to organize the militia. The posts in Wisconsin were not reoccupied after Pontiac's war and governmental control over the area was exercised from Fort Mackinac.

Under British rule, Illinois was regarded as extending to the Wabash River on the east and to the Ohio on the south. The area of Indiana thus came under the jurisdiction of Fort de Chartres; the forts at Vincennes and Ouiatenon remained empty and eventually rotted away and disappeared. Jean Baptiste Racine acted as commandant at Vincennes prior to the arrival of Lieutenant-Governor Edward Abbott.[14]

Before the adoption of the Quebec Act in 1774, the commandants of the western posts were left to their own resources in settling disputes among the inhabitants since the partial introduction of English civil law into the province of Quebec by the proclamation of 1763 did not affect the West where martial law was continued.[15] From about the beginning of British administration at Detroit, the commandants appointed judges or justices of the peace.[16] The commandant himself handled matters relating to the probate of estates. Late in 1765, Captain Sterling designated Jean Lagrange to decide disputes among the people in the Illinois settlements according to the laws and customs of the country.[17] With the consent of Gen. Thomas Gage, in December of 1768, Col. John Wilkins erected a court of judicature composed of seven persons to whom commissions of the peace were given. Authorized to hear, examine, and decide cases involving debt, property or other contests, this court was presided over by George Morgan and existed until June

[14] Edward Abbott to Sir Guy Carleton, May 26, 1777, Dunn, ed., "French Settlements on the Wabash," p. 441.

[15] Riddell, *British Rule*, p. 18, 31.

[16] *Ibid.*, p. 32, 38, 402-03; Burton, ed., *City of Detroit*, I, 167, 173, 194-95, II, 913. The judges at Detroit were Pierre St. Cosme, Gabriel Le Grand, and Philipp Dejean.

[17] Sterling to Gage, Dec. 15, 1765, Clarence W. Alvord and Clarence E. Carter, eds., *The New Régime, 1765-1767 (Colls.* Ill. State Hist. Lib., Vol. XI, *British Series,* Vol. II, Springfield, 1916) 124; Alvord, *Illinois Country,* p. 265.

1770.[18] Courts of inquiry composed of military officers were also employed in Illinois to settle disputes.

The situation in the West became progressively worse under British administration. The failure to control the Indian trade and to prevent encroachments upon Indian lands in defiance of the proclamation of 1763 caused discontent among the Indians. The curtailment of the military establishment gave greater opportunities to the traders, squatters, and criminals seeking haven in the wilderness to become a law unto themselves. The French settlers were disgruntled because of the lack of provision for civil government, and those at Kaskaskia and Vincennes sent memorials on the subject to General Gage.[19] Proposals were made by army officers at Michilimackinac and Detroit for the appointment of lieutenant governors.[20] The British inhabitants in Detroit petitioned for the formation of a civil government for some years before remedial action was taken.

By the Quebec Act of June 17, 1774, that portion of the Indian Country northwest of the Ohio River was annexed to the province of Quebec.[21] Civil government was to be introduced into the region which was to be under the governor-general at Quebec and lieutenant-governors at Detroit, Michilimackinac, Kaskaskia, and Vin-

[18] Colton Storm, "The Notorious Colonel Wilkins," of the *Ill. State Hist. Soc. Jour.*, XL (Mar. 1947), 13.

[19] Alvord, *Illinois Country*, p. 293-96; Kellogg, *British Régime*, p. 123-25; Florence G. Watts, ed., "Some Vincennes Documents of 1772," *Ind. Mag. Hist.*, XXXIV (June 1938), 208-10; Jack M. Sosin, "The French Settlements in British Policy for the North American Interior, 1760-1774," *Can. Hist. Rev.*, XXXIX (Sept. 1958), 185-208.

[20] Marjorie G. Jackson, "The Beginning of British Trade at Michilimackinac," *Minn. Hist.*, XI (Sept. 1930), 266-68. The proposal from this place was written by Robert Rogers, who commanded there during 1766-67; it is printed in *Papers of Sir Wm. Johnson*, VI, 43-58.

[21] This annexation reestablished the relationship that had existed between the region of the Great Lakes and New France before the British conquest. The ties that bound Quebec with the Upper Country—historical, geographical, economic, religious, and social—were closer than the relations of any of the English seaboard colonies with that region. The territory annexed to Quebec included the country bounded on the south by the Ohio and Mississippi Rivers and on the north and west by the domains of the Hudson's Bay Company. Modern Ontario as well as American territory was embraced in the enlarged Province of Quebec.

cennes. The first lieutenant-governor to reach his station was Capt. Henry Hamilton, who appeared at Detroit on Nov. 9, 1775.[22] The incumbent at Vincennes, Capt. Edward Abbott, remained at his post only from May 1777 to early 1778.[23] Serving in Ireland at the time of his appointment to the lieutenant-governorship of Illinois, Capt. Matthew Johnson never reached there though he saw action in America during the Revolutionary War and drew a salary as lieutenant-governor.[24] The revolt of the British seaboard colonies caused the British to withdraw Capt. Hugh Lord from Illinois in 1776, leaving as their administrator a former French military officer, Philippe François de Rastel, Sieur de Rocheblave.[25] Capt. Patrick Sinclair, who had been appointed lieutenant-governor of Michilimackinac in April of 1775, was captured by Americans when attempting to reach there through New York and did not arrive at his post until October 1779, following his release and two crossings of the Atlantic.[26] In other respects, as will be seen, hostilities in the West during the Revolutionary War prevented the British from effectuating their plan of civil government.

In conformity with the Quebec Act a more regular establishment for the settlement of legal causes was to be provided. By that act English criminal law was introduced into the province, but in controversies relating to property the old French-Canadian law was to be followed.[27] Instructions of Jan. 5, 1775 addressed to Gov. Guy Carleton directed the establishment of courts of king's bench for criminal cases and courts of common pleas for civil cases in the two districts of Quebec and Montreal. Inferior courts with both civil

[22] Burton, ed., *City of Detroit*, I, 129; Kellogg, *British Régime*, p. 131.

[23] Kellogg, *British Régime*, p. 131; Esarey, *History of Indiana*, I, 51.

[24] Kellogg, *British Régime*, p. 131; Alvord, *Illinois Country*, p. 312.

[25] Alvord, *Illinois Country*, p. 318. Concerning De Rocheblave see E. Fabre Surveyor, "Philippe François de Rastel de Rocheblave," in Robinson, *Toronto during the French Régime*, p. 233-42.

[26] William L. Jenks, "Patrick Sinclair: Builder of Fort Mackinac," *Mich. Hist. Colls.*, XXXIX (1915) 68-85.

[27] Riddell, *Michigan under British Rule*, p. 20. English criminal law had been introduced originally by the proclamation of 1763. The French-Canadian law or the custom of Paris was based on the civil law of Rome. English criminal law was regarded as preferable, because it involved the use of a jury.

and criminal jurisdiction under single judges were to be created in the districts of Detroit, Michilimackinac, Illinois, and Vincennes.[28] Governor Carleton established the courts at Quebec and Montreal early in 1777. Circumstances connected with the war prevented the execution of the plan for district courts in the West, and that region became attached for judicial purposes to the Montreal district. Since journeys to Montreal involved considerable time and expense, this was not a satisfactory arrangement for the residents of the western districts. In practice only lawsuits among the more affluent merchants at Detroit were ever taken to Montreal. Other disputants at that place resorted to the use of arbitration for the settlement of their differences. Minor disputes were adjudicated by the lieutenant-governors who had commissions as justices of the peace. Criminal cases were heard by Dejean.

An American attempt to conquer the region northwest of the Ohio River during the Revolutionary War was only partially successful. An expedition led by George Rogers Clark of Virginia captured Kaskaskia on July 4, 1778 and occupied the neighboring villages.[29] The seizure of De Rocheblave (who still represented British authority) and his transportation to Virginia marked the end of British dominion in the Illinois district. A deputation sent by Clark took Vincennes without resistance and a small American detachment was stationed there. Later that year Governor Hamilton marched from Detroit to recover the Illinois country and occupy the mouth of the Missouri. He captured Vincennes on Dec. 17, 1778, and took up winter quarters there. The more intrepid Clark made a winter march from Kaskaskia and forced the surrender of Hamilton at Vincennes in February 1779, sending him and his principal officers off to Williamsburg, Va. Clark failed in his plan to wage a campaign against Detroit, and by 1781 withdrew his forces to Louisville on the southern bank of the Ohio. The Illinois district was governed as a county of Virginia from 1778 to 1790 when Gov. Arthur St. Clair assumed jurisdiction for the Northwest

[28] *Ibid.*, p. 39; Hilda M. Neatby, *The Administration of Justice under the Quebec Act* (London, 1937), 21, 283.

[29] Alvord, *Illinois Country*, p. 326; James Alton James, *The Life of George Rogers Clark* (Chicago, 1929), 115 *et seq.*

Territory that had been created by the Continental Congress in 1787 to embrace the region northwest of the Ohio River.[30]

The treaty of Paris of Sept. 3, 1783 concluded the Revolutionary War and ceded the region south of the Great Lakes to the United States. The British evacuated New York City but continued to hold the forts along the border and on the Great Lakes,[31] in order to keep faith with the Indians and to retain control of the fur trade.[32] The retention by the British of the posts, particularly those at Detroit and Mackinac, enabled them to go on controlling a preponderant portion of the Northwest.[33]

The Royal Navy began operations on the Great Lakes in 1755, when vessels were launched at Oswego on Lake Ontario.[34] By order of Gen. Jeffery Amherst, a shipyard was established at Niagara on Navy Island, and vessels launched there aided in the defense of Detroit during 1763-64.[35] Alexander Grant, an army offi-

---

[30] In December of 1778, the appointment of county lieutenant for the county of Illinois was given to John Todd, a prominent figure in Transylvania colony (Kentucky), which he had represented in the Virginia legislature. When Todd arrived in Illinois in May 1779, Clark turned over to him the responsibility for civil government (Alvord, *Illinois Country*, p. 335-36; Edward G. Mason, "John Todd," Chicago Historical Society *Collections*, IV [1890], 285-288). Since the Virginia period of Illinois was not a foreign jurisdiction, its consideration lies outside the scope of this book.

[31] These forts were as follows: Dutchman's Point, Pointe au Fer, Oswegatchie (Ogdensburg), Oswego, Erie (Presque Isle), Niagara, Detroit, Sandusky, and Michilimackinac (Charles P. Lucas, *A History of Canada, 1763-1812*, Oxford, 1909, p. 239; Alfred L. Burt, *The United States, Great Britain and British North America from the Revolution to the Establishment of Peace after the War of 1812*, New Haven, 1940, p. 82; Canada, Public Archives, *Report on Canadian Archives*, 1890, xxxiii).

[32] Burt, *U.S., Great Britain and British N. America*, p. 82 *et seq.*; Russell, *British Régime*, p. 237-38; Wayne E. Stevens, *The Northwest Fur Trade, 1763-1800* (Urbana, 1927), p. 162-64. The treaty of Paris violated the boundary that had been agreed upon between the British and the Indians in the treaty of Fort Stanwix of 1768. The Indians contended that the British had no right to cede territory to the United States without their consent. To prevent war with the Indians, the British decided to retain control of the forts and the disputed territory.

[33] Stevens, *Northwest Fur Trade*, p. 40.

[34] George A. Cuthbertson, *Freshwater, A History and A Narrative of the Great Lakes* (New York, 1931), 53 *et seq.*

[35] Milo M. Quaife, "The Royal Navy of the Upper Lakes," *Burton Historical Collection Leaflet*, II (May 1924), 51; Russell, *British Régime*, p. 165.

cer who had had three years service in the Royal Navy and who had commanded the naval force on Lake Champlain, was put in command of the naval establishment on the Great Lakes in 1763.[36] Though designated officially as captain, Grant was called "commodore" during his long career. The vessels of the lake fleet were constructed, supplied, and operated under Grant's supervision and were employed in maintaining communications and transporting supplies and personnel. The ships were built at Niagara until 1771, when a new plant called the King's Shipyard was established at Detroit. Thereafter that lake port was the headquarters of Commodore Grant, whose residence, called Grant's Castle, was on the American side of the strait at Grosse Pointe on Lake St. Clair. An important role was played by the lake fleet during the Revolutionary War when traffic in private vessels was prohibited in order to prevent trading with the revolting colonies. In subsequent years, the Provincial Marine, as the naval vessels were called, continued to sail the lakes under Commodore Grant's direction. In addition to filling other official positions, Grant remained in charge of the naval vessels until his advanced age caused his retirement at the opening of the War of 1812.

After 1765, the Quartermaster-General's Department of the British commander in chief's headquarters controlled the Provincial Marine, first at New York and later in Canada.[37]

The opening of the lakes to privately owned ships in 1788 resulted in the appointment of another British official at Detroit. Before that time navigation on the lakes had been restricted to government naval vessels carrying the freight of traders and other private individuals. This government monopoly was maintained to prevent smuggling and to check American encroachment on the fur trade.[38] However, the service provided by the King's ships proved inadequate and greatly hindered the activities of the traders, who carried their complaints to the government. The result

[36] Milo M. Quaife, "Detroit Biographies: Commodore Alexander Grant," *Burton Hist. Coll. Leaflet,* VI (May 1928), 76; George F. MacDonald, "Commodore Alexander Grant (1734-1813)," Ontario Historical Society, *Papers and Records,* XXII (1925), 168.

[37] Cuthbertson, *Freshwater,* p. 277.

[38] Russell, *British Régime,* p. 176.

was an ordinance of April 30, 1788, opening the lakes to private commerce. To enforce certain regulations under which the trade was to be conducted, the appointment of superintendents of inland navigation at Detroit and Mackinac was provided by another ordinance of Oct. 1788.[39] Thereafter the Provincial Marine declined in importance until only half a dozen vessels were kept in commission.[40]

The British government took over the control of Indian affairs in 1755 from the individual colonies, which had previously managed their own relations with the Indians, in order to better secure the friendship and cooperation of the tribes in the war against the French. William Johnson, an Irish immigrant who had settled in the Mohawk Valley and had served for about ten years as Indian agent of New York, was appointed Superintendent of the northern district, which comprised the region north of the Potomac and Ohio rivers.[41] His initial appointment was received from Gen. Edward Braddock, and the Indian department continued to be subordinate to the commander in chief of the British army in North America. To Johnson and his assistants fell the duties of arranging conferences with the Indians, negotiating treaties, dispensing presents, and furnishing munitions of war. The Indian department was further charged in 1761 with the function of arranging for the purchase of Indian lands, and in 1764 with the regulation of trade with the Indians.

The conduct of Indian affairs remained in the Johnson family

---

[39] The post at Detroit was filled by Gregor McGregor (Quaife, ed., *Askin Papers,* I, 483), The incumbent at Mackinac for part of the period up to the American occupation was Jean L. Carignan, who was also the notary public (Reuben G. Thwaites, "At the Meeting of the Trails: the Romance of a Parish Register," Mississippi Valley Historical Association, *Proceedings,* VI, 1912-13, p. 214).

[40] A list of the vessels that comprised the Provincial Marine from 1755 to 1813 can be found in Cuthbertson, *Freshwater,* p. 277-82. The history of this fleet is yet to be written.

[41] Arthur Pound, *Johnson of the Mohawks, a Biography of Sir William Johnson* (New York, 1930), 173; Albert T. Volwiler, *George Croghan and the Westward Movement, 1741-1782* (Cleveland, 1926), 115-17. A royal commission isued to Johnson on Feb. 17, 1756 required him to observe the directions of the British commander in chief (*Papers of Sir Wm. Johnson,* II, 434-35; Pound, *Johnson,* p. 231-32).

for many years. When William Johnson's very successful incumbency of the position of Superintendent was terminated by his death in July 1774, he was succeeded by his nephew and son-in-law, Col. Guy Johnson, who had been an assistant at headquarters for many years.[42] Col. Johnson fled to Montreal in June 1775 at the outbreak of the Revolution; he continued in charge of Indian affairs in Canada until his suspension from office in February 1782 as a result of irregularities in the department. Sir. John Johnson, the son and heir of Sir William, who had also espoused the royal cause and had been forced to take refuge in Canada early in 1776, became Superintendent-General and Inspector of Indian affairs in March 1782, holding that post until its abolition in 1828.[43]

The far-flung operations of the Indian department required the services of deputies and other assistants. William Johnson appointed Daniel Claus, a German immigrant who had served as his lieutenant since 1755, as deputy for the Canadian Indians in 1760 with headquarters at Montreal where he served until 1775.[44] He was succeeded as Deputy-Superintendent by Maj. John Campbell. The experienced and able George Croghan, Indian trader and occasional Indian agent for the colony of Pennsylvania, was chosen in 1756 as deputy for the tribes in Pennsylvania and the Ohio Valley.[45] To fulfill his important mission, Croghan established his headquarters at Fort Pitt after its occupation by the British. Here he built Croghan Hall, from which he carried on his official duties and his trade and land speculating activities. On his immediate staff were two assistants, Edward Ward, his half-brother, and Thomas McKee, an old Susquehanna River Indian trader. The latter's son, Alexander McKee, acted as deputy during Croghan's absence in 1763 and 1764. Both Detroit and Michilimackinac were at first under Croghan's jurisdiction. When the district was enlarged in

[42] Duncan C. Scott, "Indian Affairs, 1763-1841," in Shortt and Doughty, eds., *Canada and Its Provinces*, IV, 705; *Papers of Sir Wm. Johnson*, IV, xi.

[43] P. H. Bryce, "Sir John Johnson, Baronet, Superintendent-General of Indian Affairs," New York State Historical Association, *Quarterly Journal*, IX (July 1928), 249; Scott, "Indian Affairs," p. 722.

[44] Pound, *Johnson*, p. 291, 424.

[45] Volwiler, *George Croghan*, p. 121.

the spring of 1766 to include the Illinois country,[46] Mackinac was placed with Niagara and the western part of Quebec (Ontario) in the same year in a middle district under Guy Johnson. Charles de Langlade, who had played a prominent part during the war in securing the support of the Northwest Indians for the French, transferred his allegiance to the British and represented them in Indian relations at Green Bay after establishing himself as a trader there in 1763.[47]

Croghan resigned as Deputy-Superintendent at Fort Pitt in 1772, following the curtailment of British activities in the West and the evacuation of the Fort Pitt garrison. Alexander McKee, who had remained as Croghan's assistant, succeeded him in the position at Fort Pitt. A Loyalist in sympathy, McKee was required by the patriots at Fort Pitt to sign a parole in April 1776. He escaped to Detroit two years later with Simon Girty, Matthew Elliott, and others.[48] McKee was appointed Deputy-Superintendent-General in December 1794 with authority to take charge of the department in the absence of Sir John Johnson, but he continued to reside at Detroit until 1796. Throughout his term of office at Detroit he had great influence among the Indians in United States territory to the south. Girty served as an interpreter and Elliott as an agent at Detroit during the Revolution and later years. The staff of the Detroit office usually included a secretary, a storekeeper, and smiths.[49] Elliott became superintendent at Detroit in 1796, and Thomas McKee was appointed to the same post at Mackinac. William Claus, a son of Daniel Claus who had been Superintendent of Indian affairs at Niagara, was appointed Deputy-Superintendent-

[46] Alvord, *Illinois Country*, p. 278.

[47] Theodore T. Brown, "Sieur Charles de Langlade," *The Wisconsin Archaeologist*, n.s., XI (July 1932), 146; Montgomery E. McIntosh, "Charles Langlade—First Settler in Wisconsin," *Parkman Club Publications*, no. 8 (Milwaukee, 1896), 216.

[48] Walter R. Hoberg, "Early History of Colonel Alexander McKee," *Pennsylvania Magazine of History and Biography*, LVIII (1934), 32; Kellogg, *British Régime*, p. 150.

[49] No adequate history of Indian affairs in the Northwest during the British period has been published.

General after McKee's death in 1799, and continued in the post until 1826.

The Indian trade of the Northwest was reopened in 1765 under a plan proposed by Sir William Johnson.[50] This system involved the issuance of licenses to traders for the conduct of trade at designated posts under the supervision of commissaries attached to the Indian department. The commissaries at Fort Pitt, Detroit, and Fort de Chartres were Alexander McKee, Jehu Hay, and Edward Cole, respectively. Benjamin Roberts resigned a commission in the British Army to accept the appointment as commissary at Mackinac where he became embroiled with Maj. Robert Rogers, the commandant, over the conduct of the Indian trade. John Askin served there as assistant commissary after 1764.

Gov. James Murray of Quebec issued licenses for carrying on trade at the western posts.[51] The traders, however, did not confine their business to the posts, because in order to get the furs they had to go out among the Indians; otherwise the unrestrained French traders would have obtained the bulk of them. Realizing that a more liberal policy was necessary and that the continuation of the commissary system would be expensive, the British government ordered in April 1768 that the regulation of the trade be turned over to the colonies.[52] The Northwest was divided among three colonies as follows: the ports on the lakes and their dependencies were assigned to Quebec, the country south of Lake Ontario to New York, and the Ohio country to Pennsylvania. The imperial commissaries were withdrawn, but the superintendents of Indian affairs and their deputies were retained for the conduct of political relations with the Indians. Under the new arrangement the governor of the Province of Quebec continued to issue licenses to traders who imported goods into the Upper Country until 1791, and with

[50] Alvord and Carter, eds., *Critical Period*, p. 273 n. 2. A roster of the officers of the Indian Department at Detroit, Sept. 5, 1778, is in *Mich. Hist. Colls.*, IX (1886), 470.

[51] Marjorie G. Reid, "The Quebec Fur-Traders and Western Policy, 1763-1774," *Can. Hist. Rev.*, VI (Mar. 1925), 22; Kellogg, *British Régime*, p. 40; Russell, *British Régime*, p. 56.

[52] Reid, "Quebec Fur-Traders" p. 25; Kellogg, *British Régime*, p. 100; Stevens, *Northwest Fur Trade*, p. 31.

the legislative council enacted measures for the regulation of the trade. The principal dependencies of Detroit were Ouiatenon, Sandusky, St. Joseph, Vincennes, Miami, and Saginaw. Outposts of Mackinac were Green Bay, Prairie du Chien, Sault Ste. Marie, La Pointe, and Grand Portage. Orders for the conduct of the trade were issued by the governor of Quebec to the commandants of Detroit and Mackinac, who also supervised political relations with the Indians.[53]

Illinois Country

The records of the British period in Illinois, 1765-78, passed into the possession of Randolph County, where Kaskaskia and Fort de Chartres were located, and St. Clair County, where Cahokia is situated. Since documents for both the French and British periods form single bodies of records and have been so handled by their custodians, the history of these records has been presented in the first chapter of this book; additional description will be given here of the content of the collections for the British period.

The Kaskaskia records are in the custody of the circuit court clerk and recorder of Randolph County at Chester, Ill. These records consist of notarial, judicial, and political papers.[54] The notarial papers have been classified and bound into the following classifications: commercial papers, 1765-78 (vol. XI); private papers, 1765-68 (vols. V and VI); and public papers, 1749-79 (vol. III).[55] A manuscript record book contains a list of notarial papers, 1722-84, a list of wills, 1765-78, and political papers for 1765-78. The French language was used through the British period, and a translation of the notarial documents, which consist mostly of transfers of real estate but also of other papers, is available.[56] A calendar of the public papers, indexes, and an abstract of the marriage contracts is in the Illinois Historical Survey of the University in Ur-

---

[53] Stevens, *Northwest Fur Trade*, p. 39-40.

[54] Alvord, "18th Cent. French Records," p. 360-61.

[55] East and Norton, "Randolph County Records," p. 257.

[56] *Ibid.*

bana.[57] Another volume contains the record of the court of judicature and judgments of the commandants, 1768-73 (p. 1-57), and
the register of the notary, 1773-83 (p. 57-257).[58] No records have
been found of the proceedings of Judge Jean Lagrange, who held
office for a brief period after 1765.[59] The Kaskaskia records were
largely microfilmed by the Illinois State Library in 1952, and copies
are in the Illinois State Archives (from which copies can be obtained), the Illinois Historical Survey, and Southern Illinois University. Translation and editorial work on the records has been
done by the Illinois Historical Survey.

Some additional Kaskaskia records found at Chester in 1950
(see the previous chapter) include a small number of notarial documents for the British period and later ones.[60]

One Kaskaskia record, which relates largely to the French period
and which has been described in the first chapter, is in the Cahokia
records at Belleville. A register of donations, it contains twenty-
four documents for the British period similar to the earlier recordings.[61]

The Cahokia records were transferred by action of the board of
supervisors of St. Clair County from the custody of the county at
Belleville to the Illinois State Archives at Springfield in 1940.[62] The
documents on the British period in this collection are few in number, a janitor having burned the bulk of them some years before
Alvord located them.[63] The surviving documents have been translated, indexed, and calendared by the Illinois State Archives.
Largely notarial in character, the documents include marriage con-

[57] Illinois University, Ill. Hist. Survey, *Guide to MS. Materials of Amer.
Origin,* p. 86. The same depository has a calendar of the court record, 1768-
75, in 101 typed pages.

[58] East and Norton, "Randolph County Records," p. 258; Clarence W.
Alvord, ed., *Cahokia Records, 1778-1790* (*Colls.* Ill. State Hist. Lib., II, *Virginia Series,* vol, I, Springfield, 1907), clii.

[59] Alvord, *Illinois Country,* p. 265.

[60] Caldwell, "Additional Kaskaskia Manuscripts," p. 192-200.

[61] Alvord, "18th Cent. French Records," p. 363-64; Norton "Perrin Collection," p. 23.

[62] Norton, "Perrin Collection," p. 22.

[63] Alvord, "18th Cent. French Records," p. 363-65; Alvord, "Ill. in the
18th Cent., A Report on the Documents in Belleville," p. 7. See Chapter One
for an account of Alvord's activities.

tracts,[64] inventories of property, and wills,[65] and a number are in print.[66] A microfilm of the Perrin collection is in the Illinois Historical Survey. Some documents originating in Cahokia are in the Otto L. Schmidt Collection in the Chicago Historical Society.

A program for collecting historical materials relating to the Northwest and Illinois was provided for by an apropriation of May 1901 by the Illinois legislature.[67] Direction of the program was placed under the trustees of the Illinois State Historical Library; its first volume of *Collections* published in 1903 embodied documents on the British period of Illinois obtained from the Canadian Archives at Ottawa.[68] Clarence W. Alvord of the University of Illinois was appointed editor in 1905, and he embarked upon extensive collecting activities in archival and manuscript depositories in Europe, the United States, and Canada. The enterprise was formalized in 1910 with the establishment of the Illinois Historical Survey in the graduate school of the University of Illinois with Alvord as director. The procurement of materials from the British archives in London began in 1906. The early transcripts from the Public Record Office were made under the direction of Hubert Hall, and later they were supplied by the firm of B. F. Stevens and Brown.[69] The transcripts include accounts from the Audit Office files of governors, agents, and others relating to the Army, forts, and the conduct of Indian affairs; from the Colonial Office Papers correspondence and reports of the colonial governors, military cor-

[64] Iben, "Marriage in Old Cahokia," p. 473-74; Margaret C. Norton, comp., "Cahokia Marriage Records," *Illinois Libraries*, XXVIII (May 1946), 260.

[65] Pease, *County Archives of Ill.*, p. 581.

[66] McDermott, *Old Cahokia*, p. 97-112. An inventory of an estate, 1773, appears in "How People Lived in Pre-Revolutionary French Illinois," *Illinois Libraries*, XXXI (Apr. 1949), 190-93.

[67] Marion Dargan, Jr., "Clarence Walworth Alvord," in William T. Hutchinson, ed., *The Marcus W. Jernegan Essays in American Historiography* (Chicago, 1937), 324.

[68] Hiriam W. Beckwith, ed., "Letters from Canadian Archives," (*Colls. Ill. State Hist. Lib.*, Vol. I, Springfield, 1903), p. 290-457. The copies were from series B and Q and included letters from lieutenant-governors at the posts in the Northwest, viz., Hamilton, Abbot, De Peyster, and from Carleton, Haldimand, and Gage, as well as letters from officers commanding other posts.

[69] Leila O. White to Gaillard Hunt, June 1, 1917, C. W. Alvord to Hunt, May 16, 1916, Library of Congress, Division of Manuscripts, Correspondence File, 679.

respondence relating to the French and Indian War and the Revolutionary War, and correspondence concerning Indian affairs.[70] Reproductions were also obtained, mostly from the British Museum, of the papers of British statesmen of the eighteenth century including Lord Chatham, the Earl of Dartmouth, the Duke of Devonshire, the Earl of Hardwicke, the Duke of Newcastle, the Earl of Shelburne, and from the Lansdowne manuscripts, generals Amherst, Clinton, Gage, and Col. Henry Bouquet.[71] From Canada materials were procured from the Provincial Archives of Quebec, the Archiepiscopal Archives of Quebec, and Laval University. Important documents relating to Indian affairs and trade came from the William Johnson papers, and from various collections in the Historical Society of Pennsylvania, including the Thomas Hutchins papers, the Dreer and Etting collections, the Wharton manuscripts, and the Gratz papers.[72] More copies on the same subject were derived from the famous Draper manuscripts of the State Historical Society of Wisconsin.[73] Transcripts obtained by Alvord from the Canadian Archives on British Illinois are among his papers in the Minnesota Historical Society.

With documents from over two dozen depositories on hand, Alvord began with Clarence E. Carter, of Miami University, the task of editing a selection for publication. Three volumes of the *British Series* entitled *The Critical Period, 1763-1765; The New Regime, 1765-1767;* and *Trade and Politics, 1767-1769* appeared in 1915, 1916, and 1921, respectively. These carefully edited works present a wealth of valuable documents on the early years of the British regime, but though the materials are on hand, the additional three volumes with which it was intended to conclude the series have not appeared.

A new program for the procurement of reproductions from the

[70] Illinois University, Ill. Hist. Survey, *Guide to MS. Materials in Foreign Depositories,* p. 2-33.

[71] *Ibid.,* p. 33-52.

[72] Illinois University, Ill. Hist. Survey, *Guide to MS. Materials of Amer. Origin, passim.*

[73] These manuscripts are described in Wisconsin, State Historical Society, *Descriptive List of Manuscript Collections of the State Historical Society of Wisconsin,* ed. by Reuben G. Thwaites (Madison, 1906), 2-104.

British Public Record Office was inaugurated by Theodore C. Pease, Alvord's successor as director of the Illinois Historical Survey, while on sabbatical leave in England in 1933. Photostats, microfilm, and microfilm enlargements were obtained for the years 1760-75.[74] Some of these documents have been published, but they relate to the years before the British occupation of Illinois.[75]

Detroit

In 1796 the notarial records of Detroit were carried across the river to Sandwich, Ontario, by the last British notary, William Monforton. The records remained in the hands of his descendants for many years until transferred by an Ontario statute of Feb. 15, 1871 to the custody of Wayne County, Mich.[76] These were volumes A, B, and C, 1737-95, but with a gap from July 11, 1784 to May 24, 1786. The missing part is said to have been stolen.[77] A fourth volume (D) containing Monforton's recordings, May 1786-July 1793, was given to Charles Frederick Labadie of Windsor in March 1858 by one of Monforton's descendants. Labadie in turn delivered the volume in November 1859 to John Stuart of that place. Eventually the volume found its way to the Canadian Archives at Ottawa.[78] That institution has copies of the earlier registers and an index for 1737-96.[79]

[74] James G. Randall, "Theodore Calvin Pease," *Ill. State Hist. Soc., Jour.,* XLI (Dec. 1948), 358.

[75] T. C. Pease, ed., *Anglo-French Boundary Disputes in the West, 1749-1763 (Colls.* Ill. State Hist. Lib., Vol. XXVII, *French Series,* Vol. II, Springfield, 1936); T. C. Pease and Ernestine Jenison, eds., *Illinois on the Eve of the Seven Years' War, 1747-1755 (Colls.* Ill State Hist. Lib., Vol. XXIX, *French Series,* Vol. III, Springfield, 1940).

[76] Burton, ed., *City of Detroit,* I, 206. The act provided for the transfer of two registry books containing a large number of entries relating to lands in Wayne County, to which the books had originally belonged, from the registrar of Essex County, Ontario, after the making of copies, to the registrar of deeds of Wayne County (Ontario, *Statutes,* 1870-71, 80-81).

[77] Lajeunesse, ed., *Windsor Border Region,* p. lxiv, n. 16.

[78] Quaife, ed., *Askin Papers,* I, 107 n. 60; Affidavit by William Monforton (a grandson of the original William Monforton), Mar. 29, 1860, affidavit by Charles F. Labadie, Feb. 24, 1860, Detroit Notarial Records, Bk. D, Burton Historical Collection, Detroit Public Library.

[79] Parker, *Guide to Materials for U.S. History,* p. 105.

Transcripts of volumes A, B, C and a photostat of volume D, and an index are in the Burton Historical Collection of the Detroit Public Library. The character of the notarial registers changed under the British government; personal transactions such as contracts, inventories of estates, wills, and marriage agreements were not so regularly recorded, transfers of real estate taking up the bulk of the space after 1769.[80] Other types of documents in the notarial records include appointments of local officials, arbitration awards, and affidavits. A number of notarial documents executed by Thomas Williams are in print.[81]

During the 1890's Clarence M. Burton obtained copies of many letters written by officers who served at Detroit from the Canadian Archives through the courtesy of Douglas Brymner, the Dominion Archivist. Bearing the title "Canadian Archives Relating to Detroit, 1760-1797," this volume of 332 pages is in the Burton Historical Collection.[82]

A volume labelled "Intercepted Correspondence 1812" in the General Records of the Department of State in the National Archives, Washington, D.C., contains some original documents, most of which had been accumulated at Detroit before the British withdrawal. These manuscripts consist of letters received by the commandants at Detroit, Maj. Patrick Murray, Maj. John Smith, and Col. Richard G. England. Many of the 144 items are holographic letters written by Alexander McKee, the British Indian agent at Fort Miamis on the Maumee River, to Maj. Smith and Col. England during 1790-94 on Indian affairs and the operations of the

---

[80] Burton, ed., *City of Detroit*, I, 174. Abstracts from the notarial books A, B, C, (1766-95) relating to land transactions are in Lajeunesse, ed., *Windsor Border Region*, p. 312-34, and in the same compilation are the texts of various types of documents in the notarial records.

[81] Quaife, ed., *Askin Papers*, I, 167-71, 172, 196-97, 198.

[82] A calendar of the correspondence between the commanding officers at Detroit and the military authorities at Quebec is in Canada, Public Archives, "Correspondence and Papers Relating to Detroit [1772-1780]," *Report*, 1882 (Ottawa, 1883), Note A, 2, p. 11-40. Some documents and other references relating to Detroit can be found in Clarence W. Alvord, ed., *Kaskaskia Records, 1778-1790* (*Colls*. Ill. State Hist. Lib., vol. V, *Va. Ser.*, vol. II, Springfield, 1909), see index under Detroit, Hamilton, etc.

American Army, which was then waging campaigns against the Indians in the Ohio country to the south. Reports and letters of McKee's subordinates in the Indian Department, Matthew Elliott, Simon Girty, and George Ironside, and of Indian traders Antoine Lasselle and H. Hay, communicating information regarding the Indians and the Americans, are also present. Other letters to the commandants are from Francis Le Maistre, military secretary to Lord Dorchester, governor of the Province of Quebec; Lord Dorchester himself; Col. A. Gordon, commanding officer at Niagara; Governor J. G. Simcoe of Upper Canada; E. B. Littlehales, major of brigade under Simcoe; and a few letters of 1796-1802 from James Green, military secretary to the governor of Quebec, to the commanding officers at Amherstburg. After the withdrawal of the British from Detroit, these documents were conveyed into Upper Canada where they were presumably captured by the American Army during the War of 1812.

A much larger quantity of transcripts was obtained by an organization founded in 1874 which took the name Michigan Pioneer and Historical Society in 1888. From an early date the Society had a committee of historians whose task was the acquisition and publication of source materials. As chairman of this committee from 1883 to 1895, Col. Michael Shoemaker—miller, farmer, and soldier —supervised the procurement of transcripts of documents in the Canadian Archives relating to the history of Michigan and the Northwest.[83] In 1887 and again in 1889 he sent his son, Bowen W. Shoemaker, to Ottawa to transcribe documents, and other persons were employed on this task in later years. By 1895 over 6,000 pages of transcripts had been acquired from the military papers (Series C) and from copies of Haldimand Papers, Bouquet Papers, and Colonial Office Papers (Series Q).[84] While transcripts were still being received, the Society began in 1886 the publication of an extensive collection of documents, which is valuable for military and

[83] Edward W. Barber, "Life and Labors of Col. Michael Shoemaker," *Mich. Hist. Colls.* XXVII (1896), 226-27; "Report of the Committee of Historians," *ibid.*, III, VI-XXVI (1881, 1883-1894/95). No report published for 1882.

[84] *Ibid.*, XXV, preface.

Indian affairs in the Northwest, local history, biography, land management, Indian trade, administration of justice, the Provincial Marine, and the navigation of the lakes.[85] The transcripts passed into the custody of the Michigan Historical Commission and were destroyed in the State Office Building fire of 1951.

Censuses giving the names of inhabitants are more numerous for Detroit during the British period. A census of August 1765 in the Manuscript Division of the Library of Congress is of unusual value since it lists the names of settlers and gives separately the number of able-bodied men, women, and children; enumerates front acreage, farm animals, and quantities of agricultural products. The Burton Historical Collection has a negative photostat of a census of 1765 giving similar information derived from the Penn Family Papers in the Historical Society of Pennsylvania. A similar census was taken by Philip Dejean on Jan. 23, 1768.[86] Other censuses ordered by Captain Lernoult (March 31, 1779)[87] and by Major De Peyster (July 16, 1782) have been published.[88] Statistics on popu-

---

[85] "The Haldimand Papers; Copies of Papers on File in the Dominion Archives at Ottawa, Canada," *ibid.*, IX-XII (1886-88), 343-658, 210-672, 319-656, 1-315. *Copies of Papers on File in the Dominion Archives at Ottawa, Canada, Pertaining to Michigan . . . ibid.*, XIX, XX, XXIII-XXV (1892-96), p. 675, 673, 680, 681, 699: It would be advisable for the historian who makes extensive use of these published documents to test their reliability by comparing some of them with the original documents in the Canadian Public Archives and with photographic reproductions from British depositories. Insofar as they were based on transcripts, the published documents are copies of copies. A useful aid for finding documents relating to persons and subjects in the foregoing volumes is in the Michigan State Historical Society, *Classified Finding List of the Collections of the Michigan Pioneer and Historical Society* (Detroit, 1952).

[86] This census is in the Gage Papers in the William L. Clements Library, Ann Arbor, Mich. enclosed in a letter from George Turnbull to Gage, Feb. 23, 1768. The part of the census relating to settlers on the south shore of the Detroit River (Windsor, Ontario) is printed in Lejeunesse, ed., *Windsor Border Region*, p. 63-64.

[87] Obtained from the Haldimand Papers in the Canadian Public Archives, it is in the *Mich. Hist. Colls.*, X (1886), 312-27, and in Lucien Brault, éd., "Recensement de Detroit en 1779," *Revue d'histoire de l'Amérique française,* V (mars 1952), 581-85.

[88] *Mich. Hist. Colls.*, X (1886), 601-13; and Lejeunesse, ed., *Windsor Border Region*, 69-74.

lation are available in censuses of 1767, 1773 and 1778.[89] A census of St. Joseph of 1780 giving the names of settlers and of slaves has been published.[90]

Land Records

By ceding the Northwest, the French obtained the agreement of the British in the Treaty of Paris of 1763 that the French grants and titles in the region would be respected. The French grants in the Illinois settlements near the Mississippi River were not interfered with by the British, and grants at Detroit and its neighborhood which were properly registered in Quebec pursuant to French law were approved.[91] Believing that many of the settlers at Vincennes were intruders without valid titles who had entered the area in violation of the proclamation of 1763, General Gage issued a proclamation on April 8, 1772 ordering them to retire from the Wabash to the English colonies.[92] They responded, however, with a letter and memorial dated Sept. 18, 1773, declaring themselves to be peaceful settlers engaged in cultivating lands granted to them by the French King or purchased by them. They asked that they be allowed to remain there and that provision be made for their government.[93] On April 2, 1773, Gage directed that a list of the settlers at Vincennes be drawn up with data as to their grants.[94] A verification of titles dated May 3, 1774 bearing the names of

[89] *Mich. Hist. Colls.,* IX (1886), 649; Lajeunesse, ed., *Windsor Border Region,* p. 82; *Mich. Hist. Colls.,* IX (1886), 469. See also Greene and Harrington, *American Population before 1790,* p. 187-92.

[90] *Mich. Hist. Colls.,* X (1886), 406-07.

[91] Gage to Dartmouth, Apr. 7, 1773, Carter, ed., *Corresp. of General Gage,* I, 347-49.

[92] Watts, ed., "Vincennes Documents of 1772," p. 202; the text is extracted therein; it also is in *A.S.P., Pub. Lands,* II, 209.

[93] The texts of the letter and of the memorial, which were obtained from the Gage papers in the William L. Clements Library, are printed in French and in English with 56 signatures in Watts, ed., "Vincennes Documents of 1772," p. 206-12.

[94] *Ibid.,* p. 203. The text is in *A.S.P., Pub. Lands,* II, 209.

eighty-eight settlers was accordingly provided.[95] No further action regarding the confirmation of the grants appears to have been taken.[96]

The occupation of the western posts by the British at once presented them with the problem of regulating settlement. The British policy was to acknowledge the Indian title to the land and to obtain cessions through negotiating treaties.[97] Relations with the Indians were precarious and to prevent hostilities with them, the British government in December 1761 specifically prohibited the securing of grants of land from them, except by the governors of the colonies with the approval of the King.[98]

The proclamation of Oct. 7, 1763 providing for the government of the territory acquired by the treaty of peace of that year contained stipulations in regard to land grants and settlement.[99] The governors and councils of the provinces of Quebec and the two Floridas were empowered to make grants to the inhabitants or to new setlers within the limits of those provinces. No grants were to be made upon unceded Indian land in any of the colonies or by the old colonies beyond the heads of the rivers emptying into the Atlantic Ocean. The region west of the mountains together with all other lands not included within the limits of the three new colonies was set aside as an Indian reserve within which all purchases of land and settlement were prohibited except with royal permission. Persons illegally occupying any of the proscribed areas were ordered to remove themselves. Because of frauds and abuses that had been committed against the Indians, no private purchases of land were to be permitted, and purchases were to be made only at public meetings conducted by the governors. The foregoing regulations in regard to land settlement and acquisition in the West were not

[95] Printed in Dunn, ed., "Documents Relating to the French Settlements on the Wabash," p. 425-27.

[96] As late as May 26, 1777, Lt. Gov. Abbott wrote from Vincennes to Gov. Carleton, requesting orders regarding lands there, for few of the French had any proper grants (Carter, ed., *Corresp. of General Gage*, I, 441).

[97] Scott, "Indian Affairs," p. 697.

[98] Buck, *Western Pennsylvania*, p. 102.

[99] Shortt and Doughty, eds., *Docs. Const. Hist. Canada*, I, 166-68.

observed because of the inability of the British authorities to enforce them.[1] The widely scattered garrisons could not prevent the entrance of settlers, who after Pontiac's War took possession of land in western Pennsylvania and in the Indian country south of the Great Lakes.[2]

The British commandants at the western posts followed the practice of issuing permits to settle and cultivate land near the posts and on the roads between them in order to provide the garrisons with sustenance. The outbreak of the Revolution brought an influx of settlers to the Detroit area. Squatters who were allowed to cultivate the land were informed by Lieutenant-Governor Hamilton that they should not regard the temporary permission as a grant.[3] Settlement progressed along the Detroit River; new lands were occupied and improved farm lands changed hands.[4] Lands were privately purchased from the Indians up and down the Detroit River and on islands in the river, especially near the close of the Revolution when it was believed that the region would be ceded to the United States.[5] American prisoners were allowed to cultivate land around Detroit during the Revolution. A record of quitrents (fees for the use of the land) received at Detroit, 1770-84, which seems to be volume 5 of a series, is in the Canadian Archives. After the war, officials, discharged soldiers, Loyalists, and former American prisoners were allowed to occupy land in and around Detroit. After Lieutenant-Governor Sinclair purchased the Mackinac Island from the Indians in 1781 as a site for a new fort, he made grants of

[1] Buck, *Western Pennsylvania*, p. 113; Bond, *Foundations of Ohio*, p. 175.

[2] Rusell, *British Régime*, p. 54-55.

[3] Henry Hamilton to Governor Frederick Haldimand, Sept. 9, 1778, *Mich. Hist. Colls.*, IX, 474.

[4] Burton, ed., *City of Detroit*, II, 937, 961; Russell, *British Régime*, p. 104, 117; Lajeunesse, ed., *Windsor Border Region*, p. lxiv.

[5] Burton, ed., *City of Detroit*, I, 274. The deed by which Alexander and William Macomb acquired Grosse Ile at the mouth of the Detroit River from the Potawatomi, a purchase which was later confirmed by Governor Simcoe and patented by the United States Government, is printed in *Mich. Hist. Colls.*, XXXV (1907), 580-83, and in John R. Command, "The Story of Grosse Ile," *Mich. Hist. Mag.*, III (1919), 130-31.

land there.[6] Charles de Langlade was given a permit for occupancy at Green Bay. To settle disputes over boundary lines, James Sterling was appointed government surveyor at Detroit in April 1774.[7] An extensive grant made by Lieutenant-Colonel Wilkins to the trading firm of Baynton, Wharton & Morgan between Prairie du Rocher and Kaskaskia was not confirmed by the governor of the province since it violated the proclamation of 1763.[8]

Records relating to land transactions during the British period of Illinois are among the county records. A record of deeds for 1768-1850 is among the Kaskaskia records in the custody of the recorder of Randolph County at Chester, Illinois.[9] Conveyances of land at Detroit were recorded by the notary, whose records are in the possession of the recorder of Wayne County at Detroit; copies are in the Burton Historical Collection. A series of books in which the quitrents mentioned earlier were received at Detroit was also kept, but the only extant volume, 1770-83, is in the Canadian Public Archives.[10]

Data on land holdings can also be derived from other sources. More comprehensive than the scanty original records are the land papers accumulated by the various boards of lands commissioners already described which include testimony as well as copies of original documents. A census of the inhabitants of Detroit taken in 1782 shows the quantity of land under cultivation and clear.[11]

---

[6] Winthrop Sargent to the Secretary of State, Sept. 30, 1796, Carter, ed., *Terr. Papers, U.S., N.W. Terr.,* III, 457. The text of a grant made by Sinclair in 1782 is in *Colls.* State Hist. Soc. Wis., XVIII, 432-34.

[7] Burton, ed., *City of Detroit,* I, 179-80.

[8] Max Savelle, *George Morgan, Colony Builder,* (New York, 1932), 59-60. The grant is printed in *A.S.P., Pub. Lands,* II, 206-07. An Indian deed for a tract conveyed to the Illinois Wabash Company, July 5, 1773 (*ibid.,* p. 117-19) bears a notation that it was registered at Kaskaskia. It is also printed in Clarence W. Alvord, ed., *The Illinois-Wabash Company Manuscript* (Privately printed by Cyrus H. McCormick, 1915).

[9] Alvord, "18th Cent. French Records," p. 361; Pease, *County Archives,* p. 554, 556; Alvord, ed., *Cahokia Records,* p. clii.

[10] Canada, Public Archives, Manuscript Division, *Preliminary Inventory, Manuscript Group 23, Late Eighteenth Century Papers* (Ottawa, 1957), 33.

[11] *Mich. Hist. Colls.,* X (1886), 601-13.

A catalog of maps, plans and surveys relating to Detroit in the Sur-
veyor-Generals' Office at Quebec is in print.[12] Collections of private papers, such as those of John Askin and others in the Burton
Historical Collection, often contain documents relative to land
grants.[13]

Land transactions at Michilimackinac, where French grants were
likewise respected, were loosely conducted during the British period without proper documentation.[14] Settlement progress was slow
at Michilimackinac and Sault Ste. Marie, but claims were eventually presented to and investigated by the land commissioners at
Detroit, and records assembled.[15]

Manuscript Collections

For military affairs in the Northwest the most important manuscripts are the papers of the British commanders in chief who
served in North America from the time of the French and Indian
War.[16] In these papers can be found correspondence with the officers who commanded the posts in the Northwest. The papers of
Maj. Gen. Jeffery Amherst, who was commander in chief when the
first posts in the Northwest were occupied in 1760, are in the Public
Record Office and in the William L. Clements Library.[17] The latter collection includes letters from Henry Gladwin and other post
commanders relating to Pontiac's War. Photostats of the Amherst

[12] *Ibid.,* XXIV (1894), 43-44.

[13] For land papers of the District of Hesse, see Chapter IV.

[14] Winthrop Sargent to the Secretary of State, Sept. 30, 1796, Carter, ed.,
Terr. Papers, NW Terr., III, 457.

[15] Testimony relating to land claims at those places is printed in "Land
Claims in Michigan," *House Report* 42, 20 Cong., 1 sess., Serial 176, p. 386-
487. Depositions regarding the occupancy of land at Mackinac before 1796
are in the papers of William Woodbridge, one of the land commissioners at
Detroit, in the Burton Historical Collection. Concerning the custody of the
records of the land office at Detroit, see Chapter I.

[16] Henry P. Beers, "The Papers of the British Commanders in Chief in
North America, 1754-1783," *Military Affairs,* XIII (Summer 1949), 79-94.

[17] *Loc. cit.* p. 86-87.

papers are in the Library of Congress and in Amherst College Library; transcripts and photostats of the Amherst College copies are in the Public Archives of Canada, and microfilm in the University of Michigan Library and the Library of Congress. Other selections relating to Pennsylvania in the French and Indian War and to Pontiac's War are in the custody of the Pennsylvania Historical and Museum Commission. The papers of Maj. Gen. Thomas Gage in the William L. Clements Library at Ann Arbor, Mich., comprise 21,000 pieces relating largely to the years 1763-75 when he served as commander in chief. The correspondence, reports, financial papers, returns, lists, proceedings of courts-martial, vouchers, warrants, maps, and other documents in the collection, supply information concerning occurrences at the posts in the West and shipbuilding, transportation, and communication on the Great Lakes and in the adjacent country.[18] Photostats of over four thousand items from the Gage papers were obtained by the Library of Congress while they were still in England.[19] A selection from the papers in print is limited to Gage's correspondence with the British officials, but it contains much data relating to the West.[20] Communications originating in that region can be found in the *Collections* of the Illinois State Historical Library already mentioned.[21] Sir Henry Clinton's papers are also available in the William L. Clements Library, hav-

----

[18] Howard H. Peckham, "Military Papers in the Clements Library," *Military Affairs*, II (Fall 1938), 126-30; Clarence E. Carter, "Notes on the Lord Gage Collection of Manuscripts," *Miss. Valley Hist. Rev.*, XV (Mar. 1929), 511-19.

[19] U.S. Library of Congress, *Report of the Librarian of Congress*, 1929, 69, 78; U.S. Library of Congress, Division of Manuscripts, *A Guide to Manuscripts Relating to American History in British Depositories Reproduced for The Division of Manuscripts of the Library of Congress*, comp. by Grace Gardner Griffin (Washington, 1946), p. 232-33.

[20] Clarence E. Carter, ed., *The Correspondence of General Thomas Gage with the Secretaries of State and with the War Office and the Treasury, 1763-1775* (New Haven, 1931-1933. 2 vols.).

[21] The correspondence of Gage with Colonel Burton and other commanders in Quebec should not be overlooked; Gage's letters concern the raising of volunteers for the campaign against Pontiac (S. Morley Scott, "Material Relating to Quebec in the Gage and Amherst Papers," *Can. Hist. Rev.*, XIX (Dec. 1938), 381 n. 11).

ing been purchased by Mr. Clements in 1926.[22] Numbering 18,500 documents of various kinds, these papers begin in 1775 but are most numerous for the years 1778 to 1782, when Clinton was commander in chief.[23]

Upon succeeding to the office of commander in chief, Sir Guy Carleton acquired possession of a collection of British Headquarters Papers to which he added his own papers during 1782-83. In 1804 Carleton's secretary deposited the papers in the Royal Institution of Great Britain in London. Transcripts of selected documents were obtained from the Carleton papers during the years 1914-21 by the Canadian Public Archives.[24] The Institution sold them in 1929 to Dr. A. S. Rosenbach, a Philadelphia dealer, who resold them in 1930 to John D. Rockefeller, Jr. The papers were deposited for five years in the New York Public Library, rearranged according to a calendar published in 1904-09,[25] photostated, and presented to Colonial Williamsburg, Inc. Other selections are in the Library of Congress.[26] The original Carleton papers were presented to Queen Elizabeth in 1957 upon the occasion of her visit to the United States to participate in the 350th anniversary celebration of the founding of Jamestown,[27] and have since been deposited in the Public Record Office in London. Colonial Williamsburg Inc. has a positive photostat of the Carleton papers and a microfilm in twenty-nine reels. Copies of the microfilm can be purchased for $175. A negative photostat of the Carleton papers is in the New York Public Library.

[22] Randolph G. Adams, "A New Library of American Revolutionary Records," *Current History*, XXXIII (Nov. 1930), 235.

[23] Michigan University, William L. Clements Library, *Guide to the Manuscript Collections in the William L. Clements Library*, comp. by Howard H. Peckham (Ann Arbor, 1942), p. 46.

[24] Canada, Public Archives, MS. Div., *Preliminary Inventory, MS. Group 23*, p. 13-16.

[25] Great Britain, Historical Manuscripts Commission, *Report on American Manuscripts in the Royal Institution of Great Britain* (London, 1904-09. 4 vols.).

[26] U.S. Library of Congress, MS. Div., *Guide to MSS. in British Depositories*, p. 190.

[27] Institute of Early American History and Culture, *News Letter*, 19 (Oct. 15, 1958), 6-7.

Positive copies of the microfilm are in the Manuscript Division of the Library of Congress and in the Canadian Public Archives. The foregoing papers are valuable for military history, local history, Indian affairs, fur trade, and genealogy, and include documents relating to the British posts in the Northwest.

The papers of other British Army officers are important for the history of the West. Maj. Gen. Frederick Haldimand, who filled military commands in Quebec during 1760-65 and commanded the forces in the province from 1778 to 1784, accumulated an extensive collection of papers to which reference has already been made in connection with the governorship of the province.[28] The papers include correspondence with the officers who commanded the posts at Detroit, Michilimackinac, Kaskaskia, and Vincennes, and correspondence (1776-83) with others on military and Indian affairs in the Northwest.[29] A variety of other documents concern all aspects of military administration in that area. Transcripts of the Haldimand papers were obtained by the Canadian Archives in the 1870's, and subsequently photostatic copies of extensive selections were procured by the Library of Congress. Many documents taken from the former collection have been published; these provide much information relative to military affairs, Indian relations, the fur trade, and navigation on the Great Lakes.[30] The Henry Bouquet papers, which came into the possession of Haldimand after Bou-

[28] Charles M. Andrews, and Frances G. Davenport, *Guide to the Manuscript Materials for the History of the United States to 1783, in the British Museum, in Minor London Archives, and in the Libraries of Oxford and Cambridge* (Washington, 1908), 105-06; Parker, *Guide Public Archives of Canada,* I, 198-210.

[29] British Museum, Department of Manuscripts, *Catalogue of Additions to Manuscripts in the British Museum, in the Years MDCCCLIV-MDCCCLX* (London, 1875. 2 vols.), I, 528, 530; Russell, *British Régime,* p. 275; Canada, Public Archives, "Haldimand Collection Calendar," *Report,* 1886, 718-25, 1887, 199-248.

[30] "Papers from the Canadian Archives," *Colls.* State Hist. Soc. Wis., XI (1888), 97-212; XII (1892), 23-132; "The Haldimand Papers, Copies of Papers on File in the Dominion Archives at Ottawa, Canada," *Mich. Hist. Colls.,* IX-XII (1886-88), 343-658, 210-672, 319-656, 1-315. Canada, General Staff, Historical Section, *A History of the Organization, Development and Services of the Military and Naval Forces of Canada from the Peace of Paris in 1763, to the Present Time* ([Ottawa] 1919. 3 vols.). Contains documents from the Haldimand papers, 1763-85.

quet's death in 1765, are also preserved in the British Museum.[31] Transcripts were obtained by the Canadian Archives, which has also published a calendar.[32] A selection from those transcripts has been published.[33] A mimeographed edition of Bouquet's papers prepared from photostats in the Library of Congress has been issued,[34] and the Pennsylvania Historical and Museum Commission which sponsored that edition has initiated the publication of the papers in letterpress with a volume on the Forbes expedition.[35]

The most important documents for the history of relations with the Indian tribes of the West during the twenty years preceding the opening of the Revolutionary War are the papers of Sir William Johnson. Accounts and vouchers covering public transactions of Sir William were buried by Sir John at the time of his flight together with other family valuables in an iron chest. In 1778 General Haldimand sent a detachment of soldiers south to Fort Johnson to recover these papers, but they found them ruined by moisture.[36] Seven bundles of Johnson papers were deposited with the Secretary of State of New York in 1801; a considerable part of these papers, included in property confiscated by New York State, was purchased at auction by John Tayler. The papers were inherited from him by Gen. John Tayler Cooper, who presented them in 1850 to the State

[31] British Museum, Dept. of MSS. *Catalogue of Additions*, I, 476-94; Andrews and Davenport, *Guide*, p. 105; Parker, *Guide Public Archives of Canada*, I, 195-98; E. Douglas Branch, "Henry Bouquet: Professional Soldier," *Pa. Mag. Hist.*, LXII (Jan. 1938), 41-51.

[32] Canada, Public Archives, "Bouquet Collection," *Report*, 1889 (Ottawa, 1890), p. 1-337.

[33] "Bouquet Papers," Mich. Hist. *Colls.*, XIX (1892), 27-295.

[34] *The Papers of Col. Henry Bouquet*, prepared by the Frontier Forts and Trails Survey, Federal Works Agency, Work Projects Administration; ed. by Sylvester K. Stevens, Donald H. Kent and Leo J. Roland (Harrisburg, 1940-43. 19 vols.).

[35] *The Papers of Col. Henry Bouquet, Volume II, The Forbes Expedition*, ed., by Sylvester K. Stevens, Donald H. Kent, and Autumn L. Leonard (Harrisburg, 1951). Not continued to date (1961). A recently discovered orderly book has been published: "The Orderly Book of Colonel Henry Bouquet's Expedition against the Ohio Indians, 1764," ed. by Edward G. Williams, *Western Pennsylvania Historical Magazine*, XLII (Mar., June, Sept. 1959), 9-33, 179-200, 283-302.

[36] Day, *Calendar*, p. 6.

Library of New York.[37] Most of these manuscripts were arranged and bound in twenty-two volumes under the direction of Dr. Edmund B. O'Callaghan from 1850 to 1855. By persevering search over a period of years, William L. Stone, Sr., succeeded in acquiring additional Johnson manuscripts from the Johnson family in England and other sources.[38] These papers were purchased by the State Library from Stone's son in 1863, and filled three more volumes. Another acquisition was made in 1866 from Henry Stevens, who had obtained a number of official papers at a sale in London. These papers consisted of warrants and accounts for Indian department disbursements under both Sir William and Guy Johnson, and a few papers relating to the war. The collection thus accumulated included 6550 papers in twenty-six volumes for the years 1733-1808. In rescuing these papers, which are indispensable for the history of one of the most stirring periods of its history, the State of New York rendered its citizens a notable service.

The preparation of the Johnson papers for publication became the lifelong occupation of Dr. Richard E. Day, an employee of the New York State Library. An extensive calendar compiled by him was published in 1909. Manuscripts destroyed by a fire in the library in 1911 included records of the Indian agency from April 1757 to February 1759, Sir William Johnson's diary of 1759 and 1761, and other records for the years 1763 to 1765.[39] This misfortune made it desirable to make up the loss as far as possible from other sources. Some transcripts that had been made before the fire by the Illinois Historical Survey were copied.[40] Abstracts were

---

[37] *The Papers of Sir William Johnson,* I, xiv; Richard E. Day, *Calendar of the Sir William Johnson Manuscripts in the New York State Library* (Albany, 1909), 5.

[38] William L. Stone, *The Life and Times of Sir William Johnson, Bart.* (Albany, 1865, 2 vols.), I, vi.

[39] *Papers of Sir Wm. Johnson,* III, 105, IV, ix; New York State Library, *94th Annual Report* (Albany, 1913), 24. The diary of Johnson's trip to Detroit in 1761 had been printed in Stone, *William Johnson,* II, 429-78 and is in the *Papers of Sir Wm. Johnson,* XIII, 215-74.

[40] Illinois University, Ill. Hist. Survey, *Guide to MS. Materials of Amer. Origin* p. 53-54. Some letters from Edward Cole to Johnson or Croghan had been printed in Clarence W. Alvord, ed., "Edward Cole, Indian Commissioner in the Illinois Country," *Ill. State Hist. Soc., Jour.,* III (Oct. 1910), 23-44.

available in Day's calendar, and complete documents comprising the earliest acquisition of 1801 had been published previously.[41] Numerous other letters written to Sir William Johnson had been published in the *Pennsylvania Archives*. The search for additional Johnson manuscripts was pursued by the successive editors in both public and private institutions in the United States and Canada, and abroad, and the yield has been sufficient to make up a number of additional volumes of Johnson papers.[42]

The Johnson papers are important not only for an understanding of Indian relations and military affairs at that time but also for the social, economic, religious, and political history of the English colonies. The papers comprise letters, journals, diaries, orders and letters, including communications to and from the officials of the Indian department, such as Croghan, Claus, McKee, and Cole, with the commanders in chief of the British army at New York, with many army officers, and with governors and other officials.

Also important for any consideration of Indian affairs are the papers of the Indian agent George Croghan in the Historical Society of Pennsylvania.[43] Soon after Croghan's death near Philadelphia in 1782, a wooden trunk containing his papers and accounts passed into the hands of Barnard and Michael Gratz, two of his

---

[41] Edmund B. O'Callaghan, ed., *The Documentary History of the State of New York* (Albany, 1849-51. 4 vols.), II, 543-1007. "Papers Relating to the Six Nations," *ibid.*, IV, 289-520, contains many Johnson letters. Other documents from the Johnson papers are in Edmund B. O'Callaghan, ed., *Documents Relative to the Colonial History of the State of New York; Procured in Holland, England, and France, by John Romeyn Brodhead, Esq., Agent, . . .* (Albany, 1853-87. 15 vols.). Vols. VI-VIII contain Johnson's correspondence for 1755 to 1774. The documents in these compilations were only referred to and were not reprinted in *The Papers of Sir William Johnson*.

[42] Data on the collections drawn upon, including the papers of the numerous military officers and civil officials who served in America during the time of Johnson's superintendency, as well as the Public Record Office, the British Museum, and the Canadian Public Archives are presented in the prefaces of the volumes of the *Papers of Sir Wm. Johnson,* in which the derivations of the individual documents are also indicated. See also Charles H. Lincoln, "Calendar of the Manuscripts of Sir William Johnson in the Library of the [American Antiquarian] Society," American Antiquarian Society, *Proceedings,* n. s., XVIII (Oct. 1907), 367-401.

[43] Volwiler, *George Croghan,* p. 349.

executors. Some of these papers were eventually given to the Society and form part of the Etting collection, named after Frank M.
Etting, a grandson of Michael Gratz. The trunk and most of the
papers, however, were transferred by the executors in 1804 to
Thomas Cadwalader, the attorney of the Croghan heirs, and remained unknown among the records of the Cadwalader firm until
they were uncovered in 1939 by the editor and research librarian
of the Historical Society of Pennsylvania, Nicholas B. Wainwright.[44] The Croghan papers in the Cadwalader collection presented to the Society included four boxes of correspondence,
diaries, and journals, and four boxes of receipted bills. Besides material relating to Croghan's trading and land activities, the papers
include letters from Sir William Johnson, military leaders, Indian
officials, and officials of the colony of Pennsylvania.

Other communications relating to Croghan's career that have
been preserved by his numerous correspondents are available in
scattered depositories. Letters to and from Croghan and instructions from the governors are in the records of the State of Pennsylvania.[45] Material of a similar character is available in the Sir William Johnson papers in the New York State Library, which have also
been published.[46] Letters from Croghan to Brig. Gen. Robert
Monckton are in the New York Public Library. The Bouquet papers
contain not only letters written by Croghan to Bouquet but to others as well. The Penn papers in the Historical Society of Pennsylvania contain an account written by Croghan of Indian affairs from
1748 to Braddock's defeat. Other Croghan items are in the Baynton,
Wharton, and Morgan papers in the Division of Public Records at
Harrisburg, Pennsylvania. The George Clinton papers, Sterling
letter book, Gage papers, and Shelburne papers in the William L.
Clements Library at Ann Arbor contain a number of Croghan

---

[44] Nicholas B. Wainwright, *George Croghan, Wilderness Diplomat* (Chapel
Hill, 1959), vii, 112-13. Wainwright has exploited Croghan's papers for his
own career, but they have not been utilized by the historians of trade and land
speculation. Some of Croghan's correspondence from this source has been published in the *Papers of Sir William Johnson.*

[45] Some of these can be found scattered in Pennsylvania (Colony and Province), *Colonial Records* (Philadelphia, 1851-53. 16 vols.).

[46] *Papers of Sir Wm. Johnson.*

manuscripts for 1751-72.[47] Other Croghan letters have been published in Massachusetts Historical Society *Collections* (4th ser., vol. IX), Alvord and Carter, eds., *The Critical Period*, and their *New Regime*, and in O'Callaghan, ed., *Documents Relative to the Colonial History of the State of New York*, vols. VI-IX.[48] The Henry Joseph collection of Gratz papers containing Croghan material has been made available on microfilm by the American Jewish Archives. Several collections in the Historical Society of Pennsylvania contain Croghan material.

The Claus papers, 1760-1826, purchased by the Canadian Public Archives in 1883 from descendants of the family at Niagara, are important for the historian of Indian affairs. They include not only the correspondence and papers of Daniel Claus and of his son William, but also the papers of Alexander McKee and of Prideaux Selby, Assistant Secretary of Indian Affairs in Upper Canada, 1792-1809.[49] The papers of McKee and Selby came into the possession of William Claus when he succeeded McKee as Deputy Superintendent-General in 1799. The collection includes correspondence with the governors of Quebec and Upper Canada, and with commandants and officials of the Indian Department at Detroit, Mackinac, Niagara, Miami Bay, Fort Miamis, Sandusky, River Raisin, Amherstburg, and Saguina (Saginaw). The Claus papers also include military commissions, land papers, diaries, notebooks, memoranda of disbursements, messages and speeches to the Indians, requisitions for and returns of Indian presents, invoices of supplies, statements of American prisoners, agents' accounts, appointments, receipts, minutes of Indian conferences, memorials, and Indian treaties. This valuable collection has been microfilmed by the Canadian Public Archives; microfilms of items relating to Alexan-

---

[47] Howard H. Peckman, ed., *George Croghan's Journal of His Trip to Detroit in 1767* (Ann Arbor, 1939), 51-55 presents a list of these manuscripts.

[48] See also "A Selection of George Croghan's Letters and Journals Relating to Tours into the Western Country—November 16, 1750-November 1765," in Reuben G. Thwaites, ed., *Early Western Travels* (Cleveland, 1904), I, 45-173.

[49] Parker, *Guide to Materials for U. S. History*, p. 106; Canada, Public Archives, Manuscript Division, *Preliminary Inventory, Manuscript Group 19, Fur Trade and Indians, 1763-1867* (Ottawa, 1954), 22. The papers include a diary of William Claus for 1770-1824.

der McKee and Arthur St. Clair were obtained by the Pennsylvania Historical and Museum Commission in 1949; other microfilm is in the State Historical Society of Wisconsin. Photostats of the Daniel Claus papers, 1716-80, were acquired by the Library of Congress in 1917. Numerous letters of Daniel Claus have been published in the *Papers of Sir William Johnson,* and in *The Correspondence of Lieut. Governor John Graves Simcoe.*

The administrative and military papers of the posts in the Northwest, except for those of Fort de Chartres and Kaskaskia, were carried off by the commandants and have largely disappeared. Such files consisted of correspondence not only with the superior officers in Canada but also with the commandants of other posts. Other documents included invoices and estimates of Indian presents, speeches to Indians and proceedings of councils, proceedings of courts of inquiry, communications on the Indian trade, reports of examining boards, reports on expenses and claims, returns of troops and of Indian department ordnance stores.[50]

Persons interested in the history of the Northwest have uncovered many documents relating to military affairs that have since been published or placed in depositiories. Papers of Robert Rogers for 1760-61 are in the New York Public Library. Papers of Maj. Henry Gladwin, commander at Detroit from 1761 to 1764, have been obtained from family sources in Yorkshire, England.[51] Papers of Col. John Bradstreet are preserved in the American Antiquarian Society, the New York Public Library, the New York State Library, and Harvard University Library.[52]

Considerable documentation exists relating to the administration of Henry Hamilton as lieutenant-governor at Detroit 1775-79 and his part in the American Revolution. It is estimated that two hun-

[50] Inventories of records of Detroit and Michilimackinac pertaining to the years 1778-84 are published in *Mich. Hist. Colls.,* XX (1892), 273-75.

[51] "The Gladwin Manuscripts," ed. by Charles Moore, *Mich. Hist. Colls.,* XXVII (1896), 605-80. These were reprinted in *Colls.* State Hist. Soc. Wis., XVIII (1908).

[52] Charles H. Lincoln, comp., "A Calendar of the Manuscripts of Col. John Bradstreet," Amer. Antiq. Soc., *Procs.,* n. s., XIX (Apr. 15, 1908), 103-81. A few letters and extracts of others are printed in "Papers Relating to the Expeditions of Colonel Bradstreet and Colonel Bouquet, in Ohio, A.D., 1764," Western Reserve and Northern Ohio Historical Society, *Tract* No. 13-14 (Feb. 1873), 5, 6 p.

dred of his letters and other papers, less than one-third of which have been printed, are available largely in the Haldimand papers in the British Museum, the Gage papers in the William L. Clements Library, the Shelburne papers and the George Germain papers in that library and in the British Museum, in the Burton Historical Collection, and in the possession of Dr. Otto Fisher of Detroit.[53] There were presented to the Houghton Library of Harvard University in 1902 by the family of one of Hamilton's brothers, pictures and landscapes by Hamilton, his journal of 1778-79, his autobiography, and a few other papers. The most important document by Hamilton, the journal (Aug. 6, 1778 to June 16, 1779) concerning his expedition against Vincennes, is in print.[54] A shorter version stopping at Oct. 6, 1778 is in the British Museum. A report written in London in 1781 (dated July 6) for Haldimand, covering from Nov. 1776 to June 1781, which is in the Germain papers in the Clements Library, has been printed several times.[55] Original letters of Hamilton and transcripts from the Canadian archives and the British archives are in the Draper Manuscripts in the State Historical Society of Wisconsin. Some letters of Capt. Henry Bird written from Detroit are in the Canadian Public Archives.[56] A meteorological journal kept at Detroit, 1781-86, by George C. Anthon, a British army surgeon, is in the New York Historical Society.

Other findings concern the Illinois country. A few papers which once formed part of the archives of Fort de Chartres and which were probably taken from acting commandant De Rocheblave by Clark and sent to Williamsburg, Va., are in the Virginia State

[53] John D. Barnhart, ed., *Henry Hamilton and George Rogers Clark in the American Revolution with The Unpublished Journal of Lieut. Gov. Henry Hamilton* (Crawfordsville, Ind., 1951), 206. Letters by Hamilton are printed in the *Colls.* of the Ill. State Hist. Lib., I (Springfield, 1903), the *Mich. Hist. Colls.*, XIX-XX; James Alton James, ed., *George Rogers Clark Papers, 1771-1781* (*Colls.* Ill. State Hist. Lib., Vols. VIII-IX, *Virginia Series*, Vols. III-IV, Springfield, 1912, 1926); and the *Colls.* State Hist. Soc. Wis., XVIII-XIX.

[54] Barnhart, ed., *Henry Hamilton*, p. 102-205.

[55] *Mich. Hist. Colls.*, IX (1886), 489-516; Great Britain, Historical Manuscripts Commission, *Report on the Manuscripts of Mrs. Stopford-Sackville, of Dayton House, Northamptonshire* (Hereford, England, 1910. 2 vols.), II, 223-48; James, ed., *Clark Papers*, VIII, 174-207; Milo M. Quaife, ed., *The Capture of Old Vincennes* (Indianapolis, 1927), 172-220.

[56] Canada, Public Archives, MS. Div., *Preliminary Inventory, MS. Group 23*, p. 42.

Library. Included in this find are letters from General Gage to Lt. Col. John Reed, 1766, to Lt. Col. John Wilkins 1768-70, two letters sent by Reed, 1769, and the proceedings of a court martial, 1766.[57] The record of proceedings of a court of inquiry held at Fort de Chartres in the case of Richard Bacon vs. George Morgan in 1770 is available in a contemporary copy in the State Historical Society of Wisconsin at Madison,[58] and the text has been published from that copy.[59] Lt. Col. John Wilkins, the commandant of the Illinois country, kept a journal of Indian affairs for the period Dec. 23, 1768 to Mar. 12, 1772, a copy of which is in the Gage Papers in the William L. Clements Library.[60] In this is recorded transactions with the Indians and information about supplies, liquor, and presents given to them. Letters written from Fort de Chartres by Ens. George Butricke, 1768-71, have been published,[61] as have others sent from the same place by Lt. Thomas Hutchins.[62] Papers of Phillipe François de Rastel, Chevalier de Rocheblave, the acting commandant of Kaskaskia, assembled from the Haldimand papers have been published.[63] De Rocheblave family papers are reported to be in the Presbytery of Notre Dame in Montreal.[64]

[57] Charles H. Ambler, ed., "Some Letters and Papers of General Thomas Gage," *The John P. Branch Historical Papers,* IV (June 1914), 86-111. These letters and those by Ensign Butricke mentioned below were reprinted in Alvord and Carter, eds., *Trade and Politics.*

[58] Wisconsin State Historical Society, *Guide to MSS.,* p. 69.

[59] John Moses, ed., "Court of Enquiry at Ft. Chartres," Chicago Hist. Soc. *Colls.,* IV (1890), 423-85.

[60] Storm, "The Notorious Colonel Wilkins," p. 17.

[61] Henry R. Stiles, ed., "Affairs at Fort Chartres, 1768-1781," *The Historical Magazine,* VIII (Aug. 1864), 257-66. Issued as a pamphlet, Albany, 1864, under Stiles's name. The letters were reprinted in Alvord and Carter, eds., *Trade and Politics, passim.*

[62] "Eight Letters of Thomas Hutchins to George Morgan," Chicago Historical Society *Bulletin,* I (May 1935), 69-78. The Morgan Papers in the Illinois Historical Survey include some letters from Hutchins. These and other sources containing letters of Hutchins were used by Anna M. Quattrocchi, Thomas Hutchins, 1730-89 (Ph.D. Dissertation, University of Pittsburgh, Pittsburgh, 1944). MS.

[63] Edward G. Mason, ed., "British Illinois; Philippe François de Rastel Chevalier de Rocheblave; Rocheblave Papers," Chicago Hist. Soc. *Colls.,* IV (1890), 382-419.

[64] Fabre-Surveyor, "De Rocheblave," p. 242.

The State Historical Society of Wisconsin has a scattering of original manuscripts relating to Wisconsin and adjacent areas. Among them are letters of the commanding officers at Mackinac, including George Etherington, Robert Rogers, Arent S. De Peyster, Patrick Sinclair, and William Doyle, and papers of Charles de Langlade, trader, Indian subagent, and militia officer at Green Bay, and miscellaneous fur trade papers.[65] These manuscripts together with reprints from numerous compilations mentioned in these pages have been published and provide valuable data concerning the fur trade, Indian relations, warfare, and white settlement of the region.[66] A few other letters, instructions, or orders of Etherington, De Peyster, and Sinclair are in the Newberry Library.[67] In print are some papers of De Peyster, a native of New York and a nephew of Peter Schuyler, as well as letters from him relating to Fort Michilimackinac, 1776-79, and to Detroit, 1779-84. These letters were obtained from the Daniel Claus Papers in the Canadian Public Archives.[68] A journal by Lt. James Gorrell, who commanded the first garrison at Green Bay during 1761-63, was found in the Maryland Historical Society by Francis Parkman. He supplied a copy of it to Lyman C. Draper, who published it with alterations and omissions.[69] The State Historical Society of Wisconsin also has reproductions from the British Public Record Office of the proceedings of important conferences held by Major Rogers with the Indians at Michilimackinac in 1767 and of the court martial at Mon-

[65] Wisconsin State Historical Society, *Descriptive List of Manuscript Collections*, p. 105.

[66] Reuben G. Thwaites, ed. "The British Regime in Wisconsin," *Colls.* State Hist. Soc. Wis., XVIII (1908), 223-468; Reuben G. Thwaites, ed., "Fur Trade on the Upper Lakes, 1778-1815," *Colls.* State Hist. Soc. Wis., XIX (1910), 234-374.

[67] Newberry Library, Edward E. Ayer Collection, *A Check List of Manuscripts in the Edward E. Ayer Collection*, comp. by Ruth L. Butler (Chicago, 1937), 26, 31, 96.

[68] Arent Schuyler De Peyster, *Miscellanies by an Officer (Colonel Arent Schuyler De Peyster, B.S.), 1774-1813*, edited by J. Watts De Peyster (New York, 1888), appendix i-xiv, xxi-xli. Some letters of Claus, Col. Guy Johnson, and John Johnson bearing on matters treated in the letters of De Peyster, 1776-1787, are on p. xlii-lvi.

[69] Lyman C. Draper, ed., "Lieut. James Gorrell's Journal," *Colls.* State Hist. Soc. Wis., I (1855), 24-48.

treal in 1768 by which Rogers was acquitted of the charge of treas-
son involving the surrender of the fort to the French.[70] A journal
by Rogers of the journey to and events at Michilimackinac, 1766-
67, has been published; the original is in the American Antiquarian
Society and a copy in the William L. Clements Library.[71] Many
letters of Rogers are in the latter depository in the papers of General
Amherst in those of Gage and George Clinton and in a special collection of Rogers' letters.[72]

Only small quantities of reproductions are to be found in other
depositories in the Midwest. The Minnesota Historical Society has
copies from the British Public Record Office and the Canadian
Public Archives of memorials of fur traders and military officers
concerning the Indians, 1765-84, and a list of Indians in the Mississippi Valley, 1766-67, as well as trade licenses.[73] Documents concerning Robert Rogers in the Minnesota Historical Society consist
of photostats of originals in the Bibliothèque St. Sulpice, Montreal,
the New York Public Library, the Public Record Office, and the
National Archives, Washington, D.C. These documents relate to
the fur trade at Michilimackinac, to Rogers' management of the
command there, to his efforts during a further sojourn in London
(1770-72) to get the British Government to pay the debts incurred
at Michilimackinac and to support a search for the Northwest Passage.[74] A collection of Carver papers in the same depository in-

[70] Wisconsin State Historical Society, *Guide*, p. 173-74. The court martial
proceedings are printed in Kenneth Roberts *Northwest Passage: Appendix,
Containing the Courtmartial of Major Robert Rogers, the Courtmartial of Lt.
Samuel Stephens and Other New Material* (Garden City, N.Y., 1937), 71-
159.

[71] "Journal of Major Robert Rogers," ed. by William L. Clements, Amer.
Antiq. Soc., *Procs.*, n.s., XXVIII (1918), 224-73.

[72] A thorough investigation of archival and manuscript sources relating to
Rogers has been made for a recent biography in which can be found a de-
scription of those sources (John R. Cuneo, *Robert Rogers of the Rangers* (New
York, 1959), 285-99.

[73] Minnesota Historical Society, *Manuscripts Collections of the Minnesota
Historical Society, Guide Number 2*, comp. by Lucile M. Kane and Kathryn
A. Johnson (St. Paul, 1955), 26, 51.

[74] *Ibid.*, p. 126-27. His proposal to the British Government relative to the
Northwest Passage, Feb. 11, 1772, is in T. C. Elliott, "The Origin of the
Name Oregon," *Oregon Historical Quarterly*, XXII (June 1921), 100-03.

cludes, in addition to his journal, reproductions of surveys and un-
validated deeds of the grant of land he received from the Indians,
and petitions to the British Government requesting reimbursement
for expenses connected with his expedition to the Mississippi River
in 1770.[75]

Materials relating to Indiana are even less plentiful. A small collection of documents relating to the French settlements on the
Wabash relates chiefly to land titles there and is mentioned in the
section on land records. Included, however, are a report by Lt.
Alexander Fraser, May 4, 1766, presenting some descriptive data
on the Illinois settlements and a journal of a trip by Thomas Hutchins from Fort Pitt to the mouth of the Ohio in 1768.[76] The Toronto
Public Library has a contemporary copy of a memorial from Edward Abbott claiming compensation from the government for property abandoned at Vincennes upon his abrupt departure from that
post early in 1778 on orders of Governor Carleton. A statement of
goods, food, and work furnished by Jean Baptiste Racine to the
Indians at Vincennes in 1773 is in the New York Public Library,
and a photostat is in the Canadian Archives. The text of an oath of
allegiance administered by the Americans to the inhabitants of
Vincennes in July 20, 1778 is valuable since it contains 182 settlers'
names.[77] The papers of Francis Vigo in the Indiana Historical Society archives contain a few land records of the 1760's and 1770's.
The Lasselle Collection in the Indiana State Library contains account books of Francis Bosseron and Hyacinth Lasselle, merchants
at Vincennes, and correspondence with merchants at Detroit and
Miamis.[78]

[75] Minnesota Historical Society, *Guide No. 2*, p. 19-20; Some of these documents are printed in John T. Lee, "Captain Jonathan Carver: Additional
Data," State Hist. Soc. Wis., *Procs.* (1912), 87-123. See also Milo M. Quaife,
"Jonathan Carver and the Carver Grant," *Miss. Valley Hist. Rev.*, VII (June
1920), 3-25.

[76] Jacob P. Dunn, ed., "Documents Relating to the French Settlements
on the Wabash," p. 408-21.

[77] Clarence W. Alvord, ed., "The Oath of Vincennes," Ill. State Hist. Soc.,
Trans. (1908), Ill. State Hist. Lib., *Pub.* No. 12, 270-76. The text with the
signatures is published therein from the Kaskaskia Records.

[78] Some of the correspondence from 1785 onward is published in Christopher B. Coleman, ed., "Letters from Eighteenth Century Merchants," *Ind.
Mag. Hist.*, V (Dec. 1909), 137-59.

The correspondence can be supplemented by numerous journals, diaries, and narratives of military officers, Indian agents, and traders. Besides geographical and travel data, these documents supply information relating to military and Indian affairs, forts, settlements, Indian trade, farming, industries, social life, and religious matters. Journals in print relating to the Northwest were written by such officers and agents as Christopher Gist, William Trent, George Croghan, George Washington, Maj. Robert Rogers, Col. Henry Bouquet, Lt. Thomas Hutchins, Lt. Diederick Brehm, Capt. John Montresor, Lt. James Gorrell, Capt. Thomas Morris, Capt. Philip Pittman, and Capt. Harry Gordon.[79] Other journals are still in manuscript; in the papers of Gen. Thomas Gage is the narrative by Lt. Alexander Fraser of a trip made from Fort Pitt to Fort de Chartres in 1765 to promote friendly relations with the Indians.[80] Jonathan Carver, who became associated with Major Rogers in his scheme to discover the Northwest Passage and who journeyed late in 1766 over Lake Michigan, across Wisconsin and up the Mississippi and Minnesota rivers, published the first description in English of that area.[81] During his service of a quarter of a century as an Indian agent George Croghan made numerous journeys on behalf of the colonies of Pennsylvania and Virginia and as deputy Indian

[79] Bibliography and data concerning these journals can be found in Solon J. Buck, *Travel and Description, 1765-1865: Together with a List of County Histories, Atlases, and Biographical Collections and a List of Territorial and State Laws.* (*Colls.* Ill. State Hist. Lib. IX, *Bibliog. Ser.*, II. Springfield, 1914); William Matthews, *American Diaries, An Annotated Bibliography of American Diaries Written Prior to the Year 1761* (Berkeley, Los Angeles, 1945); William Matthews, *Canadian Diaries and Autobiographies* (Berkeley, Los Angeles, 1950); Robert R. Hubach, *Early Midwestern Travel Narratives; an Annotated Bibliography, 1634-1850* (Detroit, 1961).

[80] Robert R. Hubach, comp., "Unpublished Travel Narratives on the Early Midwest, 1720-1850; a Preliminary Bibliography," *Miss. Valley Hist. Rev.*, XLII (Dec. 1955), 529.

[81] Jonathan Carver, *Travels of Jonathan Carver through the Interior Parts of North America in the Years 1766, 1767, and 1768* (London, 1778). See also John T. Lee, "A Bibliography of Carver's Travels," State Hist. Soc. Wis., *Procs.* (1909), 143-83. The whole subject of the authenticity of the published *Travels* and its discrepancies with the manuscript journal, of which reproductions are in the Minnesota Historical Society and the Newberry Library, is treated in Louise P. Kellogg, "The Mission of Jonathan Carver," *Wis. Mag. Hist.*, XII (Dec. 1928), 127-45.

superintendent for the British government to the Ohio and the region beyond.[82] Indian traders, such as John Patten,[83] John Jennings, William Clarkson, George Morgan, John Porteous, Patrick Kennedy, Jehu Hay, Jean B. Perrault, and Alexander Henry, Jr., also kept diaries of their travels through various parts of the Northwest.[84] These narratives constitute one of the principal sources for the history of that region.

Some of the persons mentioned above, including Hutchins, Pittman, Montresor, Gordon, and Carver, engaged in surveys while on their travels. The maps and plans of campaigns, forts, settlements, and rivers of the region which they produced enabled the British to publish the first maps based upon original surveys; hitherto they had been obliged to copy French maps.[85] Hutchins' surveys of the 1760's[86] were assembled by him in a book published in 1778 which served for many years as a guide to travellers and settlers and which

---

[82] Bibliography can be found in the works by Matthews, Volwiler, and Wainwright cited above.

[83] Documents on the captivity of Patten by the French, 1750-51, in Detroit, Canada, and France, and a map of the Ohio country attributed to him are published in Howard N. Eavenson, *Map Maker and Indian Traders; an Account of John Patten, Trader, Arctic Explorer, and Map Maker; Charles Swaine, Author, Trader, Public Official, and Arctic Explorer; Theodorus Swaine Drage, Clerk, Trader, and Anglican Priest* (Pittsburgh, 1949). One of the chapters in this book with the map had previously been published in Eavenson, "Who Made the 'Trader's Map'?" *Pa. Mag. Hist.*, LXV (Oct. 1941), 420-38. The map is also in Charles A. Hanna, *The Wilderness Trail* (New York, 1911. 2 vols.), II, 156.

[84] See the bibliographies cited above.

[85] Susan M. Reed, "British Cartography of the Mississippi Valley in the Eighteenth Century," *Miss. Valley Hist. Rev.*, II (Sept. 1915), 223; Erwin Raisz, "Outline of the History of American Cartography," *Isis*, XXVI (Mar. 1937), 378.

[86] Hutchins' plan of the Indian country in Ohio and his plan of the battle of Bushy Run were published in William Smith, *Historical Account of Bouquet's Expedition against the Ohio Indians in 1764* (Cincinnati, 1868). See also *The Courses of the Ohio River, taken by Lt. T. Hutchins, Anno 1766, and Two Accompanying Maps.* ed. by Beverly W. Bond, Jr. (Cincinnati, 1942); William L. Jenks, ed., "The Hutchins Map of Michigan," *Michigan History*, X (July 1926), 358-73. This article contains a journal by Hutchins of a tour during Apr. 4-Sept. 24, 1762 through the Indian country from Detroit; the journal is also printed in the *Sir William Johnson Papers*, X, 521-29, with a map from the Henry E. Huntington Library.

was copied by others.[87] Captain Pittman made surveys on the Mississippi River and in the Illinois country and later incorporated the data obtained in a book on that subject.[88] The manuscript reports and maps by these and other officers are in the Gage papers in the William L. Clements Library.[89] The British in 1788 also initiated hydrographic surveying on the upper Great Lakes.[90] Much of the work of these early surveyors, like that of other parts of colonial America, found its way to the British Museum in England. Archer B. Hulbert, a professor of history at Marietta College, assembled a collection of map photographs from the Crown map collection in the British Museum and placed sets in a number of American libraries.[91] Some British maps are included in a map collection selected by Louis C. Karpinski to show the gradual evolution of the Great Lakes and Michigan upon the map of North America.[92] American and English cartographers such as Lewis Evans and John Mitchell utilized the journals and maps prepared by military officers and traders in drafting maps depicting the Ohio Valley and the Old Northwest.[93] Besides geographical data, these maps fur-

[87] Thomas Hutchins, *A Topographical Description of Virginia, Pennsylvania, Maryland, and North Carolina*, ed. by Frederick C. Hicks (Cleveland, 1904. Reprinted from the original edition of 1778).

[88] Philip Pittman, *The Present State of the European Settlements on the Mississippi; with a Geographical Description of That River Illustrated by Plans and Draughts*, ed. by Frank H. Hodder (Cleveland, 1906). Originally published in 1770.

[89] Lloyd A. Brown, "Manuscript Maps in the William L. Clements Library," *The American Neptune*, I (Apr. 1941), 141-48; Michigan University, William L. Clements Library, *Guide to the Manuscript Maps in the William L. Clements Library*, comp. by Christian Brun (Ann Arbor, 1959), viii, 176-82.

[90] Roy F. Fleming, "Charting the Great Lakes," *Canadian Geograpical Journal*, XII (Feb. 1936), 69.

[91] Archer Butler Hulbert, ed., *The Crown Collection of Photographs of American Maps* (Cleveland, 1904-08. 5 vols.). A brief description appears in Grace G. Griffin, comp., *Writings in American History*, 1908, item 325. An index to the collection was published by Hulbert in 1909.

[92] Louis C. Karpinski, *Historical Atlas of the Great Lakes and Michigan, to Accompany the Bibliography of the Printed Maps of Michigan* (Lansing, 1931).

[93] Lawrence H. Gipson, *Lewis Evans; To Which Is Added Evans' A Brief Account of Pennsylvania* (Philadelphia, 1939); 56-60; Charles O. Paullin, *Atlas of the Historical Geography of the United States*, ed. by John K. Wright (Washington, New York, 1932), 13, plates 26, 89-90.

nish information relating to history, archaeology, ethnology, and natural conditions prevalent during the British regime.[94]

Inasmuch as traders who operated in the West were subject to government regulation and sometimes served as Indian subagents and militia officers, their papers reflect these activities. Most of the traders were local representatives of companies in Montreal or Philadelphia or had connections with them. Both companies and traders often became involved in land speculation, thereby subjecting themselves to the ordinances of the British Government.[95] Consequently, in addition to records relating to the business operations which are important for the economic history of the West, the papers of companies and traders contain letters, petitions, me-

[94] In addition to the titles cited above see also, British Museum, Department of Manuscripts, *Catalogue of the Manuscript Maps, Charts, and Plans, and of the Topographical Drawings in the British Museum* (London, 1844-61. 3 vols. in 4), III, 506-60; British Museum, Department of Printed Books, Map Room, *Catalogue of the Printed Maps, Plans, and Charts in the British Museum* (London, 1885. 2 vols.); Great Britain, Colonial Office Library, *Catalogue of the Maps, Plans and Charts in the Library of the Colonial Office* ([London], 1910); U.S. Library of Congress, Division of Maps, *A List of Maps of America in the Library of Congress,* comp. by Philip Lee Phillips, (Washington, 1901); Herman R. Friis, *A Series of Population Maps of the Colonies and the United States, 1625-1790* (American Geographical Society, *Mimeographed Publication* No. 3, New York, 1940), 24-46; Special Libraries Association, Geography and Map Division, Map Resources Committee, *Map Collections in the United States and Canada; a Directory.* Marie Cleckner Goodman (New York, 1954); Lloyd Arnold Brown, *Early Maps of the Ohio Valley: a Selection of Maps, Plans, and Views by Indians and Colonials from 1673 to 1783* (Pittsburgh, Pa., 1959). The Pennsylvania Historical and Museum Commission has an extensive collection of photostats of maps acquired from numerous depositories.

[95] The connections between the traders and the land companies can be traced in Clarence W. Alvord, *The Mississippi Valley in British Politics; a Study of the Trade, Land Speculation, and Experiments in Imperialism Culminating in the American Revolution* (Cleveland, 1917. 2 vols.), in which can be found extensive citations to British sources; and in Shaw Livermore, *Early American Land Companies; Their Influence on Corporate Development* (New York, 1939), 107 *et seq.* See also Kenneth P. Bailey, *The Ohio Company of Virginia and the Westward Movement, 1748-1792; a chapter in the History of the Colonial Frontier* (Glendale, Calif., 1939); Kenneth P. Bailey, ed., *The Ohio Company Papers, 1753-1817, Being Primarily Papers of the "Suffering Traders" of Pennsylvania* (Arcata, Calif., 1947); Alfred P. James, *The Ohio Company; Its Inner History* (Pittsburgh, Pa., 1959); Lois Mulkearn, ed., *George Mercer Papers Relating to the Ohio Company of Virginia* (Pittsburgh, Pa., 1954).

morials, charters, and trade licenses which would normally be in the public archives. If missing, they could no doubt be replaced from copies in the company records.

The papers of trading companies (or reproductions) are in numerous depositories in the United States, Canada, and Great Britain. A collection of the papers of B. and M. Gratz assembled from family papers and other sources is in the Missouri Historical Society and a selection of the most important documents has been published.[96] The letter books, 1723-94, account books, memoranda, lists of goods, and a ledger of Baynton, Wharton and Morgan, another Philadelphia firm that traded in the Illinois country, are in the Pennsylvania Historical and Museum Commission.[97] Original papers of George Morgan, 1766-1826, the representative of Baynton, Wharton and Morgan in Illinois, are in the Illinois Historical Survey at Urbana, Ill., and in the Carnegie Library, Pittsburgh, Pa.[98] The papers of John Askin, Indian trader and commissary of the Indian Department at Michilimackinac, 1764-79, and trader at Detroit, 1780-1802, are in the Burton Historical Collection of the Detroit Public Library and in the Canadian Archives.[99] An extensive published selection from the Askin papers pertains especially to the

[96] William V. Byars, ed., *B[arnard] and M[ichael] Gratz, Merchants in Philadelphia, 1754-1798; Papers of Interest to Their Posterity and the Posterity of Their Associates* (Jefferson City, Mo., 1916); Volwiler, *Croghan*, p. 347. The American Jewish Archives at Hebrew Union College, Cincinnati has a microfilm of Gratz papers obtained from a family collection.

[97] Morris K. Turner, "The Baynton, Wharton, and Morgan Manuscripts," *Miss. Valley Hist. Rev.*, IX (Dec. 1922), 236-41; George E. Lewis, *The Indiana Company, 1763-1798; A Study in Eighteenth Century Frontier Land Speculation and Business Venture* (Glendale, Calif., 1941), 333. The papers of both Baynton, Wharton, and Morgan and the George Morgan letter books were utilized in the compilation of the *Colls.* of the Ill. State Hist. Lib., vols. X, XI, XVI. Some references to Illinois and the Ohio will be found in "Selections from the Letter Books of Thomas Wharton, of Philadelphia, 1773-1783," *Pa. Mag. Hist.*, XXXIII (1909), 319-39, 432-53; XXXIV (1910), 41-61.

[98] Illinois University, Ill. Hist. Survey, *Guide to MS. Materials of Amer. Origin*, p. 69-70.

[99] Canada, Public Archives, MS. Div., *Preliminary Inventory, Record Group 19*, p. 11. An alphabetical list of the names of correspondents in the Askin papers is in the Canadian Public Archives.

years after 1778, since the papers for earlier years are meager.[1] The papers of William Edgar relating to his ventures in the fur trade, 1760-79, and to his partnership with Alexander and William Macomb of Detroit as suppliers to the British Army in the West, 1779-84, are in the New York Public Library.[2] Letters of Edgar and a ledger of Macomb, Edgar, and Macomb, containing a payroll of Detroit volunteers who went on the British expedition against the Americans in Kentucky in 1780, are in the Burton Historical Collection. The records of other fur traders and merchants in that depository include some of John Porteous, 1762-71, Thomas and John R. Williams, and a ledger of Jean Baptiste Barthe at Sault Ste. Marie, 1775-79. Additional papers of Thomas and John R. Williams, 1767-1854, are in Rutgers University Library. There are materials relating to shipping and shipbuilding on the Great Lakes and to the port of Detroit in the Burton Historical Collection. Papers of Robert Navarre, another Detroit official and fur trader, are in Central Michigan College Library at Mount Pleasant, Mich. The Baby family papers in the Bibliothéque St. Sulpice in Montreal contain materials relating to the fur trade at Mackinac; copies are in the Canadian Archives and in the Burton Historical Collection.

Reproductions from British Archives

Another major depository of materials relating to the Old Northwest is the Manuscript Division of the Library of Congress. These materials consist of reproductions from the principal archival and manuscript depositories of Great Britain and collections of private

---

[1] *The John Askin Papers*, ed. by Milo M. Quaife, (Detroit, 1928, 1931. 2 vols.). A list of names of persons in Detroit in 1789 taken from Ledger E of the Askin accounts is published in Burton, ed., *City of Detroit*, II, 1337-44. Besides correspondence and ledgers, the Askin papers include invoices, journals, an inventory book, and memorandum book.

[2] Canada, Public Archives, MS. Div., *Preliminary Inventory, Record Group 19*, p. 7; New York Public Library *Bulletin*, XXXV (June 1931), 345. Photostats are in the Canadian Public Archives, and typewritten copies of 21 pieces are in the Toronto Public Library.

papers. A continuous transcribing program was initiated in 1905 in the British Museum and in the Public Record Office in 1906.[3] Under a greatly expanded program inaugurated in 1927 by means of a grant from John D. Rockefeller, Jr., photostats and microfilms were obtained instead of longhand copies. In 1956 a program was initiated for substituting microfilm for the handwritten transcripts that had been procured in the early years of the program. Pertinent materials are in Audit Office Papers, Colonial Office Papers, Treasury Board Papers, War Office Papers, and Simcoe papers from the Public Record Office, as well as papers relating to the surrender of Fort Sackville (Vincennes), the Haldimand papers, and Sir William Johnson papers from the British Museum.[4]

The Library of Congress also has microreproductions of materials relating to the Old Northwest from the Canadian Public Archives. These include the papers of the Johnson family concerning Indian affairs which were carried off to Canada,[5] and correspondence between the British minister in the United States and the governors and lieutenant-governors of Canadian provinces and commanders of military forces from 1791 to about 1871.[6] A large part of the reproductions in the Library of Congress can be borrowed by institutions for research purposes.

The sources mentioned in this chapter could be used by the state archives or historical societies of the Old Northwest to reproduce and assemble complete collections of documents relating to the British regime in their particular areas. The Illinois Historical Survey has done much more in the way of research and documentation than any other agency in the region. Not until such collecting of materials has been accomplished will there be adequate documentary sources available to scholars writing on the history of the Northwest.

[3] Information on the conduct of the program is in the *Reports of the Librarian of Congress,* 1905-present.

[4] See U.S. Library of Congress, MS. Div., *Guide to MSS. Relating to American History, passim.*

[5] *Ibid.*, p. 229.

[6] *Ibid.*, p. 226-27; *Reports of the Librarian of Congress* 1930, 92; 1931, 84-85; 1933, 34.

Ecclesiastical Records

The Catholic priests in the Old Northwest remained under the juris-diction of the Bishop of Quebec throughout the British period and for some years after the cession of the region to the United States in 1783.[7] The Jesuits were expelled from Kaskaskia in 1763, and the Sulpicians withdrew from Cahokia that year. Father Sebastien L. Meurin, one of the expelled priests, soon returned, and was joined in 1768 by Father Pierre Gibault.[8] The latter was appointed vicar-general in 1769, and remained in Illinois until his removal in 1792 to New Madrid, Mo. Other priests served in Detroit and Sand-wich,[9] and in 1788 a congregation was organized on the River Raisin (Frenchtown, now Monroe, Mich.) where a settlement of French Canadians had been made in 1784.[10] In 1785, John Carroll, who had been appointed prefect apostolic of the Catholic Church in the United States in 1784, sent a priest to Illinois who established himself at Cahokia.[11] His appointee as vicar-general in Illinois coun-try, Father Pierre Huet de la Valinière, disputed the jurisdiction there with Father Gibault during 1786-87. Father Edmund Burke who was designated as vicar-general and superior of missions in Upper Canada in 1794, resided at the French settlement on the River Raisin in American territory until 1796.[12] In the same year, the transfer of authority at Detroit to the United States resulted in the transfer of ecclesiastical jurisdiction to John Carroll, who had been appointed Bishop of Baltimore in 1789.

[7] Hugh J. Somers, "The Legal Status of the Bishop of Quebec," *Cath. Hist. Rev.*, XIX (July 1933), 171.

[8] Palm, *Jesuit Missions*, p. 86-87; Fintan G. Walker, *The Catholic Church in the Meeting of Two Frontiers: the Southern Illinois Country (1763-1793)* (Washington, 1935), 34.

[9] See the detailed work based on archival sources by Paré on *The Catholic Church in Detroit*.

[10] Camillus P. Moes, "History of the Catholic Church in Monroe City and County, Mich.," *United States Catholic Historical Magazine*, II (Apr. 1888), 113-15.

[11] Walker, *Catholic Church*, p. 124; Alvord, ed., *Kaskaskia Records*, p. xxxv.

[12] Cornelius O' Brien, *Memoirs of Rt. Rev. Edmund Burke, Bishop of Zion, First Vicar Apostolic of Nova Scotia* (Ottawa, 1894), 13.

The records pertaining to the Catholic Church for 1760-96 are largely continuations of the records of the French period. Most of the churches remained in existence and continued to keep registers of baptisms, marriages, and burials. Information concerning these registers has already been given in the first chapter. A copy of the register of St. Joseph of Prairie du Rocher, 1761-99, is in the Canadian Public Archives.

The name of St. Anthony's Church at Frenchtown (Monroe, Mich.) was changed in 1845 to St. Mary's of the Immaculate Conception, and is still known by that name. That church has in its vault registers of baptisms, marriages, burials and minutes of the church committees dating back to 1794.[13] This church was served by missionaries from St. Anne's Church in Detroit, from 1788 to 1794, and entries can be found in the records of that church pertaining to the parishioners at Frenchtown. Photostats of the records are in the Burton Historical Collection.

Much correspondence between the Bishop of Quebec and the priests who served in the Illinois country and at Detroit is in the Archiepiscopal Archives of Quebec. A calendar containing entries for that correspondence has been published.[14] Transcripts of the material relating to Illinois are in the Illinois Historical Survey,[15] and numerous letters and other documents have been published,[16] as well as correspondence between the Bishop of Quebec and the Bishop of Baltimore containing references to the Old Northwest.[17]

[13] Letter from Rev. R. Francis Paquette, Pastor of St. Mary's Church, Monroe, Mich., Mar. 27, 1959.

[14] See the inventories by Ivanhöe Caron published in the *Rapport de l'archiviste de la province de Québec*, 1929-30, 47-136; 1930-31, 185-98; 199-351; 1931-32, 127-242; full titles in the bibliography.

[15] Illinois University, Ill. Hist. Survey, *Guide to MS. Material Foreign Depositories*, p. 107-08.

[16] Clarence W. Alvord, ed. "Father Pierre Gibault and the Submission of the Post Vincennes, 1778," *Amer. Hist. Rev.*, XIV (Apr. 1909), 551-57; C. W. Alvord, ed., *Kaskaskia Records*, p. 518-602; Alvord and Carter, eds., *New Regime, passim;* Alvord and Carter, eds., *Trade and Politics, passim.*

[17] Lionel St. G. Lindsay, ed., "Correspondence between the Sees of Quebec and Baltimore, 1788-1847," American Catholic Historical Society of Philadelphia, *Records*, XVIII (June, Sept., Dec. 1907), 155-89, 282-305, 434-67; Lionel St. G. Lindsay, ed., "Letters from the Archdiocesan Archives at Quebec," *ibid.*, XX (Dec. 1909), 406-30, contains letters of Gibault to Bishop Briand, 1768-88.

Considerable use has been made of the Archiepiscopal Archives of Quebec by historians, but they can still be drawn upon for an over-all treatment of the Catholic Church in the area.[18]

Some documentation can also be found in the records of the Bishop of Baltimore in the Baltimore Cathedral Archives. But since his connections with the Old Northwest were limited prior to 1796, the material is not extensive.[19] Whatever correspondence there may have been with Father Gibault and other priests in Illinois is now missing from the archives.[20] A compilation of the writings of Bishop Carroll is in preparation.[21] A collection of Gibault's papers including letters from Bishop Carroll is in the Missouri Historical Society at St. Louis.[22]

Small collections of material relating to the Catholic Church are in other depositories. The Canadian Archives has transcripts of miscellaneous records, and the reproductions from the British archives also contain data relating to the church. Other transcripts in the Quebec Archives consist of edicts, dispatches, memoirs, and correspondence, 1694-1827. The archives of the Archdiocese of Detroit in the custody of the University of Notre Dame include manuscripts dating from 1785.

The hierarchy of the Anglican Church at this time did not seem to have been especially concerned about the state of religion in Detroit. The Rev. George Mitchell arrived there in 1786 at the invitation of some officials and prominent citizens, but the English population was insufficient to support him and he departed in 1788.[23]

[18] John D. G. Shea and Peter Guilday drew upon these archives for their lives of John Carroll, and extensive use has been made of them more recently by George Paré, and F. G. Walker, and by Thomas T. McAvoy in his *The Catholic Church in Indiana, 1789-1834* (New York, 1940). McAvoy gives a useful bibliography of the manuscript sources, p. 209-12.

[19] A description of these records is in John T. Ellis, "A Guide to the Baltimore Cathedral Archives," *Cath. Hist. Rev.*, XXXII (Oct. 1946), 341-60.

[20] Alvord, ed., *Kaskaskia Records*, p. 509 n.1; McAvoy, *Catholic Church in Indiana*, p. 8.

[21] Henry J. Browne, "A New Historical Project: Editing the Papers of Archbishop John Carroll," *American Ecclesiastical Review*, CXXVII (Nov. 1952), 341-50.

[22] McAvoy, *Catholic Church in Indiana*, p. 9.

[23] Burton, ed., *City of Detroit*, II, 1228.

The lack of Anglican or other Protestant ministers obliged the lieutenant-governor to perform marriages, and baptisms of some infants of Protestant parentage were performed by the Catholic priests.[24]

24 *Ibid.*, p. 1224.

IV   The Records of Quebec and Ontario

on the British Regime

Because of the close relationships that existed between Quebec and the Old Northwest after the British conquest of Canada, many documents pertaining to that region accumulated in the records of the military governor, the civil governor, the Indian Department, the British Army commanders who were concerned with the administration of affairs in the West, and other officials. These relevant records form substantial sections of larger series concerned with the province as a whole and constitute an invaluable source for the history of the vast area that eventually became American territory. Since jurisdiction over the West was transferred to Upper Canada (Ontario) in 1791, the records of that province are of interest principally for the years 1791 to 1796, when control over the area finally passed to the United States.

PROVINCE OF QUEBEC

Brig. Gen. James Murray, who had been military governor of Quebec since 1759, was inaugurated as civil governor of Quebec on Aug. 10, 1764. The province was then provided with an official organization similar to that of the other royal colonies in North America. The governor was the direct representative of the King and had the powers of a chancellor and a vice-admiral, and for a while after 1766 he was also the military commander of the province.[1] Other officials included the following: chief justice, attorney-

[1] Duncan McArthur, "The New Regime," in Shortt and Doughty, eds., *Canada and Its Provinces*, III, 31-35; Francis J. Audet, "Gouverneurs, lieutenant-gouverneurs, et administrateurs de la province de Québec, des Bas et Haut Canadas, du Canada sous l'Union et de la puissance du Canada, 1763-1908," Royal Soc. Canada, *Procs. and Trans.* 3d. ser., II (1908), 85-124.

general, solicitor-general, surveyor-general, receiver-general of revenues, surveyor and auditor of public accounts, collector of customs, surveyor of woods, commissary of stores, adjutant general of militia, and the provincial secretary and registrar, who was also clerk of the council.[2] An executive council consisting of officials and other persons selected by the governor assisted him in the conduct of affairs.[3] There was no elective assembly prior to the Constitutional Act of 1791, though the proclamation of 1763 contained a provision for it.

Military affairs in Canada were controlled at times by the governor of Quebec and at other times by military officers. Upon establishment of the civil government in 1764, however, a northern military district was established under the command of Col. Ralph Burton.[4] The division of authority between Governor Murray and Burton resulted in strife between them, and brought about the appointment of Sir Guy Carleton in August 1766 to succeed them both.[5] When Carleton went to England for a visit in 1770, he was succeeded in the military command by Lt. Col. Augustine Prevôst. When Haldimand visited England in 1784, Lt. Gov. Henry Hamilton took over the administration of civil affairs, and Col. Barry St. Leger assumed command of the military forces. The staff of the northern military district included a deputy quarter-master general who was responsible for supplying the posts in the West.

The papers of the British commanders in chief in North America constitute an important supplementary source for Quebec's military and political affairs. Especially significant because of the length of his service are the papers of General Gage in which there are many letters to and from the brigadier generals at Quebec who

[2] James F. Kenney, "The Public Records of the Province of Quebec, 1763-1791," Royal Soc. Canada, *Procs. and Trans.*, 3d ser., sect. II, vol. XXXIV (1940), 107 *et seq.*

[3] William R. Riddell, "Pre-Assembly Legislatures in British Canada," Royal Soc. Canada, *Procs. and Trans.*, 3d ser., XII (June 1918), 111-12.

[4] S. Morley Scott, "Civil and Military Authority in Canada, 1764-1766," *Can. Hist. Rev.*, IX (June 1928), 125.

[5] Thomas Gage to Lord Barrington, Aug. 27, 1766, Carter, ed., *Corresp. of General Gage*, II, 368.

commanded the northern military district and the lieutenant-governors as well as other types of documents.[6]

The ranks of minor officials in Canada were enlarged by the British. At Montreal where the first English notary was appointed in 1762,[7] the office of sheriff was established in that year.[8] A coroner was also appointed to determine the causes of death in cases involving violence, negligence, etc.[9]

British record-making in Canada began with its conquest by the British in 1759-60. In addition to caring for the French records that were transferred to their custody, the British then started accumulating their own records. Since after 1764, (and more particularly after 1774) the military government of the Quebec Province concerned itself with the administration of affairs in the region south of the Great Lakes, its records are of particular interest for American history. The records of most of the officials and governmental bodies of Quebec have survived, but a special problem exists in the case of the official papers of the Quebec governors. Like their military contemporaries, the governors of Quebec regarded their papers as their own property and took them home to England. Consequently, except for documents which were referred to the council, few of the governors' papers remained in official hands.[10]

Governors' Papers

Insofar as possible the Canadian Public Archives has remedied the loss of the governors' papers by obtaining originals or copies from collections in England. The papers of James Murray, governor of Quebec from 1759 to 1766, were found in the possession of Mrs.

[6] S. Morley Scott, "Material Relating to Quebec in the Gage and Amherst Papers," *Can. Hist. Rev.*, XIX (Dec. 1938), 378-86.

[7] Edouard-Zotique Massicotte, "Le premier notaire anglais de Montréal, John Burke," *Bul. recherches hist.*, XXVIII (août 1922), 237-40.

[8] E.-Z. Massicotte, "Les sherifs de Montréal (1763-1923)," *Bul. recherches hist.*, XXIX (avril 1923), 107.

[9] E.-Z. Massicotte, "Les coroners de Montréal, 1764-1923," *Bul. recherches hist.*, XXIX (oct. 1923), 295.

[10] Kenney, "Public Records of Quebec," p. 108.

James Murray of Bath, England, and in 1910 transcripts were obtained.[11] A calendar of these papers was published in 1913,[12] and other letters were acquired in subsequent years.[13] Transcripts of Governor Murray's correspondence with General Haldimand are also available in the Canadian Public Archives.[14] The administration of Governor Murray is further documented in transcripts from the British Public Record Office, which will be mentioned later.

Sir Guy Carleton had several periods of service as governor of Quebec from 1766 to 1770, 1775 to 1778, 1786 to 1791, and 1793 to 1796. His papers were burned by his wife after his death in accordance with his orders,[15] and the historian of those years must therefore make use of the less extensive records preserved in Canadian and British archives. These records can be supplemented however by reference to the papers of Carleton's correspondents, such as Haldimand,[16] Lord Shelburne,[17] and General Gage.

The papers of Gen. Thomas Gage in the William L. Clements Library contain documents relating to his service as military governor of Montreal from 1760 to 1763. His jurisdiction extended only to the head of the St. Lawrence River, however, so that these manuscripts contain little relating to the Northwest during those years.[18]

---

[11] Canada, Public Archives, *Report*, 1910, 50.

[12] "Correspondence of General James Murray, 1759-1791," *ibid.*, 1912, Appendix I, 84-123.

[13] *Ibid.*, 1931, 8; 1947, ix. The acquisition of 1931 was in transcript form from the Pierpont Morgan Library, New York City, and that of 1947 was made by Gustave Lanctôt in England and consisted of letters addressed to Murray, 1760-63.

[14] Canada, Public Archives, "Haldimand Collection Calendar," *Report on Canadian Archives*, 1884, p. 70-95.

[15] Kenney, "Public Records of Quebec," p. 108; Arthur G. Bradley, *Lord Dorchester* (London, Toronto, 1926), xi. Carleton became Baron Dorchester in August 1786.

[16] Canada, Public Archives, "Haldimand Collection Calendar," *Report on Canadian Archives*, 1885, p. 236-71, covers correspondence of 1776-79; *ibid.*, 1887, 531-56, covers the years 1777-83.

[17] Parker, *Guide Public Archives of Canada*, p. 198-210; Canada, Public Archives, Manuscript Division, *Preliminary Inventory, Manuscript Group 21, Transcripts from Papers in the British Museum* (Ottawa, 1955), 17-21.

[18] John R. Alden, *General Gage in America; Being Principally a History of His Role in the American Revolution* (Baton Rogue, 1948), 55, 300.

Two letter books, Aug. 21, 1761 to Oct. 24, 1763, contain letters to Gage's subordinates and to General Amherst relating largely to military matters.[19]

The papers of General Haldimand in the British Museum and in transcript in the Canadian Public Archives are of great importance for the history of Canada and the Great Lakes region of the United States. The general served at Montreal under General Gage from 1760 to 1762, at Three Rivers in place of Colonel Burton from 1762 to 1763, again at Montreal from 1763 to 1764, and again at Three Rivers from 1764 to 1766. Returning to Canada he served as governor of Quebec and commander in chief of the military forces in the province from 1777 to 1783. For the years in Canada his papers are as complete as those for his service in other parts of North America. The collection includes correspondence with civil, military, and naval officials in Quebec and with British ministers, general orders, registers of military and naval commissions, instructions, military returns, and warrants. Included in the papers is correspondence with the British commanders in chief, Sir William Howe, Lt. Gen. Henry Clinton, and Sir Guy Carleton. The purport of these documents can be ascertained from a published calendar and a catalog.[20] Many documents from the Haldimand papers have been published;[21] a small quantity of Haldimand letters relating to Indian affairs is in the Thomas Gilcrease Institute of American History and Art at Tulsa, Oklahoma.

To build up a more complete collection of the correspondence of the early governors of Canada, Douglas Brymner, the first dominion archivist, initiated an extensive copying program in the

[19] Scott, "Material Relating to Quebec in the Gage and Amherst Papers," p. 384-85.

[20] Canada, Public Archives, "Haldimand Collection Calendar," *Report on Canadian Archives,* 1884-89 (Ottawa, 1885-90); British Museum, Dept. of MSS. *Catalogue of Additions,* I, 494-554. Haldimand's private diary for the period Jan. 1, 1786 to Aug. 12, 1790 is in the *Report on Canadian Archives* 1889, p. 123-299.

[21] See the citation in the previous chapter. Ernest A. Cruikshank, ed., *The Settlement of the United Empire Loyalists on the Upper St. Lawrence and Bay of Quinte in 1784; A Documentary Record* (Toronto, 1934), contains correspondence of May 1783-Nov. 1784, including numerous letters from and to Sir John Johnson and other British officers.

British Public Record Office. This depository contains records of the secretaries of state that are rich in material pertaining to the colonies. These records are the source for the copies of governors' papers already mentioned as well as those of other governors, lieutenant-governors, and administrators who served before 1796. These official records contain the original dispatches and enclosures received from Canada, and copies of communications and instructions sent to the governors. The series has been described as the most important collection in Canada for American history.[22] In the British Public Record Office it is known as C.O. 42 and in the Canadian Public Archives as Series Q.[23] The part relating to American history is calendared.[24]

Many topics are elucidated by the governors' correspondence. These include the administration of the western posts, Indian affairs, wars of the United States with the Indians, fur trade, the naval establishment and navigation on the lakes, Loyalist settlements, exploration, smuggling, and surveys on the lakes.[25]

Communications from Canada to the British government were dispatched in duplicate or triplicate. An extensive set of duplicates was acquired by the British Public Record Office, and in 1909 it was presented to the Canadian Public Archives. Consequently, the Archives has a file of contemporary copies for many documents in addition to the transcripts obtained over a hundred years later.

Provincial Records

The province of Quebec's civil and provincial secretaries' files was transferred to the Canadian Public Archives in 1906, and contains

[22] Parker, *Guide to Materials for U.S. History*, p. 154-55.

[23] C.O. for Colonial Office papers and Q for Quebec papers.

[24] Canada, Public Archives, [Calendar of] State Papers—Governors' Correspondence, Minutes of Council, Miscellaneous Letters and Papers, [1760-99], *Report on Canadian Archives*, 1890 (Ottawa, 1891). A list of the commissions and instructions issued to the governors of Canada can be found in Charles M. Andrews, "List of the Commissions and Instructions Issued to the Governors and Lieutenant Governors of the American and West Indian Colonies from 1609 to 1784," Amer. Hist. Asso. *Ann. Rep.*, 1911, I, 423-25.

[25] Charles O. Paullin and Frederic L. Paxson, *Guide to the Materials in London Archives for the History of the United States since 1783* (Washington, 1914), 278.

other executive records. These records (Series S) include petitions, letters, and reports addressed to the governor and his civil secretary, drafts of outgoing letters, proclamations, ordinances, commissions, court records, bonds, licenses and certificates, militia records, and civil service records.[26] Some of these records begin in 1760; others begin years later; all extend well into the nineteenth century. Much of the correspondence has been lost, particularly the outgoing letters, drafts of which do not start until 1796. The ordinances, proclamations, and other issuances of the military reign, 1759-64, have also been lost, but they have been recovered as far as possible from the British archives and collections in Canadian depositories, and published.[27] These decuments are also in print for later years down to 1791.[28] The foregoing records are voluminous and varied in con-

[26] An early description of these records can be found in Quebec (Province) Legislative Council, "Report of the Committee of Quebec on the Ancient Archives [Mar. 1790]," in Canada, Public Archives, *Report Concerning the Public Archives for the Year 1904* (Ottawa, 1905), Appendix D, *passim*. See also Kenney, "Public Records of Quebec," p. 113-14; Canada, Public Archives, Manuscript Division, *Preliminary Inventory, Record Group 4, Civil and Provincial Secretaries' Offices, Canada East, 1760-1867, Record Group 5, Civil and Provincial Secretaries' Offices, Canada West, 1788-1867* (Ottawa, 1953), 9-13.

[27] Canada, Public Archives, "Ordinances, Proclamations, etc., Issued by the Military Governors of Quebec, Montreal, and Trois Rivières, from the Capitulation of Quebec until the Establishment of the Civil Government on August 10, 1764," in *Report of the Public Archives* 1918 (Ottawa, 1920), Appendix B. For an earlier compilation of such documents see Jacques Viger, éd., *Règne militaire en Canada; ou administration judiciaire de le pays par les anglais du 3 septembre 1760 au 10 août 1764; manuscrits recueillis et annotés* (Montréal, 1870).

[28] Canada, Public Archives, "Ordonnances faites pour la province de Québec par le gouverneur et la conseil de la dite province depuis le commencement du gouvernement civil," in *Report of the Public Archives,* 1913 (Ottawa, 1915), Appendice E, p. 48-91; Canada, Public archives, "Ordinances made for the Province of Quebec by the Governor and Council of the said Province, from 1768 until 1791, being a Continuation of the Ordinances published as Appendix "E" of the Report of the Public Archives for 1913," in *Report,* 1914-1915 (Ottawa, 1916), Appendix C; Canada, Public Archives, "Proclamations Issued by the Governor-in-Chief from the Establishment of Civil Government on August, 10, 1764 until the Partition of the Province of Quebec into the Provinces of Upper and Lower Canada, on December 26, 1791," in *Report,* 1918 (Ottawa,, 1920), Appendix C, p. 401-71. See also Ontario, Department of Public Records and Archives, *Proclamations [Issued] by [the] Governors and Lieutenant Governors of Quebec and Upper Canada [1760-1840],* in *Fourth Report,* 1906 (Toronto, 1907). Proclamations, ordinances, and other documents were issued contemporaneously in broadside form or as supple-

tent and can be used for research on many subjects.[29] Many documents relate to Pontiac's conspiracy and Indian affairs, trade, and treaties in the West from 1761 onward.[30]

Important also for American history are the records of the Governor-General's Office (Series G) in the Canadian Archives. These include dispatches from the British Colonial Office to the governors of Quebec, 1784-90, to the governors of Canada, 1791-1909, and to the lieutenant-governors of Upper Canada, 1796-1841.[31] A calendar of the series for 1784-1841 has been published.[32] Replies to the dispatches are missing for the early years; drafts start in 1792 and the fair copies in letters-sent books start in 1799. But the Public Archives has transcripts of replies from the governors and lieutenant-governors to the colonial secretaries in the Colonial Office Papers of the Public Record Office, London. Other letters received by the governors are in bound volumes, and there are miscellaneous records for the last quarter of the eighteenth century.[33]

In the administration of Indian affairs, the province of Quebec continued to concern itself with Indians in United States territory. In Upper Canada after 1791, this interest continued not only until the transfer of territory in 1796, but for many years thereafter while British traders operated in American territory. When Col. Guy and Sir John Johnson fled to Canada early in the Revolutionary War, they took with them some valuable records relating to the administration of the northern Indian department in the preceding years.[34]

---

ments to *The Quebec Gazette* from 1764. Bibliography regarding them with library locations and places of publication is in Marie Tremaine, *A Bibliography of Canadian Imprints, 1751-1800* (Toronto, 1952); see also Charles R. Brown, "Bibliography of Quebec or Lower Canada Laws," *Law Library Journal,* XIX (Jan. 1927), 90-109. The items listed in Tremaine's bibliography have been microfilmed by the National Library of Canada; copies sell for $175.

[29] Gustave Lanctôt, *Les Archives du Canada* (Lévis, 1926), 12.

[30] Parker, *Guide to Materials for U.S. History,* p. 178-80.

[31] Canada, Public Archives, Manuscript Division, *Preliminary Inventory, Record Group 7, Governor General's Office* (Ottawa, 1953), 7.

[32] Canada Public Archives, *Report of the Public Archives,* 1930-33, 1935-38. (Ottawa, 1931-34, 1936-39). See the list, *ibid.,* 1949, 456. Because of the great importance of this series, its 436 volumes have been microfilmed.

[33] Canada, Public Archives, MS. Div., *Preliminary Inventory* RG 7, p. 10, 11-13.

[34] Parker, *Guide to Materials for U.S. History,* p. 2, 181.

These and similar records of later dates were kept for many years in the office of the secretary of Indian affairs at Montreal.

Custody of Indian affairs records was transferred in 1867 to the Office of the Superintendent of Indian Affairs for the federal government after the formation of the confederation of Canadian provinces. The records of the Indian Department, which were transferred to the Canadian Archives in 1907, include much important material relating to the United States. Records of the Superintendent of Indian Affairs for the Northern Department include Sir William Johnson's correspondence, 1756-72, with some memoranda and minutes of Indian councils.[35] The superintendents (Sir William and Col. Guy Johnson) kept a journal of their activities and of the minutes of councils with the Indians, 1755-72, 1779-80. The correspondence of Sir John Johnson, Superintendent-General after 1782, that of other officials of the Indian Department, and requisitions, reports, memoranda, etc. cover the period from 1791 to 1828. Somewhat more voluminous are the letters-received and other documents of William Claus, the Deputy-Superintendent-General, 1797-1830.[36] Part of the records of the Indian Department have been microfilmed by the Canadian Public Archives. Photostats of some of the records are in the Minnesota Historical Society collections,[37] and microfilm copies are in the State Historical of Wisconsin collections,[38] and in the Library of Congress.[39] Many documents from the Indian Department records relating to the superintendency of Sir William Johnson are in his published papers, which draw more largely, however, upon the Johnson papers described in Chapter III. Other papers of William Claus are in the Daniel Claus papers described in Chapter III.

The Indian Department records contain much material relating

[35] Canada, Public Archives, Manuscript Division, *Preliminary Inventory, Record Group 10, Indian Affairs* (Ottawa, 1951), 3.

[36] Texts of treaties with the Chippewa, 1781, at Mackinac Island, and 1786, at Bois Blanc Island are in Canada, *Indian Treaties and Surrenders, from 1680 to [1903]* (Ottawa, 1905-12. 3 vols.).

[37] Minnesota Historical Society, *MSS. Colls., Guide No. 2*, p. 33.

[38] Wisconsin, State Historical Society, *Guide Supplement No. One*, p. 21.

[39] U.S. Library of Congress, MS. Div., *Guide to MSS. Relating to Amer. History*, p. 229-30.

to the western Indians and to military affairs. The proceedings of councils at Detroit with Pontiac in 1766 and with the Huron, Ottawa, Chippewa, Shawnee, Six Nations, and Potawatomi tribes, 1781-90, are documented. There are also minutes of proceedings of congresses at Niagara with the Chippewa and Ottawa from Mackinac and Green Bay, the Huron from Detroit, and Indians from Lake Superior and Green Bay. Other minutes concern conferences at Fort Pitt in 1765 with the Shawnee, Delaware, Seneca, and Sandusky Indians. Proceedings of conferences held in the fall of 1764 with the Delawares and Shawnee on the upper Muskingum River by Colonel Bouquet were transmitted by Alexander McKee. Letters from Indian officials, including George Croghan, Alexander McKee, Matthew Elliott, Prideaux Selby, from Army officers at Detroit, Mackinac, and the Illinois country are in the Johnsons' correspondence. Extracts of a journal kept by McKee at Fort Pitt, Oct. 1773-May 1774, record talks to Shawnee chiefs, data on Indians, occurrences at the fort, and activities of the militia. Deeds, lists and descriptions of land transferred by the Huron, Ottawa, Chippewa, and Potawatomi in the neighborhood of Detroit are also in the Indian Department records.

Indian trade licenses and related papers are also among the records of the Indian Department. The collection includes duplicates of the licenses which were issued to the traders, usually accompanied by bonds, declarations supplying the information necessary for filling in the licenses, and consolidated returns summarizing the data on the licenses.[40] In 1924 the foregoing materials were examined by Prof. Wayne E. Stevens of Dartmouth College, an historian of the fur trade, and as a result of his examination he spent the summer of 1925 with an assistant under the sponsorship of historical societies of the Upper Mississippi Valley working on the records. They abstracted the licenses for 1768-75, and some declarations and photostated consolidated returns for 1777-91. Copies of the materials obtained are in the Minnesota Historical Society, the State

[40] "Report to Accompany Abstracts and Returns of Indian Trade Licenses," by Wayne E. Stevens, in Abstracts of Indian Trade Licenses in Canadian Archives, Ottawa, 1767-1776, Burton Historical Collection; Stevens, *Northwest Fur Trade*, p. 188. The text of a trade license issued by Carleton at Quebec on Apr. 15, 1769 is in Jacob R. Marcus, ed., *American Jewry Documents Eighteenth Century, Primarily Hitherto Unpublished Manuscripts* (Cincinnati, 1959), 398-99.

Historical Societies of Wisconsin and Iowa, the Burton Historical Collection, the Illinois Historical Survey, and the University of Saskatchewan Library; photostats of the licenses are on file at the University of Toronto Library. A sample of a consolidated return is in print, obtained from the Colonial Office Papers in the Public Record Office, London.[41] The British trade licenses, like the French voyageurs' contracts, have been neglected by the historians of localities. Since the British traders were required to give the names of all their employees, these records are genealogically valuable.

The records of Quebec's legislative and executive councils passed into the custody of a successor body, the Privy Council. Subsequently, the minutes of the councils disappeared, so the Canadian Public Archives transcribed the copies in the Board of Trade papers in the British Public Record Office.[42] When received in Canada, these copies became part of the Q series. The original minutes and other records of the executive and legislative councils of Quebec were found, however, in records received by the Canadian Public Archives from the Privy Council in 1907.[43] The accession included minute books of both councils, 1764-91, land board books, 1787-1791, reports of committees, and commissions.[44] Copies of the council minutes of 1778 to 1784 from the Haldimand papers have been calendared.[45] Selections from the minutes have been published in Doughty and Shortt's *Constitutional Documents.*

Judicial Records

The judicial records of the Quebec province are of little significance for the history of the West, since the records of the court of king's bench which had criminal jurisdiction for the whole province have

[41] Charles E. Lart, "Fur Trade Returns 1767," *Can. Hist. Rev.,* III (Dec. 1922), 351-58. See also Kellogg, *British Régime,* p. 102-03, 138-39, 140, 144, 146, 176, 181 for data relative to the licenses issued.

[42] Canada, Public Archives, *Report,* 1892, ii.

[43] Parker, *Guide to Materials for U.S. History,* p. 31-32.

[44] Kenney, "Public Records of Quebec," p. 111; Canada, Public Archives, Manuscript Division, *Preliminary Inventory, Record Group 1, Executive Council, Canada, 1764-1867* (Ottawa, 1953), 9. The minutes have been microfilmed.

[45] Canada, Public Archives, *Report,* 1886, 584-90.

been destroyed or lost.[46] As far as the history of the West is concerned this loss is not important, because few criminal cases were ever reported from that region.

The judicial archives in the courthouse at Montreal contain the records of several courts: for the court of common pleas, which handled civil matters, there are five registers in English, 1776-87, for causes involving over five pounds, and seven registers in French, 1776-91, for causes of over ten pounds.[47] Two English minute books for causes of over ten pounds can also be found in these records. The records of the prerogative court include two series of bound volumes containing acts of guardianship and marriage contracts.[48] The years covered extend from 1776 to 1799, but some volumes for 1780 are missing. Some cases tried in Montreal had their origins in what became American territory.

The notarial records of Quebec, Montreal, and Three Rivers, which form part of the judicial records of those places, were described in the second chapter. Since Montreal continued to be the center of the fur trade after the British conquest, the notarial records there contain many *engagements* of voyageurs and clerks and agreements between individuals and the companies engaged in the fur trade.[49] The transcripts obtained by Clarence M. Burton during 1895-98 cover the years down to 1820. These are now in the Burton Historical Collection of the Detroit Public Library and transcripts are available in the Canadian Public Archives. The contents of the *engagements* can be ascertained from a published calendar.[50] The notarial records are valuable for social, economic, and family history.

[46] Neatby, *Administration of Justice*, p. 128-29; Kenney, "Public Records of Quebec," p. 128-29; Henri Roy, "Les dossiers aux Archives judiciaires de Québec," *Bul. recherches hist.*, LI (jan.-fév. 1945), 65.

[47] Neatby, *Admin. of Justice*, p. 362-63. A schedule of causes tried in this court in 1787 is in *Mich. Hist. Colls.*, XI (1887), 624-25.

[48] *Ibid.*, p. 365.

[49] Canada, Public Archives, *Report*, 1883, 2; Parker, *Guide Public Archives of Canada*, p. 67.

[50] Quebec (Province) Archives, "Répertoire des engagements pour l'ouest conservés dans les Archives judiciaires de Montréal," en Quebec (Province) Archives, *Rapport de l'archiviste de la province de Québec*, 1932-33, 1942-43, 1943-44, 1944-45, 1945-46, 1946-47 (Québec, 1933, 1943-47), 245-304, 261-397, 335-444, 307-401, 225-340, 299-369.

Censuses

Censuses were infrequent in Quebec during the British regime. The Archives of the Seminary of Quebec has a census for 1762 which has been copied by the Quebec Provincial Archives.[51] In the latter depository is a census of Montreal and Three Rivers of 1765.[52] Although these censuses give only the names of the heads of families, they also show the number of married or single women, boys and girls under and over fifteen, men and women servants, and foreigners and refugees, the quantity of land, and the number of farm animals. Other materials supplement the formal censuses. The head of the chimney sweeps of Quebec prepared each year a list of citizens showing those who had paid for his work and those who had not. The list constitutes a directory of Quebec families.[53] A register of Canadian military officers for the year 1767 is also in print.[54]

Military Records

When the British army withdrew from Canada in 1870, the records of the military headquarters at Montreal were sent to Halifax for shipment to England. As a result of negotiations conducted with the London War Office in 1873, by the Canadian Archivist Douglas Brymner, it was agreed that the major portion of the records should remain in Canada and be deposited in the archives at Ottawa. This acquisition amounted to 200,000 documents, extending from 1761 for more than a century. Designated as Series C, the collection consists mainly of the papers of the military secretary of the British Government to the Canadian commander in chief, who was usually

[51] Amédée Gosselin, éd., "Le recensement du gouvernement de Québec en 1762," Quebec (Province) Archives, *Rapport de l'archiviste de la province de Québec,* 1925-26 [Québec, 1926], p. 1-143.

[52] "Le recensement des gouvernements de Montréal et des Trois-Rivières [1765]," *ibid.,* 1936-37 [Québec, 1937], p. 1-121.

[53] F.-J. Audet, "Les habitants de la ville de Québec en 1769-1771," *Bul. recherches hist.,* XXVII (mars, avril, juillet, août, 1921), 81-88, 119-25, 218-24, 247-52.

[54] Caron, *Colonisation de la province de Québec,* p. 251-62.

the governor of the Quebec province.[55] Most of the documents date from 1786 and become numerous only after 1791. The governor's papers constitute the bulk of the correspondence on military affairs in earlier years, particularly the private papers of Governor Haldimand. Series C consists of correspondence with the British War Office, the Admiralty, and the Treasury as well as with Canadian officials, and a variety of other documents such as reports, instructions, memorials, orderly books, journals, accounts, surveys, certificates, requisitions, circulars, payrolls, petitions, returns, maps, estimates, and proceedings.[56] The collection is arranged in groups of volumes relating to chaplains, commissariat, horse corps, Indians, medical matters, military posts, settlers, relations with the United States, and barracks. A partial card index for the series and indexes to volumes have been prepared by the Canadian Public Archives and a detailed inventory giving the contents of each volume with an analytical index has been published.[57] A list of the subject titles of the volumes composing the various groups is also in print.[58] Much material concerning the administration of the Northwest during the British regime can be found in these military papers.

The military papers also include correspondence and other records relating to the Provincial Marine that operated on the Great Lakes. The records in Series C date from 1776 onward.[59] Logbooks of several vessels which served on the Great Lakes during the later years of the war, including the *Angelica, Dunmore, General Gage,* and the *Welcome* are in the Burton Historical Collection.[60] Other material is contained in the papers of the British commanders in chief, including some for earlier years particularly in the Gage papers, as well as in the papers of the governors of Quebec and Upper

[55] Kenney, "Public Records of Quebec," p. 122-23.

[56] Parker, *Guide Public Archives of Canada,* p. 69-74.

[57] Ernest A. Cruikshank, *Inventory of the Military Documents in the Canadian Archives* (Ottawa, 1910). Cruikshank, who was an officer in the Canadian militia, was keeper of these military manuscripts from 1908 to 1911.

[58] Canada, Public Archives, Manuscript Division, *Preliminary Inventory, Record Group 8, British Military and Naval Records* (Ottawa, 1954), 7-12.

[59] Cruikshank, *Inventory of Military Documents,* p. 126; Canada, Public Archives, *Preliminary Inventory, RG 8,* p. 11; Parker, *Guide to Materials for U.S. History,* p. 28.

[60] Russell, *British Regime,* p. 277.

Canada. Besides correspondence, the Haldimand papers contain accounts, reports, returns, and miscellaneous papers relating to the Provincial Marine, 1774-84.[61] The naval establishment on the Great Lakes was also the subject of correspondence between the British governors in Canada and the Colonial Office; consequently the transcripts from series C.O. 42 of the records of that office in the Canadian Public Archives include pertinent material.[62] Much correspondence of Alexander Grant, the commodore of the Provincial Marine, will be found in the preceding sources, and in the Askin and the Simcoe papers. The papers of Alexander Harrow, a British naval officer on the Great Lakes, are in the Burton Historical Collection.

District of Hesse

As long as the British held the forts at Detroit and Mackinac, they were governed by Canada. The western portion of the province of Quebec above Montreal received a considerable influx of Loyalists and other settlers from the United States in the years immediately after the Revolution. For their benefit and for that of the citizens of Detroit, four new judicial districts were created in that part of the province which became Upper Canada (Ontario) by the governor's proclamation of July 24, 1788.[63] These districts were Lunenberg, Mecklenberg, Nassau, and Hesse; the last-named embraced the territory from Long Point on Lake Erie to Detroit and the other western settlements.[64] Since Detroit, Mackinac and their environs belonged by law to the United States, the limits of the district were not exactly defined.[65]

[61] British Museum, Dept. of MSS., *Catalog*, 1875, I, 530, 534, 542; Canada, Public Archives, "Haldimand Collection Calendar," *Report on Canadian Archives*, 1887, p. 467-535.

[62] Paullin and Paxson, *Guide to the Materials in London Archives*, p. 262.

[63] Neatby, *Admin. of Justice*, p. 284; Riddell, *British Rule*, p. 47; Kenney, "Public Records of Quebec," p. 125.

[64] Neatby, *Admin. of Justice*, p. 285-287.

[65] The proclamation stated that the district of Hesse was "to comprehend all the residue of Our said province, in the Western or inland parts thereof, of the entire breadth, from the Southerly to the Northerly boundaries of the same . . ." (Shortt and Doughty, eds., *Docs. Const. Hist. Canada*, II, 954).

Judicial systems were set up in the districts. The governor designated three Detroit residents, Jacques Duperon Baby, Alexander McKee, and William Robertson, as the justices of the court of common pleas of the district of Hesse, but since two of the appointees were merchants, among whom most of the litigation arose, the inhabitants as well as the appointees themselves protested and asked for the appointment of a qualified, salaried judge.[66] The result was the appointment of William D. Powell as district judge. Powell was a native of Boston who had studied law in Massachusetts and England and had practiced in Montreal. Powell opened the court of common pleas at L'Assomption (now Sandwich) across the river from Detroit on July 16, 1789, and resided in Detroit where most of the business of the court originated. Possessed of unlimited civil jurisdiction, this court could only commit for trial in criminal cases. Officials associated with the court were the clerk, bailiffs, and a sheriff.[67]

Other courts also operated within the district of Hesse. The prerogative court held by Judge Powell proved wills, issued letters of administration to the estates of intestates and debtors, and appointed legal guardians for infants. Sessions of this court were held from July 2, 1789 to 1792. It ceased in the latter year, following the enactment of a statute by the Upper Canada legislature on Oct. 15, 1792 providing that cases involving property and civil rights were to be handled according to English law.[68] The responsibility for preserving peace and punishing minor offenses was put in the hands of eight justices of the peace who were appointed to the district in 1788.[69] Sitting together as a court of quarter sessions, the justices had power to try by jury all criminal cases; in practice, however,

[66] Neatby, *Admin. of Justice*, p. 294-95; Riddell, *British Rule*, p. 53-54; Burton, ed., *City of Detroit*, I, 210-11; William R. Riddell, *The Life of William Dummer Powell, First Judge at Detroit and Fifth Chief Justice of Upper Canada* (Lansing, 1924), 57-58.

[67] The sheriff was Gregor McGregor, who was also the superintendent of inland navigation at Detroit; the clerk was Thomas Smith; and the coroner was George Meldrum.

[68] Riddell, *British Rule*, p. 369.

[69] *Ibid.*, p. 60; Burton, ed., *City of Detroit*, I, 210; Lajeunesse, ed., *Windsor Border Region*, 106, list the justices as follows: Alexander Grant, Guillaume La Motte, St. Martin Adhemar, William Macomb, Joncaire de Chabert, Alexander Maisonville, William Caldwell, and Matthew Elliott. The justices of the peace also performed marriages.

they sent all capital crimes to the court of oyer and terminer (to hear and determine by a court of assize) and general gaol (jail) delivery. The court of oyer and terminer and general gaol delivery met at Sandwich with Judge Powell on the bench to try cases of murder, burglary, and larceny.[70] An act of 1792 gave power to two justices forming a court of requests to try cases involving not more than 40 shillings.[71] The introduction of English law in 1792 necessitated the formation of a probate court in Upper Canada and of surrogate courts in the four districts.[72] These surrogate courts probated wills and issued letters of administration for the property of intestates. The court of quarter sessions was transferred from Detroit to Sandwich in 1796.

Legislation passed by the first legislature of Upper Canada modified the judicial system of the districts. To introduce English institutions as well as English law into the province, Governor Simcoe obtained the passage of a law on July 7, 1794 which abolished the courts of common pleas and placed full civil and criminal jurisdiction in a single court of the king's bench, thereby discontinuing all district courts modeled on the French system.[73] Deprived of his judgeship in the district of Hesse, Powell was commissioned in July 1794 as a member of the new provincial court and left Detroit for Newark (Niagara). However, the abolition of the courts of common pleas worked a hardship on people with small claims and caused legislation to be passed in 1794 for the establishment of district courts with jurisdiction where sums of twenty shillings to fifteen pounds were involved. The district court for the Western District met at Detroit under Judge James Harfly from 1794 until the beginning of the British evacuation in 1796.[74]

[70] Riddell, *British Rule*, p. 60-61.

[71] *Ibid.*, p. 267; William R. Riddell, *The Life of John Graves Simcoe, First Lieutenant-Governor of the Province of Upper Canada, 1792-96* (Toronto, 1926). 177-78; J. H. Aitchison, "The Courts of Requests in Upper Canada," *Ontario History*, XLI (1949), 125-32.

[72] The wills of Alexander Grant, Matthew Elliott, John White, John Butler, Joseph Brant, and others obtained from the records of the probate court of Upper Canada are in A. F. Hunter, ed., "The Probated Wills of Men Prominent in the Public Affairs of Early Upper Canada," Ont. Hist. Soc. *Papers and Records*, XXIII (1926), 328-59; XXIV (1927), 381-409.

[73] Riddell, *British Rule*, p. 358-59; Riddell, *Powell*, p. 80-82.

[74] Riddell, *British Rule*, p. 362-63; Burton, ed., *City of Detroit*, I, 232.

The records of most of the courts handling matters within American territory during the period from 1789 to 1796 are still extant. With the abolition of the court of common pleas for the District of Hesse in 1794, its records were transferred to the newly created court of king's bench. The records of the former court were missing for many years, but were accidentally discovered in 1910 upon the occasion of a visit by Clarence M. Burton to the vaults in Osgoode Hall, the home of Toronto, Ontario's high courts. The box, in which one of the missing court of common pleas minute books for the Western District was found, also contained the original court records for the old districts of Hesse, Mecklenberg, and Lunenberg.[75] On a visit to the same depository in 1913, William R. Riddell, the principal authority on the history of the courts, found the first volume of the original record for the court of common pleas for Hesse.[76] These records were soon published by the Province of Ontario.[77] They are complete except for the periods from Sept. 24, 1789 to May 19, 1791, Mar. 22 to Aug. 21, 1792, and Sept. 5, 1792 to Sept. 12, 1793; these periods had been cut out of the volume for some unknown reason. A few errors were observed by Riddell in the first printed edition of the records for the court of common pleas, and he republished them in correct form.[78] These records are useful for business, industrial and local history, biography, and land transactions.

Records are also extant for some of the other courts. The records of the prerogative court were found by Clarence M. Burton in the registrar's office at Chatham, Kent County, Ontario.[79] A photostat entitled "Register of His Majesty's Prerogative Court for the District of Hesse, 2nd July 1789" in the Burton Historical Collection covers the period from July 2, 1789 to Aug. 11, 1791. The records of the court of oyer and terminer and general gaol delivery, 1792-94,

[75] Ontario, Department of Public Records and Archives, *Records of the Courts of Justice of Upper Canada, Fourteenth Report of the Department of Public Records and Archives*, 1917, (Toronto, 1918), v. Hereinafter cited by report number.

[76] *Ibid.*, p. vi; Riddell, *British Rule*, p. 419.

[77] See the title in the note above.

[78] The text appears in Riddell, *British Rule*, p. 72-264, 268-332.

[79] *Ibid.*, p. 369, 479.

are in the Ontario Department of Public Records and Archives at Toronto and have been printed.[80] The Ontario Archives has the records for the court of king's bench of Upper Canada.[81] Except for presentments of the grand juries of April and July 1795, no records for the Detroit court of general quarter sessions of the peace are extant,[82] nor are there any records of the Detroit district court which met to try cases involving small monetary amounts.[83] Records for the court of assize and the court of nisi prius, which held sessions in the Western District during 1794-96, and the court of requests are also missing.[84] Copies of the judicial records of the District of Hesse are in the Canadian Public Archives.

An act of Upper Canada of July 9, 1793 provided for the validation of marriages which had been publicly contracted before a magistrate, a commanding officer or other person in public employ and the recording of testimony.[85] Marriages performed in Detroit during the period 1772-1794 were recorded under this act. The register shows the names of the marrying parties and of the officiating magistrate or other official, the date of marriage, and the date of registration. The register of marriages for the District of Hesse is in the Essex Historical Society, Windsor, Ont., and data drawn from it has been published.[86]

The papers of various governmental officials have also contributed to the documentation of affairs in the District of Hesse. A voluminous collection of the papers of William Dummer Powell in the Toronto Public Library includes papers concerning the administration of justice, the business of the Detroit land board, and his reports to Lord Dorchester.[87] Other Powell papers in the Canadian Public Archives contain correspondence, militia papers, and

[80] *Ibid.*, p. 333-55.
[81] Riddell, *Powell*, p. 91.
[82] Riddell, *British Rule*, p. 363.
[83] *Ibid.*
[84] *Ibid.*, p. 268, 361.
[85] The text of the act is in Canada, Public Archives, *Report*, 1921, Appendix, F, 409-12; W. R. Riddell, "The Law of Marriages in Upper Canada," *Can. Hist. Rev.*, II (Sept. 1921), 226.
[86] William R. Riddell, "Some Marriages in Old Detroit," *Mich. Hist. Mag.*, VI (1922), 111-30. Sample entries are in Lajeunesse, ed., *Windsor Border Region*, p. 200-01.
[87] Toronto Public Library, *Guide to MS. Coll.*, p. 66-67.

letters to his wife.[88] A great grandson, Commodore Amelius Jarvis, of Toronto, reputedly possessed other papers.[89] James (Jacques Duperon) Baby of Detroit was a member of the Executive and Legislative Councils and lieutenant-colonel of the Kent County militia after 1793. A small quantity of papers relating to his militia command are in the Toronto Public Library. John Askin and Alexander McKee were both connected with the militia of Detroit and Essex County, and pertinent materials are in their papers in the Canadian Public Archives.

ONTARIO (UPPER CANADA)

Government

An important change in the government of Canada resulted from the passage of the constitutional act of June 10, 1791 by the British Parliament.[90] The new provinces of Upper and Lower Canada created by that act were formed on Dec. 26, 1791 from the old province of Quebec. The British adopted the act because of the increase in population, the need to meet a demand for more representative institutions, and the desirability of separating the English from the French to overcome the constitutional difficulties that had rankled one side or the other ever since the British conquest.[91] The act provided for the establishment of legislative councils and assemblies for the provinces, and allowed the adoption of English civil law in place of the French for the new districts populated by British subjects. The western districts of the old province of Quebec, including that of Hesse, were comprised in Upper Canada, which lay immediately north of Lakes Ontario and Erie. The lieutenant-governors of the two provinces came under the authority of the governor-general at Quebec, but in practice this subordination was not enforced, and the lieutenant-governor of Upper Canada

[88] Canada, Public Archives, *Report,* 1904, xix, mentions the purchase of Powell papers. Canada, Public Archives, MS. Div., *Preliminary Inventory MS. Group 23,* p. 37-38.

[89] Riddell, *Powell,* preface, 192.

[90] Shortt and Doughty, eds., *Docs. Const. Hist. Canada,* II, 1031-51. A proclamation of Nov. 18, 1791 made the act effective in the two provinces on Dec. 26, 1791.

[91] Kennedy, *Constitution of Canada,* p. 84; Duncan McArthur, "Upper Canada," in Shortt and Doughty, eds., *Canada and Its Provinces,* III, 171.

functioned independently.[92] In military affairs, however, the governor-general did exercise supreme command, thus continuing the
role of the governor-general of the province of Quebec.[93]

The government of Upper Canada was inaugurated on July 9,
1792 at Kingston with the appointment of the chief officials as executive councillors and the taking of the oath as lieutenant-governor by Col. John Graves Simcoe.[94] Other officials included the
following:[95]

Chief Justice	William Osgoode
Receiver-General	Peter Russell
Attorney-General	John White
Solicitor-General	Robert Gray
Surveyor-General	David W. Smith
Naval Officer	Alexander Grant
Superintendent of Indian Affairs	Col. John Butler
Military Secretary	Maj. Edward B. Littlehales
Aide-de-camp	Lt. Thomas Talbot
Civil Secretary	William Jarvis
Clerk of the Executive Council	John Small
Assistant to the Surveyor-General	Thomas Ridout
	William Chewett
Clerk of the Legislative Council	Peter Clark
Sheriff	Alexander Macdonell
	William Coffin

[92] Charles Lucas, *A History of Canada, 1763-1812* (Oxford, 1909), 271, 279.

[93] G. R. Pearkes, "The Evolution of the Control of His Majesty's Forces," *Canadian Defence Quarterly*, X (July 1933), 467.

[94] Later in the same month the seat of government was moved to Newark (Niagara), and in 1797, after Fort Niagara was transferred to the United States, it moved to York. The name of this place was changed in 1834 to Toronto, by which it had been known prior to 1792. Simcoe had served in America during the Revolution in command of the Queen's Rangers. He maintained his headquarters and residence at Niagara in Navy Hall, which had originally been built for the use of the officers of the naval establishment.

[95] Riddell, *Simcoe*, p. 155, 169; Frank Yeigh, *Ontario's Parliament Buildings; or a Century of Legislation, 1792-1892, a Historical Sketch* (Toronto, 1893), 11; Jessee E. Middleton and Fred Landon, *The Province of Ontario, a History* (Toronto, 1927. 4 vols.), I, 45.

The legislature of the province consisted of the Legislative Council or upper house and the General Assembly. The members of the Legislative Council were appointed for life and included some of the executive councillors. This body possessed the power to veto bills passed by the assembly. Its first meeting occurred at Kingston on July 16, 1792. The assembly first convened at Newark on September 17 and held regular sessions thereafter. The elected representatives in the assembly from Kent County, both residents of Detroit, were Francis Baby and William Macomb. Another Detroiter, David W. Smith, represented Suffolk and Essex Counties. Some of the earliest legislation of Upper Canada concerned Detroit, though it was not mentioned by name because legally it was in American territory.

The Executive Council consisted of the chief justice, the receiver-general, the surveyor-general, and other persons appointed by Lieutenant-Governor Simcoe. Members of this body from Detroit were James Baby, a prominent merchant there, and Alexander Grant, the commander of the British navy on the Great Lakes.[96] Baby and Grant served for many years on this council as well as on the Legislative Council. The Executive Council performed consultative and fiscal functions, advising the governor on administrative matters and land grants, and passing the budget in a perfunctory manner. In the judicial field the council considered criminal cases and appeals and appeals in civil cases.

A decree of July 16, 1792 provided a new system of local government composed of nineteen counties for Upper Canada. The last named of these counties, Kent, was "to comprehend all the country not being territories of the Indians, not already included in the several counties herein before described, extending northward to the boundary line of Hudson's Bay, including all the territory to the westward and southward of the said line, to the utmost extent of the country commonly called or known by the name of Canada."[97] The confines of the county were worded thus indefinitely so as to include territory south of the lakes that had been ceded by

[96] Middleton and Landon, *Province of Ontario*, I, 45.

[97] Ontario, Dept. of Public Records and Archives, *Proclamations by Govrs. and Lt. Govrs.*, p. 179.

treaty to the United States but not actually transferred. So elastic were the southern and western boundaries of Kent County that they could be regarded as extending to the Ohio and Mississippi Rivers. For practical purposes, however, Kent County included the town of Detroit, a strip four miles deep along the upper Detroit River and south of Lake St. Clair and north of the Latranche or Thames River in the present Essex County.[98] The chief town of Kent County was Detroit, where the county government was centered. Essex County comprised the rest of the western peninsula between Lake St. Clair and Lake Erie.

At the time of the formation of the counties, the districts established in 1788 were given English names. Lunenberg, Mecklenberg, Nassau, and Hesse were changed to Eastern, Midland, Home, and Western, respectively. Lieutenants of counties appointed by Governor Simcoe under another act of the parliament had authority to designate magistrates and to nominate militia officers. James Baby became lieutenant of Kent County, and the same position was given to Alexander McKee for Essex.

Under the terms of the Jay treaty of Nov. 19, 1794 that settled matters in dispute between the United States and Great Britain, the British agreed to evacuate the forts in American territory along the Canadian border. Lt. Col. John F. Hamtramck of the U.S. Army took possession of Detroit on July 11, 1796; two days earlier Fort Miamis was occupied.[99] The British officials and many Detroit inhabitants moved across the Detroit River into Essex County, settling at Sandwich or Amherstburg, or participating in the founding of Malden (which eventually became Windsor, Ontario). A detachment of American soldiers under Maj. Henry Burbeck received the transfer of Mackinac on Sept. 1, 1796. The British garrison there moved to St. Joseph Island, where a new fort was already under construction.[1]

In 1792, the old province of Quebec passed its jurisdiction over

---

[98] Lajeunesse, ed., *Windsor Border Region*, p. lxxxv.

[99] Henry P. Beers, *The Western Military Frontier, 1815-1846* (Philadelphia, 1935), 4.

[1] Joseph and Estelle Bayliss, *Historic St. Joseph Island* (Cedar Rapids, Ia., 1938), 22-25.

the western country to the newly-formed government of Upper Canada. The new administration took over the functions which had been performed in Quebec in July 1792, but most of the administrative records were not transferred from the former seat of government. In most cases, these were an integral part of the records of Quebec povince and could not be easily separated for the purpose of transfer, with the result that most Toronto records date from the year 1792.

Simcoe Papers

The most important manuscripts relating to Upper Canada during the years 1792 to 1796 are the papers of John Graves Simcoe. When he retired from the governorship in the latter year he carried off his records to his home at Wolford Lodge in Devonshire, England, where they remained in the possession of his descendants. Transcripts of some Simcoe papers were obtained by George Coventry in 1860 for the Library of Parliament and in 1881 by the Canadian Public Archives, which also copied the Coventry transcripts. John Ross Robertson, publisher of the Toronto *Evening Telegram* and a collector of Canadiana, borrowed a box of the original papers in 1906, copied them, and returned them to England in 1907.[2] Robertson subsequently presented these transcripts to the Canadian Public Archives, where they were collated with the originals.[3] Some years later the original papers passed into the possession of a great grandson of Governor Simcoe, Willoughby P. Cole, of Southhampton, England. While the papers were in his hands, the Canadian Archives in 1921 had copies made of documents which had not previously been transcribed.[4] The original Simcoe papers were purchased by R. S. McLaughlin of Oshawa, Ont. and presented to

[2] Toronto Public Library, *Guide to MS. Coll.*, p. 83.

[3] Canada, Public Archives, *Report*, 1921, 9. Canada, Public Archives, MS. Div., *Preliminary Inventory, MS. Group 23*, p. 36-37. Copies of the Robertson transcripts and of the Canadian Public Archives transcripts are in the Toronto Public Library.

[4] Canada, Public Archives, *Report*, 1926, 12; 1929, 5, 12; 1931, 5. Name and subject indexes to the Simcoe papers are in the Canadian Public Archives.

the University of Toronto Library in 1946.[5] The original papers were restored to their rightful home when they were deposited in the Ontario Department of Public Records and Archives in 1952. The collection consists of a large number of letter books, bundles of loose papers, and a diary and water color sketches by Mrs. Simcoe.[6]

Other Simcoe manuscripts relating to the administration of Upper Canada are in the Sir Henry Clinton papers in the William L. Clements Library. Simcoe's letter book for 1791-93 is in the Henry E. Huntington Library at San Marino, Calif.

An extensive selection of Simcoe papers has been published, based chiefly on the Simcoe transcripts in the Canadian Public Archives. Other documents in the collection were drawn from the John Askin papers, the David W. Smith papers, the Claus papers, the Diocesan archives of Quebec, and from other collections.[7] The volumes contain correspondence with officials in England, Upper Canada and Lower Canada, with military officers, naval officers and Indian agents. Besides the governor's own letters the volumes include correspondence between subordinate officials, memoranda, notes, Indian speeches, memorials, proceedings of Indian conferences, and journals.

The Simcoe papers are valuable for civil administration, military and naval affairs, Indian relations and trade, navigation and shipbuilding on the lakes, land management, ecclesiastical affairs, local history, biography, boundary disputes, and economic and social life. In regard to Indian relations these were particularly crucial

[5] *Can. Hist. Rev.*, XXVII (June 1946), 230.

[6] The diary had been published from a transcript obtained before the removal of the Simcoe papers from England (John R. Robertson, ed., *The Diary of Mrs. John Graves Simcoe, Wife of the First Lieutenant Governor of the Province of Upper Canada, 1792-6* (Toronto, 1911.)

[7] Ernest A. Cruikshank, ed., *The Correspondence of Lieut. Governor John Graves Simcoe, with Allied Documents Relating to His Administration of the Government of Upper Canada* (Toronto, 1923-31. 5 vols.). The incidents of a tour made by Simcoe to Detroit in 1793 are recounted in a journal kept by his secretary and have been published: Henry Scadding, ed., *Journal Written by Edward Baker Littlehales . . . of an Exploratory Tour, Partly in Sleighs But Chiefly on Foot, from Navy Hall, Niagara, to Detroit. Made in the Months of February and March A. D. 1793, by His Excellency Lieut-Gov. Simcoe* (Toronto, 1889).

years, since the United States Army was then engaged in military campaigns against the Indians north of the Ohio River in territory the United States had never previously occupied. The Simcoe papers reveal information concerning the activities of the British among the Indians in American territory south of Detroit.

Provincial Records

The records of the Executive Council of Upper Canada were transferred by the Privy Council to the Canadian Public Archives in 1907. The Executive Council had kept the records relating to state matters separate from those relating to lands, and these were classified by the Public Archives as Series E and Series L, respectively. The state records (Series E) were further subdivided into minute books (E-1) containing a chronological record of the decisions of the council, 1797-1841 (1792-96 are in L 3); draft minutes and reports (E-2); and Upper Canada state papers (E-3), consisting of case files on the subjects taken up by the council.[8] Other subdivisions containing papers antedating 1796 are the archives, consisting of typed copies of documents concerning the constitutional development of Canada (E 9); and audit records (E 15). These records, and particularly series E 3, for which a calendar has been prepared, are valuable for biographies, genealogies, and administrative, legal, judicial, military, economic, religious, and local history. Typewritten copies of the minutes for 1792-96 are available in the Toronto Public Library. Many items relating to the United States are in the records.[9]

Other records of the province were kept by its secretary. A series designated as "Upper Canada sundries" contains letters, petitions, and reports from correspondents resident in North America.[10] A

[8] Canada, Public Archives, Manuscript Division, *Preliminary Inventory, R. G. 1, Exec. Council,* p. 9; W. G. Ormsby, "The Upper Canada State Papers: An Untapped Research Source," *Ontario History,* XLIII (Jan. 1951), 29-34. The state papers for 1792-1840 and the minutes for 1791-1867 have been microfilmed; positive copies are in the Ontario Department of Public Records and Archives.

[9] Parker, *Guide to Materials for U.S. History,* p. 32.

[10] Canada, Public Archives, *Preliminary Inventory, R.G. 5, Civil and Provincial Secretaries' Offices,* p. 18.

file of commissions and letters patent issued for appointments to offices includes commissions to justices of the peace in the District of Hesse, 1788-92. The secretary was also the custodian of a file of proclamations issued by the provincial government. A compilation of proclamations gathered from the official records and other sources has been published.[11] Other correspondence relating to Upper Canada is in the records of the Governor-General's Office already described in this chapter.

The proceedings of the Legislative Assembly of Upper Canada were recorded in journals and ordered to be printed. The originals are believed to have been destroyed in the burning of the government buildings at Toronto by American forces in 1813,[12] and the printed copies have disappeared. Fortunately, however, copies of the journals had been regularly dispatched to the Colonial Office in London and transcripts of these copies were obtained by the Canadian government in 1855 and placed in the Library of Parliament.[13] This set is not complete, as the journals for the assembly of 1794 are incomplete and those for 1795, 1796, and 1797 are missing.[14] Typewritten copies of the London journals were made in 1886 and deposited in the Departmental Office, Public Library, Osgoode Hall, Toronto, and in the Public Archives at Ottawa.[15] Later the manuscript proceedings of the assembly for June 2-11, 1794 were found among some old papers in the Parliament Building. Still other copies of the journals are in the Toronto Public Library. The copies in the Library of Parliament at Ottawa were used by the Ontario Department of Public Records and Archives for

---

[11] Ontario, Dept. of Public Records and Archives, *Proclamations [Issued] by [the] Governors and Lieutenant Governors of Quebec and Upper Canada [1760-1840], Fourth Report . . . 1906* (Toronto, 1907).

[12] Joseph-Edmond Roy, "Les archives du Canada, à venir à 1872," Royal Soc. Canada, *Procs. and Trans.,* 3d ser., IV (1910), 101; Ontario, Dept. of Public Records and Archives, *Sixth Report,* 1909, xi; J. Franklin Jameson, "Colonial Assemblies and Their Legislative Journals," Amer. Hist. Asso., *Ann. Rep.,* 1897, 407; Matilda Edgar, *Ten Years of Upper Canada, the Ridout Letters* (Toronto, 1890), 186.

[13] Ontario, Dept. Public Records and Archives, *Sixth Report,* 1909, xi.

[14] *Ibid.,* p. xi.

[15] *Ibid.,* p. xi, 53; see Jameson, "Colonial Assemblies," p. 405 and 407-08 for a list of the journals.

printing the journals.[16] The proceedings of the Legislative Council are also in print.[17]

Publication of the statutes of Upper Canada began in 1793 when those for the first session of 1792 and the second session of 1793 were issued at Niagara in separate editions.[18] These, together with the laws of the third and fourth sessions were issued by Gideon Tiffany at Niagara with an imprint of 1795, but were actually published in the spring of 1796.[19] This edition was also issued later in 1796 by Tiffany with the laws of the fifth session. The laws for 1792-93 were republished again in 1922.[20] The early editions of the laws are extremely rare; a reprint of the early laws would be a useful publication.

The papers of many early Upper Canadian officials will be of great value in the documentation relating to affairs in American territory. In addition to serving as acting governor after the departure of Simcoe in 1796, Peter Russell was Receiver-General and a member of the Executive and Legislative Councils of Upper Canada from 1792 to 1808. His papers in the Toronto Public Library contain material relating to public accounts and legislative matters as well as administrative affairs.[21] The published collection derived from those papers and other sources is important since it deals with the transfer of the border posts to the United States and with relations between the British and the Indians in American territory

[16] Ontario, Dept. of Public Records and Archives, *The Journals of the Legislative Assembly of Upper Canada for the Years 1792, 1793, 1794 (partly), 1798, 1799, 1800, 1801, 1802, 1803, 1804, Sixth Report,* 1909 (Toronto 1911).

[17] Ontario, Dept. of Public Records and Archives, *The Journals of the Legislative Council of Upper Canada for the Years 1792, 1793, 1794, 1798, 1799, 1800, 1801, 1802, 1803, 1804, 1805, 1806, 1807, 1808, 1810, 1811, 1812, 1814, 1819, Seventh Report,* 1910 (Toronto, 1911).

[18] Tremaine, *Bibliography of Canadian Imprints,* p. 405.

[19] *Ibid.,* p. 466; W. George Easkins, "The Bibliography of Canadian Statute Law," *Law Library Journal,* I (Oct. 1908), 64.

[20] Canada, Public Archives, "Statutes of Upper Canada, 1792-1793," *Report of the Public Archives for the Year 1921* (Ottawa, 1922), Appendix F, p. 373-425.

[21] Toronto Public Library, *Guide to MS. Coll.* p. 74-75.

during subsequent years.[22] Another member of the Executive Council and Chief Justice of Upper Canada (1792-94) was William Osgoode, whose correspondence is in the Law Society of Upper Canada, Osgoode Hall, Toronto.[23] A diary of June 21, 1792-April 5, 1794, by John White, the first Attorney-General, recording a journey from Montreal to Kingston and events at the latter place and Niagara, is in the Toronto Public Library, and a photostat from the original is in the Canadian Public Archives.[24] Some papers of William Jarvis, the civil secretary, and of his wife, are in the Canadian Public Archives.[25] In 1958, the latter institution acquired letters written by White to Samuel Shepherd, his brother-in-law, 1792-99.

Land Records

The settlement of the western part of the Quebec Province by Loyalists from the United States began after the Revolution along the upper St. Lawrence, the Bay of Quinte, the Niagara River, and the Detroit River.[26] Between 1783 and 1789 locations of land were

---

[22] Ernest A. Cruikshank and A. F. Hunter, eds., *The Correspondence of Peter Russell with Allied Documents Relating to His Administration of the Government of Upper Canada . . .* (Toronto, 1932-36. 3 vols.).

[23] More important for his official activities, however, are transcripts of his letters in the Canadian Public Archives, Series Q, in the University of Toronto Library, and in the Ontario Department of Public Records and Archives, which have been drawn upon for a small published collection, "Letters from The Honorable Chief Justice William Osgoode," ed. by William Colgate, *Ontario History*, XLVI (Spring, Summer 1954), 77-95, 149-68.)

[24] Canada, Public Archives, MS. Div., *Preliminary Inventory, MS. Group 23*, p. 38.

[25] *Ibid.*, p. 37. See also "Letters from the Secretary of Upper Canada and Mrs. Jarvis to Her Father, the Rev. Samuel Peters, D.D. [1792-1813]," Women's Canadian Historical Society, Toronto, *Transactions*, XXIII (1923), 11-63.

[26] George C. Patterson, *Land Settlement in Upper Canada, 1783-1840* (Ontario, Dept. of Public Records and Archives, *Sixteenth Report*, 1920, Toronto, 1921), 32. The diary of a traveller on the Detroit River in 1787 records the names of settlers along the east bank of the river south of Sandwich as follows: Alexander McKee, William Caldwell, Charles McCormack, Robert Eurphleet, Anthony St. Martins, Matthew Elliott, Henry Bird, Thomas McKee, and Simon Girty (Middleton and Landon, *Province of Ontario*, I, 34.) The grants of land obtained by the foregoing men (among whom were officials at

assigned to Loyalists and disbanded troops by deputy surveyors on the authority of certificates issued by the governor, the acting governor, or the deputy surveyor-general. An appointment as deputy surveyor for Niagara and Detroit was given to Philip R. Frey, who was sworn in at Detroit by William Monforton on Mar. 30, 1785.[27] He first located at Niagara, since there was little business in Detroit at that time. In 1788, however, he moved to Detroit, where he became subordinate to the land board of the District of Hesse.

The influx of settlers necessitated an expansion of the administrative machinery, and in 1789 land boards were created in the districts into which the western part of the province had been divided the preceding year. The boards took over from the governor and council the function of approving land titles in order to eliminate the delays that had been experienced previously by claimants.[28] The boards passed upon the applications for land grants, issued certificates for permission to settle for presentation to the deputy surveyor, and sent their reports to the governor. Organized at Detroit in August 1789, the land board of the District of Hesse was composed of Maj. Patrick Murray, William D. Powell, Alexander McKee, William Robertson, and Alexander Grant.[29] The commandant at Detroit usually presided; Major Murray was succeeded by Maj. John Smith and Smith by Col. Richard England. An increase of the business before the board caused its membership to be enlarged on May 1, 1791 by the addition of several prominent loyalists, including John Askin, George Leith, and Montigny

---

Detroit) from the Indians in 1783 and the years following were confirmed by order of Lord Dorchester in 1788 (Lajeunesse, *Windsor Border Region,* p. ciii). For an account of the settlement of the Canadian side of the Detroit River and lists of settlers thereon, see *ibid.,* p. cii-cxxix, 357-60.

[27] Willis Chipman, "The Life and Times of Major Samuel Holland, Surveyor General, 1764-1801," Ont. Hist. Soc., *Papers, and Records,* XXI (1924), 52-53. Holland, an engineer officer who had served with the British Army in America, had been appointed Surveyor-General of Quebec and Surveyor-General of the northern district of North America in March 1764, but prior to the Revolution he was engaged in surveys on the coast.

[28] Patterson, *Land Settlement,* p. 24.

[29] Ontario, Dept. of Public Records and Archives, "Board of Land Office for the District of Hesse, 1789-1794, Minutes of Meetings, etc.," *Third Report,* 1905 (Toronto, 1906), 2.

de Louvigny. Though the board had received over three hundred applications by the fall of 1791, the issuance of location certificates was delayed by disputes over Indian titles and by the lack of qualified surveyors.[30] The board was placed in a position to issue certificates when it signed a treaty with the Indians on May 21, 1790 providing for a cession of land already occupied for the most part under Indian grants or by transfer from speculators. Patrick McNiff succeeded to the deputy surveyorship in 1789, and during the following years was occupied in making surveys from Long Point to Detroit. The lands along the Detroit River had to be resurveyed to settle boundary disputes between settlers because the French survey describing the grants had been lost.[31] To accelerate the work of the land board, the District of Hesse was reduced to the counties of Essex and Kent in 1792. The Executive Council of Upper Canada decided that the land boards were no longer needed, and terminated them on Nov. 6, 1794. Thereafter, certificates of recommendation for two hundred acres were issued by magistrates, and locations were made by the deputy surveyor. This practice ceased in December 1795, and afterward applications for land were made to the provincial government.

Records relating to land grants in Upper Canada, including the District of Hesse and the counties of Essex and Kent, were accumulated by various agencies of the governments of Quebec Province and after 1791 by the Province of Upper Canada (Ontario). The Executive Council minute books, containing the decisions of the land committees on petitions for land grants, were transferred in 1907 to the Canadian Public Archives.[32] The first two volumes of the minutes of Quebec (also called "Land Books" Series L 1), for Feb. 17, 1787 to Dec. 24, 1791, are concerned chiefly with early grants to Loyalists in Ontario.[33] Certified copies of these minutes

[30] Alfred L. Burt, *The Old Province of Quebec* (Toronto, 1933), 395-97.

[31] MacDonald, "Alexander Grant," p. 171.

[32] Parker, *Guide to Materials for U.S. History*, p. 31-32; Canada, Public Archives, *Report*, 1908, p. 17.

[33] Canada, Public Archives, MS. Div., *Preliminary Inventory R.G. 1, Exec. Council*, p. 12; James J. Talman, "Early Ontario Land Records as a Source of Local History," *Western Ontario Historical Notes*, VIII (Sept. 1950), 131-32; Parker, *Guide to Materials for U.S. History*, p. 32; Kenney, "Public Records of Quebec," p. 111.

have been made available for researchers, and portions of the books relating to Upper Canada have been published.[34] Land transactions in Ontario have been recorded in the minute book series, volumes 18 and 19, covering 1787-91 and 1792-96. These minute books provide a key to the petitions which will be mentioned later. Photostats of the minute books are in the Ontario Department of Public Records and Archives at Toronto. A chronological record can be found in the minutes books of the land regulations and their administration, and of the decisions of the land committee relative to land matters in the Hesse District.

The most voluminous land papers are the petitions or applications from individuals for land grants dating from 1788. These and a variety of miscellaneous land records were also transferred from the Privy Council to the Canadian Public Archives in 1907. The petitions (Series L 3) are arranged by year and alphabetically by name to correspond to numbered references in the minute books of the Executive Council. Earlier unnumbered petitions are arranged in the same manner. These petitions have been indexed on three by five cards and microfilmed. Some of the early ones have been published, including many from residents of Detroit.[35] A register of patents (the issuance of which did not start until May 1795) is in the Crown Lands Office, Parliament Building, Toronto. An index of patents in the Office of the Provincial Secretary in the same building is an aid to finding the area in which a settler located and facilitates searching in local registry offices.[36]

The land board of Hesse district kept minutes of its transactions and sent copies regularly to the governor in council at Quebec. The

[34] Ontario, Dept. of Public Records and Archives, *Grants of Crown Lands in Upper Canada, 1787-1791," Seventeenth Report*, 1928 (Toronto, 1929). The preceding title is continued for 1792-96 (*ibid.*, 1929.)

[35] Ernest A. Cruikshank, ed., "Petitions for Grants of Land, 1792-6," Ont. Hist. Soc., *Papers and Records*, XXIV (1927), 17-144; continued for 1796-99, *ibid.*, XXVI (1930), 97-379.

[36] Talman, "Early Ontario Land Records," p. 132. See also United Empire Loyalist Centennial Committee, Toronto, *The Centennial of the Settlement of Upper Canada by United Empire Loyalists 1784-1884; the Celebrations at Adolphustown, Toronto, and Niagara, with an Appendix Containing a Copy of the U.E. List Preserved in the Crown Lands Department at Toronto* (Toronto, 1885), p. [125]-334.

records of the land board passed into the possession of the government of Upper Canada and were eventually acquired by the Ontario Department of Public Records and Archives from the Department of Lands, Forests, and Mines. The published minutes of the board supply information regarding residents of Detroit who acquired land on the Canadian side of the Detroit River.[37]

The records of the Heir and Devisee Commission created under an Upper Canada statute of 1797 to clarify land titles in the province contain documents relating to residents of Detroit who obtained land in Upper Canada. The commission considered claims of those holding land as heirs, devisees or assignees of the original nominees and issued patents for approved claims, provided that the surveyor-general reported valid titles. The records include certificates issued by the Hesse District land board on the qualifications of petitioners to receive grants of land, schedules of certificates accompanying reports of the land board, certificates by individuals as to improvements of lots in the settlement near the mouth of the Detroit River, permits by Major Murray to occupy lots, and certificates of recommendation for land grants.[38]

Other land records relating to the period before 1796 are in the Canadian Archives. These include minutes and correspondence of the Hesse District land board; correspondence and accounts regarding the collection of the King's rents, taxes, and quitrents at Detroit, 1775-84, correspondence between the commandants at Detroit and the governors at Quebec, a list of French concessions at Detroit, lists of settlers on the east side of the Detroit River and north of Lake Erie, instructions on surveys, and letters of the deputy surveyor, Patrick McNiff. There are also land certificates, acknowledgments, affidavits, bonds, deeds, grants, licenses of occupation, land receipts, certificates of character and performance of settlement duties, land exchanges and surrenders, recommendations for land grants, vouchers, regulations, instructions, and re-

[37] Ontario, Dept. of Public Records and Archives, *Board of Land Office for the District of Hesse, 1788-1794, Minutes of Meetings, etc., Third Report,* 1905. (Toronto, 1906). Other records of the board were reported to be missing (*ibid.,* cxxxi, p. 189).

[38] Canada, Public Archives, *Preliminary Inventory, R.G. 1, Exec. Council,* p. 14-15.

ports.[39] Rolls of United Empire Loyalists are also in the Canadian Public Archives.[40] The lack of public vital statistics records in Ontario necessitates the use of the land records as an index to the citizens of the province prior to commencement of registers of vital statistics in 1869.

Important materials relating to lands in Ontario were accumulated in the Office of the Surveyor-General of Quebec before 1791 and thereafter in the Office of the Surveyor-General of Upper Canada. The records of the former officer eventually passed into the possession of the Department of Lands and Forests at Quebec and include letters received and copies of instructions to surveyors.[41] The letters sent after 1767 as well as surveyor reports and field notes are missing.[42] At an unknown date, correspondence with the land boards and the deputy surveyors in Upper Canada was removed from these records for transmittal to the provincial government, of that province, and they are now in the Ontario Department of Public Records and Archives. Materials are available in the same depository relating to the administration of lands from other sources.[43] Maps transferred from Quebec are in the Division of Surveys of the Department of Lands and Forests in Toronto.[44]

The records of the Surveyor-General of Upper Canada are in the Department of Lands and Forests and in the Department of Public Records and Archives in Toronto. The collection includes correspondence with land boards and deputy surveyors, transcripts of surveyors' field notes, instructions to surveyors, orders in coun-

[39] *Ibid.*, p. 12-14; Canada, Public Archives, *Report,* 1908, 19; Parker, *Guide to Materials for U.S. History,* p. 32.

[40] Canada, Public Archives, *Report on Manuscript Lists in the Archives Relating to the United Empire Loyalists, with Reference to Other Sources,* comp. by William Wilfred Campbell [Ottawa?], 1909.

[41] Kenney, "Public Records of Quebec," p. 119-20.

[42] *Ibid.*, p. 120.

[43] Ontario, Dept. of Public Records and Archives, *Third Report,* p. xxiii-xxv, xxxii.

[44] A list of maps in the Surveyor-General's Office, Quebec, Nov. 12, 1790, is in Ontario, Dept. of Pub. Records and Archives, *Seventeenth Report,* 1928, p. 131-32. A catalog of maps in that office relating to Detroit and vicinity and Michilimackinac is in *Mich. Hist. Colls.,* XXIV (1885), 43-44.

cil, copies of patents, lists of settlers, maps, and diaries.[45] An extensive selection from these records was microfilmed by the Canadian Public Archives on thirty-five reels in 1959. A small quantity of materials derived from these records illustrates their character and value for the history of settlements in the region.[46] A photostat of a map of Detroit prepared by Patrick McNiff in 1791, obtained from the original in England, is in the William L. Clements Library. In 1796, McNiff presented another map of Detroit to Gen. Anthony Wayne, based in part on the 1791 map and showing the land owners on the American side of the Detroit River. The Division of Surveys of the Ontario Department of Lands and Forests has materials by McNiff in the surveyors' letters, field notes, and maps, but none by deputy surveyor Phillip R. Frey. Other surveyor-general's records relating to lands in Ontario from 1792 onward are in the Canadian Public Archives,[47] where there are also transcripts dated 1764-89 of documents in the Library of Parliament,[48] and cartographic materials received with the land papers.[49]

The papers of David William Smith, Surveyor-General of Upper Canada from 1792 to 1804, were purchased for £32 by the Toronto Public Library in 1888. The collection contains much material of an official nature relating to lands in Ontario and Detroit, including correspondence, returns of lands granted by the Executive Council up to 1797, and accounts, 1792-1802, as well as private letters.[50] Copies of the Smith papers are in the Ontario Department of Public Records and Archives.

[45] Patterson, *Land Settlement in Upper Canada,* p. 253-54; Alexander Fraser, "The Ontario Archives," Amer. Hist. Assoc., *Ann. Rep.,* 1911, I, 356.

[46] J. J. Murphy, ed., "Documentary History of the First Surveys in the Province of Ontario," Association of Ontario Land Surveyors, *Proceedings,* No. 13 (1898), 196-231.

[47] Canada, Public Archives, *Report,* 1908, p. 19; Canada, Public Archives, *Preliminary Inventory, R.G. 1, Exec. Council,* p. 15.

[48] Canada, Public Archives, *Report,* 1930, ix.

[49] These are listed together with other maps in the collections of transcripts and the original records in Canada, Public Archives, *Catalogue of Maps, Plans and Charts in the Map Room of the Dominion Archives,* classified and indexed by H. R. Holmden (Ottawa, 1912).

[50] Toronto Public Library, *Guide,* p. 84-85.

No guide to the public records of Ontario has been published. Since the records are divided among the Ontario Department of Public Records and Archives, the Canadian Public Archives, and public offices of Ontario, a guide or inventory which would bring together in one place information regarding the records would be extremely helpful. The preparation of such an inventory should take precedence over the publication of documents. The *Ontario Series* of the *Publications* of the Champlain Society, to which the Government of Ontario makes a financial contribution, contains some volumes of selected documents on the British period.[51] Compilations of limited geographical scope, like that by Cruikshank on Niagara,[52] could be undertaken for places in the United States, such as Mackinac and Vincennes.

Reproductions from British Archives

Inasmuch as the Canadian civil and military officials were in constant communication with the governmental departments in Great Britain to which they were subordinate, the original records in Canada can be supplemented by transcripts of records at the British Public Record Office in London.[53] The papers of the officials

[51] Richard A. Preston, ed., *Kingston before the War of 1812; a Collection of Documents* (Toronto, 1959). The documents in this compilation are from originals or transcripts in the Canadian Public Archives and other sources, and relate to the settlement of United Empire Loyalists and the establishment of Kingston. Maps and rolls of names are included. Another volume in this series, frequently cited in these pages, is that by Lajeunesse on the *Windsor Border Region*. Since it is devoted to the eighteenth century when the governing officials of the area were located at Detroit and includes numerous documents drawn up there, it is of considerable value for the history of Detroit, though Lajeunesse was mainly concerned with the neighboring city of Windsor and the Canadian shore of the Detroit River. Another in this series is Edith G. Firth, ed., *The Town of York, 1793-1815; a Collection of Documents of Early Toronto* (Toronto, 1962). The volume contains letters and/or information on William D. Powell, Matthew Elliott, Alexander McKee, and Angus Mackintosh.

[52] Ernest A. Cruikshank, ed., "Records of Niagara [1778-1792], Niagara Historical Society, *Publications*, Nos. 38-41 (1927-30). Continued for later years, *ibid*.

[53] Descriptions of these records together with some administrative history of the agencies which created them can be found in Charles M. Andrews,

who headed those departments have historical importance, as well as the papers of provincial Canadian governors and military officers who served in Canada and the American colonies. Many collections of papers are preserved in the British Museum,[54] and others are in other depositories in Great Britain[55] and in the United States.

Guide to the Materials for American History to 1783, in the Public Record Office of Great Britain (Washington, 1912. 2 vols.); Paullin and Paxson, *Guide to the Materials in London Archives;* and in Great Britain, Public Record Office, *A Guide to the Manuscripts Preserved in the Public Record Office,* comp. by M. S. Guiseppi (London, 1923-24. 2 vols.); for further information, see Great Britain, Public Record Office, *Guide to the Contents of the Public Record Office, Volume I, Legal Records, etc., Volume II, State Papers and Departmental Records* (London, 1963. 2 vols.). Works on the administrative history of the agencies and on archive and manuscript collections will be found listed in Stanley Pargellis and D. J. Medley, eds., *Bibliography of British History; The Eighteenth Century, 1714-1798* (Oxford, 1951); Lillian M. Penson, ed., "Bibliography," in J. Holland Rose, A. P. Newton, and E. A. Benians, gen. eds., *The Old Empire from the Beginnings to 1783 (The Cambridge History of the British Empire,* Vol. I, New York, Cambridge, England, 1929), 824-88; Arthur G. Doughty and R. G. Trotter, "Bibliography," in *Canada and Newfoundland, op. cit.,* VI (New York, Cambridge, 1930), 813-85. Records of the British Foreign Office are not without some pertinence; they are described in Daniel H. Thomas and Lynn M. Case, eds., *Guide to the Diplomatic Archives of Western Europe* (Philadelphia, 1959), 98-124. For current bibliography regarding the British archives see *Archives, the Journal of British Records Association,* no. 1- 1949- (London, 1949-). See also Virginia 350th Anniversary Celebration Consultants in History and Archives to the Joint Commission, *The Search Room Catalogues and Other Finding Aids to the Records Preserved in the Public Record Office* (Charlottesville, 1957); Virginia Colonial Records Project, *The British Public Record Office; History, Description, Record Groups, Finding Aids, and Materials for American History with Special Reference to Virginia* (Richmond, Va., 1960).

[54] Charles M. Andrews, and Frances G. Davenport, *Guide to the Manuscripts Materials for the History of the United States to 1783, in the British Museum, in Minor London Archives, and in the Libraries of Oxford and Cambridge* (Washington, 1908); Arundell J. K. Esdaile, *The British Museum Library; A Short History and Survey* (London, 1946).

[55] Jessie E. Beckman, "The British Historical Manuscripts Commission," *The American Archivist,* VII (Jan. 1944), 41-48; John Franklin Jameson, "Guide to the Items Relating to American History in the Reports of the English Historical Manuscripts Commission and Their Appendixes," Amer. Hist. Asso., *Ann. Rep.,* 1898, 611-700; Great Britain, Historical Manuscripts Commission, *A Guide to the Reports on Collections of Manuscripts of Private Families, Corporations and Institutions in Great Britain and Ireland Issued by the Royal Commissioners for Historical Manuscripts* (London, 1914, 1935. 2 vols.). There has been under way for some years a National Register of Archives, cov-

These sources have been drawn upon for reproductions by numerous institutions in both the United States and Canada.

The Canadian Public Archives, established in 1872 as the Archives Branch in the Department of Agriculture, initiated a transcribing program in the British archives in 1882. During the early years transcripts were obtained of material relating to the French and Indian War, and of selected documents relating to Canada from the year 1760 in the correspondence of the governors, lieutenant-governors, and administrators of Quebec, Lower Canada, and Upper Canada in the Colonial Office Papers of the British Public Record Office in London.[56] While the transcribing was still going forward, the Public Archives which designated the transcripts as Series "Q" began publishing calendars of the correspondence in 1890.[57] Descriptions of this series, including enclosures originating at the British posts in the West, are also in print.[58] These documents comprise the most important collection in the Public Archives of material relating to American history. A special search was made for instructions to governors, which were scattered in several series in the Colonial Office Papers; copies were made of them from 1763 onward,[59] and a compilation of these for

ering family papers and institutional archives; it also has in its custody the results of a survey of ecclesiastical archives made by the Pilgrim Trust (Great Britain, Historical Manuscripts Commission, *Bulletin of the National Register of Archives,* Nos. 1-8, London, Nov. 1948-1956); Lionel W. Van Kersen, "The National Register of Archives," *American Archivist,* 23; 319-37 (July 1960).

56 The progress of the program can be traced in the *Reports on Canadian Archives,* 1883 onward.

57 The calendars appear in numerous reports published between 1890 and 1945 and cover the correspondence of the years 1760 to 1841. The calendars on materials dated before 1796 are in the reports for 1890-1892. A complete list of the calendars is in Canada, Public Archives, Manuscript Division, *Preliminary Inventory, Manuscript Group 11, Public Record Office, London, Colonial Office Papers* (Ottawa, 1952), 31-32. See also Canada, Public Archives, "Guide to Calendars of Series and Collections in the Public Archives," *Report,* 1949 (Ottawa, 1950), 453, and the bibliography of this book.

58 Parker, *Guide to the Public Archives,* p. 99-161; Canada, Public Archives, *Preliminary Inventory, MS. Group 11,* p. 31-35; Parker, *Guide to the Materials for U.S. History,* p. 154-73.

59 Canada, Public Archives, *Report,* 1892, i; Canada, Public Archives, MS. Div., *Preliminary Inventory, MS. Group 11,* p. 47; Charles M. Andrews, "List of the Commissions and Instructions," p. 424-26.

the years 1763-87 is in print.[60] Transcripts of the correspondence between the British commanders in chief in North America and the Secretary of State concerned with the colonies in that hemisphere are also of great historical value. These records were formerly classified in the Colonial Office Papers as "America and the West Indies" and reclassified as "C.O.5."[61] Other transcripts were derived from the Board of Trade papers,[62] the War Office, the Admiralty, and the Treasury Solicitor. Photostats of maps were also obtained.

The Canadian Public Archives inaugurated a microfilming program in the Public Record Office in 1950,[63] and began another in 1952 of series C.O.42, transcripts of which were already available in Ottawa designated as series Q.[64] These transcripts were made, however, at a time when permission had not been given for the copying of minutes, notes, etc., which had been added to the documents by the British officials. Since these annotations were regarded as valuable and since microproductions usually provide an exact copy of the original documents (thereby eliminating copyists' errors), a microfilming program was begun. The microfilm camera has also replaced longhand copying for other materials.

Manuscript Collections

A number of volumes in the military papers (Series C) of the Canadian Public Archives are of considerable importance for the study of Indian affairs in Quebec and in Upper Canada after 1791. Correspondence of the military secretary with officials of the Indian Department, and army officers is in this series.[65] In these

[60] Canada, Public Archives, "Instructions to Governors [Colonial Office Records, 1763-1787]," *Report Concerning Canadian Archives* . . . 1904 (Ottawa, 1905), Appendix E, p. 191-286.

[61] Parker, *Guide to Material U.S. History*, p. 115.

[62] Canada, Public Archives, "Calendar of Series C.O. 42," *Report of the Public Archives* 1921 (Ottawa, 1922), Appendix D, p. 283-359. This calendar covers Jan. 1763-Apr. 1821.

[63] Canada, Public Archives, *Report*, 1950, 14.

[64] *Ibid.*, 1952, 18-19; 1953-54, 20-21; 1955-58, 43.

[65] Parker, *Guide to Public Archives Canada*, p. 72.

military records is to be found much information regarding the western Indians, the campaign conducted against them by the American army, the treaty of Greenville, and Indian relations in the United States up to the War of 1812.

The North West Company was formed during the American Revolution by a number of Montreal firms and traded for nearly a half a century on the western lakes, the country to the west and the north and on the Upper Mississippi River.[66] Its center of operations in the West was at Grand Portage, Minn., located at the lake end of the portage extending from Lake Superior to the navigable waters of the Pigeon River.[67] Agents of the company were located at Detroit and Milwaukee in the 1790's, and about 1800 a post was established at Pembina, on the Red River, a point which later proved to be in American territory (North Dakota).[68] Subsequently the company's operations were extended to the Missouri River and the Minnesota River, and it inevitably came into conflict with the Hudson's Bay Company. The two companies were finally united in 1821, and part of the North West Company's records were transferred to the Hudson's Bay Company. Other records were later sold at auction and became scattered in numerous depositories, including the Canadian Public Archives, the University of Toronto Library, the Toronto Public Library, the McGill University Library, and the Burton Historical Collection.[69] Copies of other documents, which had been collected by the first Baron Strathcona, were purchased by the Canadian Public Archives in 1955.[70] The Archives later acquired the papers of Simon McGillivray, containing correspondence, memoranda, and diaries. Accounts, agreements, auto-

[66] Gordon C. Davidson, *The Northwest Company* (Berkeley, 1918); Harold A. Innis, "The North West Company," *Can. Hist. Rev.*, VIII (Dec. 1927), 311-12.

[67] Solon J. Buck, "The Story of Grand Portage," *Minn. Hist.*, V (Feb. 1923), 14-27.

[68] John P. Pritchett, "Some Red River Fur Trade Activities," *Minn. Hist.*, V (May 1924), 404.

[69] William S. Wallace, *The Pedlars from Quebec, and Other Papers on the Nor'westers* (Toronto, 1954), vii; Marjorie E. W. Campbell, *The Northwest Company* (New York, 1957), 285-90; Canada, Public Archives, *Preliminary Inventory MS. Group 19*, p. 12, 15, 16-19.

[70] Canada, Public Archives, *Report*, 1955-58, 30-31.

biographical notes, letters, journals, reminiscences, narratives, and sketches have been published.[71] As recently as 1954 the Canadian Public Archives purchased three volumes kept by Angus Mackintosh, the North West Company agent at Detroit, containing letters, 1793-1803, a petty ledger, 1806-15, and inventories, 1819-22.[72] Other papers of Angus and Alexander Mackintosh are in the Burton Historical Collection. Some reproductions of North West Company papers are in the Minnesota Historical Society collections.[73]

The Hudson's Bay Company, which was chartered by the British Government in 1670, possessed trading and administrative rights in western Canada. Its records are of some significance for the history of the Northwest because it operated a number of posts in American territory adjacent to the boundary west of Grand Portage, and settlers at the colony established by Lord Selkirk on the Red River in the company's territory migrated to and traded with Fort Snelling at the junction of the Mississippi and Minnesota Rivers. The records of the company are preserved in its London office and constitute the largest and most valuable body of documents relating to Canada outside of public archives.[74] Under an

[71] Louis F. R. Masson, *Les Bourgeois de la Compagnie du Nord-Ouest Récits de voyages et rapports inédits relatifs au nord-oeust canadien* (Québec, 1889-90. 2 vols.); Canada, Public Archives, "North-Western Explorations," *Report*, 1890 (Ottawa, 1891), Note C, p. 48-66; William S. Wallace, ed., *Documents Relating to the North West Company* (Toronto, 1934). Wallace's book includes the minutes of meetings of the company at Grand Portage and Fort William, 1801-1807, and other documents from the Canadian Public Archives and the Montreal notarial records, as well as the Hudson's Bay Company House in London, the Bibliothèque de St. Sulpice in Montreal, the Edgar papers in the Detroit Public Library, and other places. A letter and two partnership agreements of 1787 are in R. Harvey Fleming, "McTavish Frobisher and Company of Montreal," *Can. Hist., Rev.*, X (June 1929), 145-52.

[72] Canada, Public Archives, *Report*, 1953-54, 15.

[73] Minnesota Historical Society, *MSS. Colls. Guide No. 2*, p. 21, 28, 34, 41, 47, 63, 84, 107. A record of a case tried by the court of king's bench at Montreal, involving a dispute over trading rights at Grand Portage in which the North West Company was the defendant, is printed in Grace L. Nute, ed., "A British Legal Case and Old Grand Portage," *Minn. Hist.*, XXI (June 1940), 117-48.

[74] R. H. G. Leveson-Gower, "The Archives of the Hudson's Bay Company," The Beaver, CCLXIV (1933), 40-42; CCLXV (1934), 19-21, 37-39; CCLXVI (1935), 22-24; Arthur S. Morton, "Business Methods and the Archives of the Hudson's Bay Company," Canadian Historical Association, *Re-*

agreement concluded in Oct. 1949, the Canadian Public Archives and the company have jointly microfilmed its records.[75] The Canadian Archives has reproductions of the papers of Thomas Douglas, fifth Earl of Selkirk, concerning the Red River settlement and his conflict with the North West Company.[76] A microfilm of these Selkirk papers is in the Manitoba Legislative Library, Archives Branch. Some original records relating to the same subjects are also in the Canadian Archives.[77] Transcripts obtained by Agnes C. Laut from the records of the Hudson's Bay Company and from the Selkirk papers are in the Newberry Library, Chicago,[78] and additional copies of correspondence from the Selkirk papers preserved at St. Mary's Isle, Scotland, for 1806-24, and materials relating to the Hudson's Bay Company are in the Minnesota Historical Society collections.[79] Documents have been published from this collection and others from the archiepiscopal archives in Quebec relating to missions established in the upper Mississippi River region under the sponsorship of Lord Selkirk.[80] The availability of the Hudson's Bay Company records in the Canadian Public Archives makes pos-

port, 1938, 134-44; E. E. Rich, "The Hudson's Bay Company's Activities; Forthcoming Publication of Documents by Hudson's Bay Company Records Society," *Pacific Historical Review*, VII (Sept. 1938), 267-73. A series of volumes has since been edited by Rich and published as the *Hudson's Bay Company Series* by the Champlain Society, but the volumes thus far published do not relate to American territory except in the Oregon country.

[75] Canada, Public Archives, *Report*, 1950, 13-14; 1952, 16-18; 1953-54, 21-22; 1955-58, 44-46.

[76] Canada, Public Archives, MS. Div., *Preliminary Inventory, MS. Group 19*, p. 25-27; Chester B. Martin, *Lord Selkirk's Work in Canada* (Oxford, 1916), 8; Chester B. Martin, ed., *Red River Settlement: Papers in the Canadian Archives Relating to the Pioneers* (Ottawa, 1910); "Selkirk Settlement; Letter Book of Captain Miles MacDonnell (From Archives: Selkirk Correspondence.)" in Canada, Public Archives, *Report*, 1886 (Ottawa, 1887), Note F, clxxxvii-ccxxv.

[77] Canada, Public Archives, *Preliminary Inventory, R.G. 4*, p. 15.

[78] Newberry Library, Chicago, *Edward E. Ayer Collection; A Checklist of Manuscripts in the Edward E. Ayer Collection*, comp. by Ruth L. Butler (Chicago, 1937), 60-61. Miss Laut was the author of *The 'Adventurers of England' on Hudson Bay; A Chronicle of the Fur Trade in the North* (Toronto, Glasgow, 1914).

[79] Minnesota Historical Society, MSS. Coll., *Guide No. 2*, p. 44, 62-63, 78, 84, 85, 135-36.

[80] Grace Lee Nute, ed., *Documents Relating to Northwest Missions, 1815-1827* (St. Paul, 1942).

sible the preparation of definitive studies regarding its operations.[81]

No program for the publication of comprehensive compilations of documents has been undertaken by the Canadian Public Archives, since the institution has been too busy assembling materials and bringing them under control to attempt to initiate such a program. As the citations in these pages show, however, it has published some of the primary documents such as ordinances and proclamations as well as calendars of correspondence.[82] More recently, it has published a much needed series of preliminary inventories covering holdings of records, reproductions, and manuscripts, which enable investigators to ascertain more easily the nature of those holdings. Positive copies of microfilmed reproductions from foreign archives and of the other holdings of the Public Archives, whenever they are available, are loaned for research purposes.

Very few of the manuscript depositories in Canada have published guides. Until these become available or until the union catalog of manuscripts now under way is compiled, it will be difficult to locate materials. Directories of historical societies and libraries provide the names of institutions which might have pertinent material.[83] The Canadian Public Archives has inaugurated a cooperative program with historical societies for the preparation of inventories of their records.

---

[81] Prof. Rich utilized the records in the preparation of *The History of the Hudson's Bay Company, 1670-1870* (London, 1958-59. 2 vols.). The notes and bibliography omitted from the published work are available in an annotated copy in the Canadian Public Archives.

[82] See also William P. M. Kennedy, ed., *Statutes, Treaties and Documents of the Canadian Constitution, 1713-1929* (Toronto, 1930).

[83] See American Association for State and Local History, *Directory [of] Historical Societies and Agencies in the United States and Canada, 1963* (Madison, Wis., 1963), 83-87; and the latest edition of the *American Library Directory*, which includes Canadian libraries. Canadian authorities have given consideration to the preparation of inventories and guides and the publication of documents, and have initiated programs (as indicated in the present work) that will no doubt serve as examples to private depositories; see George W. Brown, "The Problem of Public and Historical Records in Canada," *Can. Hist. Rev.*, XXV (Mar. 1944), 1-5; Canada, Royal Commission on National Development in the Arts, Letters, and Sciences, 1949-1951, *Royal Commission Studies; a Selection of Essays Prepared for the Royal Commission on National Development in the Arts, Letters and Sciences* (Ottawa, 1951), containing articles by C. P. Stacey on "Canadian Archives," p. 231-48, and by W. L. Morton on "Historical Societies and Museums," p. 249-59.

Ecclesiastical Records

The advent of British rule in Canada resulted in the introduction of Protestant churches. Chaplains of the Church of England connected with the British military forces began conducting services in Quebec and Montreal in 1760, and soon afterwards at Three Rivers.[84] A clergyman from New York began Anglican services at Sorel in 1784. John Stuart, a missionary of the Society for the Propagation of the Gospel in Foreign Parts, of London, England, was sent to the western district of Quebec Province, traveled as far as Niagara in 1784, and settled at Kingston in the following year. Robert Addison, an Anglican minister sent to Niagara in 1792, served as chaplain to the army and to the assembly of Upper Canada, missionary to the Indians, and parish priest. A Presbyterian church was organized in Quebec soon after the conquest, and in 1786, one was founded in Montreal.[85] Other early parishes of the Anglican Church were St. John at Sandwich (1802), St. James at Toronto (1803), and Cornwall (1802).

The work of preserving and collecting the diocesan archives was undertaken about 1926 by an historical records committee of the Church Society of the Diocese of Quebec.[86] A search in the recesses of the cathedral brought to light a small group of parchments consisting of crown commissions, letters patent, and letters testimonial relating to the parishes of Quebec and Ontario. A collection of Bishop Mountain's correspondence which had been sent from England by descendants of his family to the bishopric was

[84] Henry C. Stuart, *The Church of England in Canada 1759 to 1793* (Montreal, 1893), 7-14; Thomas R. Millman, *Jacob Mountain, First Lord Bishop of Quebec; A Study in Church and State* (Toronto, 1947), 36-37.

[85] William Gregg, *Short History of the Presbyterian Church in the Dominion of Canada from the Earliest to the Present Time* (Toronto, 1893), 18-19.

[86] Arthur R. Kelley, "The Quebec Diocesan Archives, A Description of the Collection of Historical Records of the Church of England in the Diocese of Quebec," Quebec (Province) Archives, *Rapport de l'archiviste de la province de Québec pour 1946-1947* (Québec, [1947]), 184. Kelley was a member of the committee.

also turned over to the records committee.[87] These three groups, designated as series A, B, and C, all begin in 1793. A transcribing program was intiated in 1930 with financial assistance from the Canadian Government to build up a collection of documents for the period 1759 to 1793 which continued for many years. Transcripts were obtained from the archives of the Society for the Propagation of the Gospel, the Canadian Public Archives, the Sewell papers in the Diocese of Ontario Synod Office at Kingston, the Henry Scadding collection in the Toronto Public Library, and other places.[88] The transcripts are designated as series D, and a digest of the collection has been published.[89] The materials assembled by the records committee have been housed since 1932 in the Quebec Provincial Archives. Reproductions from the archives of the Society for the Propagation of the Gospel in Foreign Parts in the Canadian Public Archives include correspondence from the missionaries and journals of the society.[90]

Though Protestant churches in Quebec were not required to keep registers of vital statistics until the passage of the registration act of 1795, there are registers which begin much earlier. Copies of the

[87] *Ibid.*, p. 185, 212-19; Arthur R. Kelley, ed., "Jacob Mountain, First Lord Bishop of Quebec; A Summary of His Correspondence and of Papers Related Thereto for the Years 1793 to 1799 Compiled from Various Sources," *ibid.*, 1942-1943, 179.

[88] Kelley, "Quebec Diocesan Archives," p. 185-86, 233-34; Toronto Public Library, *Guide*, p. 79.

[89] Arthur R. Kelley, "Church and State Papers for the Years 1759 to 1786, Being a Compendium of Documents Relating to the Establishment of Certain Churches in the Province of Quebec," Quebec (Province), Archives, *Rapport*, 1948-1949, p. 293-340. A. H. Young, ed., "The Rev. Robert Addison; Extracts from the Reports and (Manuscript) Journals of the Society for the Propagation of the Gospel in Foreign Parts," Ont. Hist. Soc. *Papers and Records*, XIX (1922), 171-91. Thomas R. Millman, *Jacob Mountain, First Lord Bishop of Quebec; A Study in Church and State, 1793-1825* (Toronto, 1947), 303-05.

[90] S. Kula, "Archives of the Church of England Missionary Societies in the Public Archives of Canada," Committee on Archives of the United Church of Canada, *Bulletin*, XI (1958), 15-16. The Canadian Public Archives microfilmed the records of the Society relating to Canada during 1952-55, and has also prepared an alphabetical index of names of correspondents and an index of places. Reproductions from the archives of the S.P.G. and of the Bishop of London are also in the Library of Congress, Washington, D. C. (U.S. Library of Congress, MS. Div., *Guide to MSS. British Depositories*, p. 186-87, 196-98).

registers of the Holy Trinity Anglican Church at Quebec, 1768-1800, and of St. Andrews Presbyterian Church at Quebec, 1770-1829, are in the Canadian Public Archives. The registers of the Anglican Christ Church at Montreal begin in 1766, and since that church maintained the only available records for births, marriages, and burials, it was used by other Protestants, including Presbyterians, Methodists, Congregationalists, and even Jews and some Roman Catholics and Negro slaves.[91] Part of the register is in print.[92] The Scotch Presbyterian Church at Montreal was established in 1786, but its registers do not start until 1796.[93] Since many of the traders in the West were Scotchmen from Montreal, these registers contain entries relating to them and their families. A copy of the register of the Protestant parish and garrison at Three Rivers, 1768-92, is in the Canadian Public Archives.

Registers kept by Protestant ministers in the early settlements of Upper Canada could also be of historical value. The register maintained by Stuart at Kingston contains the names of residents in those settlements, which were peopled largely by Loyalists who emigrated from the United States after the Revolutionary War.[94] The same observation applies to the registers of the Anglican churches at Niagara,[95] Cornwall, Sandwich,[96] Ernesttown (now Bath) and Fredericksburgh.[97] Copies of the Cornwall and Sandwich church records are in the Canadian Public Archives. The

[91] R. W. McLachlan, "Notes on the Protestant Church Registers of Montreal," *Canadian Antiq. and Numismat. Jour.*, 3d ser., XII (July 1915), 125-27; E.-Z. Massicotte, "Les mariages mixtes à Montreal, dans les temples protestantes au 18 siècle." *Bull. recherches hist.*, XXI (mars 1915), 84-86.

[92] Canada, Public Archives, "Copy of the Register of the Parish of Montreal, Commencing the 5th October 1766, Ending the 5th September 1787, by the Rev. Mr. D. C. Delisle," *Report on Canadian Archives*, 1885 (Ottawa, 1886), Note A, lxxx-xciv.

[93] McLachlan, "Church Registers of Montreal," p. 127.

[94] A. H. Young, ed. The Parish Register of Kingston, *Upper Canada, 1785-1811* (Kingston, Ont., 1921).

[95] Janet Carnochan, ed., "Early Records of St. Mark's and St. Andrews' Churches, Niagara," *Ont. Hist. Soc. Papers and Records*, III (1901), 7-85.

[96] The registers of this church date from 1802 (Lajeunesse, ed., *Windsor Border Region*, p. cxxi.

[97] "[Registers of Marriages, Baptisms and Burials of Rev. John Langhorn, 1787-1813]," *Ont. Hist. Soc. Papers and Records*, I (1899), 13-70.

registers of St. Andrew's Presbyterian Church at Williamstown, 1779-1817, are in the Ontario Archives and a photostat is in the Canadian Public Archives. Robert McDowall, a Presbyterian minister, performed many marriages and baptisms for residents of Fredericksburgh, Ernesttown, Adolphustown, Richmond, and Hallowell. The register, 1800-36, kept by him is in Queen's College Library, Kingston, and an abstract from it has been published.[98] An abstract of a marriage and baptismal register by a Lutheran minister, 1793-1832, is also available.[99]

The Church of the Assumption on the south side of the Detroit River was the only Catholic parish in the southwestern part of Upper Canada before the transfer of authority at Detroit and continued to be the only parish for some years afterwards.[1] The Rev. Edmund Burke moved over to the British side in 1796 and for five years traveled among the settlements ministering to the needs of the Catholics among the new English, Scotch, and Irish settlers.[2] St. Peter's Church was started on the Thames River eleven miles west of Chatham in 1802, being visited once a month by the priest from the Church of the Assumption at Sandwich.[3] The registers of St. Peter's Church begun in 1802 contain information about French families of Kent, Essex, and Lambton Counties, Ontario, whose forbears were active in American territory. Members of these families migrated in the nineteenth century to the forests of Michigan. James Baby, a former resident of Detroit, participated about 1806 in the founding of St. Paul's Church at Toronto.

[98] "Rev. Robert McDowall's Register," *ibid.*, p. 70-108.

[99] "Lutheran Church [Ebenezer Church, Fredericksburgh, Lennox County] Record, 1793-1832 [1850]," *ibid.*, VI (1904-1905), 137-59.

[1] Concerning the Church of the Assumption see Chapter II.

[2] O'Brien, *Edmund Burke*, p. 39-42.

[3] Theodore Martin, "History of St. Peter's Parish, 1802-1947," Kent Historical Society, *Papers and Addresses*, 7 (1951), 18.

V   Bibliographical Sources

BIBLIOGRAPHIES

Beers, Henry P. *Bibliographies in American History: Guide to Materials for Research.* New York, H. W. Wilson, 1942. Reprinted Pageant Books, Inc., Paterson, N.J., 1959.
———. *The French in North America: A Bibliographical Guide to French Archives, Reproductions, and Research Missions.* Baton Rouge, Louisiana State University Press, 1957.
Brown, Charles R. "Bibliography of Quebec or Lower Canada Laws." *Law Library Journal*, XIX (Jan. 1927), 90-109.
Buck, Solon J. *Travel and Description, 1765-1865; Together with a List of County Histories, Atlases, and Biographical Collections and a List of Territorial and State Laws* (*Collections* of the Illinois State Historical Library, Vol. IX, *Bibliographical Series*, Vol. II). Springfield, 1914.
Canada, Public Archives. *Catalogue of Maps, Plans and Charts in the Map Room of the Dominion Archives.* Classified and Indexed by H. R. Holmden (*Publications* of the Canadian Archives, No. 8). Ottawa, Government Printing Bureau, 1912.
Detroit Institute of Arts. *The French in America, 1520-1880; an Exhibition Organized by the Detroit Institute of Arts to Commemorate the Founding of Detroit by Antoine de Lamothe Cadillac in the Year 1701* [Catalog, Detroit]. 1951.
Dionne, Narcisse E. *Inventaire chronologique des cartes, plans, atlas relatifs à la Nouvelle-France et à la province de Québec, 1508-1908.* Québec, 1909. Published also in the *Proceedings and Transactions* of the Royal Society of Canada, 3d ser., II, pt. II (1908), 1-124.
Doughty, Arthur G. and Trotter, Reginald G. "Bibliography—The Manuscript Sources of Canadian History; Printed Works." in Rose, J.

195

Holland, Newton, A. P., and Benians, E. A., eds. *The Cambridge History of the British Empire, vol. VI, Canada and Newfoundland.* New York, The Macmillan Company; Cambridge, England, At the University Press, 1930, p. 813-85.

Eakins, W. George. "The Bibliography of Canadian Statute Law." *Law Library Journal,* I (Oct. 1908), 61-78.

Garique, Philip. *A Bibliographical Introduction to the Study of French Canada.* Montreal, Dept. of Sociology and Anthropology, McGill University, 1956.

Gauthier, Henri. *Sulpitiana.* Montréal, Bureau des oeuvres pariossiales de St.-Jacques, 1926.

Greenly, Albert H. *A Selective Bibliography of Important Books, Pamphlets, and Broadsides Relating to Michigan History.* Lunenburg, Vt., The Stinehour Press, 1958.

Griffin, Appleton P. C. "Bibliography of the Discovery and Exploration of the Mississippi Valley," in Knox College, Library. *An Annotated Catalogue of Books Belonging to the Finley Collection on the History and Romance of the Northwest.* Galesburg, Ill., Knox College, 1924, p. 47-67.

————. "Discovery of the Mississippi; Bibliographical Account of the Travels of Nicolet, Allöuez, Marquette, Hennepin, and La Salle in the Mississippi Valley." *The Magazine of American History,* IX (Mar., Apr. 1883), 190-99, 273-80.

Harrisse, Henry. *Notes pour servir à l'histoire, à la bibliographie et à la cartographie de la Nouvelle-France et des pays adjacents, 1545-1700.* Paris, Librairie Tross, 1872.

Hubach, Robert R. *Early Midwestern Travel Narratives; an Annotated Bibliography, 1634-1850.* Detroit, Wayne State University Press, 1961.

Lanctôt, Gustave. *L'oeuvre de la France en Amérique du Nord; bibliographie selective et critique.* Montréal et Paris, Fides, 1951.

Lee, John T. "A Bibliography of Carver's Travels." *Proceedings* of the State Historical Society of Wisconsin (1909), 143-83.

Marcel, Gabriel A. *Cartographie de la Nouvelle France; supplément à l'ouvrage de M. Harrisse.* Paris, Maisonneuve Frères et Cie, 1885. Published also in *Revue de géographie,* XVI (1885), 186-94, 282-89, 359-65, 442-47; XVII (1885), 50-57.

Matthews, William. *American Diaries, an Annotated Bibliography of American Diaries Written Prior to the Year 1761* (University of California, *Publications in English,* XVI. Berkeley, Los Angeles, University of California Press, 1945.

————. *Canadian Diaries and Autobiographies.* Berkeley, Los Angeles, University of California Press, 1950.

Michigan State Historical Society. *Classified Finding List of the Collections of the Michigan Pioneer and Historical Society.* Detroit, Wayne State University Press, 1952.

Neill, Edward D. and Winsor, Justin. "Critical Essay on the Sources of Information—Discovery Along the Great Lakes." in Winsor, Justin, ed. *Narrative and Critical History of America.* Boston, New York, Houghton, Mifflin and Company, 1884. IV, 196-200.

Pargellis, Stanley M. and Medley, D. J., eds. *Bibliography of British History, The Eighteenth Century, 1714-1789.* Oxford, At the Clarendon Press, 1951.

Penson, Lillian M., ed. "Bibliography." in Rose, J. Holland, Newton, A. P., and Benians, E. A., gen. eds. *The Old Empire from the Beginnings to 1783 (The Cambridge History of the British Empire, Vol. I).* New York, Macmillan; Cambridge, University Press, 1939. p. 824-88.

Quebec (Province) Archives. "Bibliographie de généalogies et histoires de familles." Quebec (Province) Archives. *Rapport de l'archiviste de la province de Québec, 1940-41.* Québec, 1941. p. 95-332.

Special Libraries Association, Geography and Map Division, Map Resources Committee. *Map Collections in the United States and Canada; A Directory.* Marie Cleckner Goodman, chairman. New York, Special Libraries Association, 1954.

Stewart, John Hall. *France, 1715-1815; a Guide to Materials in Cleveland.* Cleveland, Western Reserve University Press, 1942.

Tanghe, Raymond. *Bibliography of Canadian Bibliographies; Bibliographie des bibliographies canadiennes.* Toronto, University of Toronto Press, 1960.

Toronto Public Library. *A Bibliography of Canadiana; Being Items in the Public Library of Toronto, Canada, Relating to the Early History and Development of Canada.* Ed. by Frances M. Staton and Marie Tremaine, Toronto, 1934.

————. *A Bibliography of Canadiana, First Supplement Being Items in the Public Library of Toronto, Canada, Relating to the Early History and Development of Canada.* Ed. by Gertrude M. Boyle. Toronto. 1960.

Tremaine, Marie. *A Bibliography of Canadian Imprints, 1751-1800.* Toronto, University of Toronto Press, 1952.

U.S. Library of Congress. *The National Union Catalog of Manuscript Collections, 1959-1961; Based on Reports from American Reposi-*

tories of Manuscripts. Ann Arbor, Mich., J. W. Edwards, Publisher, 1962.

U.S. Library of Congress, Division of Maps. *A List of Maps of America in the Library of Congress.* Comp. by Philip Lee Phillips. Washington Government Printing Office, 1901.

Vollmar, Edward R., S.J. *The Catholic Church in America: An Historical Bibliography.* New Brunswick, The Scarecrow Press, 1956.

Walter, Frank K., and Doneghy, Virginia. *Jesuit Relations and Other Americana in the Library of James F. Bell; a Catalogue.* Minneapolis, University of Minnesota Press, 1950.

Winsor, Justin. "Father Louis Hennepin and His Real or Disputed Discoveries (Bibliographical)," in his *Narrative and Critical History of America.* Boston, New York, Houghton, Mifflin and Company, 1884, IV, 247-56.

———. "Joliet, Marquette and La Salle: Historical Sources and Attendant Cartography." in his *Narrative and Critical History of America.* Boston, New York, Houghton, Mifflin and Company, 1884. IV, 377-94.

ARCHIVES AND MANUSCRIPTS

Burton, Clarence Monroe. Papers, 1889-1926. Detroit Public Library, Burton Historical Collection.

Carnegie Institution of Washington, Department of Historical Research. Correspondence Files.

Quattrocchi, Anna N. Thomas Hutchins, 1735-1789. (Ph.D. Dissertation University of Pittsburgh). Pittsburgh, 1944.

U.S. Library of Congress, Manuscript Division. Correspondence Files of the Manuscript Division.

U.S. National Archives

U.S. Department of the Interior, General Land Office. Letters Received from the Surveyor General of the Northwest (Ohio). Record Group 49.

U.S. Department of the Interior, General Land Office. Letters Received from the Surveyors General. Record Group 49.

U.S. Department of the Interior, General Land Office. Letters Sent to Registers and Receivers. Record Group 49.

U.S. Department of the Interior, General Land Office. Letters Sent to Surveyors General. Record Group 49.
U.S. Department of the Interior, General Land Office. Private Land Claim Dockets. Record Group 49.
U.S. Department of the Interior, General Land Office. Register of Letters Received from Surveyors General. Record Group 49.
U.S. Surveyor General of the Northwest, Letters Received. Record Group 49.

PRINTED ARCHIVES AND MANUSCRIPTS

Alvord, Clarence W., ed. *Cahokia Records, 1778-1790* (*Collections* of the Illinois State Historical Library, Vol. II, *Virginia Series*, Vol. I). Springfield, Ill., 1907.
—— "Edward Cole, Indian Commissioner in the Illinois Country." Illinois State Historical Society, *Journal*, III (Oct. 1910), 23-44.
—— *The Illinois Wabash Company Manuscript.* Privately printed by Cyrus H. McCormick, 1915.
——, ed. *Kaskaskia Records, 1778-1790* (*Collections* of the Illinois State Historical Library, Vol. V, *Virginia Series*, Vol. II). Springfield, Ill., 1909.
——, ed. "The Oath of Vincennes." Illinois State Historical Society, *Transactions* (1908), Illinois State Historical Library *Publication*, No. 12, 270-76.
—— and Carter, Clarence E., eds. *The Critical Period, 1763-1765* (*Collections* of the Illinois State Historical Library, Vol. X, *British Series*, Vol. I). Springfield, Ill., 1915.
—— and ——, eds. *The New Régime, 1765-1767* (*Collections* of the Illinois State Historical Library, Vol. XI, *British Series*, Vol. II). Springfield, Ill., 1916.
—— and ——, eds. *Trade and Politics, 1767-1769.* (*Collections* of the Illinois State Historical Library, Vol. XVI, *British Series*, Vol. III). Springfield, Ill., 1921.
Ambler, Charles H., ed. "Some Letters and Papers of General Thomas Gage." Randolph Macon College, *The John P. Branch Historical Papers*, IV, No. 2 (June 1914), 86-111.
Audet, F.-J. "Les habitants de la ville de Québec en 1769-1771." *Bulletin des recherches historiques*, XXVII (mars, avril, juillet, août, 1921), 81-88, 119-25, 218-24, 247-52.
Bailey Kenneth P., ed. *The Ohio Company Papers, 1753-1817, Being*

Primarily Papers of the "Suffering Traders" of Pennsylvania. Arcata, Calif., 1947.

Barnhart, John D., ed. *Henry Hamilton and George Rogers Clark in the American Revolution with The Unpublished Journal of Lieut Gov. Henry Hamilton.* Crawfordsville, Ind., R. E. Banta, 1951.

Beaudet, Louis, Abbé, éd. *Recensement de la ville de Québec pour 1716.* Québec, Impr. A. Coté et cie, 1887.

Beckwith, Hiram W., ed. "Letters from Canadian Archives." (*Collections* of the Illinois State Historical Library, Vol. I). Springfield, 1903. p. 290-457.

Brault, Lucien, éd. "Documents inédits, recensement de Détroit, 1779." *Revue d'histoire de l'Amérique française*, V (mars, 1952), 581-85.

Brown, Lloyd Arnold. *Early Maps of the Ohio Valley: a Selection of Maps, Plans, and Views by Indians and Colonials from 1673 to 1783.* Pittsburgh, Pa., University of Pittsburgh Press, 1959.

Burton, Clarence M., ed. "Cadillac Papers." (*Michigan Historical Collections*, Vols. XXXIII-XXXIV). Lansing, 1904-05. p. 36-715, 11-214.

————, ed., "Cadillac's Records." (*Michigan Historical Collections*, Vol. XXXIV). Lansing, 1905. p. 215-302.

Byars, William V ., ed., *B[arnard] and M[ichael] Gratz, Merchants in Philadelphia, 1754-1798. Papers of Interest to Their Posterity and the Posterity of Their Associates.* Jefferson City, Mo., The Hugh Stevens Printing Co., 1916.

Canada. *Indian Treaties and Surrenders from 1680 to [1903]* Ottawa, 1905-12. 3 vols. in 2.

Canada, General Staff, Historical Section. *A History of the Organization, Development and Services of the Military and Naval Forces of Canada, from the Peace of Paris in 1763, to the Present Time, with Illustrative Documents.* [Ottawa] 1919.

Canada, Public Archives. "Copy of the Register of the Parish of Montreal, Commencing the 5th October 1766, Ending the 5th September 1787, by the Rev. Mr. D. C. Delisle." *Report on Canadian Archives*, 1885. Ottawa, 1886. Note "A", lxxx-xciv.

————. "Correspondence and Papers Relating to Detroit [1772-80]." *Report on Canadian Archives*, 1882. Ottawa, 1883. Note A—2, 11-40.

————. "Correspondence of General James Murray, 1759-1791." *Report of the Work of the Archives Branch*, 1912. Ottawa, 1913. Appendix I, p. 84-123.

————. "Instructions to Governors [Colonial Office Records 1763-87]."

Report Concerning Canadian Archives, 1904. Ottawa, 1905. Appendix E, p. 191-286.

———. "North-Western Exploration." *Report on Canadian Archives,* 1890. Ottawa, 1891. Note C, p. 48-66.

———. "Ordinances Made for the Province of Quebec by the Governor and Council of the said Province, from 1768 until 1791, being a Continuation of the Ordinances published as Appendix 'E' of the Report of the Public Archives for 1913." *Report of the Public Archives,* 1914-15. Ottawa, 1916. Appendix C.

———. "Ordinances, Proclamations, etc., Issued by the Military Governors of Quebec, Montreal, and Trois Rivières, from the Capitulation of Quebec until the Establishment of the Civil Government on August 10, 1764." *Report of the Public Archives,* 1918. Ottawa, 1920. Appendix B.

———. "Ordonnances faites pour la province de Québec par le gouverneur et la conseil de la dite province depuis le commencement du gouvernement civil." *Report of the Public Archives,* 1913. Ottawa, 1915. Appendice E, p. 48-91.

———. "Proclamations Issued by the Governor-in-Chief from the Establishment of Civil Government on August 10, 1764 until the Partition of the Province of Quebec into the Provinces of Upper and Lower Canada, on December 26, 1791." *Report of the Public Archives,* 1918. Ottawa, 1920. Appendix C, p. 401-71.

———. "Recensement des habitans de la ville & gouvernement des Trois Rivières, tel qu'l a ete pris au mois de septembre mil sept cent soixante." *Report of the Public Archives,* 1918. Ottawa, 1920. p. 158-89.

———. "Selkirk Settlement, Letter Book of Captain Miles MacDonnell (From Archives: Selkirk Correspondence)." *Report on Canadian Archives,* 1886. Ottawa, 1887. Note F, p. clxxxvii-ccxxv.

———. "Statutes of Upper Canada, 1792-1793." *Report of the Public Archives,* 1921. Ottawa, 1922. Appendix F, p. 373-425.

Carnochan, Janet, ed. "Early Records of St. Mark's and St. Andrews' Churches, Niagara." Ontario Historical Society. *Papers and Records,* III (1901), 7-85.

Carter, Clarence E., ed. *The Correspondence of General Thomas Gage with the Secretaries of State, and with the War Office and the Treasury 1763-1775 (Yale Historical Publications, Manuscripts and Edited Texts,* XII). New Haven, Yale University Press; London, Humphrey Milford, Oxford University Press, 1931-33. 2 vols.

Cleary, Francis, ed. "Baptisms (1761 to 1786), Marriages (1782-1786), and Deaths (1768 to 1786), Recorded in the Parish Registers of Assumption, Sandwich." Ontario Historical Society, *Papers and Records,* VII (1906), 31-97.

Coleman, Christopher B., ed. "Letters from Eighteenth Century Indiana Merchants." *Indiana Magazine of History,* V (Dec. 1909), 137-59.

Colgate, William, ed. "Letters from The Honorable Chief Justice William Osgoode." *Ontario History,* XLVI (Spring, Summer 1954), 77-95, 149-68.

"Comptes et mémoires du Poste Vincennes." *Bulletin des recherches historiques,* LX (juillet, août, sept. 1954), 141-45.

Cruikshank, Ernest A., ed. *The Correspondence of Lieut. Governor John Graves Simcoe, with Allied Documents relating to His Administration of the Government of Upper Canada.* Toronto, Ontario Historical Society, 1923-31. 5 vols.

————, ed. "Petitions for Grants of Land, 1792-6." Ontario Historical Society, *Papers and Records,* XXIV (1927), 17-144; XXVI (1930), 97-379.

————, ed. "Records of Niagara [1778-1792]." (Niagara Historical Society, *Publications,* Nos., 38-41), Niagara, Ontario, 1927-30.

————, ed. *The Settlement of the United Empire Loyalists on the Upper St. Lawrence and Bay of Quinte in 1784; a Documentary Record.* Toronto, Ontario Historical Society, 1934.

———— and Hunter, A. F., eds. *The Correspondence of The Honorable Peter Russell with Allied Documents Relating to His Administration of the Government of Upper Canada during the Official Term of Lieut.-Governor J. G. Simcoe . . .* Toronto, Ontario Historical Society, 1932-36. 3 vols.

De Peyster, Arent Schuyler. *Miscellanies by an Officer (Colonel Arent Schuyler de Peyster, B. S.), 1774-1813.* Ed. by J. Watts de Peyster. New York, A. E. Chasmer and Co., 1888.

Draper, Lyman C., ed. "Canadian Documents." (*Collections* of the State Historical Society of Wisconsin, Vol. V). Madison, 1868. p. 64-108.

————, ed. "The Mission to the Ouabache." Indiana Historical Society, *Publications,* III, No. 4 (1902), 253-330.

Dunn, Caroline and Dunn, Eleanor, trans. "Indiana's First War." Indiana Historical Society, *Publications,* VIII, No. 2 (1924), 71-143.

Dunn, Jacob Piatt., ed. "Documents Relating to the French Settlements on the Wabash." Indiana Historical Society, *Publications,* II, No. 11 (1894), 403-442.

Elliott, Richard R., trans. and ed. "Account Book of the Huron Mission at Detroit and Sandwich (1740-1751) [by Fathers Pierre Potier and Armand de la Richardie]." Ontario, Department of Public Records and Archives. *Fifteenth Report* . . . , 1918-19. Toronto, 1920, p. 689-715.

Eschmann, C. J., trans. "Kaskaskia Church Records." Illinois State Historical Society, *Transactions* (1904), Illinois State Library, *Publication*, No. 9, 394-413.

———, ed. "Prairie du Rocher Church Records." Illinois State Historical Society, *Tranactions,* (1903), Illinois State Historical Library, *Publication*, No. 8, 128-49.

Firth, Edith G., ed. *The Town of York, 1793-1815; a Collection of Documents of Early Toronto* (The Champlain Society, Ontario Series, Vol. V). Toronto, University of Toronto Press, 1962.

Frontier Forts and Trails Survey, Federal Works Agency, Work Projects Administration. *The Expedition of Baron de Longueuil; a Preliminary Report Commemorating the 200th Anniversary* (*Northwestern Pennsylvania Historical Series,* ed. by Sylvester K. Stevens and Donald H. Kent). Harrisburg, Pennsylvania Historical Commission, 1940.

———. *The Papers of Col. Henry Bouquet* (*Northwestern Pennsylvania Historical Series.* ed. by Sylvester K. Stevens and Donald H. Kent). Harrisburg, Pennsylvania Historical Commission, 1940-43. 19 vols.

———. *Wilderness Chronicles of Northwestern Pennsylvania.* Ed. by Sylvester K. Stevens and Donald H. Kent. Harrisburg, Pennsylvania Historical Commission, 1941.

Gates, Charles M., ed. *Five Fur Traders of the Northwest; Being the Narrative of Peter Pond and the Diaries of John Macdonell, Archibald H. McLeod, Hugh Faries, and Thomas Connor.* Minneapolis, Society of the Colonial Dames of America, The University of Minnesota Press, 1933.

Gosselin, Amédée, ptre., éd. "Le recensement du gouvernement de Québec en 1762." Quebec (Province) Archives. *Rapport de l'archivist de la province de Québec,* 1925-26. Québec, 1926. p. 1-143.

Grenier, Fernand, éd. *Papiers Contrecoeur et autres documents concernant le conflit anglo-français sur l'Ohio de 1745 à 1756* (*Publications* des Archives du Séminaire de Québec, Vol. I.) Québec, Les Presses Universitaires Laval, 1952.

Hough, Franklin B., ed. *Diary of the Siege of Detroit in the War with Pontiac; Also a Narrative of the Principal Events in the Siege by Major Robert Rogers; a Plan for Conducting Indian Affairs, by Colonel Bradstreet; and Other Authentic Documents, Never Before Printed.* Albany, J. Munsell, 1860.

"How People Lived in Pre-Revolutionary French Illinois." *Illinois Libraries*, XXXI (Apr. 1949), 190-93.

Hulbert, Archer Butler, ed. *The Crown Collection of Photographs of American Maps*. Cleveland, Arthur H. Clark, 1904-08. 5 vols.

——, ed. *The Crown Collection of Photographs of American Maps; a Collection of Original Photographs, Carefully Mounted, of Maps Important Historically Yet Hitherto Unpublished, Contained in the British Museum and Other Foreign Archives Especially Chosen and Prepared to Illustrate the Early History of America . . . Index.* Cleveland, A. H. Clark, 1909.

Hunter, A. F., ed. "The Probated Wills of Men Prominent in the Public Affairs of Early Upper Canada." Ontario Historical Society, *Papers and Records*, XXIII (1926), 328-59; XXIV (1927), 381-409.

Hutchins, Thomas, "Eight Letters of Thomas Hutchins to George Morgan." Chicago Historical Society, *Bulletin*, I (May 1935), 69-78.

James, James Alton, ed. *George Rogers Clark Papers, 1771-1781 (Collections* of the Illinois State Historical Library, Vol. VIII, XIX, *Virginia Series*, Vol. III, IV). Springfield, 1912, 1926.

Jarvis, William. "Letters from the Secretary of Upper Canada and Mrs. Jarvis to Her Father, the Rev. Samuel Peters, D.D. [1792-1813]." Women's Canadian Historical Society Toronto, *Transactions*, XXIII (1923), 11-63.

Kellogg, Louise Phelps, ed. *Early Narratives of the Northwest, 1634-1699 (Original Narratives of Early American History*, ed. by J. Franklin Jameson). New York. C. Scribner's Sons, 1917.

Kennedy, William P. M., ed. *Statutes, Treaties and Documents of the Canadian Constitution, 1713-1929*. Toronto, London, Oxford University Press, 1930.

Kilroy, Margaret Claire. "In the Footsteps of the Habitant on the South Shore of the Detroit River." Ontario Historical Society, *Papers and Records*, VII (1906), 26-30.

Lajeunesse, Ernest J., ed. *The Windsor Border Region Canada's Southernmost Frontier; a Collection of Documents* (The Champlain Society, *Ontario Series*, Vol. IV). Toronto, University of Toronto Press, 1960.

Lambing, Andrew A., trans. and ed. *The Baptismal Register of Fort Duquesne (from June, 1754, to Dec., 1756)*. Pittsburgh, Myers, Shinkle & Co., 1885. Reprinted by the Catholic Historical Society of Western Pennsylvania, Pittsburgh, Pa., 1954.

——, trans. and ed. "Register of the Baptisms and Internments Which

Took Place at Fort Duquesne during the Years 1753-1756." *American Catholic Historical Researches,* I (1884), 60-73, 109-18, 138-54; II (1885), 18-25.

Langlade, Charles de. "Langlade Papers—1737-1800." (*Collections* of the State Historical Society of Wisconsin, Vol. VIII). Madison, 1879. p. 209-23.

Lapalice, Ovid-M.-H., éd. "Registre du Fort de la Presque Isle." *Canadian Antiquarian and Numismatic Journal,* XI, 3d ser., (Oct. 1914), 168-70.

Lart, Charles E., ed. "Fur-Trade Returns, 1767." *Canadian Historical Review,* III (Dec. 1922), 351-58.

Lemay, Hugolin Père, éd. "Le registre du fort de la Presqu'île pour 1753." *Bulletin des recherches historiques,* XLIV (juillet 1938), 204-11.

Lindsay, Lionel, St. George, ed. "Correspondence between the Sees of Quebec and Baltimore, 1788-1847." American Catholic Historical Society of Philadelphia, *Records,* XVIII (June, Sept., Dec. 1907), 155-89, 282-305, 434-67.

———, ed. "Letters from the Archdiocesan Archives at Quebec." American Catholic Historical Society of Philadelphia, *Records,* XX (Dec. 1909), 406-30.

"Lutheran Church [Ebenezer Church, Fredericksburgh, Lennox County] Records, 1793-1832 [1850]," Ontario Historical Society, *Papers and Records,* VI (1904-1905), 137-59.

McDermott, John F., ed. *Old Cahokia; a Narrative and Documents Illustrating the First Century of its History.* St. Louis Historical Documents Foundation, 1949.

McNiff, Patrick. *Patrick McNiff's Plan of the Settlements at Detroit, 1796; Reproduced in Collotype Facsimile from the Original Manuscript in the Clements Library.* With a Note by F. Clever Bald. Ann Arbor, University of Michigan Press, 1946.

Marcus, Jacob Rader, ed. *American Jewry Documents Eighteenth Century; Primarily Hitherto Unpublished Manuscripts (Publications* of the American Jewish Archives, No. III). Cincinnati, The Hebrew Union College Press, 1959.

Margry, Pierre A., éd. *Découvertes et établissements des français dans l'ouest et dans le sud de l'Amérique Septentrionale 1614-1754; mémoires et documents originaux recueillis et publiés par P. Margry.* Paris. D. Jouaust. 1876-86. 6 vols.

———, éd. *Mémoires et documents pour servir à l'histoire des origines françaises des pays d'outre-mer; découvertes et établissements des français dans l'ouest et dans le sud de l'Amérique Septentrionale (1614-1754).* Paris, Maisonneuve et cie, 1879-88. 6 vols.

Martin, Chester B., ed. *Red River Settlement; Papers in the Canadian Archives Relating to the Pioneers.* Ottawa, 1910.

Mason, Edward G., ed. "British Illinois: Philippe François de Rastel Chevalier de Rocheblave. Rocheblave Papers." (Chicago Historical Society, *Collections,* Vol. IV). Chicago, 1890. p. 360-419.

———, ed. "John Todd." (Chicago Historical Society, *Collections,* Vol. IV). Chicago, 1890. p. 285-88.

Masson, Louis F. R., éd. *Les bourgeois de la Compagnie du Nord-Ouest; récits de voyages et rapports inédits relatifs au nord-ouest canadien.* Québec, de l'Imprimerie Général A. Coté et Cⁱᵉ 1889-90. 2 vols.

Michigan Pioneer and Historical Society. "Bouquet Papers." (*Michigan Historical Collections,* Vol. XIX). Lansing, 1892. p. 27-295.

———. *Copies of Papers on File in the Dominion Archives at Ottawa Canada, Pertaining to Michigan, As Found in the Reports on American Colonies, Military Dispatches, Bouquet Papers, and Haldimand Papers* (*Michigan Historical Collections,* Vols. XIX, XX). Lansing, 1892.

———. *Copies of Papers on File in the Dominion Archives at Ottawa, Canada, Pertaining to Michigan, As Found in the Colonial Office Papers* (*Michigan Historical Collections,* Vols. XXIII, XXIV, XXV). Lansing, 1893, 1895, 1896.

———. "The Haldimand Papers, Copies of Papers on File in the Dominion Archives at Ottawa, Canada." (*Michigan Historical Collections,* Vols. IX-XI). Lansing, 1886-87. p. 343-658, 210-672, 319-656.

Montreal, Notre-Dame Church. *Premier registre de l'église Notre-Dame de Montréal.* Montréal, Edition des Dix, 1961.

Moore, Charles, ed. "The Gladwin Manuscripts." (*Michigan Historical Collections,* Vol. XXVII). Lansing, 1896. p. 605-80.

Moses, John, ed. "Court of Enquiry at Ft. Chartres." (Chicago Historical Society, *Collections,* Vol. IV). Chicago, 1890. p. 420-85.

Mulkearn, Lois, ed. *George Mercer Papers Relating to the Ohio Company of Virginia.* Pittsburgh, University of Pittsburgh Press, 1954.

Munro, William B., ed. *Documents Relating to the Seigniorial Tenure in Canada, 1598-1854, With a Historical Introduction and Explanatory Notes* (Champlain Society, *Publications,* Vol. III). Toronto, The Champlain Society, 1908.

Murphy, J. J., ed. "Documentary History of the First Surveys in the Province of Ontario." Association of Ontario Land Surveyors, *Proceedings*, No. 13 (1898), 196-231.

New France. *Ordonnances, commissions, etc. etc., des gouverneurs et intendants de la Nouvelle-France, 1639-1706*. Par Pierre-Georges Roy. Beauceville, P. Q., 1924. 2 vols.

New France, Conseil supérieur de Québec. *Jugements et délibérations du Conseil souverain de la Nouvelle-France, 1663-1710*. Québec, Imp. A. Coté et Cⁱᵉ, 1885-91. 6 vols.

———. *Lettres de noblesse, généalogies, érections de comtés et baronnies insinuées par le Conseil souverain de la Nouvelle-France*. Par Pierre-Georges Roy. (*Archives de la Province de Québec*, Vol. 10). Beauceville, P. Q., 1920. 2 vols.

New France, Laws, Statutes, etc. *Édits, ordonnances royaux, déclarations, et arrêts du Conseil d'état du roi concernant le Canada*. Québec, De la presse à vapeur de E. R. Fréchette, 1854-56. 3 vols.

Norton, Margaret C., ed. *Illinois Census Returns 1810, 1818*. (*Collections* of the Illinois State Historical Library, Vol. XXIV, *Statistical Series*, Vol. II). Springfield, 1935.

Nute, Grace Lee, ed. *Documents Relating to Northwest Missions, 1815-1827* (The Clarence Walworth Alvord Memorial Commission of the Mississippi Valley Historical Association, *Publications* No. 1). St. Paul, 1942.

O'Callaghan, Edmund B., ed. *The Documentary History of the State of New York*. Albany, Weed, Parsons & Co., Public Printers, [vols. 1-3], Charles Van Benthuysen, Public Printers [vol. 4], 1849-51. 4 vols.

———, ed. *Documents Relative to the Colonial History of the State of New York: Procured in Holland, England, and France, by John Romeyn Brodhead, Esq., Agent* . . . Albany, Weed, Parsons and Company, Printer, 1853-87. 15 vols.

Ontario, Department of Public Records and Archives. "Board of Land Office for the District of Hesse, 1789-1794; Minutes of Meetings, etc." *Third Report of the Department of Public Records and Archives, 1905*. Toronto, 1906. p. 1-291.

———. *Grants of Crown Lands in Upper Canada, 1787-1791. Seventeenth Report* . . . 1928. Toronto, 1929.

———. *Grants of Crown Lands, etc., in Upper Canada, 1792-1796. Eighteenth Report* . . . 1929. Toronto, 1930.

———. *The Journals of the Legislative Assembly of Upper Canada for* the Years 1792, 1793, 1794 (partly), 1798, 1799, 1800, 1801, 1802, 1803, 1804. Sixth Report . . . 1909. Toronto, 1911.

————. *The Journals of the Legislative Council of Upper Canada for the Years 1792, 1793, 1794, 1798, 1799, 1800, 1801, 1802, 1803, 1804, 1805, 1806, 1807, 1808, 1810, 1811, 1812, 1814, 1819. Seventh Report* . . . 1910. Toronto, 1911.

————. *Proclamations [Issued] by Governors and Lieutenant Governors of Quebec and Upper Canada [1760-1840]. Fourth Report* . . . 1906. Toronto, 1907.

————. *Records of the Courts of Justice of Upper Canada. Fourteenth Report* . . . 1917. Toronto, 1918.

Ott, E. R., trans. and ed. "Selections from the Diary and Gazette of Father Pierre Potier, S.J. (1708-1781)." *Mid-America*, XVIII n.s. VII (July, Oct. 1936), 199-207, 260-65.

"Papers Relating to the Expeditions of Colonel Bradstreet and Colonel Bouquet, in Ohio, A.D., 1764." Western Reserve and Northern Ohio Historical Society, *Tract* No. 13-14 (Feb. 1873).

Paré, George, and Quaife, Milo M., eds. "The St. Joseph Baptismal Register." *Mississippi Valley Historical Review*, XIII (Sept. 1926), 201-39.

Pease, Theodore C., ed. *Anglo-French Boundary Disputes in the West, 1749-1763 (Collections* of the Illinois State Historical Library, Vol. XXVII, *French Series*, Vol. II). Springfield, 1936.

————, and Jenison, Ernestine, eds. *Illinois on the Eve of the Seven Years' War, 1747-1755 (Collections* of the Illinois State Historical Library, Vol. XXIX, *French Series*, Vol. III). Springfield, 1940.

————, and Werner, Raymond C., eds. *The French Foundations, 1680-1693 (Collections* of the Illinois State Historical Library, Vol. XXIII, *French Series*, Vol. I). Springfield, Ill., 1934.

Pennsylvania (Colony). *Colonial Records*. Philadelphia, J. Severns & Co., 1851-53. 16 vols.

————. *Papers Relating to the French Occupation in Western Pennsylvania, 1631-1764 (Pennsylvania Archives*, 2d ser., Vol. VI). Harrisburg, 1891.

————. *Pennsylvania Archives* [1st ser.]. Ed. by Samuel Hazard. Philadelphia, J. Severns & Co., 1852-56. 12 vols.

Pennsylvania Historical and Museum Commission. *The Papers of Henry Bouquet, Volume II, The Forbes Expedition*. Ed. by Sylvester K. Stevens, Donald H. Kent, and Autumn L. Leonard. Harrisburg, 1951.

Preston, Richard A., ed. *Kingston before the War of 1812: a Collection of Documents (Publications* of the Champlain Society, *Ontario Series,* Vol. III). Toronto, The Society, 1959.

———, and Lamontagne, Leopold, trans. and ed. *Royal Fort Frontenac (Publications* of the Champlain Society, *Ontario Series,* Vol. II). Toronto, The Society, 1958.

Quaife, Milo M., ed. *The Capture of Old Vincennes; The Original Narratives of George Rogers Clark and of His Opponent Gov. Henry Hamilton.* Indianapolis, The Bobbs-Merrill Company, 1927.

———, ed. *The John Askin Papers (Burton Historical Records,* Vols. I-II). Detroit, Detroit Library Commission, 1928, 1931. 2 vols.

———, ed. *The Development of Chicago, 1674-1914, Shown in a Series of Contemporary Original Narratives.* Chicago, The Caxton Club, 1916.

———, ed. *The Western Country in the 17th Century; Memoirs of Lamothe Cadillac and Pierre Liette.* Chicago, Lakeside Press, 1947.

Quebec (Province). *Cadastres abrégés des seigneuries.* Québec, 1863. 6 vols.

Quebec (Province) Archives. "Aveu et dénombrement de messire Louis Normand, prêtre du séminaire de Saint-Sulpice de Montréal, au nom et comme fondé de procuration de messire Charles-Maurice le Pelletier, supérieur du séminaire de Saint-Sulpice, de Paris, pour la seigneurie de l'île de Montréal (1731)." *Rapport de l'archiviste de la province de Québec,* 1941-42. Québec, 1942. p. 1-176.

———. *Collection de manuscrits contenant lettres, mémoires, et autres documents, historiques relatifs à la Nouvelle-France, recueillis aux archives de la province de Québec, ou copiés à l'étranger; mis en ordre et édités sous les auspices de la législature de Québec, avec table etc.* Québec, 1883-85. 4 vols.

———. "Correspondance échangée entre la Cour de France et le gouverneur de Frontenac, pendant sa première administration (1672-1682)." *Rapport de l'archiviste de la province de Québec,* 1926-27. [Québec, 1927]. p. 3-144.

———. "Correspondance échangée entre la Cour de France et le gouverneur de Frontenac, pendant sa seconde administration (1689-1699)." *Rapport de l'archiviste de la province de Québec,* 1927-28, 1928-29. [Québec, 1928, 1929]. p. 3-211, 247-384.

———. "Correspondance échangée entre la Cour de France et l'intendant Talon pendant ses deux administrations dans la Nouvelle-France." *Rapport de l'archiviste de la province de Québec,* 1930-31 [Québec, 1931]. p. 1-182.

———. "Correspondance entre M. de Vaudreuil et la Court." *Rapport de l'archiviste de la province de Québec,* 1938-39, 1939-40, 1942-43, 1946-47. [Québec, 1939, 1940, 1943, 1947]. p. 10-179, 355-463, 399-443, 371-460.

―――. "Lettres et mémoires de l'Abbé de l'Isle-Dieu." *Rapport de l'archiviste de province de Québec,* 1935-36, 1936-37, 1937-38. [Québec, 1936, 1937, 1938]. p. 275-410, 331-459, 147-253.

―――. *Papier terrier de la Compagnie des Indes Occidentales, 1667-1668. Publié par Pierre-Georges Roy. (Archives de la province de Québec).* Beauceville, P.Q., 1931.

―――. "Le premier recensement de la Nouvelle-France [1666]." *Rapport de l'archiviste de la province de Québec,* 1935-36. [Québec, 1936]. p. 1-154.

―――. "Le recensement des gouvernements de Montréal et des Trois-Rivières [1765.]." *Rapport de l'archiviste de la province de Québec,* 1936-37. [Québec, 1937]. p. 1-121.

―――. "Recensement des habitants de la ville et gouvernement des Trois-Rivières [sept. 1760]." *Rapport de l'archiviste de la province de Québec,* 1946-47. [Québec, 1947]. p. 3-53.

Quebec (Province) Parliament. *Édits, ordonnances, déclarations et arrêts relatifs à la tenure seigneuriale; demandes par une adresse de l'assemblée législative 1851.* Québec, 1852.

―――. *Nouvelle-France, documents historiques; correspondance échangée entre les autorités françaises et les gouverneurs et intendants, volume I.* Québec, 1893.

"[Registers of Marriages, Baptisms and Burials of Rev. John Langhorn, 1787-1813]," Ontario Historical Society, *Papers and Records,* I (1899), 13-70.

"Rev. Robert McDowall's Register," Ontario Historical Society, *Papers and Records,* I (1899), 70-108.

Roberts, Kenneth L. *Northwest Passage,* Volume II: "Appendix, Containing the Courtmartial of Major Robert Rogers [1768] the Courtmartial of Lt. Samuel Stephens, and Other New Material." Garden City, N. Y., Doubleday, Doran & Company, 1937.

Roy, Pierre-Georges, éd. "Le premier recensement nominal de Québec [1666]." *Bulletin des recherches historiques,* XXXVII (juin, juillet 1931), 321-31, 385-404.

Schmitt, Edmond, J. P., Rev., trans. "The Records of the Parish of St. Francis Xavier at Post Vincennes, Ind." American Catholic Historical Society, *Records,* XII (Mar., June, Sept. 1901), 41-60, 193-211, 322-36.

Shea, John D. G., ed. *Discovery and Exploration of the Mississippi Val-*

ley; with the Original Narratives of Marquette, Allouez, Membré, Hennepin, and Anastase Douay. New York, Redfield, 1852.

————, ed. *Early Voyages Up and Down the Mississippi, by Cavelier, St. Cosme, Le Sueur, Gravier, and Guignas.* Albany, J. Munsell, 1861.

————. *Registres des baptesmes et sepultures qui se sont faits au Fort Duquesne pendant les années 1753, 1754, 1755 & 1756.* Nouvelle York, 1859.

Shortt, Adam, and Doughty, Arthur G., eds. *Documents Relating to the Constitutional History of Canada, 1759-1791.* Ottawa, J. de L. Taché, 1918. 2 vols.

Stiles, Henry R., ed. "Affairs at Fort Chartres, 1768-1781." *Historical Magazine*, VIII (Aug. 1864), 257-66.

Sullivan, James; Flick, Alexander C.; Lauber, Almon W.; and Hamilton, Milton W., eds. *The Papers of Sir William Johnson.* Albany, University of the State of New York, 1921-62. 13 vols. A chronological list of documents is in XIII, 735-1026.

Tetu, Henri, et Gagnon, Charles-Octave, éds. *Mandements, lettres pastorales et circulaires des évêques de Québec.* Québec, Imprimerie générale A. Coté et Cⁱᵉ, 1887-88. 4 vols.

Thwaites, Reuben Gold, ed. "The British Regime in Wisconsin." (*Collections* of the State Historical Society of Wisconsin, Vol. XVIII). Madison, 1908. p. 223-468.

————, ed. *The French Regime in Wisconsin, 1634-1760* (*Collections* of the State Historical Society of Wisconsin, Vols. XVI-XVIII). Madison, 1902, 1906, 1908. 3 vols.

————, ed. "Fur-Trade on the Upper Lakes, 1778-1815." (*Collections* of the State Historical Society of Wisconsin, Vol. XIX). Madison, 1910. p. 234-374.

————, ed. "Important Western State Papers." (*Collections* of the State Historical Society of Wisconsin, Vol. XI). Madison, 1888. p. 26-63.

————, ed. *The Jesuit Relations and Allied Documents: Travels and Explorations of the Jesuit Missionaries in New France, 1610-1791; the Original French, Latin, and Italian Texts, With English Translations and Notes; Illustrated by Portraits, Maps, and Facsimiles.* Cleveland, The Burrows Brothers Company, 1896-1901. 73 vols.

————, ed. "The Mackinac Register, 1725-1821: Register of Marriages in the Parish of Michilimackinac; 1695-1821: Register of Baptisms of the Mission of St. Ignace de Michilimackinac; 1743-1806: Register of Interments." (*Collections* of the State Historical Society of Wisconsin, Vols. XVIII, XIX). Madison, 1908, 1910, p. 469-513, 1-162.

————, ed. "Missions des Hurons du Détroit, 1733-56." *The Jesuit Relations* . . . Cleveland, The Burrows Brothers Co., 1900. LXIX, 240-77, LXX, 19-77.

Viger, Jacques, éd. *Règne militaire en Canada; ou administration judiciaire de ce pays par les anglais du 8 septembre, 1760 au août 1764; manuscrits recueillis et annotés* (Société Historique de Montréal, *Mémoires*). Montréal, 1870.

Wallace, William Stewart, ed. *Documents Relating to the North West Company* (*Publications* of the Champlain Society). Toronto, The Champlain Society, 1934.

Watts, Florence G., trans. and ed. "Some Vincennes Documents of 1772." *Indiana Magazine of History*, XXXIV (June 1938), 199-212.

Wharton, Thomas. "Selections from the Letter Books of Thomas Wharton of Philadelphia, 1773-1783." *Pennsylvania Magazine of History and Biography*, XXXIII (1909), 319-39, 432-53; XXXIV (1910), 41-61.

Whittlesey, Charles, ed. *Papers Relating to the Expeditions of Colonel Bradstreet and Colonel Bouquet in Ohio, A.D., 1764.* (Western Reserve and Northern Ohio Historical Society, *Tract*, Nos. 13-14). Cleveland, 1873.

Williams, Edward G., ed. "The Orderly Book of Colonel Henry Bouquet's Expedition Against the Ohio Indians, 1764," *Western Pennsylvania Historical Magazine*, XLII (Mar., June, Sept. 1959), 9-33, 179-200, 283-302.

Young, A. H., ed. *The Parish Register of Kingston, Upper Canada, 1785-1811.* Kingston, Ont., The British Whig Publishing Co., 1921.

————, ed. "The Rev. Robert Addison; Extracts from the Reports and (Manuscript) Journals of the Society for the Propagation of the Gospel in Foreign Parts." Ontario Historical Society, *Papers and Records*, XIX (1922), 171-91.

JOURNALS

Bonnecamps, Père Joseph Pierre de. "Account of the Voyage on the Beautiful River Made in 1749, Under the Direction of Monsieur de Celoron, by Father Bonnecamps." in Thwaites, Reuben G., ed.

Jesuit Relations and Allied Documents . . . Cleveland, 1900. LXIX, 150-99. Reprinted in *Ohio Archaeological and Historical Quarterly*, XXIX (Oct. 1920), 397-423.

Boucherville, M. de. "Relation des aventures de M. de Boucherville à son retour des Scioux, en 1728 et 1729, suivie d'observations sur les moeurs, coutumes, &c de ces sauvages." in Bibaud, Michel, *Bibliothèque canadienne*, III (juin-oct. 1826), 11-15, 46-50, 36-39, 127-30, 166-67.

Brehm, Diederick. "Lieut. Diederick Brehm." Ed. by Gideon D. Scull. *New England Historical and Genealogical Register*, XXXVII (1883), 21-26.

Burton, M. Agnes, ed., Ford, R. Clyde, trans. *Journal of Pontiac's Conspiracy, 1763.* Detroit, 1912.

Céloron, Pierre-Joseph. "Celoron's Journal [1749]." Ed. by A. A. Lambing. *American Catholic Historical Researches*, II (1885), 61-76, 103-13, 132-46, III (1886), 21-33, 68-71.

Carver, Jonathan. *Travels of Jonathan Carver Through the Interior Parts of North America in the Years 1766, 1767, and 1768.* London, J. Walter, 1778.

Chaussegros de Léry, Joseph-Gaspard. "Journal de Joseph-Gaspard Chaussegros de Léry, lieutenant des troupes, 1754-1755." Quebec (Province) Archives, *Rapport de l'archiviste de la province de Québec*, 1927-28. [Québec, 1928]. p. 355-429.

————. "Journal de la campagne faite par le détachement du Canada sur les Chicachas en février 1740 au nombre de 201 français . . ." Quebec (Province) Archives, *Rapport de l'archiviste de la province de Québec*, 1922-23 [Québec, 1923]. p. 157-65.

————. "Les journaux de campagne de Joseph-Gaspard Chaussegros de Léry." Quebec (Province) Archives, *Rapport de l'archiviste de la province de Québec*, 1926-27, 1927-28, 1928-29 [Québec, 1927, 1928, 1929]. p. 331-405, 355-429, 227-45.

————. *Journal of Chaussegros de Léry.* Ed. by Sylvester K. Stevens, and Donald H. Kent, trans. by Frontier Forts and Trails Survey, Work Projects Administration, Federal Works Agency (*Northwestern Pennsylvania Historical Series*). Harrisburg, 1939.

Croghan, George. *George Croghan's Journal of His Trip to Detroit in 1767; With His Correspondence Relating Thereto: Now Published for the First Time from the Papers of General Thomas Gage in the William L. Clements Library.* Ed. by Howard H. Peckham. Ann Arbor, University of Michigan Press; London, Humphrey Milford, Oxford University Press, 1939.

————. "George Croghan's Journal, 1759-1763; from the Original in the Cadwalader Collection of the Historical Society of Pennsylvania." Ed. by Nicholas B. Wainwright. *Pennsylvania Magazine of History and Biography*, LXXI (Oct. 1947), 303-444.

————. "A Selection of George Croghan's Letters and Journals Relating to Tours into the Western Country—November 16, 1750-November 1765." in Thwaites, Reuben Gold, ed. *Early Western Travels* . . . Cleveland, Arthur H. Clark Company, 1904. I, 45-173.

Delisle, Legardeur. "A Search for Copper on the Illinois River: The Journal of Legardeur Delisle, 1772." Ed. by Stanley Faye. Illinois State Historical Society, *Journal*, XXXVIII (Mar. 1945), 38-57.

Galinée, De Bréhant de. "Exploration of the Great Lakes, 1669-1670 by Dollier de Casson and De Bréhant de Galinée; Galinée's Narrative and Maps with an English Version, Including all the Map-Legends." Trans. and ed. by James H. Coyne. Ontario Historical Society, *Papers and Records*, IV (1903), 1-89.

Gist, Christopher. *Christopher Gist's Journals with Historical, Geographical, and Ethnological Notes*. Ed. by William M. Darlington. Pittsburgh, J. R. Weldin & Co., 1893.

Gordon, Harry. "Gordon's Journal, May 8, 1766-December 6, 1766." in Alvord, Clarence W. and Carter, Clarence E., eds. *The New Régime, 1765-1767 (Collections* of the Illinois State Historical Library, Vol. XI, *British Series*, Vol. II). Springfield, Ill., 1916. p. 290-311.

Gorrell, James. "Lieut. James Gorrell's Journal." (*Collections* of the State Historical Society of Wisconsin, Vol. I). Madison, 1855. p. 24-48.

————. "Lieut. James Gorrell's Journal from Montreal on the Expedition Commanded by Major Wilkins." *Maryland Historical Magazine*, IV (June 1909), 183-87.

Haldimand, Frederick. "Private Diary of Gen. Haldimand," Canada, Public Archives. *Report on Canadian Archives*, 1889. Ottawa, 1890. p. 123-299.

Hamilton, Henry. "Account of the Expedition of Lieut. Gov. Hamilton." (*Michigan Historical Collections*, Vol. IX). Lansing, 1908. p. 489-516. Journal of Aug. 6, 1778-June 16, 1779.

————. "Report by Lieut.-Governor Henry Hamilton on His Proceedings from Nov., 1776, to June, 1781." in Great Britain, Historical Manuscripts Commission, *Report on the Manuscripts of Mrs. Stopford-Sackville of Dayton House, Northhampshire*. Hereford, England, 1910. II, 223-48.

Henry, Alexander. *Alexander Henry's Travels and Adventures in the*

Years 1760-1776. Ed. by Milo M. Quaife. (Chicago, R. R. Donnelley & Sons Company, 1921.

Hutchins, Thomas. *The Courses of the Ohio River, Taken by Lt. T. Hutchins, Anno 1766, and Two Accompanying Maps.* Ed. by Beverly W. Bond, Jr. Cincinnati, Historical and Philosophical Society of Ohio, 1942.

————. "Western Pennsylvania in 1760; a Journal of a March from Fort Pitt to Venango, and from Thence to Presqu'Isle." *Pennsylvania Magazine of History and Biography,* II (1878), 149-53.

Jennings, John. "John Jennings' Journal at Fort Chartres, and Trip to New Orleans, 1768." *Pennsylvania Magazine of History and Biography,* XXXI (1907), 304-10.

————. "John Jennings' Journal, from Fort Pitt, to Fort Chartres in the Illinois Country, March-April 1766," *Pennsylvania Magazine of History and Biography,* XXXI (1907), 145-56.

"Journal of the Siege of Fort Detroit by the Confederate Indian Nations, Acting Under Pontiac [1763]." in Schoolcraft, Henry R. *Information Respecting the History, Condition and Prospects of the Indian Tribes of the United States.* Philadelphia, Lippincott, Grambo & Co., J. B. Lippincott & Co., 1851-57. 6 vols. II (1852), 242-304.

"Journal or History of a Conspiracy by the Indians Against the English, and of the Siege of Fort Detroit, by Four Different Nations, Beginning on the 7th of May, 1763." (*Michigan Historical Collections,* Vol. VIII). Lansing, 1886. p. 266-339.

La Pause, Jean-Guillaume-Charles de Plantavit de Margon, Chevalier de. "Les mémoires du Chevalier de la Pause." Quebec (Province) Archives. *Rapport de l'archiviste de la province de Québec,* 1932-33. [Québec], 1933. p. 305-91.

————. "Mémoire et observations sur mon voyage au Canada." Quebec (Province) Archives, *Rapport de l'archiviste de la province de Québec,* 1931-32. [Québec], 1932. p. 3-46.

————. "Les papiers La Pause." Quebec (Province) Archives, *Rapport de l'archiviste de la province de Québec, 1933-34.* [Québec], 1934. p. 65-231.

La Vérendrye, Pierre Gaultier de Varennes, Sieur de. *Journals and Letters of Pierre Gaultier de Varennes de La Vérendrye and His Sons, with Correspondence between the Governors of Canada and the French Court, Touching the Search for the Western Sea.* Ed. by Lawrence J. Burpee. (The *Publications* of the Champlain Society, Vol. [VI]). Toronto, The Champlain Society, 1927.

Legardeur de Saint Pierre, Jacques Repentigny. "Memoir or Summary

Journal of the Expedition of Jacques Repentigny Legardeur de Saint Pierre, Knight of the Royal and Military Order of Saint Louis, Captain of a Company of Troops Detached from the Marine in Canada, Charged with the Discovery of the Western Sea." Canada, Public Archives. *Report on Canadian Archives, 1886.* Ottawa, 1887. p. clviii-clxix.

Littlehales, Edward B., *Journal Written by Edward Baker Littlehales . . . of an Exploratory Tour, Partly in Sleighs But Chiefly on Foot, from Navy Hall, Niagara, to Detroit, Made in the Months of February and March, A.D. 1793 by His Excellency Lieut.-Gov. Simcoe.* Ed. by Henry Scadding. Toronto, 1889. Originally published in the *Canadian Literary Magazine,* May 1834; also published in the London and Middlesex Historical Society, *Transactions,* VIII (1917), 5-18.

Marin, Joseph de la Marque, Sieur. "Marin versus La Vérendrye." Ed. by Grace, Lee Nute. *Minnesota History,* XXXII (Winter 1951), 226-38.

Montrésor, John. "Journal of John Montrésor's Expedition to Detroit in 1763." Ed. by John C. Webster. Royal Society of Canada, *Proceedings and Transactions,* 3d ser., XXII, sect. II (May 1927), 8-31.

――――, and Montrésor, James. *The Montrésor Journals.* Ed. by Gideon D. Scull (*Collections* of the New York Historical Society, 1881). New York, 1882.

Morgan, George. "Morgan's Journal, September 30, 1767-November 1, 1767." in Alvord, Clarence W. and Carter, Clarence E., eds. *Trade and Politics, 1767-1769 (Collections* of the Illinois State Historical Library, Vol. XVI, *British Series,* Vol. III). Springfield, 1921. p. 67-71.

――――. "Voyage Down the Mississippi, November 21, 1766-December 18, 1766." in Alvord, Clarence W. and Carter, Clarence E., eds. *The New Régime, 1765-1767 (Collections* of the Illinois State Historical Library, Vol. XI, *British Series,* Vol. II). Springfield, Ill., 1916. p. 1-64.

Morris, Thomas. "Journal of Captain Thomas Morris, of His Majesty's XVII Regiment of Infantry [Aug.-Sept. 1764]." in his *Miscellenies in Prose and Verse.* London, Printed for James Ridgway, 1791. p. 1-39. Also published in Thwaites, Reuben G., ed. *Early Western Travels, 1748-1846.* Cleveland, Arthur H. Clark Company, 1904. I, 301-28; in the *Magazine of History,* extra no. 76 (1922), 5-29;

and in Peckham, Howard H., ed. in the *Old Fort News*, VI (Feb. 1941), 3-11.

Passerat de la Chapelle, Baron. "La Chapelle's Remarkable Retreat Through the Mississippi Valley, 1760-61." Trans. and ed. by Louise P. Kellogg. *Mississippi Valley Historical Review*, XXII (June 1935), 63-81.

"The Pontiac Manuscript: Journal or History of a Conspiracy by the Indians Against the English, and of the Siege of Fort Detroit, by Four Different Nations, Beginning on the 7th of May, 1763." Trans. by Rudolph Worch and F. Krusty (*Michigan Historical Collections*, VIII). Lansing, 1886. p. 266-339.

Porteous, John. "From Fort Niagara to Mackinac in 1767." Ed. by F. Clever Bald. *Inland Seas*, II (Apr. 1946), 86-97. Reprinted from Algonquin Club of Detroit, *Historical Bulletin*, No. 2 (Mar. 1938).

———. "Schenectady to Michilimackinac 1765 & 1766." Journal of John Porteous. Ed. by Fred C. Hamil. Ontario Historical Society, *Papers and Records*, XXXIII (1939), 75-98.

Radisson, Pierre Esprit. *The Explorations of Pierre Esprit Radisson; from the Original Manuscript in the Bodleian Library and the British Museum*. Ed. by Arthur T. Adams. Minneapolis, Ross & Haines, Inc., 1961.

———. *Voyages of Peter Esprit Radisson, Being an Account of His Travels and Experiences Among the North American Indians, from 1652 to 1684*. Ed. by Gideon D. Scull (The *Publications* of the Prince Society, Vol. 16). Boston, The Prince Society, 1885. Reprint, New York, Peter Smith, 1943.

Rogers, Robert. "Journal of Robert Rogers the Ranger on His Expedition for Receiving the Capitulation of the Western French Posts (October 20, 1760 to February 14, 1761)." Ed. by Victor H. Paltsits. New York Public Library, *Bulletin*, XXXVII (Apr. 1933), 261-76.

———. *Journals of Major Robert Rogers: Containing Account of the Several Excursions He Made Under the Generals Who Commanded Upon the Continent of North America, during the Late War*. Ed. by Franklin B. Hough. Albany, Joel Munsell's Sons, 1883. Originally published in London in 1765.

———. "Rogers's Michilimackinac Journal [Sept. 21, 1766-July 3, 1767]." Ed. by William L. Clements. American Antiquarian Society, *Proceedings*, n.s., XXVIII, pt. 2 (Oct. 1918), 224-73.

Rutherford, Lt. "Rutherford's Narrative—an Episode in the Pontiac

War, 1763; an Unpublished Manuscript by Lieut. Rutherford of the Black Watch." Canadian Institute, *Transactions*, III (Sept. 1893), 229-51.

Simcoe, Mrs. John G. *The Diary of Mrs. John Graves Simcoe, Wife of the First Lieutenant Governor of the Province of Upper Canada, 1792-6.* Ed. by John R. Robertson. Toronto, W. Briggs, 1911.

Tonty, Henri de. *Relation of Henry de Tonty, Concerning the Explorations of La Salle from 1678 to 1683.* Trans. by Melville B. Anderson. Chicago, The Caxton Club, 1898.

Trent, William. *Journal of Captain William Trent from Logstown to Pickawillany, A.D. 1752; Now Published for the First Time From a Copy in the Archives of the Western Reserve Historical Society, Cleveland, Ohio, Together with Letters of Governor Robert Dinwiddie; an Historical Notice of the Miami Confederacy of Indians; a Sketch of the English Post at Pickawillany, with a Short Biography of Captain Trent, and Other Papers Never before Printed.* Ed. by Alfred T. Goodwin. Cincinnati, R. Clarke & Co. for W. Dodge, 1871.

Weiser, Conrad. "The Journal of Conrad Weiser, Esqr., Indian Interpreter, to the Ohio [1748]." in Thwaites, Reuben G., ed. *Early Western Travels.* Cleveland, Arthur H. Clark Company, 1904. I, 21-44.

INVENTORIES, GUIDES, CALENDARS, ETC.

American Association for State and Local History. *Directory [of] Historical Societies and Agencies in the United States and Canada, 1963.* Madison, Wis., 1963.

Andrews, Charles M. *Guide to the Materials for American History to 1783, in the Public Record Office of Great Britain* (Carnegie Institution of Washington, *Publication* No. 90-A, Vol. I). Washington, 1912.

————. "List of the Commissions and Instructions Issued to the Governors and Lieutenant Governors of the American and West Indian Colonies from 1609 to 1784." American Historical Association, *Annual Report*, 1911, I, 393-528.

————, and Davenport, Frances G. *Guide to the Manuscript Materials for the History of the United States to 1783, in the British Museum, in Minor London Archives, and in the Libraries of Oxford and Cambridge* (Carnegie Institution of Washington, *Publication* No. 90). Washington, 1908.

Biggar, Henry P. "The Public Archives at Ottawa." Institute of Historical Research, *Bulletin,* II (Feb. 1925), 66-79; III (June 1925), 38-44.

British Museum, Department of Manuscripts. *Catalogue of Additions to the Manuscripts in the British Museum, in the Years MDCCCLIV-MDCCCLX.* London, 1875. 2 vols.

———. *Catalogue of the Manuscript Maps, Charts, and Plans, and of the Topographical Drawings in the British Museum.* London, 1844-61. 3 vols. in 4.

British Museum, Department of Printed Books, Map Room. *Catalogue of the Printed Maps, Plans, and Charts in the British Museum.* London, 1885. 2 vols.

Canada, Bureau of Statistics. *Chronological List of Canadian Censuses.* Ottawa, 1942.

———. "Chronological Summary of Population Growth in Canada, with Sources of Information, 1605-1931." *Seventh Census of Canada,* 1931. Ottawa, 1933-36. 13 vols. I, 133-53.

Canada, Department of Agriculture. "Censuses of Canada, 1665 to 1871." *Census of Canada, 1870-71.* Vol. 14. Ottawa, 1876.

Canada, Public Archives. "Abstracts of the Actes de foy et hommage (Fealty Rolls)." *Report on Canadian Archives,* 1885. Ottawa, 1886. p. 1-29, 31-76.

———. "Bouquet Collection." *Report on Canadian Archives,* 1889. Ottawa, 1890.

———. "Calendar of Manuscripts in the Archives of the Chicago Historical Society." *Report on Canadian Archives,* 1905. Ottawa, 1906. I, xxxii-xlvii.

———. "Calendar of Miscellaneous State Papers Addressed by the Secretaries of State for the Colonies to the Governors General or Officers Administering the Province of Lower Canada from 1784-1841 (Series G of Public Archives)." *Report of the Public Archives,* 1938. Ottawa, 1939. Appendix I, p. 1-15.

———. "Calendar of Series C. O. 42 [Great Britain, Public Records Office, Colonial Office Papers]." *Report of the Public Archives,* 1921. Ottawa, 1922. Appendix D, p. 283-359.

———. "Calendar of State Papers, Addressed by the Secretaries of State for the Colonies to the Governors General or Officers Administering the Province of Lower Canada, from 1787 until 1841 (Series G of Public Archives)." *Report of the Public Archives,* 1930-32. Ottawa, 1931-33. Appendix A.

———. "Calendar of State Papers, Addressed by the Secretaries of

State for the Colonies to the Lieutenant Governors or Officers Administering the Province of Upper Canada, 1796-[1841]." *Report of the Public Archives,* 1933, 1935-37. Ottawa, 1934, 1936-38. Appendixes.

———. "[Calendar of] State Papers—Governors' Correspondence, Minutes of Council, Miscellaneous Letters and Papers [1760-1799]." *Report on Canadian Archives,* 1890. Ottawa, 1891.

———. "[Calendar of] State Papers—Lower Canada [1791-1800]." *Report on Canadian Archives,* 1891-92. Ottawa, 1892-93. p. 1-200. 1800-07. *ibid.,* 1892. Ottawa, 1893. p. 153-285.

———. "[Calendar of] State Papers—Upper Canada [1791-1801]." *Report on Canadian Archives,* 1891. Ottawa, 1892. p. 1-177. 1801-07. *ibid.,* 1892. Ottawa, 1893. p. 286-399.

———. *Catalogue of Maps, Plans and Charts in the Map Room of the Dominion Archives.* Comp. by H. R. Holmden (*Publications* of the Canadian Archives No. 8). Ottawa, 1912.

———. "Guide to Calendars of Series and Collections in the Public Archives." *Report of the Public Archives,* 1949. Ottawa, 1950. p. 451-59.

———. *A Guide to the Documents in the Manuscript Room at the Public Archives of Canada, Vol. I.* Comp. by David W. Parker (*Publications* of the Archives of Canada No. 10). Ottawa, 1914.

———. "Haldimand Collection, Calendar." *Report on Canadian Archives,* 1884-89. Ottawa, 1885-90.

———. *Index to Reports of Canadian Archives from 1872 to 1908* (*Publications* of the Canadian Archives No. 1). Ottawa, 1909.

———. *Inventory of the Military Documents in the Canadian Archives.* Comp. by Ernest A. Cruikshank (*Publications* of the Canadian Archives No. 2). Ottawa, 1910.

———. "Papers in the Possession of Mr. C. M. Burton, of Detroit." *Report on Canadian Archives,* 1905. Ottawa, 1906. I, xxiv-xxxii.

———. *Report on Manuscript Lists in the Archives Relating to the United Empire Loyalists, with Reference to Other Sources.* Comp. by William Wilfred Campbell. [Ottawa?] 1909.

———. "Summary of Documents in Paris Made by the Late Mr. Edouard Richard [Colonial Archives, Series B]." *Report on Canadian Archives,* 1899 (*Supplement*), 1904, 1905. Ottawa, 1901, 1904, 1905.

———. "Synopsis of Manuscript Documents Relating to Canada Examined at the Ministère de la Marine, Paris, Colonial Archives, Canada—Correspondance Générale [Series C11A]." Comp. by

Joseph Marmette. *Report on Canadian Archives, 1885-87.* Ottawa, 1886-88.

———, Manuscript Division. *Inventaire provisoire; fonds des manuscrits, no. 1, Archives nationales, Paris, Archives des colonies.* Ottawa, 1952.

———, ———. *Inventaire provisoire, fonds des manuscrits, no. 2, Archives de la marine, no. 3, Archives nationales, no. 4, Archives de la guerre, Paris.* Ottawa, 1954.

———, ———. *Preliminary Inventory, Manuscript Group 8, Quebec Provincial and Local Records; Manuscript Group 9, Provincial, Local and Territorial Records.* Ottawa, 1961.

———, ———. *Preliminary Inventory, Manuscript Group 11, Public Record Office, London, Colonial Office Papers.* [Ottawa], 1952.

———, ———. *Preliminary Inventory, Manuscript Group 18, Pre-conquest Papers.* Ottawa, 1954.

———, ———. *Preliminary Inventory, Manuscript Group 19, Fur Trade and Indians, 1763-1867.* Ottawa, 1954.

———, ———. *Preliminary Inventory, Manuscript Group 21, Transcripts from Papers in the British Museum.* Ottawa, 1955.

———, ———. *Preliminary Inventory, Manuscript Group 23, Late Eighteenth Century Papers.* Ottawa, 1957.

———, ———. *Preliminary Inventory, Record Group 1, Executive Council, Canada, 1764-1867.* Ottawa, 1953.

———, ———, *Preliminary Inventory, Record Group 4, Civil and Provincial Secretaries Offices, Canada East, 1760-1867; Record Group 5, Civil and Provincial Secretaries' Offices, Canada West, 1788-1867.* Ottawa, 1953.

———, ———, *Preliminary Inventory, Record Group 7, Governor General's Office.* [Ottawa], 1953.

———, ———. *Preliminary Inventory, Record Group 8, British Military and Naval Records.* Ottawa, 1954.

———, ———. *Preliminary Inventory, Record Group 10, Indian Affairs.* Ottawa, 1951.

Caron, Ivanhoë. "Les archives de l'archevêché de Québec." Société canadienne d'histoire de l'église catholique, *Rapport,* 1934-35, 65-73.

———. "Inventaire de la correspondance de Mgr. Jean-François Hubert, évêque de Québec et de Mgr. Charles-François Bailly de Messein, son coadjuteur." Quebec (Province) Archives. *Rapport de l'archiviste de la province de Québec,* 1930-31. [Québec], 1931. p. 199-351.

————. "Inventaire de la correspondance de Mgr. Jean-Olivier Briand, évêque de Québec, 1741 a 1794." Quebec (Province) Archives. *Rapport de l'archiviste de la province de Québec, 1929-30.* [Québec], 1930, p. 47-136.

————. "Inventaire de la correspondance de Mgr. Louis-Philippe Mariaucheau d'Esgly, évêque de Québec [1740 à 1791]." Quebec (Province) Archives. *Rapport de l'archiviste de la province de Québec.* 1930-31. [Québec], 1931, p. 185-98.

————. "Inventaire de la correspondance de Mgr. Pierre-Denaut, évêque de Québec, 1794 à 1806." Quebec (Province) Archives. *Rapport de l'archiviste de la province de Québec, 1931-32.* [Québec], 1932, p. 127-242.

————. "Inventaire des documents concernant l'église du Canada sous le régime français." Quebec (Province) Archives. *Rapport de l'archiviste de la province de Québec,* 1939-40, 1940-41, 1941-42. [Québec], 1940-42, p. 155-353, 333-473, 178-298.

Day, Richard E., comp. *Calendar of the Sir William Johnson Manuscripts in the New York State Library.* Albany, University of the State of New York, 1909.

Duboscq, Guy. "Inventaire des archives départementales, communales et hospitalières se rapportant à l'histoire ecclésiastique." *Revue d'histoire de l'église de France,* XXXVI (1950), 70-75; XXXVIII (1952), 90-91.

East, Ernest E., and Norton, Margaret C. "Randolph County Records: an Inventory of Microfilm Copies in the Illinois State Library." *Illinois Libraries,* XXXV (June 1953), 256-62.

Ellis, John T. "A Guide to the Baltimore Cathedral Archives." *Catholic Historical Review,* XXXII (Oct. 1946), 341-60.

Esdaile, Arundell J. K. *The British Museum Library; a Short History and Survey.* London, George Allen & Unwin, Ltd., 1946.

France, Archives nationales. *Le fonds du Conseil d'état du roi aux Archives nationales; guide des recherches.* Par Michel Antoine. Paris, Imprimerie nationale, 1955.

France, Direction des archives de France. *État des inventaires des archives nationales, départmentales, communales et hospitalières; supplément (1937-1954).* Paris, Imprimerie nationale, 1955.

————. *Guide des recherches dans les fonds judiciares de l'ancien régime.* Par Michel Antoine, Henri-François Buffet, Suzanne Clémencet, Ferreol de Ferry, Monique Langlois, Yvonne Lanhers, Jean-Paul Laurent, Jacques Meurgey de Typigny. Paris, Imprimerie nationale, 1958.

France, Ministère de la France d'Outre-Mer, Service des archives. *Inventaire analytique de la correspondance générale avec les colonies, départ, série B (déposée aux Archives nationales), I, registres 1 à 37 (1654-1715).* Par Étienne Taillemite. Paris, 1959.

Gingras, Achille, Frère. *Répertoire des sources manuscrites de l'histoire religieuse canadienne en Europe surtout à Paris, à Rome et à Londres, de 1608 a 1860.* Lévis, P. Q., Les Frères de l'Instruction Chrétienne Saint-Romuald d'Etchemin, 1958-59.

Great Britain, Colonial Office, Library. *Catalogue of the Maps, Plans and Charts in the Library of the Colonial Office.* [London], 1910.

————, Historical Manuscripts Commission. *A Guide to the Reports on Collections of Manuscripts of Private Families, Corporations and Institutions in Great Britain and Ireland Issued by the Royal Commissioners for Historical Manuscripts.* London, 1914, 1935. Pts. I-II.

————, ————. *Report on American Manuscripts in the Royal Institution of Great Britain Presented to Parliament by Command (Report on Historical Manuscripts, Unnumbered Series).* London, 1904-09. 4 vols.

————, ————. National Register of Archives. *Bulletin of the National Register of Archives,* No. 1-12, London, 1948-63.

Great Britain, Public Record Office. *Guide to the Contents of the Public Record Office, Volume I, Legal Records, etc., Volume II, State Papers and Departmental Records; Revised and Extended to (1960) from the Guide by the Late M. S. Giuseppi, F.S.A.* London, Her Majesty's Stationery Office, 1963.

————, Public Record Office. *A Guide to the Manuscripts Preserved in the Public Record Office.* Comp. by M. S. Giuseppi. London, 1923, 1924. 2 vols.

————, ————. *Guide to the Public Records, Part I, Introductory.* London, 1949.

Hale, Richard W., Jr. *Guide to Photocopied Historical Materials in the United States and Canada.* Ithaca, Cornell University Press, 1961.

Hamer, Philip M., ed. *A Guide to Archives and Manuscripts in the United States.* Compiled for the National Historical Publications Commission. New Haven, Yale University Press, 1961.

Historical Records Survey, Illinois. *Guide to Depositories of Manuscript Collections in Illinois.* Chicago, June 1940.

————, Michigan. *Guide to Church Vital Statistics Records in Michigan: Wayne County.* Detroit, Apr. 1942.

————, ————. *Inventory of the Church Archives of Michigan; The*

Roman Catholic Church: Archdiocese of Detroit. Detroit, July 1941.

———, Minnesota. *Guide to Depositories of Manuscript Collections in the United States: Minnesota.* St. Paul, Mar. 1941.

———, Missouri. *Guide to Depositories of Manuscript Collections in the United States: Missouri.* St. Louis, 1940.

———, ———. *Guide to Vital Statistics; Church Records in Missouri.* St. Louis, Apr. 1942.

———, Pennsylvania. *Guide to Depositories of Manuscript Collections in Pennsylvania.* Ed. by Margaret S. Eliot and Sylvester K. Stevens, Harrisburg, 1939.

———, Wisconsin. *Guide to Depositories of Manuscript Collections in Wisconsin.* Madison, Jan. 1941.

Hubach, Robert R. "Unpublished Travel Narratives of the Early Midwest, 1720-1850: a Preliminary Bibliography." *Mississippi Valley Historical Review,* XLII (Dec. 1955), 525-48.

Illinois, University, Illinois Historical Survey. *Guide to Manuscript Materials of American Origin in the Illinois Historical Survey.* Comp. by Marguerite Jenison Pease (Illinois Historical Survey, *Publication* No. 6). Urbana, Ill., 1956.

———, ———. *Guide to Manuscript Materials Relating to Western History in Foreign Depositories Reproduced for the Illinois Historical Survey.* Comp. by Marguerite Jenison Pease (Illinois Historical Survey, *Publication* No. 5). Urbana, 1956.

Jameson, John Franklin. "Guide to the Items Relating to American History in the Reports of the English Historical Manuscripts Commission and Their Appendixes." American Historical Association, *Annual Report,* 1898, 611-708.

Kelley, Arthur R., ed. "Church and State Papers for the Years 1759 to 1786, Being a Compendium of Documents Relating to the Establishment of Certain Churches in the Province of Quebec." Quebec (Province) Archives. *Rapport de l'archiviste de la province de Québec,* 1948-49. [Québec, 1950], p. 293-340.

———. "Jacob Mountain First Lord Bishop of Quebec, a Summary of His Correspondence and of Papers Related Thereto for the Years 1793 to 1799 Compiled from Various Sources." Quebec (Province) Archives. *Rapport de l'archiviste de la province de Québec,* 1942-43. [Québec], 1943, p. 177-260.

———. "The Quebec Diocesan Archives; a Description of the Collection of Historical Records of the Church of England in the Diocese of Quebec." Quebec (Province) Archives. *Rapport de l'archiviste de la province de Québec,* 1946-47 [Québec, 1948], p. 181-298.

Kenney, James F. *The Public Records of the Province of Quebec 1763-1791.* Reprinted from the Royal Society of Canada, *Transactions,* 3d ser., XXXIV, sect. II (1940), 87-133.

Kula, S. "Archives of the Church of England Missionary Societies in the Public Archives of Canada." Committee on Archives of the United Church of Canada, *Bulletin,* XI (1958), 8-17.

Lanctôt, Gustave. *Les archives du Canada.* Lévis, P. Q., La Cie de publication de Lévis, 1926.

Leland, Waldo G. *Guide to Materials for American History in the Libraries and Archives of Paris, Volume I, Libraries* (Carnegie Institution of Washington, *Publication* No. 392, Vol. I). Washington, 1932.

————, and Meng, John J., and Doysié, Abel. *Guide to Materials for American History in the Libraries and Archives of Paris, Volume II, Archives of the Ministry of Foreign Affairs* (Carnegie Institution of Washington, *Publication* No. 392). Washington, 1943.

Lincoln, Charles H. "A Calendar of the Manuscripts of Col. John Bradstreet in the Library of the American Antiquarian Society." American Antiquarian Society, *Proceedings,* n.s., XIX (Apr. 15, 1908), 103-81.

————. "Calendar of the Manuscripts of Sir William Johnson in the Library of the [American Antiquarian] Society." American Antiquarian Society, *Proceedings,* n.s., XVIII (Oct. 1907), 367-401.

Manitoba, Legislative Library, Archives Branch. *Preliminary Inventory.* Winnipeg, 1955.

Massicotte, Edouard-Zotique. "Arrêts, édits, ordonnances, mandements et règlements conservés dans les archives du Palais de Justice de Montréal; première partie 1653-1700." Royal Society of Canada, *Proceedings and Transactions,* 3d ser., X, sect. I (Dec. 1917, Mar. 1918), 147-74; XII, sect. I (Dec. and Mar. 1919), 209-23.

————. "Les arrêts, édits, ordonnances, mandements et règlements conservés à Montréal." *Bulletin des recherches historiques,* XXXIV (sept. 1928), 520-27.

————. "Congés et permis déposés ou enregistrés à Montréal sous la régime français." Quebec (Province) Archives. *Rapport de l'archiviste de la province de Québec,* 1921-22. [Québec], 1922. p. 189-225.

————. *Montréal sous le régime français; répertoire des arrêts, édits,*

mandements, ordonnances et règlements conservés dans les archives au Palais de Justice de Montréal, 1640-1760. Montréal,
1919.

Matteson, David M. *Lists of Manuscripts Concerning American History
Preserved in European Libraries and Noted in Their Published
Catalogues and Similar Printed Lists* (Carnegie Institution of
Washington, *Publication* No. 359). Washington, 1925.

Meilleur-Barthe, J.-B. "Inventaire sommaire des archives conservés au
Palais de Justice des Trois-Rivières." Quebec (Province) Archives.
Rapport de l'archiviste de la province de Québec, 1920-21. [Qué-
bec], 1921. p. 328-49.

Michigan, University, William L. Clements Library of American History. *Guide to the Manuscript Collections in the William L. Clements Library*. Comp. by Howard H. Peckham. Ann Arbor, University of Michigan Press, London, Humphrey Milford, Oxford University Press, 1942.

———, ———. *Guide to the Manuscript Maps in the William L.
Clements Library*. Comp. by Christian Brun. Ann Arbor, The
University of Michigan, 1959.

Minnesota Historical Society. *Manuscripts Collections of the Minnesota Historical Society, Guide Number 2*. Comp. by Lucile M.
Kane and Kathryn A. Johnson. St. Paul, 1955.

Newberry Library, Edward E. Ayer Collection. *A Check List of Manuscripts in the Edward E. Ayer Collection*. Comp. by Ruth Lap-
ham Butler, Chicago, The Newberry Library, 1937.

———, ———. *List of Manuscript Maps in the Edward E. Ayer Collection*. Comp. by Clara A. Smith, Chicago, 1927.

New France, Conseil supérieur de Québec. "Analytical table of the
Judgments and Deliberations of the Supreme Council from the
11th of January 1717 to the [22d of December 1739]." Quebec
(Province) Secretary, *Report of the Secretary and Registrar of
the Province of Quebec*, 1892-93 (Quebec, Parlement, *Sessional
Papers*, 1892, Vol. 2, 1893, Vol. 2). Quebec, 1892-93, p. 167-228,
126-236.

———, ———. *Inventaire des insinuations du Conseil souverain de
la Nouvelle-France*. Par Pierre-Georges Roy (*Archives de la province de Québec* [no. 6]). Beauceville, P. Q., 1921.

———, ———. *Inventaire des jugements et délibérations du Conseil
supérieur de la Nouvelle-France de 1717 à 1760*. Par Pierre-
Georges Roy. Beauceville, P. Q., 1932-35. 7 vols.

————, Cour de la prévôté de Québec. *Inventaire des insinuations de la prévôté de Québec.* Par Pierre-Georges Roy (*Archives de la province de Québec*). Beauceville, P. Q., 1936. 3 vols.

————, Intendant. *Inventaire des ordonnances des intendants de la Nouvelle-France, conservés aux Archives provinciales de Québec.* Par Pierre-Georges Roy (*Archives de la province de Québec*). Beauceville, P. Q., 1919. 4 vols.

New York Historical Society. *Survey of the Manuscript Collections in the New York Historical Society.* New York, 1941.

Ouellet, Fernand. "Inventaire de la saberdache de Jacques Viger." Quebec (Province) Archives. *Rapport de l'archiviste de la province de Québec,* 1955-56 et 1956-57. [Québec, 1958]. p. 31-176.

Pargellis, Stanley M. and Cuthbert, Norma B. "Loudoun Papers (a) Colonial, 1756-58, (b) French Colonial, 1742-53." *Huntington Library Bulletin,* no. 3 (Feb. 1933), 97-107.

Parker, David W. *A Guide to the Documents in the Manuscript Room at the Public Archives of Canada.* Vol. I (*Publications* of the Archives of Canada No. 10). Ottawa, 1914.

————. *Guide to the Materials for United States History in Canadian Archives* (Carnegie Institution of Washington, *Publication* No. 172). Washington, 1913.

Paullin, Charles O. and Paxson, Frederic L. *Guide to the Materials in London Archives for the History of the United States Since 1783* (Carnegie Institution of Washington, *Publication* No. 90-B). Washington, 1914.

Pease, Marguerite Jenison. "Archives in Randolph County; a Revised Inventory." *Illinois Libraries,* XLIII (June 1961), 433-48.

Pease, Theodore C. *The County Archives of the State of Illinois* (*Collections* of the Illinois State Historical Library, Vol. XII, *Bibliographical Series,* Vol. III). Springfield, 1915.

Pennsylvania Historical and Museum Commission. *Preliminary Guide to the Research Materials of the Pennsylvania Historical and Museum Commission.* Harrisburg, 1959.

Provost, Honorius, Rev. "Inventaire des documents concernant l'histoire du Canada conservés aux archives de Chicago." *Revue d'histoire de l'Amérique française,* IV (sept., déc. 1950, mars, 1951), 294-302, 453-58, 591-600.

Quebec (Province) Archives. "Les congés de traite sous le régime français au Canada." *Rapport de l'archiviste de la province de Québec,* 1922-23. [Québec], 1923, p. 191-265.

―――. *Index du Bulletin des recherches historiques, organe du Bureau des archives, 1895-1925.* Par Pierre-Georges Roy (*Archives de la province de Québec*). Beauceville, P. O., 1925-26. 4 vols.

―――. *Inventaire des concessions en fief et seigneurie, fois et hommages et aveux et dénombrements conservés aux archives de la province de Québec.* Par Pierre-Georges Roy (*Archives de la province de Québec*). Beauceville, P. Q., 1927-29. 6 vols.

―――. *Inventaire des greffes des notaires du régime français.* Par Pierre-Georges Roy et Antoine Roy (*Archives de la province de Québec*). Québec, 1942-60. 19 vols.

―――. "Répertoire des engagements pour l'ouest conservés dans les Archives judiciaires de Montréal [1670-1821]." *Rapport de l'archiviste de la province de Québec*, 1929/30-1932/33, 1942/43-1946/47. [Québec], 1930-33, 1943-47. 1929/30—1944/45, par Edouard-Zotique Massicotte; 1945-46 par Louis Chaboillez et J. G. Beek; 1946-47 par Jean-Jacques Lefebvre.

Quebec (Province) Judicial archives. *Inventaire des contrats de mariage du régime français conservés aux Archives judiciaires de Québec.* Par Pierre-Georges Roy (*Archives de la province de Québec*). Quebec, 1937-38. 6 vols.

―――. *Inventaire des registres de l'état civil conservés aux Archives judiciaires de Québec.* Par Pierre-Georges Roy. Beauceville, P. Q., 1921.

―――. *Inventaire des testaments, donations et inventaires du régime français conservés aux Archives judiciaires de Québec.* Par Pierre-Georges Roy. (*Archives de la province de Québec*). Québec, 1941. 3 vols.

Quebec (Province) Secretary. "An Analytical Index of the Archives of Montreal from 1651 [to 1695]." Comp. by Eudore Evanturel. *Fourth [-Fifth] Report of the Secretary of the Province of Quebec, Registrar's Division*, 1889/90-1890/91 (Quebec, Parlement, *Sessional Papers*, 1890, Vol. 24, pt. 2). Quebec, 1890-91. p. 73-91, 79-298.

―――. "Analytical Table of the Unpublished Documents Relating to the History of New France Transcribed from the Originals of Paris and London and Now in the Custody of the Office of the Registrar of the Province of Quebec." *First Report of the Secretary of the Province of Quebec, Registrar's Division*, 1886-87 (Quebec, Parlement, *Sessional Papers*, 1888, Vol. 21, pt. 2). Quebec, 1888. Annex 10, p. 68-263.

―――. "Catalogue of the Volumes and Registers Found in the Vaults of the Superior Court at Montreal." *Third Report of the Secretary of the Province of Quebec, Registrar's Division,* 1888-89 (Quebec, Parlement, *Sessional Papers,* 1890, Vol. 23, pt. 2). Quebec, 1890. p. 131-38.

————. "Chronological List or Index of Grants en Fief and Royal Ratifications of Grants en Fief Made in New France to the Time of Its Cession to the British Crown in 1760." *Report of the Secretary and Registrar of the Province of Quebec,* 1892 (Quebec, Parlement, *Sessional Documents,* 1892, Vol. 26, pt. 2). Quebec, 1893. p. 120-66.

————. "Civil Registers of the Prévoté of Quebec." *First Report of the Secretary of the Province of Quebec, Registrar's division,* 1886-87 (Quebec, Parlement, *Sessional Papers,* 1888, Vol. 21, pt. 2). Quebec, 1888. p. 62-66.

————. "List of Historical Records Actually in the Vaults of the Provincial Registrar." *Third Report of the Secretary of the Province of Quebec, Registrar's Division,* 1888-89 (Quebec, Parlement, *Sessional Papers,* 1890, Vol. 23, pt. 2). Quebec, 1890. p. 128-29.

————. "List of the Historical Volumes and Registers in the Vault of the Department of the Registrar of the Province of Quebec." *Report of the Secretary and Registrar,* 1904 (Quebec, Parlement, *Sessional Papers,* 1905, Vol. 38, pt. 2). Quebec, 1904. p. 6-18.

————. "List of the Registers Transferred from the Archives Office, St. Ann Street, to the Registrar's Department." *Second Report of the Secretary of the Province of Quebec, Registrar's Division,* 1887-88 (Quebec, Parlement, *Sessional Papers,* 1889, Vol. 22, pt. 2). Quebec, 1889, p. 9-13.

Roy, Joseph-Edmond. "Les archives du Canada, à venir à 1872." Royal Society of Canada, *Proceedings and Transactions,* 3d ser., IV (1910), 57-123.

————. *Rapport sur les archives de France relatives à l'histoire du Canada (Publications* des Archives du Canada No. 6). Ottawa, 1911.

Stevens, Sylvester K. and Kent, Donald H. *Pennsylvania Sources in Various Western Depositories; a Preliminary Checklist.* Harrisburg, 1949.

Surrey, Mrs. Nancy Maria (Miller). *Calendar of Manuscripts in Paris Archives and Libraries Relating to the History of the Mississippi Valley to 1803.* Washington, Carnegie Institution of Washington, 1926-28. 2 vols.

Survey of Federal Archives, Illinois. *Inventory of Federal Archives in* the States, Series VIII, The Department of the Interior, No. 12, Illinois. Chicago, 1941.

——, Minnesota. *Inventory of Federal Archives in the States, Series VIII, The Department of the Interior, No. 22, Minnesota.* St. Paul, Minn., 1941.

——, Wisconsin. *Inventory of Federal Archives in the States, Series VIII, The Department of the Interior, No. 48, Wisconsin.* Madison, 1939.

Thomas, Daniel H. and Case, Lynn M., eds. *Guide to the Diplomatic Archives of Western Europe.* Philadelphia, University of Pennsylvania Press, 1959.

Toronto Public Library. *Guide to the Manuscript Collection in the Toronto Public Libraries.* Toronto, Toronto Public Libraries, 1954.

United Empire Loyalist Centennial Committee, Toronto. *The Centennial of the Settlement of Upper Canada by United Empire Loyalists 1784-1884; The Celebrations at Adolphustown, Toronto, and Niagara; with an Appendix Containing a Copy of the U. E. List Preserved in the Crown Lands Department at Toronto.* Toronto, Rose Publishing Co., 1885. Appendix, p. [125]-334.

U.S. Library of Congress, Manuscript Division. *Handbook of Manuscripts in the Library of Congress.* Washington, 1918.

——, ——. *A Guide to Manuscripts Relating to American History in British Depositories Reproduced for the Division of Manuscripts of the Library of Congress.* Comp. by Grace Gardner Griffin. Washington, Government Printing Office, 1946.

——, Photoduplication Service. *A Guide to the Microfilm Collection of Early State Records.* Prepared by the Library of Congress in Association with the University of North Carolina; Collected and Compiled under the direction of William Sumner Jenkins; Edited by Lillian A. Hamrick. Washington, 1950. *Supplement,* 1951.

U.S. National Archives. *Preliminary Inventory of the Land-Entry Papers of the General Land Office.* Comp. by Harry P. Yoshpe and Philip P. Brower. (*Preliminary Inventory,* No. 22). Washington, 1949.

Vachon, André. "Inventaire critique des notaires royaux des gouvernements de Québec, Montréal et Trois-Rivières (1663-1764)." *Revue d'histoire de l'Amérique française,* IX (déc 1955, mars 1956), 423-38, 546-61; X (juin, sept., déc. 1956), 93-103, 257-63, 381-90; XI (juin, sept., déc. 1957), 93-106, 270-76, 400-06.

Virginia Colonial Records Project. *The British Public Record Office; History, Description, Record Groups, Finding Aids, and Materials for American History with Special Reference to Virginia* (Virginia

Colonial Records Project, *Special Reports* 25, 26, 27, 28, Virginia State Library *Publication* No. 12). Richmond, Va., 1960.

Virginia 350th Anniversary Celebration Consultants in History and Archives to the Joint Commission. *The Search Room Catalogues and Other Finding Aids to the Records Preserved in the Public Record Office, London* (Virginia Colonial Records Project, *Special Report* No. 27). Charlottesville, 1957.

Wisconsin, State Historical Society, Library. *Descriptive List of Manuscript Collections of the State Historical Society of Wisconsin . . .* Ed. by Reuben G. Thwaites. Madison, The Society, 1906.

———. *Guide to the Manuscripts of the Wisconsin Historical Society.* Comp. by Alice E. Smith. Madison, 1944.

———. *Guide to the Manuscripts of the State Historical Society of Wisconsin, Supplement Number One.* Comp. by Josephine L. Harper and Sharon C. Smith. Madison, 1957.

Wroth, Lawrence C., and Annan, Gertrude L., comps. "Acts of French Royal Administration Concerning Canada, Guiana, the West Indies, and Louisiana, Prior to 1791." New York Public Library, *Bulletin,* XXXIII (Oct., Dec. 1929), 789-800, 868-93; XXXIV (Jan.-Mar. 1930), 21-55, 87-126, 155-93. Reprinted, New York, New York Public Library, 1930.

PRINTED SOURCES

American State Papers; Documents, Legislative, and Executive of the Congress of the United States. Ed. by Walter Lowrie and Matthew St. Clair Clarke. Washington, Gales and Seaton, 1832-61. 38 vols. *Public Lands,* Vol. I-VIII (1789-1837). Washington, 1832-61.

Canada, Public Archives. *Report of the Public Archives,* 1873-1955/58. Ottawa, 1874-1959. The reports for 1873-80 are included in the *Report of the Minister of Agriculture;* those for 1873-1924 are also in the *Sessional Papers* of Parliament; also separately published from 1881.

Carter, Clarence E., ed. *The Territorial Papers of the United States.* Washington, Government Printing Office, 1934-50. Vols. II-IV, *Northwest Territory;* VII-VIII, *Indiana Territory;* X-XII, *Michigan Territory;* XVI-XVII, *Illinois Territory.*

Edgar, Lady Matilda. *Ten Years of Upper Canada in Peace and War, 1805-1815; Being the Ridout Letters . . .* Toronto, William Briggs, 1890.

Hutchins, Thomas. *A Topographical Description of Virginia, Pennsylvania, Maryland, and North Carolina.* Ed. by Frederick C. Hicks. Cleveland, The Burrows Brothers Company, 1904.

Illinois, Auditor of Public Accounts. *Biennial Report,* 1882. Springfield, 1882.

Illinois, Laws, Statutes, etc. *Laws of the State of Illinois,* 1855, 1879. Springfield, 1855, 1879.

Illinois, State Historical Library. *Biennial Report of the Board of Trustess,* 1889/90-1928/30. Springfield, Danville, 1891-1931.

Michigan Pioneer and Historical Society. *Michigan Historical Collections,* I-XL, 1874/76-1929. Lansing, 1877-1929. Title varies; published from 1915 as *Michigan Historical Collections.* Vols. XXXIX-XL published by the Michigan Historical Commission.

Michigan Pioneer and Historical Society. "Report of the Committee of Historians." *Michigan Historical Collections,* III, VI-XXVI (1881, 1883-94/95). Lansing, 1881, 1884-96.

Miller, Hunter, ed. *Treaties and Other International Acts of the United States of America.* Washington, Government Printing Office, 1931-48. 8 vols.

New York, State Library. *94th Annual Report,* 1911. Albany, University of the State of New York, 1913.

Ontario, Department of Public Records and Archives. *First [-Twentieth] Report of the Department of Public Records and Archives of Ontario,* 1903-33. Toronto, 1904-34. No reports published for 1921-27, 1934-date.

Ontario, Laws, Statutes, etc. *Statutes of the Province of Ontario.* Toronto, 1871.

Pittman, Philip. *The Present State of the European Settlements on the Mississippi, With a Geographical Description of That River Illustrated by Plans and Draughts.* Ed. by Frank H. Hodder. Cleveland, Arthur H. Clark Company, 1906.

Quebec (Province) Archives. *Rapport de l'archiviste de la province de Québec,* 1920/21-1957/58 et 1959/60. [Québec], 1921-61.

Quebec (Province) Legislative Council. "Report of the Committee of Quebec on the Ancient Archives [Mar. 1790]." in Canada, Public Archives, *Report Concerning the Public Archives,* 1904. Ottawa, 1905. Appendix D, p. 82-189.

Quebec (Province) Secretary. *Report of the Secretary and Registrar,* 1886/87-1920/21. Quebec, 1888-1921.

Smith, William H., ed. *The St. Clair Papers; The Life and Public Services of Arthur St. Clair . . . With His Correspondence and Other Papers.* Cincinnati, Robert Clarke & Co., 1882. 2 vols.

U.S. Congress. "Land Claims in Michigan; Report of the Committee on Public Lands, of the House of Representatives of the U. States, in Relation to Claims to Lands in the Territory of Michigan, Jan. 2, 1828." *House Report* 42, 20 Congress, 1 Session. Washington, 1828. Serial 176. Reprinted in *American State Papers, Public Lands.* Washington, Duff Green, 1834. IV, 695-879.

U.S. General Land Office. *Annual Report,* 1817-1957. The reports for the years 1817-48 are in U.S. Treasury Department, *Annual Report of the Secretary of the Treasury on the State of the Finances;* 1849-1957 are in U.S. Department of the Interior, *Annual Report of the Secretary of the Interior.*

U.S. Laws, Statutes, etc. *The Statutes at Large of the United States of America,* 1789-date. Boston, C. C. Little and J. Brown, 1845-51; Boston, Little, Brown and Company, 1855-73; Washington, Government Printing Office, 1875-date.

U.S. Library of Congress. *Report of the Librarian of Congress,* 1866-1960. Washington, Government Printing Office, 1866-1961.

Wilson, Joseph S. "Special Report by Joseph S. Wilson in Regard to Surveying Archives of Missouri, Iowa, and Wisconsin [May 26, 1866]; Report of the Secretary of the Interior, Nov. 19, 1866." *House Executive Document* 1, 39 Congress, 2 Session, Washington, 1866. p. 400-11. Serial 1284.

SECONDARY PUBLICATIONS

A. Books

Alden, John R. *General Gage in America; Being Principally a History of His Role in the American Revolution.* Baton Rouge, Louisiana State University Press, 1948.

Alvord, Clarence W. *The Illinois Country, 1673-1818 (The Centennial History of Illinois,* Vol. I). Springfield, Illinois Centennial Commission, 1920.

———. *The Mississippi Valley in British Politics; a Study of the Trade, Land Speculation, and Experiments in Imperialism Culminating in the American Revolution.* Cleveland, Arthur H. Clark Company, 1917. 2 vols.

Andrews, Roger. *Old Fort Mackinac on the Hill of History.* Menominee, Mich., Herald-Leader Press, 1938.

Bailey, Kenneth P. *The Ohio Company of Virginia and the Westward Movement, 1748-1792; a Chapter in the History of the Colonial Frontier.* Glendale, Calif., Arthur H. Clark Company, 1939.

Bayliss, Joseph and Estelle. *Historic St. Joseph Island.* Cedar Rapids, Ia., The Torch Press, 1938.

Beers, Henry P. *The Western Military Frontier, 1815-1846* (University of Pennsylvania, Ph.D. Dissertation). Philadelphia, Privately Printed, 1935.

Belting, Natalia M. *Kaskaskia Under the French Regime (Illinois Studies in the Social Sciences,* Vol. XXIX, No. 3). Urbana, University of Illinois Press, 1948.

Bond, Beverley W., Jr. *The Foundations of Ohio (The History of the State of Ohio,* ed. by Carl Wittke, Vol. I). Columbus, State Archaeological and Historical Society, 1941.

Brebner, John B. *The Explorers of North America, 1492-1806 (The Pioneer Histories,* ed. by V. T. Harlow and J. A. W. Williamson). New York, The Macmillan Company, 1933.

Breese, Sidney. *The Early History of Illinois from Its Discovery by the French in 1673, Until Its Cession to Great Britain in 1763* . . . Chicago, E. B. Myers & Company, 1884.

Buck, Solon J. and Buck, Elizabeth H. *The Planting of Civilization in Western Pennsylvania.* Pittsburgh, University of Pittsburgh Press, 1939.

Burpee, Lawrence J. *The Discovery of Canada.* Toronto, Macmillan Company of Canada, Limited, 1944.

––––––. *The Search for the Western Sea; the Story of the Exploration of North-western America.* Toronto, Macmillan Company, 1935. 2 vols.

Burt, Alfred L. *The Old Province of Quebec.* Toronto, The Ryerson Press; Minneapolis, University of Minnesota Press, 1933.

––––––. *The United States, Great Britain and British North America from the Revolution to the Establishment of Peace after the War of 1812.* New Haven, Yale University Press; Toronto, The Ryerson Press, 1940.

Burton, Clarence M. *Cadillac's Village, or Detroit under Cadillac with List of Property Owners and a History of the Settlement from 1701 to 1710.* Detroit, 1896.

––––––, and others, eds. *The City of Detroit, Michigan, 1701-1922.* Detroit, Chicago, The S. J. Clarke Publishing Company, 1922. 5 vols.

Cadden, John P. *The Historiography of the American Catholic Church, 1785-1943* (The Catholic University of America, *Studies in Sacred Theology* No. 82). Washington, Catholic University of America Press, 1944.

Caldwell, Norman W. *The French in the Mississippi Valley, 1740-1750 (Illinois Studies in Social Sciences,* Vol. XXVI, No. 3). Urbana, University of Illinois Press, 1941.

Campbell, Marjorie E. W. *The Northwest Company.* New York, St. Martin's Press, 1957.

Canada, Royal Commission on National Development in the Arts, Letters, and Sciences, 1949-1951. *Royal Commission Studies; a Selection of Essays Prepared for the Royal Commission . . .* Ottawa, 1951.

Caron, Ivanhoë. *La colonisation de la province de Québec; débuts du régime anglais, 1760-1791.* Québec, 1923.

Carter, Clarence E. *Great Britain and the Illinois Country, 1763-1774.* Washington, America Historical Association, 1910.

Crouse, Nellie M. *In Quest of the Western Ocean.* New York, William Morrow & Co., 1928.

Cuneo, John R. *Robert Rogers of the Rangers.* New York, Oxford University Press, 1959.

Curry, Cora C. *Records of the Roman Catholic Church in the United States as a Source of Authentic Genealogical and Historical Material* (National Genealogical Society, *Genealogical Publications* No. 5). Washington, 1935.

Cuthbertson, George A. *Freshwater; a History and a Narrative of the Great Lakes.* New York, The Macmillan Company, 1931.

Davidson, Gordon C. *The Northwest Company* (University of California, *Publications in History,* Vol. VII). Berkeley, University of California Press, 1918.

De Brumath, A. Leblond. *Bishop Laval (The Makers of Canada Series,* Vol. 2). Toronto, Morang & Co., Limited, 1906.

DeVoto, Bernard. *The Course of Empire,* With Maps by Erwin Raisz. Boston, Houghton, Mifflin, 1952.

Dictionary of American Biography. Ed. by Allen Johnson and Dumas Malone. New York, Charles Scribner's Sons, 1928-36. 20 vols.

Dictionary of National Biography. Ed. by Sir Leslie Stephen and Sir Sidney Lee. London, Oxford University Press, 1921-22. 21 vols. Reprint edition.

Dorrance, Ward A. *The Survival of the French in the Old District of Sainte Genevieve* (University of Missouri, Ph.D. Dissertation). Columbia, Mo., 1935.

Doughty, Arthur G. *The Canadian Archives and Its Activities.* Ottawa, F. A. Acland, 1924.

Downes, Ralph C. *Council Fires on the Upper Ohio; a Narrative of*

Indian Affairs in the Upper Ohio Valley Until 1795. Pittsburgh, University of Pittsburgh Press, 1940.

Eavenson, Howard N. *Map Maker and Indian Traders; an Account of John Patten, Trader, Arctic Explorer, and Map Maker; Charles Swaine, Author, Trader, Public Official, and Arctic Explorer; Theodorus Swaine Drage, Clerk, Trader, and Anglican Priest.* Pittsburgh, University of Pittsburgh Press, 1949.

Esarey, Logan. *History of Indiana from Its Exploration to 1922.* Dayton, Ohio, Dayton Historical Publishing Co., 1922-23. 3 vols.

Farmer, Silas. *The History of Detroit and Michigan, or The Metropolis Illustrated; a Chronological Cyclopaedia of the Past and Present, Including a Full Record of Territorial Days in Michigan and the Annals of Wayne County.* Detroit, Silas Farmer & Co., 1884. 2 vols.

Fite, Emerson D. and Freeman, Archibald. *A Book of Old Maps, Delineating American History from the Earliest Days Down to the Close of the Revolutionary War.* Cambridge, University Press, 1926.

Folwell, William W. *A History of Minnesota.* St. Paul, Minnesota Historical Society, 1921-30. 4 vols.

Fowle, Otto. *Sault Ste. Marie and Its Great Waterways.* New York, G. P. Putnam's Sons, 1925.

Friis, Herman R. *A Series of Population Maps of the Colonies and the United States, 1625-1790* (American Geographical Society, *Mimeographed Publication* No. 3). New York, 1940.

Gipson, Lawrence H. *Lewis Evans; To Which Is Added Evans' A Brief Account of Pennsylvania.* Philadelphia, Historical Society of Pennsylvania, 1939.

————. *Zones of International Friction North America, South of the Great Lakes Region, 1748-1754 (The British Empire before the American Revolution,* Vol. IV). New York, Alfred A. Knopf, 1939.

————. *Zones of International Friction; The Great Lakes Frontier, Canada, the West Indies, India, 1748-1754 (The British Empire before the American Revolution,* Vol. V). New York, Alfred A. Knopf, 1942.

Greene, Evarts B., and Harrington, Virginia D. *American Population before the Federal Census of 1790.* New York, Columbia University Press, 1932.

Gregg, William. *Short History of the Presbyterian Church in the Dominion of Canada from the Earliest to the Present Time.* Toronto. Printed for the Author by C. Blackett Robinson, 1893.

Hammang, Francis H. *The Marquis de Vaudreuil; New France at the Beginning of the Eighteenth Century.* Bruges, Belgium, Descleé de Brouwer, 1938.

Hanna, Charles A. *The Wilderness Trail; or, the Ventures and Adventures of the Pennsylvania Traders on the Allegheny Path.* New York and London, G. P. Putnam's Sons, 1911. 2 vols.

Hughes, Thomas A. *History of the Society of Jesus in North America, Colonial and Federal.* London, New York, Longmans, Green, and Co., 1907-17. 3 vols.

Hunter, William A. *Forts on the Pennsylvania Frontier, 1753-1758.* Harrisburg, Pennsylvania Historical and Museum Commission, 1960.

Innis, Harold A. *The Fur Trade in Canada; an Introduction to Economic History.* Toronto, University of Toronto Press, 1956.

Jacobs, Wilbur R. *Diplomacy and Indian Gifts; Anglo-French Rivalry Along the Ohio and Northwest Frontiers, 1748-1763.* Stanford, Calif., Stanford University Press, 1950.

James, Alfred P. *The Ohio Company: Its Inner History.* Pittsburgh, University of Pittsburgh Press, 1959.

James, James A. *The Life of George Rogers Clark.* Chicago, University of Chicago Press, 1928.

Karpinski, Louis C. *Historical Atlas of the Great Lakes and Michigan, to Accompany the Bibliography of the Printed Maps of Michigan.* Lansing, 1931.

Kellogg, Louise P. *The British Régime in Wisconsin and the Northwest.* Madison, State Historical Society of Wisconsin, 1935.

————. *The French Régime in Wisconsin and the Northwest.* Madison, State Historical Society of Wisconsin, 1925.

Kennedy, William P. M. *The Constitution of Canada, 1534-1937; an Introduction to Its Development, Law and Custom.* London, New York, Toronto, Oxford University Press, 1938.

Kent, Donald H. *The French Invasion of Western Pennsylvania, 1753.* Harrisburg, Pennsylvania Historical and Museum Commission, 1954.

Kuczynski, Robert R. *Birth Registration and Birth Statistics in Canada* (The Institute of Economics of the Brookings Institution, *Publication* No. 38). Washington, 1930.

Laut, Agnes C. *The 'Adventures of England' on Hudson Bay; a Chronicle of the Fur Trade in the North (Chronicles of Canada Series,* ed. by George M. Wrong and H. H. Langton). Toronto, Glasgow, Brook & Company, 1914.

Law, John. *The Colonial History of Vincennes Under the French, British and American Governments.* Vincennes, Ind., Harney, Mason & Co., 1858.

Leacock, Stephen B. *Montreal Seaport and City.* New York, Doubleday, Doran & Company, Inc., 1945.

Le Jeune, Louis-Marie. *Dictionnaire général de biographie, histoire, littérature, agriculture, commerce, industrie et des arts, sciences, moeurs, coutumes, institutions, politiques et religieuses du Canada.* Ottawa, Université d'Ottawa, 1931. 2 vols.

Lewis, George E. *The Indiana Company, 1763-1798; a Study in Eighteenth Century Frontier Land Speculation and Business Venture (Old Northwest Historical Series,* Vol. IV). Glendale, Calif., Arthur H. Clark Company, 1941.

Livermore, Shaw. *Early American Land Companies; Their Influence on Corporate Development.* New York, Humphrey Milford, Oxford University Press, 1939.

Lucas, Charles P. *A History of Canada, 1763-1812.* Oxford, At the Clarendon Press, 1909.

Lux, Leonard. *The Vincennes Donation Lands* (Indiana Historical Society, *Publications,* Vol. 15, No. 4). Indianapolis, 1949.

McAvoy, Thomas T. *The Catholic Church in Indiana, 1789-1834.* (Columbia University, Ph.D. Dissertation). New York, Columbia University Press, 1940.

McInnis, Edgar. *Canada, a Political and Social History.* New York, Toronto, Rinehart & Company, Inc., 1959.

Martin, Chester B. *Lord Selkirk's Work in Canada (Oxford Historical and Literary Studies,* Vol. 7). Oxford, At the Clarendon Press, 1916.

Mason, Edward G. *Kaskaskia and Its Parish Records: Old Fort Chartres; and Col. John Todd's Record-Book (Fergus Historical Series* No. 12). Chicago, 1881.

Maxwell, Moreau S. and Binford, Lewis H. *Excavation of Fort Michilimackinac, Mackinac City, Michigan, 1959 Season.* (Michigan State University *Publications of the Museum, Cultural Series,* vol. 1, no. 1). East Lansing, 1961.

Melançon, Arthur. *Liste des missionaires—jésuites, Nouvelle-France et Louisiane, 1611-1800.* Montréal, Collège Sainte-Marie, 1929.

Middleton, Jesse E., and Landon, Fred. *The Province of Ontario, a History, 1615-1927.* Toronto, The Dominion Publishing Company, Limited, 1927. 4 vols.

Millman, Thomas R. *Jacob Mountain: First Lord Bishop of Quebec; a*

Study in Church and State (University of Toronto Studies, History and Economic Series, Vol. X). Toronto, University of Toronto Press, 1947.

Morton, Arthur S. *A History of the Canadian West to 1870-71; Being a History of Rupert's Land (The Hudson's Bay Company's Territory) and of the Northwest Territory (Including the Pacific Slope).* London, New York, T. Nelson & Sons, Ltd., [1939]

Mulvey, Mary D. *French Catholic Missionaires in the Present United States (1604-1791)* (The Catholic University of America, *Studies in American Church History,* Under the direction of Rt. Rev. Msgr. Peter Guilday, Vol. XXIII). Washington, 1936.

Munro, William B. *The Seigniorial System in Canada; a Study in French Colonial Policy (Harvard Historical Studies,* Vol. XIII). New York, Longmans, Green, and Co., 1907.

Neal, Frederick. *The Township of Sandwich (Past and Present).* Windsor, Ont., The Record Printing Co., Limited, 1909.

Neatby, Hilda M. *The Administration of Justice Under the Quebec Act.* London, Humphrey Milford, Oxford University Press; Minneapolis, The University of Minnesota Press, 1937.

Neill, Edward D. *The History of Minnesota: from the Earliest French Exploration to the Present Time.* Minneapolis, Minnesota Historical Company, 1882.

Nute, Grace Lee. *Caesars of the Wilderness: Médard Chouart, Sieur des Groseilliers, and Pierre Esprit Radisson, 1618-1710.* New York, London, D. Appleton-Century Company, 1943.

———. *The Voyageur.* New York, London, D. Appleton and Company, 1931.

———. *The Voyageur's Highway; Minnesota's Border Lake Land.* St. Paul, The Minnesota Historical Society, 1941.

O'Brien, Cornelius. *Memoirs of Rt. Rev. Edmund Burke, Bishop of Zion, First Vicar Apostolic of Nova Scotia.* Ottawa, Thoburn & Co., 1894.

Palm, Sister Mary B. *The Jesuit Missions of the Illinois Country, 1673-1763* (St. Louis University, Ph.D. Dissertation). St. Louis, 1931.

Paré, George. *The Catholic Church in Detroit, 1701-1888.* Detroit, The Gabriel Richard Press, 1951.

Patterson, George C. *Land Settlement in Upper Canada, 1783-1840* (Ontario, Dept. of Public Records and Archives, *Sixteenth Report,* 1920). Toronto, 1921.

Paullin, Charles O. *Atlas of the Historical Geography of the United States.* Ed. by John K. Wright (Carnegie Institution of Washington, *Publication* No. 401). Washington, New York, Published Jointly by the Carnegie Institution of Washington and the American Geographical Society of New York, 1932.

Paxson, Frederic L. *History of the American Frontier, 1763-1893.* Boston, Houghton Mifflin Company, 1924.

Perrin, J. Nick. *Perrin's History of Illinois.* Springfield, Illinois State Register, 1906.

Phillips, Paul C. and Smurr, J. W. *The Fur Trade.* Norman, University of Oklahoma Press, 1961. 2 vols.

Pierce, Bessie L. *A History of Chicago.* New York, London, Alfred A. Knopf, 1937-57. 3 vols.

Priestley, Herbert I. *France Overseas Through the Old Regime; a Study of European Expansion.* New York, London, D. Appleton-Century Company, 1939.

Pound, Arthur. *Johnson of the Mohawks; a Biography of Sir William Johnson.* New York, The Macmillan Company, 1930.

Quaife, Milo M. *Wisconsin: Its History and Its People, 1634-1924.* Chicago, The S. J. Clarke Publishing Co., 1924. 4 vols.

Rich, Edwin E. *The History of the Hudson's Bay Company, 1670-1870.* London, The Hudson's Bay Record Society, 1958-59. 2 vols.

Riddell, William R. *The Life of John Graves Simcoe, First Lieutenant-Governor of the Province of Upper Canada, 1792-96.* Toronto, McClelland & Stewart, 1926.

———. *The Life of William Dummer Powell, First Judge at Detroit and Fifth Chief Justice of Upper Canada.* Lansing, Michigan Historical Commission, 1924.

———. *Michigan Under British Rule, Law and Law Courts, 1760-1796.* Lansing, Michigan Historical Commission, 1926.

Robinson, Percy J. *Toronto During the French Régime; a History of the Toronto Region from Brûlé to Simcoe, 1615-1793.* Toronto, The Ryerson Press; Chicago, University of Chicago Press, 1933.

Roy, Joseph-Edmond. *Histoire du notariat au Canada.* Lévis, Imprimé à la Revue du notariat, 1899-1902. 4 vols.

Rupp, Israel D. *Early History of Western Pennsylvania, and of the West, and of Western Expeditions and Campaigns, from MDCCLIV to MDCCCXXXIII.* Pittsburgh, D. W. Kauffman; Harrisburg, W. O. Hickok, 1846.

Russell, Nelson V. *The British Régime in Michigan and the Old Northwest, 1760-1796.* Northfield, Minn., Carleton College, 1939.

Savelle, Max. *George Morgan, Colony Builder.* New York, Columbia University Press, 1932.

Scanlan, Peter L. *Prairie du Chien: French, British, American.* Menasha, Wis., George Banta Publishing Company, 1937.

Shortt, Adam, and Doughty, Arthur G., eds. *Canada and Its Provinces: a History of the Canadian People and Their Institutions.* Toronto, Printed by T. & A. Constable at The Edinburgh University Press for the Publishers Association of Canada, Limited, 1914-17. 23 vols.

Slick, Sewell E. *William Trent and The West.* Harrisburg, Pa., Archives Publishing Co. of Pennsylvania, Inc., 1947.

Smith, William. *Historical Account of Bouquet's Expedition Against the Ohio Indians in 1764.* Cincinnati, Robert Clarke & Co., Reprint of the London edition by T. Jefferies, 1766.

Sosin, Jack M. *Whitehall and the Wilderness; the Middle West in British Colonial Policy, 1760-1775.* Lincoln, Nebr., University of Nebraska Press, 1961.

Stevens, Wayne E. *The Northwest Fur Trade, 1763-1800* (University of Illinois, *Studies in the Social Sciences,* Vol. XIV, No. 3). Urbana, University of Illinois, 1928.

Stone, William L. *The Life and Times of Sir William Johnson, Bart.* Albany, J. Munsell, 1865. 2 vols.

Stuart, Henry C. *The Church of England in Canada, 1759-1793, From the Conquest to the Establishment of the See of Quebec.* Montreal, John Lovell & Son, 1893.

Sulte, Benjamin. *Histoire des canadiens-français, 1608-1880; origine, histoire, religion, guerres, découvertes, colonisation, coutumes, vie domestique, sociale et politique, développement, avenir.* Montréal, Wilson & Cie, 1882-84. 8 vols.

Tanguay, Cyprien. *Dictionnaire généalogique des familles canadiennes depuis la fondation de la colonie jusqu'à nos jours.* Montréal, E. Senécal & Fils, 1871-90. 7 vols.

————. *Répertoire général du clergé canadien, par ordre chronologique depuis la fondation de la colonie jusqu'à nos jours.* Québec, C. Darveau, 1868.

Thwaites, Reuben G. *France in America, 1497-1763* (*The American Nation; a History,* Vol. 7, ed. by Albert B. Hart). New York, London, Harper & Brothers, 1905.

Treat, Payson J. *The National Land System, 1785-1820.* New York, E. B. Treat & Company, Publishers, 1910.

Trudel, Marcel. *L'église canadienne sous le régime militaire, 1759-1764.* Montréal, Les études de l'institut d'histoire de l'Amérique française, 1956.

Tucker, Sara Jones. *Indian Villages of the Illinois Country* (Illinois State Museum, *Scientific Papers*, Vol. II, pt. I, *Atlas*). Springfield, 1942.

Volwiler, Albert T. *George Croghan and the Westward Movement, 1741-1782*. Cleveland, Arthur H. Clark Company, 1926.

Wade, Mason. *The French Canadians, 1760-1945*. Toronto, The Macmillan Company of Canada, Limited, 1955.

Wainwright, Nicholas B. *George Croghan, Wilderness Diplomat*. Chapel Hill, Published for the Institute of Early American History and Culture by the University of North Carolina Press, 1959.

Walker, Fintan G. *The Catholic Church in the Meeting of Two Frontiers: The Southern Illinois Country (1763-1793)* (The Catholic University of America, *Studies in American Church History*, Vol. XIX). Washington, Catholic University Press, 1935.

Wallace, Paul A. W. *Conrad Weiser, 1696-1760, Friend of Colonist and Mohawk*. Philadelphia, University of Pennsylvania Press; London, Humphrey Milford, Oxford University Press, 1945.

Wallace, William Stewart, ed. *The Encyclopedia of Canada*. Toronto, University Associates of Canada Limited, 1935-37. 6 vols.

———. *The Pedlars from Quebec, and Other Papers on the Nor'-westers*. Toronto, The Ryerson Press, 1954.

Wheat, Carl I. *Mapping the Trans-Mississippi West, 1540-1861, Volume One, the Spanish Entrada to the Louisiana Purchase, 1540-1804*. San Francisco, The Institute of Historical Cartography, 1957.

Winsor, Justin. *Cartier to Frontenac; Geographical Discovery in the Interior of North America in Its Historical Relations, with Full Cartographical Illustrations from Contemporary Sources*. Boston and New York, Houghton, Mifflin and Company, 1894.

———, ed. *Narrative and Critical History of America*. Boston, New York, Houghton, Mifflin and Company, 1884-89. 8 vols.

Wittke, Carl. *A History of Canada*. New York, F. S. Crofts & Co., 1933.

Wood, William C. H., *et al*, eds. *The Storied Province of Quebec Past and Present*. Toronto, Dominion Publishing Company, Limited, 1931-32. 5 vols.

Wrong, George M. *The Rise and Fall of New France*. New York, Macmillan Company, 1928. 2 vols.

Yeigh, Frank. *Ontario's Parliament Buildings; or, a Century of Legislation, 1792-1892; a Historical Sketch*. Toronto, Williamson Book Company, Ltd., 1893.

B. ARTICLES

Adair, E. R. "The Evolution of Montreal under the French Regime." Canadian Historical Association, *Report*, 1942, 20-41.

Adams, Randolph G. "A New Library of American Revolutionary Records." *Current History*, XXXIII (Nov. 1930), 234-38.

Aitchison, J. H. "The Courts of Requests in Upper Canada." *Ontario History*, XLI (1949), 125-32.

Alvord, Clarence W. "Eighteenth Century French Records in the Archives of Illinois." American Historical Association, *Annual Report*, 1905, I, 353-66.

———. "Father Pierre Gibault and the Submission of Post Vincennes, 1778." *American Historical Review*, XIV (Apr. 1909), 544-57.

———. "The Finding of the Kaskaskia Records." Illinois State Historical Society, *Transactions* (1906), Illinois State Historical Library, *Publication* No. 11, 27-31.

———. "Illinois in the Eighteenth Century; a Report on the Documents in Belleville, Illinois." Illinois State Historical Library, *Bulletin*, I, No. 1 (1905), 7-38.

———. "The Old Kaskaskia Records." Chicago Historical Society, *Proceedings*, III (1906), 33-57.

———, and Pease, Theodore C. "Archives of the State of Illinois." American Historical Association, *Annual Report*, 1909, 383-463.

Archambault, A.-S. "Les registres de l'état civil de la province de Québec." *Revue trimestrielle canadienne*, IV (mai 1918), 52-68.

Audet, Francis-J. "Gouverneurs, lieutenant-gouverneurs, et administrateurs de la province de Québec, des Bas et Haut Canadas, du Canada sous l'Union et de la puissance du Canada, 1763-1908." Royal Society of Canada, *Proceedings and Transactions*, 3d ser., II (1908), 85-124.

Auger, Roland-J. "Registre des abjurations (1662-1757)." Société généalogique canadienne-française, *Mémoires*, V (juin 1953), 243-46.

Bannon, John F. "The Saint Louis University Collection of Jesuitica Americana." *Hispanic American Historical Review*, XXXVII (Feb. 1957), 82-88.

Barber, Edward W. "Life and Labors of Col. Michael Shoemaker." (*Michigan Historical Collections*, Vol. XXVII). Lansing, 1897. 209-33.

Baudot, M. "Les archives départementales, centres de la documentation régionale," *La gazette des archives*, n.s., no. 9 (jan. 1961), 46-55.

Baudry, René. "Les archives de France et l'histoire du Canada." dans *Mélanges offerts par ses confrères étrangers à Charles Braibant.* Bruxelles, Comité des Mélanges Braibant, 1959. p. 31-42.

Beckham, Jessie E. "The British Historical Manuscripts Commission." *American Archivist,* VII (Jan. 1944), 41-48.

Beers, Henry P. "The Papers of the British Commanders in Chief in North America." *Military Affairs,* XIII (Summer 1949), 79-94.

Bellemare, Raphael. "Vice-rois et lieutenants généraux des rois de France, en Amérique." Société historique de Montréal, *Mémoires et documents relatifs à l'histoire du Canada.* Montréal, Duvernay, fréres, 1859. III, 97-122.

Beuckman, Frederick. "The Commons of Kaskaskia, Cahokia, and Prairie du Rocher. *Illinois Catholic Historical Review,* I (Apr. 1919), 405-12.

Bonin, M.-R., P.S.S. "Les archives sulpiciennes source d'histoire ecclésiastique." Société canadienne d'histoire de l'église catholique, *Rapport,* 1934-35, 39-50.

Bonnault, Claude de, éd. "Le Canada militaire état provisoire des officiers de milice de 1641 à 1760." Quebec (Province) Archives. *Rapport de l'archiviste de la province de Québec,* 1949-50 et 1950-51. [Québec, 1952] p. 261-527.

Bovey, Wilfred. "Some Notes on Arkansas Post and St. Philippe in the Mississippi Valley." Royal Society of Canada, *Proceedings and Transactions,* 3d ser., XXXIII, sect. II (May 1939), 29-47.

Branch, E. Douglas. "Henry Bouquet: Professional Soldier." *Pennsylvania Magazine of History and Biography,* LXII (Jan. 1938), 41-51.

Brown, George W. "The Problem of Public and Historical Records in Canada." *Canadian Historical Review,* XXV (Mar. 1944), 1-5.

Brown, Lloyd A. "Manuscript Maps in the William L. Clements Library." *American Neptune,* I (Apr. 1941), 141-48.

Brown, Theodore T. "Sieur Charles de Langlade." *Wisconsin Archeologist,* n.s., XI (July 1932), 143-47.

Browne, Henry J. "A New Historical Project: Editing the Papers of Archbishop John Carroll." *American Ecclesiastical Review,* CXXVII (Nov. 1952), 341-50.

Bryce, P. H. "Sir John Johnson, Baronet; Superintendent-General of Indian Affairs." New York State Historical Association, *Quarterly Journal,* IX (July 1928), 233-71.

Buck, Solon J. "The Story of Grand Portage." *Minnesota History,* V (Feb. 1923), 14-27.

Burton, Clarence M. "Citizens and Families of Early Detroit; Directory of Cadillac's Village, 1701-1710—Detroit Residents in 1789—in 1795—Detroit in 1820—The Prominent Families and Names of the Day." in *The City of Detroit, Michigan, 1701-1922* Detroit, S. J. Clarke Publishing Co., 1922. II, 1314-1404.

———. "Detroit Rulers, French Commandants in This Region from 1701 to 1760." (*Michigan Historical Collections,* Vol. XXXIV). Lansing, 1905. p. 303-40.

Caldwell, Norman W. "Additional Kaskaskia Manuscripts." *Illinois Libraries,* XXXIV (May 1952), 192-204.

Caron, Ivanhoë. "Les censitaires du côteau Saint-Geneviève (banlieue de Québec) de 1636 à 1800." *Bulletin des recherches historiques,* XXVII (avril, mai, juin, 1921), 97-108, 129-46, 161-76.

———. "Le diocèse de Québec; divisions et subdivisions de 1674 à 1844." Société canadienne d'histoire de l'église catholique, *Rapport,* 1937-38, 11-47.

———. "Les évêques de Québec, leurs procureurs et leurs vicaires généraux, à Rome, à Paris et à Londres, (1734-1834)." Royal Society of Canada, *Proceedings and Transactions,* 3d ser., XXIX, sect. I (May 1935), 153-78.

Carr, Paul O. "The Defense of the Frontier, 1760-1775." (University of Iowa, *Studies in the Social Sciences,* Vol. X, No. 3, Nov. 1, 1934). Iowa City [1935?]. p. 46-59.

Carrière, Gaston. "Sources de notre histoire religieuse: les archives." *Recherches sociographiques,* I (avril-juin 1960), 189-206.

Carter, Clarence E. "Notes on the Lord Gage Collection of Manuscripts." *Mississippi Valley Historical Review,* XV (Mar. 1929), 511-19.

"Charles F. Gunther Collection." Illinois State Historical Society, *Journal,* XIII (Oct. 1920), 401-03.

Chipman, Willis. "The Life and Times of Major Samuel Holland, Surveyor General, 1764-1801." Ontario Historical Society, *Papers and Records,* XXI (1924), 11-90.

Command, John R. "The Story of Grosse Ile." *Michigan History Magazine,* III (1919), 126-32.

Conger, John L. "Report on the Public Archives of Michigan." American Historical Association, *Annual Report,* 1905, I, 369-76.

Crossman, Daniel L. "How the Last French Claim to a Michigan Farm Was Extinguished." (*Michigan Historical Collections,* Vol. XIV). Lansing, 1890. p. 644-50.

Dargan, Marion, Jr. "Clarence Walworth Alvord." in Hutchinson, William T., ed. *The Marcus W. Jernegan Essays in American Historiography.* Chicago, University of Chicago Press, 1937. p. 323-38.

DeLand, Charles E. "The Verendrye Explorations and Discoveries." (*South Dakota Historical Collection,* Vol. VII). Pierre, S. Dak., 1914. p. 99-322.

Delanglez, Jean. "The Discovery of the Mississippi: Primary Sources." *Mid-America,* XXVII (Oct. 1945), 219-31.

————. "Franquelin—Mapmaker." *Mid-America,* XXV (Jan. 1943), 29-74.

————. "The Genesis and Building of Detroit," *Mid-America,* XXX (Apr. 1948), 75-104.

————. "A Mirage: The Sea of the West." *Revue d'histoire de l'Amérique française,* I (déc 1947, mars 1948), 346-81, 541-68.

————. "The Sources of the Delisle Map of America, 1703." *Mid-America,* XXV (Oct. 1943), 275-98.

Diller, Aubrey. "Maps of the Missouri River before Lewis and Clark." in Montagu, M. F., Ashley, ed. *Studies and Essays in the History of Science and Learning Offered in Homage to George Sarton.* New York, Henry Scheman, 1946. p. 503-19.

Doughty, Arthur G. "Sources for the History of the Catholic Church in the Public Archives of Canada." *Catholic Historical Review,* XIX (July 1933), 148-66.

Douville, Raymond. "Short Sketch of the Archives of Three Rivers." *American Archivist,* X (July 1947), 263-68.

East, Ernest E. "Historical Treasures of Randolph County." *Illinois Libraries,* XXXV (Apr. 1953), 161-70.

Eavenson, Howard N. "Who Made the 'Trader's Map'?" *Pennsylvania Magazine of History and Biography,* LXV (Oct. 1941), 420-38.

Elliott, Richard R. "The Recollect Priests Who Officiated at the Church of Saint Anne, Detroit, from 1701 to 1782, and as Chaplains at Fort Pontchartrain, During the French Régime." (*Michigan Historical Collections,* Vol. XXXV). Lansing, 1907, p. 267-72.

Elliott, T. C. "The Origin of the Name Oregon." *Oregon Historical Quarterly,* XXII (June 1921), 91-115.

Fabre Surveyer, E. "Philippe François de Rastel De Rocheblave," in Robinson, Percy J. *Toronto During the French Régime; a History of the Toronto Region from Brûlé to Simcoe, 1615-1793.* Toronto, The Ryerson Press; Chicago, University of Chicago Press, 1933, p. 233-42.

Fleming, R. Harvey. "McTavish, Frobisher and Company of Montreal." *Canadian Historical Review,* X (June 1929), 136-52.

Fleming, Roy F. "Charting the Great Lakes." *Canadian Geographical Journal*, XII (Feb. 1936), 69-77.

Fraser, Alexander. "The Ontario Archives." American Historical Association, *Annual Report*, 1911, I, 353-63.

Gareau, J.-B. "La prévôté de Québec, ses officiers, ses registres." Quebec (Province) Archives. *Rapport de l'archiviste de la province de Québec*, 1943-44. [Québec], 1944. p. 51-146.

Garraghan, Gilbert J. "The Ecclesiastical Rule of Old Quebec in Mid-America." *Catholic Historical Review*, XIX (Apr. 1933), 17-32.

Godbout, Archange, Père. "Nos ancêtres au XVIIe siècle, dictionnaire généalogique et bio-bibliographique des familles canadiennes." Quebec (Province) Archives, *Rapport de l'archiviste de la province de Québec*, 1951-52 et 1952-53, 1953-54 et 1954-55, 1955-56 et 1956-57, 1957-58 et 1958-59, 1959-60. [Québec 1954-61] p. 447-544, 443-536, 377-489, 381-440, 275-354.

Greene, Jack P. "The Publication of the Official Records of the Southern Colonies." *William and Mary Quarterly*, 3d ser., XIV (Apr. 1957), 268-80.

Gumm, Clark L. "The Foundation of Land Records." *Our Public Lands*, VII (Oct. 1957), 4-5, 12-14.

Hamilton, Raphael N. "The Early Cartography of the Missouri Valley." *American Historical Review*, XXXIX (July 1934), 645-62.

Harrison, Robert W. "Public Land Records of the Federal Government." *Mississippi Valley Historical Review*, XLI (Sept. 1954), 277-88.

Hoberg, Walter R. "Early History of Colonel Alexander McKee." *Pennsylvania Magazine of History and Biography*, LVIII (1934), 26-36.

Holbrook, Franklin F. "The Survey in Retrospect." *Western Pennsylvania Historical Magazine*, XIX (Dec. 1936), 293-304.

Iben, Icko. "Notes from the Work Shop, Marriage in Old Cahokia." *Illinois Libraries*, XXVI (Nov. 1944), 473-83.

Innis, Harold A. "The North West Company." *Canadian Historical Review*, VIII (Dec. 1927), 308-21.

Jackson, Marjorie G. "The Beginning of British Trade at Michilimackinac." *Minnesota History*, XI (Sept. 1930), 231-70.

Jameson, John Franklin. "The Colonial Assemblies and Their Legislative Journals." American Historical Association, *Annual Report*, 1897, 403-53.

Jenks, William L., ed. " 'The Hutchins' Map of Michigan." *Michigan History Magazine*, X (July 1926), 358-73.

248 *The French and British in the Old Northwest*

————. "Patrick Sinclair, Builder of Fort Mackinac." (*Michigan Historical Collections,* Vol. XXXIX). Lansing, 1915. p. 61-85.

Karpinski, Louis C. "Manuscript Maps Relating to American History in French, Spanish, and Portuguese Archives." *American Historical Review,* XXXIII (Jan. 1928), 328-30. Also published in the *Mississippi Valley Historical Review,* XIV (Dec. 1927), 437-39.

————. "Michigan and the Great Lakes upon the Map, 1636-1802." *Michigan History Magazine,* XXIX (July-Sept. 1945), 291-312.

Keeler, Lucy E. "Old Fort Sandoski of 1745 and the Sandusky Country." Ohio Archaeological and Historical Society, *Publication,* XVII (1908), 357-430.

Keith, Julia H. "History of Grosse Isle." (*Michigan Historical Collections,* Vol. XXXV). Lansing, 1907. p. 583-604.

Kellogg, Louise P. "Copper Mining in the Early Northwest." *Wisconsin Magazine of History,* VIII (Dec. 1924), 146-59.

————. "The Mission of Jonathan Carver." *Wisconsin Magazine of History,* XII (Dec. 1928), 127-45.

————. "Search for Wisconsin Manuscripts in Canada." Wisconsin Historical Society, *Proceedings,* LIX (1912), 36-42.

Kent, Donald H. "Preserving Pennsylvania's Historical Heritage Photographically." *Pennsylvania History,* XVII (Oct. 1950), 302-14.

Krauskopf, Francis. "The Documentary Basis for La Salle's Supposed Discovery of the Ohio River." *Indiana History,* XLVII (June 1951), 143-53.

Lapalice, Ovide M.-H. "Le premier registre d'état civil de Montréal." *Canadian Antiquarian and Numismatic Journal,* 3d ser., VIII (Oct. 1911), 171-98.

————. "Les premières pages du registre de la paroisse de Montréal." *Canadian Antiquarian and Numismatic Journal,* 3d ser., X (Oct. 1913), 214-37.

————. "Registre du Fort de la Presque Isle." *Canadian Antiquarian and Numismatic Journal,* 3d ser., XI (Oct. 1914), 168-70.

Le Bel, E. C. "History of Assumption, the First Parish in Upper Canada." Canadian Catholic Historical Association, *Report,* 1954.

Lee, John T. "Captain Jonathan Carver: Additional Data." State Historical Society of Wisconsin, *Proceedings,* 1912, 87-123.

Leveson-Gower, R. H. G. "The Archives of the Hudson's Bay Company." *The Beaver,* CCLXIV (1933), 40-42; CCLXV (1934), 19-21, 37-39; CCLXVI (1935), 22-24.

Levron, Jacques. "Les registres paroissiaux et d'état civil en France." *Archivum,* IX (1959), 55-100.

Lindsay, Lionel St.G., Abbé. "The Archives of the Archbishopric of Quebec." American Catholic Historical Society, *Records*, XVIII (1907), 8-11.

McArthur, Duncan. "The Ontario Archives and the Historical Societies." Ontario Historical Society, *Papers and Records*, XXXI (1936), 5-10.

MacDonald, George F. "Commodore Alexander Grant (1734-1813)." Ontario Historical Society, *Papers and Records*, XXII (1925), 167-81.

McIntosh, Montgomery E. "Charles Langlade—First Settler in Wisconsin." (Parkman Club *Publications* No. 8). Milwaukee, 1896. p. 205-23.

McLachlan, R. W. "Notes on the Protestant Church Registers of Montreal." *Canadian Antiquarian and Numismatic Journal*, 3d ser., XII (July 1915), 121-35.

Maheux, Arthur. "Les archives du séminaire de Québec." *Le Canada français*, XXVII (fév. 1940), 503-08.

Mahieu, Bernard. "Les archives de l'église catholique en France." *Archivum*, IV (1954), 89-104.

Martin, Theodore. "History of St. Peter's Parish 1802-1947." Kent Historical Society, *Papers and Addresses*, 7 (1951), 18-29.

Mason, Edward G. "The Kaskaskia Parish Records." (*Michigan Historical Collections*, Vol. V). Lansing, 1884, p. 94-109.

Massicotte, Edouard-Zotique. "Les actes des trois premiers tabellions de Montréal, 1648-1657." Royal Society of Canada, *Proceedings and Transactions*, 3d ser., IX, sect. I (Sept. 1915), 189-204.

———. "Les archives judiciaires de Montréal." *Bulletin des recherches historiques*, XXXII (avril 1926), 226-28.

———. "Les coroners de Montréal, 1764-1923." *Bulletin des recherches historiques*, XXIX (oct. 1923), 295-97.

———. "Les coroners du XVIIe et du XVIIIe siècles." *Bulletin des recherches historiques*, XL (oct. 1934), 617-20.

———. "Daniel de Greysolon, sieur du Lhut, Claude de Greysolon, sieur de la Tourette, et Jean-Jacques Patron." *Bulletin des recherches historiques*, XXXIII (mars 1927), 139-47.

———. "Les greffiers de Montréal sous le régime français, 1648-1760." *Bulletin des recherches historiques*, XXXI (avril 1925), 114-19.

———. "Les huissiers de Montréal sous le régime français." *Bulletin des recherches historiques*, XXXII (fév. 1926), 79-92.

———. "Inventaire des actes de foi et hommage conservés aux Archives judiciaires de Montréal." Quebec (Province) Archives.

Rapport de l'archiviste de la province de Québec, 1921-22. Québec, 1922, p. 102-08.

———. "L'inventaire des biens de Lambert Closse." *Bulletin des recherches historiques*, XXV (jan. 1919), 16-31.

———. "Les juges de Montréal sous le régime français, 1648-1760." *Bulletin des recherches historiques*, XXVII (juin 1921), 177-83.

———. "Les mariages mixtes à Montréal, dans les temples protestantes au 18e siècle." *Bulletin des recherches historiques*, XXI (mars 1915), 84-86.

———. "La maréchaussee à Montréal." *Bulletin des recherches historiques*, XXII (jan. 1916), 16-18.

———. "Mémento historique de Montréal, 1636-1760." Royal Society of Canada, *Proceedings and Transactions*, 3d ser., XXVII, sect. I (May 1933), 111-31.

———. "La population de Montréal en 1673." *Canadian Antiquarian and Numismatic Journal*, 3d ser., XI (Oct. 1914), 141-67.

———. "Le premier notaire anglais de Montréal, John Burke." *Bulletin des recherches historiques*, XXVIII août 1922), 237-40.

———. "Les procureurs fiscaux et royaux à Montréal sous le régime français." *Bulletin des recherches historiques*, XXXII (juillet 1926), 393-97.

———. "Les sherifs de Montréal (1763-1923)." *Bulletin des recherches historiques*, XXIX (avril 1923), 107-14.

———. "Les syndics de Montréal." *Bulletin des recherches historiques*, XXIII (août 1917), 240-43.

———. Les tribunaux et les officiers de justice, à Montréal, sous le régime français, 1648-1760." Royal Society of Canada, *Proceedings and Transactions*, 3d ser., X, sect. I (Dec. 1916), 273-303.

Moes, Camillus P. "History of the Catholic Church in Monroe City and County, Mich." *United States Catholic Historical Magazine*, II (Apr. 1888), 113-52.

Monicat, Jacques. "Les archives notariales." *Revue historique*, CCXIV (juillet-sept., 1955), 1-9.

Morin, Victor. "Esquisse biographique de Jacques Viger." Société Royale du Canada, *Mémoires*, ser. 3, XXXII, sect. 1, (mai 1938), 183-90.

Morton, Arthur S. "The Business Methods and the Archives of the Hudson's Bay Company." *Canadian Historical Association, Report*, 1938, 134-44.

———. "La Vérendrye: Commandant, Fur-Trader and Explorer." *Canadian Historical Review*, IX (Dec. 1928), 284-98.

Munro, William B. "The Coureurs de Bois." Massachusetts Historical Society, *Proceedings*, LVII (Oct. 1923-June 1924), 192-205.

Norton, Margaret C. "Cahokia Marriage Records." *Illinois Libraries,* XXVIII (May 1946), 260-72.

———. "The J. Nick Perrin Collection." *Illinois Libraries,* XXII (Oct. 1940), 22-24.

———. "The Oldest Extant Civil Record West of the Alleghenies." *Illinois Libraries,* XXXI (Apr. 1949), 187-89.

———. "The Resources of the Illinois State Archives." *Illinois Libraries,* XXXVI (Jan. 1954), 33-41.

Nute, Grace Lee., ed. "A British Legal Case and Old Grand Portage." *Minnesota History,* XXI (June 1940), 117-48.

———. "Posts in the Minnesota Fur-trading Area, 1660-1855." *Minnesota History,* XI (Dec. 1930), 353-85.

Ormsby, W. G. "The Upper Canada State Papers: an Untapped Research Source." *Ontario History,* XLIII (Jan. 1951), 29-34.

Pandzić, Basile, O.F.M. "Les archives générales de l'ordre des frères-mineurs." *Archivum,* IV (1954), 153-64.

Paré, George. "The St. Joseph Mission." *Mississippi Valley Historical Review,* XVII (June 1930), 24-54.

Pargellis, Stanley M. and Cuthbert, Norma B. "Loudoun Papers: (a) Colonial, 1756-58, (b) French Colonial, 1742-53." *Huntington Library Bulletin,* No. 3 (Feb. 1933), 97-107.

Parkman, Francis. "Early Unpublished Maps of the Mississippi and the Great Lakes." in his *La Salle and the Discovery of Great West.* Boston, Little, Brown, and Company, 1879, p. 449-58.

Pattison, William D. "Use of the U.S. Public Land Survey Plats and Notes as Descriptive Sources." *Professional Geographer,* n.s., VIII (Jan. 1956), 10-14.

Pearkes, G. R. "The Evolution of the Control of His Majesty's Canadian Forces." *Canadian Defence Quarterly,* X (July 1933), 465-80.

Pease, Theodore C. "Otto Leopold Schmidt: 1863-1935." Illinois State Historical Society, *Journal,* XXVIII (Jan. 1936), 225-36.

Peckham, Howard H. "Military Papers in the Clements Library." *Military Affairs,* II (Fall 1938), 126-30.

Pelzer, Louis. "The Private Land Claims of the Old Northwest Territory." *Iowa Journal of History,* XII (July 1914), 373-93.

Perrin, J. Nick. "The Oldest Civil Record in the West." Illinois State Historical Society, *Transactions* (1901), Illinois State Historical Library, *Publication* No. 6, 63-65.

Phillips, Paul C. "Vincennes in Its Relation to French Colonial Policy." *Indiana Magazine of History*, XVII (Dec. 1921), 311-38.

Pritchett, John P. "Some Red River Fur-Trade Activities." *Minnesota History*, V (May 1924), 401-23.

Quaife, Milo M. "Detroit Biographies: Commodore Alexander Grant." *Burton Historical Collection Leaflet*, VI (May 1928), 65-80.

———. "Jonathan Carver and the Carver Grant." *Mississippi Valley Historical Review*, VII (June 1920), 3-25.

———. "The Royal Navy of the Upper Lakes." *Burton Historical Collection Leaflet*, II (May 1924), 49-64.

Raisz, Erwin. "Outline of the History of American Cartography." *Isis*, XXVI (Mar. 1937), 373-89.

Randall, James G. "Theodore Calvin Pease." Illinois State Historical Society, *Journal*, XLI (Dec. 1948), 353-65.

Reed, Susan M. "British Cartography of the Mississippi Valley in the Eighteenth Century." *Mississippi Valley Historical Review*, II (Sept. 1915), 213-24.

Reid, Marjorie G. "The Quebec Fur-Traders and Western Policy, 1763-1774." *Canadian Historical Review*, VI (Mar. 1925), 15-32.

Rich, Edwin E. "The Hudson's Bay Company's Activities; Forthcoming Publication of Documents by Hudson's Bay Company Record Society." *Pacific Historical Review*, VII (Sept. 1938), 267-73.

Riddell, William R. "The Law Marriage in Upper Canada." *Canadian Historical Review*, II (Sept. 1921), 226-48.

———. "Pre-Assembly Legislatures in British Canada." Royal Society of Canada, *Proceedings and Transactions*, 3d ser., XII, sect. II (June 1918), 109-34.

———. "Some Marriages in Old Detroit." *Michigan History Magazine*, VI (1922), 111-30.

Robinson, Doane. "Vérendrye's Farthest West." State Historical Society of Wisconsin, *Proceedings*, LXI (1913), 146-50.

Rogers, Richard R. "Historical Cartography of the Great Lakes (1569-1746)." Michigan Academy of Sciences, *Papers*, XXXIV (1948), 175-84.

Roussier, Paul, "Le dépôt des papiers publics des colonies." *Revue d'histoire moderne*, IV (juillet-août 1929), 241-62.

———. "Les origines du dépôt des papiers publics des colonies: le dépôt de Rochefort (1763-1790)." *Revue de l'histoire des colonies françaises*, XVIII (1st trimestre 1925), 21-50.

Roy, Henri. "Les dossiers aux Archives judiciaires de Québec." *Bulletin des recherches historiques*, LI (jan.-fév. 1945), 65.

Roy, Léon. "The Keeping of Church Registers of Juridical Status in the Province of Quebec." Quebec (Province) Archives, *Rapport de l'archiviste de la province de Québec, 1959-60* [Québec], 1961, p. 167-229.

Roy, Pierre-Georges. "Les archives de la province de Québec." *Bulletin des recherches historiques*, XXXII (avril 1926), 193-208.

————. "Les commissaires ordinaires de la marine en la Nouvelle-France." *Bulletin des recherches historiques*, XXIV (fév. 1918), 51-54.

————. "Les commissions des gouverneurs de la Nouvelle-France." *Bulletin des recherches historiques*, XXI (mai 1915), 139-43.

————. "Les conseillers au Conseil souverain de la Nouvelle-France." Royal Society of Canada, *Proceedings and Transactions*, 3d ser., IX, sect. I (Sept. 1915), 173-87.

————. "La maréchaussée de Québec sous le régime français." Royal Society of Canada, *Proceedings and Transactions*, 3d ser., XII, sect. I (Dec. 1918, Mar. 1919), 189-92.

————. "La Prévôté de Québec." Royal Society of Canada, *Proceedings and Transactions*, 3d ser., X (Sept. 1916), 119-28.

————. "Les lettres de naturalité sous le régime française." *Bulletin des recherches historiques*, XXX (août 1924), 225-32.

————. "Les notaires au Canada sous le régime français." Quebec (Province) Archives. *Rapport de l'archiviste de la province de Québec, 1921-22.* [Québec], 1922, p. 1-58.

————. "Les officiers d'état-major des gouvernements de Québec, Montréal et Trois-Rivères sous le régime français; notes biographiques." *Revue canadienne*, n.s., XX (nov. 1917), 375-84; XXI (jan.-avril 1918), 75-79, 210-20, 276-95; XXII (sept.-déc. 1918), 214-21, 290-300, 375-81, 432-46; XXIII (jan.-juin, 1919), 51-55, 130-41, 218-24, 299-301, 360-75, 439-56; XXIV (juillet-déc. 1919), 53-61, 131-38, 210-20, 286-302, 366-78, 442-58; XXV (jan.-avril 1920), 47-59, 212-19, 280-94.

————. "Les secrétaires des gouverneurs et intendants de la Nouvelle-France." *Bulletin des recherches historiques*, XLI (fév. 1935), 74-107.

Roy, Régis. "Les intendants de la Nouvelle-France." Royal Society of Canada, *Proceedings and Transactions*, 2d ser., IX, sect. I (May 1903), 65-107.

Scott, Canon. "The Catholic Church in the Province of Quebec, from Its Beginning to Our Time." in Wood, William C. H., Atherton, William H., and Conklin, Edwin P., eds. *The Storied Province of*

Quebec Past and Present. Toronto, Dominion Publishing Company, Limited, 1931-32. 5 vols. I, 474-527.

Scott, Duncan C. "Indian Affairs, 1763-1841." in Shortt, Adam, and Doughty, Arthur G., eds. *Canada and Its Provinces; a History of the Canadian People and Their Institutions by One Hundred Associates.* Edinburgh, Printed by T. & A. Constable at the Edinburgh University Press for the Publishers Association of Canada Limited, Toronto, 1914, IV, 695-725.

Scott, S. Morley. "Civil and Military Authority in Canada, 1764-1766." *Canadian Historical Review,* IX (June 1928), 117-36.

————. "Material Relating to Quebec in the Gage and Amherst Papers." *Canadian Historical Review,* XIX (Dec. 1938), 378-86.

Shiels, W. Eugene. "The Jesuits in Ohio in the Eighteenth Century." *Mid-America,* XVIII, n.s. VII (Jan. 1936), 27-47.

Somers, Hugh J. "The Legal Status of the Bishop of Quebec." *Catholic Historical Review,* XIX, (July 1933), 167-89.

Sosin, Jack M. "The French Settlements in British Policy for the North American Interior, 1760-1774." *Canadian Historical Review,* XXXIX (Sept. 1958), 185-208.

Sparks, Edwin E. "The Record of a Lost Empire in America." *Chautauquan,* XXXIII (Aug. 1901), 478-86.

Storm, Colton. "The Notorious Colonel Wilkins." Illinois State Historical Society, *Journal,* XL (Mar. 1947), 7-22.

Streeter, Floyd B. "The Burton Historical Collection of the Detroit Public Library." *Americana Collector,* I (Jan. 1926), 124-34.

Taillemite, Étienne. "Les archives de la France d'Outre-Mer." *Gazette des archives,* n.s., no. 22 (juillet 1957), 6-22.

Talman, James J. "Early Ontario Land Records as a Source of Local History." *Western Ontario Historical Notes,* VIII (Sept. 1950), 130-34.

Tanguay, Cyprien, Mgr. "Les registres de l'état civil." *Bulletin des recherches historiques,* XXXIX (avril 1933), 247-49.

Thompson, Joseph J. "The Cahokia Mission Property." *Illinois Catholic Historical Review,* V (Jan.-Apr. 1923), 195-217; VI (Jan.-Apr. 1924), 99-135.

Thwaites, Reuben G. "At the Meeting of the Trails: the Romance of a Parish Register." *Mississippi Valley Historical Association, Proceedings,* VI (1912-13), 198-217.

Trowbridge, Frederick N. "Confirming Land Titles in Early Wisconsin." *Wisconsin Magazine of History,* XXVI (Mar. 1943), 314-22.

Turner, Morris K. "The Baynton, Wharton, and Morgan Manuscripts." *Mississippi Valley Historical Review*, IX (Dec. 1922), 236-41.

Utley, George B. "Source Material for the Study of American History in the Libraries of Chicago." Bibliographical Society of America, *Papers*, XVI, pt. I (1922), 17-46.

Van Kersen, Lionel W. "The National Register of Archives." *American Archivist*, XXIII (July 1960), 319-37.

Verrier, Louis-Guillaume. "Les registres de l'amirauté de Québec." *Rapport de l'archiviste de la province de Québec*, 1920-21. [Québec], 1921, p. 106-31.

Winsor, Justin. "The Maps of the Seventh Century Showing Canada." in his *Narrative and Critical History of America*. (Boston, New York, Houghton, Mifflin and Company, 1884), IV, 377-94.

W[oltz], L. O. "Source Material of the Detroit Public Library as Supplied by the Acquisition of the Burton Historical Collection." *Michigan History Magazine*, VI (1922), 386-99.

Wood, George A. "Céloron de Blainville and French Expansion in the Ohio Valley." *Mississippi Valley Historical Review*, IX (Mar. 1923), 302-19.

Wood, William. "The New Provincial Archives of Quebec." *Canadian Historical Review*, II (June 1921), 126-54.

Wroth, Lawrence C. "The Jesuit Relations from New France." Bibliographical Society of America, *Papers*, XXX, pt. 2 (1936), 110-49.

Index

Abbot, Edward letters of, 111 n 68; lt. gov. at Vincennes, 99, 101; memorial of, 135; requests orders *re* lands, 118 n 96

Acadia, 1

Accounts, Askin, 141 n 1; Assumption mission, 92; Baynton, Wharton and Morgan, 140; traders, 135; Indian agents, 129; Indian disbursements, 126; Johnson, 125; military, 160, 161; North West Co., 186, 187; Upper Canada, 174; western posts, 79 n 80

Actes de foi et hommage, 73, 75

Acts, royal, 35, 50, 70, 71, 74

Acts of possession, 3, 37

Addison, Robert, Anglican minister, 190, 191

Adhemar, St. Martin, apptd. j. p., 162 n 69

Adjurations, 88 n 20

Adjutant general of militia, Quebec, 148

Administration, archives *re*, 24, 74-75, 78, 172

Admiralty court, Quebec, estab., 63

Adolphustown, Ont., 193

Agriculture, govt. aid, 15, 33; production, 36, 116; supervised by comdt., 13. *See also* Farm lands

Albany, N.Y., Indian trade at, 16

Allegheny Mountains, 9; boundary of Illinois dist., 12

Allegheny River, fort on, 9; La Salle reaches, 2

Allegheny-Ohio route, Iroquois dominate, 9

Allen, John, 28

Almoner, Detroit, 15

Alvord, Clarence W., dir. of Ill. Hist. Surv., 27; finds Cahokia archives, 110; finds Kaskaskia archives, 23-24; obtains archive reproductions, 29, 111; papers, 112

American Antiquarian Society, *mss. held by*: Bradstreet, 130 n 52, Johnson, 127 n 42, Rogers' journal, 134

American Bottom, settlement on, 15

American Jewish Archives, Hebrew Union College, Gratz papers, 129, 140 n 96

American State Papers, Public Lands, docs. *re* priv. land claims, 47

Americans, capture Sinclair, 101; capture Vincennes, 102; encroach on fur trade, 104; prisoners, 129; take prisoners to Williamsburg, 102. *See also* United States

Amherst, Jeffery, corresp. with Gage, 151; order *re* shipyard, 103; papers, 112, 121, 122, 134

Amherst College Library, Amherst papers, 122

Amherstburg, Ont., corresp., of officers, 115, 129; Detroiters settle at, 169

Angelica, logbook, 160

Anglican Church, in Canada, 190; inactivity in Detroit, 145. *See also* Church of England

Anthon, George C., meteorological jour., 131

Appointments, Detroit, 114; Indian agents, 129; Montreal, 34; Upper Canada, 173

257

Apprenticeship, papers, 11
Arbitration, awards at Detroit, 114; decisions, 11; used to settle disputes, 102
Archaeology, land surveys and sites, 48; maps and, 139
Archbishop of Paris, archives, 90
Archbishop of Quebec, archives, 87, 88 and n 20
Archbishop of Rouen, archives, 90
Archbishops, archives, 90
Archdiocese of Detroit, archives, 145
Archiepiscopal Archives of Quebec, 87-88; docs. pub., 144, 188; reproductions from, 112
Archivists. *See* Brymner, Caron, Day, Doughty, Doysié, Evanturel, Lanctôt, Leland, Lindsay, Margry, Massicotte, O'Callaghan, Richard, Roy
Archivum Romanum Societatis Iesu, 89
Arkansas district, 12
Arkansas Post, attached to Illinois commandery, 12
Arkansas River, 2
Army. *See* British Army; Military officers; U.S. Army
Askin, John, asst. commissary at Mackinac, 108; land board member, 176; militia officer, 166; papers, 121, 140, 141 n 1, 161, 166, 171
Assumption Church, Ont., 91-93, 193
Atlantic coast, surveys on, 176 n 27
Atlantic Ocean, 118
Attorney, Montreal, 65
Attorney-General, New France, functions, 64
Attorney–General, Quebec, 147
Attorney-General, Upper Canada, 167
Auctions, 11
Auditor of public accounts, Quebec, 148

Audrain, Francis, clk. to Bd. Land Commrs. at Detroit, 43
Audrain, Peter, clk. to Bd. Land Commrs. at Detroit, 43
Autobiographies, French, 51; Hamilton, 131
Aveux et dénombrements, 73

Baby, Francis, member of Gen. Assembly of Upper Canada, 168
Baby, Jacques Duperon, apptd. j. p., 162; founder of church at Toronto, 193; lt. of Kent Co., 169; member of Exec. Council, 168; papers, 166
Baby family, papers, 141
Backus, Elijah, 41 n 59
Bacon, Francis, 132
Baird, Samuel, land surv. in Indiana, 40
Baltimore Cathedral Archives, 145
Baptismal registers, described, 58
Baptisms, Detroit, 146; Ontario, 194. *See also* Parish registers
Barns, 31
Barracks, archives *re*, 160
Bath, Ont., Anglican church registers, 192
Baumer, ———, carries off notarial records, 40 n 55
Bay of Quinte, settlement on, 175
Baynton, John. *See* Baynton, Wharton, and Morgan
Baynton, Wharton and Morgan, land grant in Illinois, 120; mss., 128, 140
Beaufort, France, refugees from Canada settle near, 67
Beauharnois, François, papers, 68
Beaujeu, Daniel-Hyacinthe-Marie Liénard de, papers, 83
Beaver pelts, 16, 17, 18
Bégon, Michel, order *re* land titles, 72
Bellestre, Marie-François Picote de, surrenders Detroit, 95

Bradstreet, John, campaigns in West, 95-96; papers, 130

Brant, Joseph, will, 163 n 72

Breese, Signey, finds French records, 26

Brehm, Diederick, jour., 136

Briand, Jean-Oliver, bishop of Quebec, corresp., 88 n 20, 144 n 17

British, activities in Amer. terr., 172; carry off Detroit land records, 43; criminal law introd. into Quebec, 101; dominion in Illinois terminated, 102; evacuate New York City, 103; exped. agst. Kentucky, 141; fur-trade system, 18; land-grant policy, 117-18; *occupy:* Detroit, 15, Illinois, 96, western posts, 95; publish maps of Northwest, 137; recognize Indian title to land, 118; record-keeping methods, 40; relations with Indians in U.S. terr., 174; rent land at Michilimackinac, 22; retire from Illinois, 101; settlements, 48; surrender Northwest posts, 42. *See also* England; English colonies; Great Britain

British archives, reproductions from, 111, 141, 153

British Army, archives *re*, 111; corresp., 114, 115; examining bd. reports, 130; in Northwest, 95-97; officers' corresp., 121, 122, 123, 124, 151 n 21, 156, 185; officers govern western posts, 97; returns, 122, 130, 151, 161. *See also* British Army, Commander in Chief, and names of officers

British Army, Commander in Chief, archives *re* Provincial Marine, 160; commands officers in the West, 97; controls Indian Dept., 105; corresp., 127, 185; papers, 121, 123, 148-49

British Army, Commander of the

British Army—*Cont.*
Forces (Canada), archives, 142, 159-61, 185; authority in Upper Canada, 167; govs. as, 147, 151; papers transcribed, 115

British Army, Northern Military District, administers affairs in the West, 149; estab. in Quebec, 148

British Army, Quartermaster General's Department, controls Provincial Marine, 104

British Government, Carver petitions, 134; colonial charters, 38; corresp., 151; regulation of land speculation, 139; Rogers' debts, 134

British Headquarters papers, 123

British Historical Manuscripts Commission, 183 n 55

British Indian Department, accounts, 126; agents apptd., 106-07; commissaries apptd., 108; corresp., 114, 185; estab., 105; ordnance returns, 130. *See also* Superintendent of Indian Affairs; and names of officials

British manuscripts, reproductions, 141-42

British Museum, depository of mss., 183; *mss. held by:* Bouquet, 125, Germain, 131; Haldimand, 131, 142, 151, Hamilton, 131, Johnson, 127 n 42, 142, maps, reproductions from by: Ill. Hist. Surv., 112, Lib. Cong., 142

British Navy, estab. on Great Lakes, 103. *See also* Provincial Marine

British Secretaries of State, papers transcribed, 152

British soldiers, occupy western posts, 95

Brotier, Gabriel, saves Jesuit archives, 89

Brymner, Douglas, assists Burton, 114; collects docs., 34; initiates

Brymner—*Cont.*
copying program, 151; negotiates transfer of military records, 159
Buchet, Joseph, dep. intendant in Illinois, 14
Budget, 63
Bulletin des recherches historiques, 78
Burbeck, Henry, receives poss. of Mackinac, 169
Burial registers, described, 58; Ft. Presque Isle, 58. *See also* Parish registers
Burke, Edmund, Catholic priest in Upper Canada, 193; resides on River Raisin, 143
Burton, Clarence M., collecting activities, 33-35; inspects ct. records in Toronto, 164; transcripts obtained by, 114, 158
Burton, Ralph, commands northern mil. dist., 148, 151; corresp., 122 n 21
Burton Historical Collection, *archives held by*: census of Detroit, 36, land records, 44, logbooks of naval vessels, 160, notarial archives of Detroit, 32; register of French families, 33; founded, 34; *mss. held by*: Askin, 121, 140, Assumption Church, 92, Cadillac, 35, Hamilton, 131, Harrow, 161, Mackintosh, 187, North West Co., 186, payroll of Detroit volunteers, 141, Porteous, 141, Williams, 141, Woodbridge, 121 n 15; *reproductions obtained by*: Cadillac doc., 35, Canadian Indian Dept. records, 157, Penn, 116, prerogative court Hesse district, 164, parish registers, 57, 144; *transcripts obtained by*: Baby, 141, intendants' registers, 44, land records, 43, 120, notarial archives of Detroit, 114, notarial archives of Montreal, 33, 75, 76,

Burton Historical Collection—*Cont.*
158, parish registers, 56, 92, Potier's diary, 93
Bushy Run, plan of battle, 137 n 86
Business, archives re, 75, 79, 164; contracts, 11
Butler, John, Supt. of Indian Affairs, 167; will, 163 n 72
Butricke, George, letters pub., 132

Cadillac, Antoine Laumet de la Mothe, Sieur de, archives re, 35; establishes Detroit, 6; forwards land conveyances to Paris, 43; grants land on Detroit R., 21 and n 81; inventory of property, 33; list of men with, 33 n 25; mss., 35; memoirs, 52 n 18; notarial archives of, 32-33; trade monopoly at Detroit, 17
Cadwalader, Thomas, 128
Cahokia, Ill., 54; archives transf. to Ill. State Arch., 110; estab., 19; French records, 29; list of inhabitants, 39; located in St. Clair Co., 109; obtains copies of Kaskaskia records, 23; officials, 14; parish registers, 56; removal of records from, 25; Sulpicians withdraw from, 143. *See also* Tamaroa mission
Caldwell, William, apptd. j. p., 162 n 69; obtains land grant in Ontario, 175 n 26
Calendars, archives of New France, 77; Bouquet papers, 125; Bradstreet papers, 130 n 52; British sec. of state, 152 n 24; British transcripts, 184 n 57; Cahokia records, 110; Colonial Office dispatches, 152 n 24; corresp. of Detroit officers, 114 and n 82; corresp. of Bishop of Quebec, 144; *engagements,* 158; French archives, 37-38, 78 n 79, 79 n 81; genealogy, 86

Detroit, Mich.—*Cont.*
resides in, 162, 163; priests serve
in, 143, 144; removal of inhabitants from, 169; removal office
Surv. Gen. to, 46; residents acquire
land in Ontario, 169; seat of Kent
Co., 168, 169; settlers, 33 and n 25
and 26, 119, 141 n 1; shipyard
estab. at, 104; Simcoe tour to,
171 n 7; supt. of inland navigation
at, 105; surrendered to British, 15;
surv., 120; trade center, 16; trade
monopoly at, 17; transf. to U.S.,
42. *See also* Burton Historical Collection
Detroit land board, 165
Detroit land office, 43
Detroit Public Library, Burton's coll.
given to, 35. *See also* Burton Historical Collection
Detroit River, 55, 169; first passage,
2; land grants on, 21, 22; mission
estab. on, 91; settlement on, 119,
175, 176, 179
Devonshire, Duke of (William Cav-
endish, 4th duke), papers, 112
Diaries, 136; among Ontario land
records, 181; British officers, 136,
137; Claus, 129; Croghan, 128;
French, 51; Haldimand, 151 n 20;
Johnson, 126, 127; McGillivray,
186; Marin, 8 n 32; Potier, 93;
Simcoe, 171; Upper Canada, 181;
White, 175. *See also* Journals
Diocese of Belleville, parish registers,
55
Diocese of Ontario (Anglican), Se-
well papers, 191
Diocese of Quebec, archives, 171
Diocese of Quebec (Anglican), 190
Diplomatic archives, guide, 183 n 53
Discovery, bibliog. *re*, 52 n 19; pub.
docs., 37. *See also* Exploration
District of Hesse. *See* Hesse district
Dollier de Casson, François, 2

Donations, 11; Illinois, 25, 26, 110;
Quebec, 71 n 47
Dorchester, Lord. *See* Carleton, Guy
Doughty, Arthur G., 27 n 6
Douglas, Thomas. *See* Selkirk, Lord
Dowries, 26
Doyle, William, letters, 133
Doysié, Abel, 31, 35
Drage, Theodorus S., 137 n 83
Draper, Lyman C., coll., 112, 131;
edits Gorrell's jour., 133; obtains
transcripts, 36
Dreer collection, 112
Duluth, Daniel Greysolon, Sieur, list
of docs., 75 n 69; establishes Ft.
St. Joseph, 4; takes poss. of Sioux
country, 3; trader, 16
Dunmore, logbook, 160
Duquesne, Ange de Menneville, Mar-
quis de, 84
Dutch, trade with Iroquois, 16
Dutchman's Point, 103 n 31

East Florida, estab., 98
East St. Louis, Ill., 14
Eastern district, Ont., estab., 169
Ecclesiastical affairs, Simcoe papers
and, 171
Ecclesiastical archives, British Can-
ada, 190-93; Old Northwest, 55-
59; New France, 85-93; survey of
British, 184 n 55
Economic conditions, Illinois, 31;
Simcoe papers and, 171
Economic history, 83 n 97; archives
re, 172; censuses and, 81; Detroit,
92; English colonies, 127; New
France, 69, 71; notarial records
and, 158; traders' mss., 139
Edgar, William, papers, 141, 187 n
71
Elliott, Matthew, 182 n 51; apptd.
j. p., 162 n 69; escapes to Detroit,
107; letters, 115, 156; obtains land

France, Ministry—*Cont.*
14; transcripts of land conveyances from, 43-44
France, Ministry of War, archives, 30, 79
Franciscans, arrive in Canada, 53
Franklin, Pa., site of Ft. Machault, 9
Franquelin, Jean-Baptiste-Louis, 52 n 19
Fraser, Alexander, jour., 135, 136
French, disgruntled under British rule, 100; evacuate western Pennsylvania, 10; explore the West, 1-2; maps, 137; occupy Miss. Valley, 30; Patten captive of, 137 n 83; record-keeping methods, 40; settlements, 48; surrender western forts, 95-96; title to the West, 9; warned off from the Ohio Valley, 10; withdraw from West, 5
French and Indian War, 10 n 39, 22, 23, 121; corresp. *re,* 112; transcripts *re,* 184
French Canadians, settle at Frenchtown, 143; settle in Michigan, 193
French Creek, fort on, 9
The French Foundations, 1680-1693, 30
French officers, corresp., 31
French soldiers, in the West, 4, 6; lists, 50; reach Illinois dist., 13
Frenchtown, Mich., parish register, 144; settlement, 143
Frey, Philip R., dep. surv. at Detroit, 176, 181
Friars Minor, archives destroyed, 90
Frontenac, Louis de Buade, Count de Palluau et de, corresp. pub., 80
Frontenac, Minn., 7
Frontier Forts and Trails Survey, 37, 84 n 3
Fur trade, 83 n 97; Amer. encroachment, 104; archives *re,* 75-76, 158; British, 103; centers in Northwest, 8; contracts with *engagés,* 18; con-

Fur trade—*Cont.*
trolled by govt., 16-18; intendants' orders *re,* 70; license system, 17; mss. *re,* 124; Michilimackinac, 96; Montreal center for, 64; need for hist. work on, 18 n 66; New France, 61; papers, 133, 141. *See also* Indian trade; Trade licenses; Traders
Fur traders, Edgar, 141; memorials, 134; Porteous, 141; supervised by comdts., 13; Williams, 141.

Gage, Thomas, consents to ct. in Illinois, 99; corresp., 148, 150; letters, 111 n 68; memorialized, 100; orders evacuation of Vincennes, 117; papers, 112, 122, 132, 134, 136, 150-51, 160
Gagnon collection, 93
Galinée, René de Bréhant de, 2
Genealogical sources, French Illinois, 42; New France, 72; Montreal dist., 75; Quebec, 73. *See also* Censuses; Church registers; Parish registers; Registers of civil status
Genealogy, archives *re,* 75, 76, 172; censuses and, 81; French families of Detroit, 57; Indian-trade licenses, 157; mss. *re,* 124; Quebec, 86
General Gage, logbook, 160
General Land Office. *See* U.S. General Land Office
Georgetown University Archives, parish registers, 56
Georgian Bay, 1
Geography, docs. *re,* 37, 136
Germain, George, papers, 131
Germany, natives naturalized in New France, 70 n 39
Gibault, Pierre, Rev., arrives in Illinois, 143; corresp., 144 n 17, 145
Gifts, 11
Gingras, Achille, archival investig. by, 90 n 31

Green Bay, Wis.—*Cont.*
lease, 76 n 73; trade licenses for,
76 n 73; trader, 50. *See also* Fort
La Baye; La Baye
Green, James, corresp., 115
Groséilliers Médard Chouart, Sieur
des, trader, 16; visits L. Superior, 2
Grosse Ile, deed of purchase, 119 n 5
Grosse Pointe, Grant locates on, 104
Guardians, appts., 25, 72, 158, 162
Guilday, Peter, 145 n 18
Gunther, Charles F., coll., 49
Gulf Coast, 12
Gulf of Mexico, 2; Le Sueur returns
to, 5

Haldimand, Frederick, letters, 111 n
68; order *re* Detroit archives, 32;
orders rescue of Johnson papers,
125; papers, 115, 124, 141, 142,
150-51, 157, 160, 161; request *re*
land titles at Vincennes, 21; serves
in Canada, 151; visits England,
145
Halifax, Nova Scotia, 159
Hall, Hubert, 111
Hallowell, Ont., 193
Hamilton, Henry, goes to Vincennes,
98; letters of, 111 n 68; papers,
130-31; reaches Detroit, 101; taken
prisoner to Virginia, 102; takes
over admin. in Quebec, 148; warn-
ing *re* settlement around Detroit,
119
Hamtramck, John F., takes poss. of
Detroit, 169
Haran, Gui-Louis, 67
Hardware, 16
Hardwicke, Earl of (Philip Yorke),
papers, 112
Harfly, James, judge at Detroit, 163
Harmar, Josiah, 40
Harrow, Alexander, papers, 161
Harvard University Library, Brad-

Harvard University Library—*Cont.*
street papers, 130; Hamilton pa-
pers, 131
Hay, H., 115
Hay, Jehu, commissary at Detroit,
108; diary, 137
Hebrew Union College. *See* American Jewish Archives
Heir and Devisee Commission, 179
Henry, Alexander, Jr., 137
Henry E. Huntington Library, mss.
re Indians, 51; map of Indian country, 137 n 86; Simcoe papers, 171;
Vaudreuil papers, 50
Henry, William, 39
Hesse district, archives, 161-66;
comm. of j. p., 173; composed of
Essex and Kent Cos., 177; ct.
records, 164; cts. abolished, 163;
estab., 161; incorporated into Up-
per Canada, 166; judge, 32; judi-
cial organization, 162; land ar-
chives, 177-79; prerogative ct.
archives, 164; register of marriages,
165; renamed, 169
Historical societies, 80; directory,
189 n 83
Historical Society of Pennsylvania,
Croghan papers, 127-28; Dreer
coll., 112; Etting coll., 112; Penn
papers, 116, 128
History, maps and, 139
Holland, Samuel, surv. gen. of Que-
bec, 176 n 27
Home district, estab., 169
Horse corps, archives *re*, 160
Houses, 31
Howard, William, 96
Howe, William, 151
Hudson's Bay, 168
Hudson's Bay Company, 100 n 21;
acquires North West Co. records,
186; archives, 187-88
Hulbert, Archer B., 138
Huron Indians, council proc., 156;

Mackinac Island, Mich., fortified, 97; purchased from Indians, 119; treaty with Chippewa, 155 n 36

Mackinaw City, Mich., 6

Mackintosh, Alexander, 182 n 51; papers, 187

Mackintosh, Angus, Northwest Co. agent, 187

McLaughlin, R. S., purchases Simcoe papers, 170

McNiff, Patrick, apptd. dep. surv., 177; letters, 179; map of Detroit, 181

Macomb, Alexander, acquires Grosse Ile, 119 n 5; papers, 141

Macomb, Edgar, and Macomb, ledger, 141

Macomb, William, acquires Grosse Isle, 119 n 5; apptd. j.p., 162 n 69; member of Gen. Assembly, 168; papers, 141

McTavish Frobisher and Company, 187 n 71

Makarty-Mactique, Major, letters, 50

Madeline Island, 6

Magistrates, apptd. in Upper Canada, 169; issue land certificates, 177; notaries function as, 11

Maisonville, Alexander, apptd. j.p., 169 n 69

Malden, Ont., settlement, 169

Mandan Indians, La Vérendrye visits, 8

Manitoba Legislative Library, Archives Branch, Selkirk papers, 188

Mankato, Minn., 5

Manuscript collectors, obtain archival reprods., 80. *See also* Burton, Clements, Coventry, Draper, Dreer, Fisher, Gunther, Mason, Robertson, Scadding, Schmidt, Stone, Tayler, Verreau, Viger

Manuscripts, Illinois country, 49-52; New France, 83-85; Northwest, 121-41, 185-89, union catalog, 85.

Manuscripts—*Cont.*
See also names of places and persons

Maps, Detroit, 21 n 81, 121, 180 n 44; Gage papers, 122; engineers, 52; explorers, 52; French, 81; Kingston, Ont., 182 n 51; land, 46 n 88; Michigan, 137 n 86; Michilimackinac, 180 n 44; military, 160; Northwest, 137; Ohio country, 137 n 83; Ohio R., 84; Ontario land surveys, 180-81; Pennsylvania, 139 n 94; population, 139 n 94; reprods. of British, 185. *See also* Cartography

Margry, Pierre, transl. of comp. by, 34-35

Marin, Joseph de la Marque, Sieur de, 8

Marin, Paul de la Marque, Sieur de, 8

Marin, Philippe-Denis, Sieur de, diary, 8 n 32

Marin, Pierre-Paul de la Malgue (Marque), Sieur de, builds fort, 9; papers, 83

Marine commissary, Montreal, 65

Marquette, Jacques, voyage down the Miss. R., 2

Marriage contracts, 11; Detroit, 33, 114; Illinois, 26 and n 96, 109, 110; Montreal, 34, 75 n 66, 158; New France, 71

Marriages, Assumption Church, 92 n 36; Hesse district, 162 n 69, 165; Montreal, 192; Ontario, 193; performed by comdts., 11, 97, 146; registers, 58; validated in Detroit, 165. *See also* Parish registers

Martial law, prevails in West, 99

Martin, Félix, 93

Maryland Historical Society, Gorrell's jour., 133

Mason, Edward G., coll. mss., 26, 49

Massicotte, Edouard-Zotique, 65 n 14

Maumee, Ohio, 4

Milwaukee, Wis., agent of North West Co., 186
Minerals, search for, 8, 17
Mining concession, Renault, 20
Mining engineer, 20
Minnesota, French in, 3; fur trade, 18; land records, 46; Marin's activities in, 8; trade in, 8
Minnesota Historical Society, Alvord papers, 112; Canadian Indian Dept. records, 155; *reproductions obtained by*, Carver's narrative, 136 n 81; fur traders' mss., 134; Indian trade licenses, 156; North West Co., 187; *transcripts held by*: notarial archives of Montreal, 76; Selkirk papers, 188
Minnesota River, Carver goes up, 136; Ft. Snelling on, 187 Le Sueur on, 5; North West Co. operates on, 186
Minors, 11. *See also* Guardians
Minute books, notarial, 11
Missionaries, active in West, 6; arrive in Canada, 53; chaplains at Fort de Chartres, 18; docs. by, 51; docs. pub. *re*, 81; names appear on registers, 58; Protestant, 190-91; serve at western posts, 11. *See also* Franciscans; Friars Minor, Jesuits; Recollects; Sulpicians
Missions, 83 n 97; archives *re*, 86-93; corresp., 86, 87; Detroit, 17; estab., 54; docs. pub. *re*, 37; Mississippi River, 188
Mississippi Company, succeeds Company of the Indies, 20. *See also* Company of the West Indies
Mississippi River, 50; boundary of Quebec province, 100 n 21; Carver's exped., 135-36; communication to L. Erie, 6-7; confirmation land claims on, 38; discovery, 2; encroaches on Ft. de Chartres, 23; exploration, 1-2; floods Ft. de

Mississippi River—*Cont.*
Chartres, 96; floods Kaskaskia, 23; fort on, 6; Illinois settlements, 14; Indian trade, 186; maps, 52 n 19; missions, 188; passage from L. Superior, 5; Perrot on, 4; posts withdrawn from, 5; settlements, on, 9; surveys on, 138; trade licenses for, 76 n 73
Mississippi Valley, archives *re* Indians, 134; church archives *re*, 88; French occupation, 6, 7, 30; mss. on, 32
Missouri Historical Society, Gibault papers, 145; Gratz papers, 140; mss. *re* Illinois, 51; parish registers of Illinois, 56
Missouri River, boundary of Illinois dist., 12; La Vérendryes reach, 9; maps, 52 n 19; North West Co. operates on, 186
Missouri Valley, cartography, 52 n 19
Mitchell, George, Rev., arrives in Detroit, 145
Mitchell, John, cartographer, 138
Montforton, William, apptd. notary at Detroit, 98; carries off notarial archives, 32, 113
Monkton, Robert, 128
Monongahela River, 10
Monroe, Mich., Catholic church 143; parish registers, 144
Montreal, 35; admin. dist. estab. at, 64; agents in West, 139; Anglican church registers, 192; capitulation of French, 10, 22, 65-66, 95, 97; census, 159; church registers, 192; connection with West, 64; ct. estab., 101; dep. intendant, 65; Ft. Presque Isle burial register, 58; fur trade, 16, 18; Haldimand mil. gov., 150-51; hqrs. Canadian Indian dept., 106; Johnson flees to, 106; judicial archives, 33-34, 74-76, 158, 187 n 78; judicial dist., 102; list of

New France—*Cont.*
16-18; govt., 61-65; govt. of West,
10-11; judicial archives; 69, 71;
jurisdiction over Detroit, 15; land
grants, 69 n 32, 72-73; notarial
records, 68; officials, 62-65; officials' papers carried off, 66-67;
pub. docs. *re*, 77-78; royal govt.
estab., 62; ties with Upper Country, 100 n 21. *See also* Canada;
Montreal; Prévôté of Quebec;
Quebec (Province)
New France, Comptroller of the
Marine, records to be carried to
France, 66
New France, Governor; abolishes
sedentary comd. at Detroit, 16;
archives removed to France, 66;
docs. pub. *re*, 81; letters, 49; powers, 62, 63; recommends comdts.,
10
New France, Intendant, archives, 44,
66, 69, 70, 72; dep. at Montreal,
65; docs. pub. *re*, 81; land records,
44, 72-74; powers, 62-64
New France, Sovereign Council, composition, 53, 64; ordinance *re*
parish registers, 72
New France, Superior Council, archives, 44, 69-70; orders enforced
by intendant, 63; powers, 63, 64;
records to remain in New France,
66, 68; transcripts of archives obtained by Burton, 33; transcripts
of land records, 43
New France, Treasurer, archives, 66
New Madrid, Mo., Gibault removes
to, 143
New Orleans, La., ct., 13; distant
from Illinois, 12
New York (City), 101, 104, 127;
British evacuate, 100
New York (Colony), control of Indian trade, 108; Indian agent, 105;

New York (Colony)—*Cont.*
Jesuit archives *re*, 86; La Pause
serves in, 81
New York (State), confiscates Johnsons' property, 125
New York, Secretary of State, Johnson papers deposited with, 125
New York Historical Society, Anthon's jour., 131; De Lotbinière letters, 50
New York Public Library, Carleton
papers, 123; *mss. held by*: Bradstreet, 130, De Lotbinière, 50,
Edgar, 141, Monkton, 128, Racine's statement *re* Indian supplies,
135, Rogers, 130, 134
New York State Library, Bradstreeet
papers, 130; Johnson papers, 126
Niagara, N. Y., Anglican church
registers, 192; base for La Salle, 3;
corresp. *re*, 129; control of Indian
affairs, 107; dep. surv. at, 176;
diary *re* events at, 175; docs. pub.
re, 182; held by British, 103 n 31;
Indian congresses, 156; shipyard
at, 103, 104; statutes pub. at, 174;
Stuart travels to, 190; Supt. of Indian affairs, 107
Niagara River, portage, 2; settlement
on, 175
Nicolet, Jean, discovers Wis., 1
Niles, Mich., ment., 4
North America, archives *re* missions,
89; French royal acts *re*, 50; map,
138
North Dakota, La Vérendrye in, 8
North West Company, disposition of
records, 186; docs. pub., 187 and
n 71; operations, 186
Northwest, annexed to Quebec, 100;
archives *re*, 90 n 31; 160; controlled
by British, 103; docs. pub., *re*, 37,
81, 115-16; embraced in Indian
Country, 98; lawsuits from tried in
Montreal, 102; mss. *re*, 124; maps,

Northwest—*Cont.*
137; reproductions *re,* 30-31;
transcripts *re,* 115; travels in, 136,
137. *See also* Great Lakes; Old
Northwest; Upper Country; West;
Western posts
Northwest Passage, Rogers' interest,
134, 136
Northwest Territory, created, 102-
103; jurisdiction over Detroit and
Mackinac, 42; settlement of land
claims in, 38
Notarial archives, Detroit, 32, 44,
113-14, 120; Illinois, 25-29, 109-
11; Indiana, 40; Montreal, 33, 74-
75, 158; New France, 67-68;
Quebec, 71, 158; Three Rivers, 77,
158
Notaries, Detroit, 15, 98; file traders'
engagements, 18; functions, 11;
Illinois, 98; Kaskaskia, 99; Montreal, 65 n 14, 149; New France,
64; Vincennes, 21, 99
Nova Scotia, 1

Oath of allegiance, taken by inhabi-
tants at Vincennes, 135
O'Callaghan, Edmund B., arranges
Johnson papers, 126
Ohio, land records, 46, 47 n 97
Ohio Company of Virginia, 139 n 95
Ohio country, campaigns in, 115;
control of Indian trade, 108; fur
trade, 18; map, 137 n 83, 86; plan
of, 137 n 86
Ohio River, 38; Americans invade
north of, 102; boundary of Illinois
dist., 12, 99; boundary of northern
Indian suptcy., 105, 137; English
on, 9; Ft. Duquesne on, 9; Ft.
Massac on, 7; Hutchins' trip, 135;
journal of voyage down, 84; La
Salle reaches, 2; map, 84; mil.
campaigns north of, 172; route
from L. Erie, 9; south. bound. of
Quebec, 100; trip down, 135

Ohio Valley, Croghan Dep. Supt. of
Indian Affairs, 106; French warned
off, 10; maps, 138, 139 n 94; occupation by French, 83; part of attached to Canada, 12
Old Northwest, confirmation of land
claims, 44-45; ecclesiastical archives, 86; maps, 138; pub. of
censuses proposed, 31 n 17. *See
also* Great Lakes: Northwest;
West
O'Leary, P.M., 26 n 1, 86 n 10
Ontario, ecclesiastical archives, 91-
93, 192-93; forms part of Quebec,
100 n 21; land records, 177-81;
publishes French docs., 81; settlement, 92, 161, 175; vital statistics, 180
Ontario, Crown Lands Office, patents
for land, 178
Ontario, Department of Lands and
Forests, archives, 180-81
Ontario, Department of Lands, Forest, and Mines, Hesse district archives, 179; maps, 180
Ontario, Department of Public Records and Archives, *archives held
by*: church register, 193, ct. of
king's bench, 165, cts. of Hesse
dist., 165, land board Hesse dist.,
179, land records, 180-81; publishes legis. jour., 173; reproductions of Exec. Council records, 172
n 8, 178; Simcoe papers, 171;
transcripts obtained by: Osgoode
papers, 175 n 23, Smith papers,
181
Ontario, Legislature, enactment for
transfer of Detroit records, 113 n
76
Orderly books, 160; Bouquet, 125
Orders, 127
Ordnance stores, returns, 130
Oregon country, 188 n 74
Osgoode, William, chief justice, 167;
papers, 175

Settlement—*Cont.*
tario; 92, 161, 175; prohibited in Northwest, 118; western Quebec, 175. *See also* names of places

Settlements, plans, 137

Settlers, archives *re,* 160; Detroit, 116, French fur traders become, 18

Seven Years' War, 10 n 39. *See also* French and Indian War

Sewell papers, 191

Shawnee Indians, council proc., 156

Shea, John D. G., 56, 57-58, 145 n 18

Shelburne, Earl of (Sir William Petty, 2nd Earl of Shelburne and 1st Marquess of Lansdowne), papers, 112, 128, 131, 150

Shepherd, Samuel, 175

Sheriff, Hesse district, 162; Montreal, 65 and n 14, 149; Upper Canada, 167

Shipbuilding, Great Lakes, 171, mss. *re,* 122, 141

Shipping, mss. *re,* 141

Shipyard, Detroit, 104; Niagara, 103, 104

Shoemaker, Bowen W., 115

Shoemaker, Michael, 115

Simcoe, James G., 115, 163; appoints lts. of counties, 169; confirms deed to Grosse Ile, 119 n 5; inaugurated, 167; papers, 142, 161, 170-72

Sinclair, Patrick, grants lands on Mackinac Island, 119; letters, 133; reaches Michilimackinac, 101

Sioux country, French take poss., 3; trade licenses for, 76 n 73

Sioux Indians, 54; peace with Chippewa, 5; trade with, 4

Six Nations, council proc., 156; docs. pub. *re,* 127 n 41

Sketches, Simcoe (Mrs.), 171

Slaves, 117; data *re* on registers, 58; Detroit, 36

Small John, 167

Smith, David W., apptd. surv. gen.,

Smith, David—*Cont.*
167; member of Gen. Assembly, 168; papers, 171, 181

Smith, John, 114; comdt. at Detroit, 176

Smith, Thomas, 162 n 67

Smuggling, 104, 152

Social history, 83 n 97, 158, 171; archives *re,* 75; censuses and, 81; church registers and, 58; Johnson papers and; 127; Montreal, 74; New France, 69, 71

Social life, docs. *re,* 136

Society for the Propagation of the Gospel in Foreign Parts, London, 190, 191

Society of Jesus. *See* Jesuits

Soldiers, docs. by, 51; *engagements,* 34

Solicitor-General, Quebec, 148

Solicitor-General, Upper Canada, 167

Sorel, Protestant services in, 190

South Dakota, La Vérendryes in, 9

Southern Illinois University, microfilms of Illinois records, 28, 110

Southampton, England, Simcoe papers in, 170

Spain, surrenders Floridas, 97

Spanish, settlements, 48

Springfield (Ill.) land office, custody of records, 41

Squatters, 100

Starved Rock, fort at, 3

State Historical Society of Iowa, British Indian Dept. records, 157

State Historical Society of Wisconsin, ct. of inquiry record, 132; Draper mss., 112, 131; Hamilton papers, 131, 133; Langlade papers, 50; mss. of British officers, 133; *reproductions obtained by*: Canadian Indian Dept., 155, 157, French archives, 36, parish registers of Mackinac, 57; *transcripts obtained*

U. S. District Court—*Cont.*
decision *re* grant at Sault Ste. Marie, 22
U. S. General Land Office, priv. land claim records, 46-48
U. S. Government, issues patent for Grosse Ile, 119 n 5
U. S. Library of Congress, Manuscript Division, censuses of Detroit, 36, 116; *reproductions obtained by*: Amherst papers, 122, Bouquet papers, 125, Bishop of London, 191 n 90, British archives, 141, Canadian Indian Dept., 155, Carleton papers, 123, 124, Claus papers, 130, French archives, 30, 31, 37, 80, 82 n 97, Gage papers, 122, Haldimand papers, 124 map of the Ohio, 84, Society for the Propagation of the Gospel, 191 n 90
U. S. National Archives, corresp. British Army officers and Indian agents, 114-15, docs. *re.* Rogers, 134; General Land Office records, 45 n 82, 47 n 97
U. S. National Park Service, microfilms of Illinois records, 28, 87
U. S. Supreme Court, decision *re* grant at Sault Ste. Marie, 22
U. S. Surveyor General of Illinois and Missouri Territories, records transf. to, 45
U. S. Surveyor General Northwest of the Ohio, distrib. of records, 45
U. S. Surveyor General of Minnesota Territory, land records transf. to, 46
U. S. Surveyor General of Wisconsin and Iowa Territories, transf. of records to, 45
U. S. Surveyors general, records to be transf. to states, 46 n 88; survey records, 45
U. S. Treasury Department, General Land Office estab. in, 47 n 95; re-

U. S. Treasury Department—*Cont.*
ceives reports on Illinois land claims, 41
University of Chicago Library, reproductions French mss. in, 31-32; microfilm of translation of Margry, 35
University of Illinois, borrows French records, 24. *See also* Illinois Historical Survey
University of Michigan Library, Amherst papers, 122
University of Notre Dame, mss. *re* church, 145; reproductions of Roman archives, 91
University of Pittsburgh, Darlington Memorial Library, calendar of French *docs.* 38
University of Saskatchewan Library, reproductions of Canadian Indian Dept. records, 157
University of Toronto Library, Indian trade licenses, 157; North West Co. mss., 186, Osgoode papers, 175 n 23; Simcoe papers, 171
Upper Canada, admin. of Indian affairs, 154; archives, 130, 173-82; control of mil. affairs, 167; created, 1, 166; jurisdiction of cts., 168; land records, 172; local govt. estab., 168; officials, 167; officials' papers, 174; probate ct. estab., 163; statutes pub.; 174; transcripts *re,* 184; vicar general, 143. *See also* Ontario
Upper Canada, Executive Council, archives, 172; duties, 168; land books, 177
Upper Canada, Legislative Assembly, journals lost, 173; powers, 168
Upper Canada, Legislative Council, powers, 168; proceedings pub., 174
Upper Canada, Lieutenant Governor, corresp., 129, 184; dispatches to,

Upper Canada, Lieut. Gov.—*Cont.*
154; papers, 160. *See also* Simcoe,
John G.
Upper Canada (Province), Surveyor
General, 167; archives, 180, 181
Upper Country, archives missing, 78;
defined, 5 n 18. *See also* North-
west; Old Northwest; West; West-
ern posts
Ursulines, care for Cadillac's daugh-
ter, 33
Utica, Ill., 4; site of Jesuit mission, 54

Vatican archives, reproductions from,
88 n 20
Vaudreuil-Cavagnal, Pierre de Ri-
gaud, Marquis de, carries papers to
France, 66; corresp. pub., 80; let-
ters of, 68; papers, 31 n 17, 50 n 10
Verreau, Hospice, collects mss., 83
Versailles, 66, 67
Viger, Jacques, coll. mss., 53, 83
Vigo, Francis, papers, 135
Villiers, Louis Coulon de, 10
Villiers, Pierre-Joseph Neyon de,
leaves Ill., 96
Vincennes, François, Marie Bissot,
Sieur de, founds Fort Vincennes, 7;
grants land, 21
Vincennes, Ind., 81; Abbot abandons
property in, 135; corresp. *re*, 124;
evacuation ordered, 117; Hamilton's exped. agst., 131; Harmar at,
40; land claims, 38 and n 45, 40;
lt. gov. apptd., 100, 101; list of families, 40 n 58; list of settlers, 117-
18, notary, 11, 99; oath by inhabitants, 135; parish registers, 56;
settlers memorialize Gen. Gage,
100, 117; taken by Americans, 102;
trade permit, 76 n 73; traders, 135.
See also Fort Sackville
Vincennes land office, records land
grants, 43
Virginia (Colony), Croghan agent

Virginia (Coloney)—*Cont.*
for, 136; Hamilton and De Rocheblave taken to, 102; land cession
by, 38 n 45; sends out Washington,
10
Virginia State Library, Ft. de Chartres records, 131-32
Vital statistics, required in Canada,
191. *See also* Censuses; Parish
registers
Voyageurs, archives *re,* 34
Voyageurs, contracts in Montreal archives, 75, 76, 158; licenses sold to,
18
Vocabularies, Huron-French, 93

Wabash River, 12; area east of transf.
to Canada, 12; boundary of British
Illinois, 99; fort on, 6, 7; land
grants on, 21; land titles, 135
Wainwright, Nicholas B., 128
War of 1812, archives *re,* 186; rec-
ords captured during, 115
Ward, Edward, 106
Warehousemen, 18
Warrants,   Indian   disbursements,
126; military, 122
Washington, George, 10; jour., 136
Waterford, Pa., site of Ft. Le Boeuf,
9
Wayne County, Mich., land records,
42, 44, 113 n 76, 120; list of land
claims, 22 n 82; notarial archives,
32, 113
Wayne, Anthony, map presented to,
181
Welcome, logbook, 160
Werner, Raymond C., 30
West, criminal cases, 158
West, archives of New France *re,* 65;
divided into districts, 98; explora-
tion, 84; French reach, 1-2; Gage
papers *re,* 122; govt. by British,
97-109. *See also* Northwest; Old
Northwest; Upper Country

The manuscript was edited by Richard Dey. The book was designed by Sylvia Winter. The text typeface is Linotype Caledonia designed by W. A. Dwiggins in 1940. The display face is Linotype Bodoni designed by Giambattista Bodoni at the end of the 18th century.

Printed on Warren's Olde Style Antique, and bound in Lindenmeyer Schlosser's Elephant Hide paper over boards. Manufactured in the United States of America.